Kentucky's JOSEPH C.S. BLACKBURN

Kentucky's Joseph C.S. Blackburn

Soldier, Statesman
and a
Friend of All

Elizabeth Rouse Fielder

AP™
Acclaim Press
MORLEY, MISSOURI

Acclaim Press
— Your Next Great Book —

P.O. Box 238
Morley, MO 63767
(573) 472-9800
www.acclaimpress.com

Book Design: Rodney Atchley
Cover Design: M. Frene Melton

ISBN: 978-1-948901-02-4 | 1-948901-02-1
Library of Congress Control Number: 2018907355

First Printing 2018
Printed in the United States of America
10 9 8 7 6 5 4 3 2 1

Contents

Special thanks to the following for their assistance researching material for this book: Jennifer A. Bartlett, Head of Reference Services, University of Kentucky (UK) Library; Gordon E. Hogg, Director, UK Special Collections Library; Ruth Bryan, CA, UK Director of Archives & University Archives, Lexington, KY; The Library of Congress, Washington, D.C.; The Filson Historical Society, Louisville, Kentucky; The Kentucky Historical Society, Frankfort, Kentucky; The Woodford County Historical Society, Versailles, Kentucky; The Harrodsburg Historical Society, Harrodsburg, Kentucky; *The Woodford Sun*, Clippings from *The Blue-grass Clipper*, Versailles, Kentucky; the Kentucky Genealogical Society, Frankfort, Kentucky; the University of Virginia Special Collections, Charlottesville, VA; and Jonelle Fisher, Midway, Kentucky.

Special gratitude to the following for the editorial review and assistance: Dr. James Klotter, Kentucky State Historian, Georgetown, Kentucky; T. J. Anderson III, Hollins University Creative Writing Chair, Roanoke, Virginia; Joseph Manning, Editor, Louisville, Kentucky; Jay Hopkins, Frankfort, Kentucky; and Hap Houlihan, Lexington, Kentucky.

Heartfelt gratitude to my husband, Tom Fielder, for his consistent love and support and to our wonderful son, Graham, and my amazing step-children Kristin, Vaughan, and Austin. Gratefulness for Grandmother Terese Blackburn Lane Wise Rouse, who preserved records, letters, books, and memorabilia all her life that my father Owen Conner Rouse, Jr. and his half-brother, Joseph Blackburn Wise, also preserved over their lifetimes, and to my siblings Owen Rouse and Judith Grady for their support.

—Elizabeth Rouse Fielder

Prologue

Joseph Blackburn was a tall, lean, athletic man who walked with purpose and energy. He had clear blue eyes that captured his audience while drawing them in with his clear arguments. He was well informed, instinctively perceptive, and delivered fiery speeches in the chambers of the United States House and Senate, making him a well-known and formidable political foe in his day. Audiences leaned forward to hear his debates. Trained as a lawyer with a gift for the dramatic flair yet steeled by the decisive action required on the battlefields, he stood his ground when defending the people of his agrarian Woodford County, Kentucky, located in the heart of the Bluegrass Region in central Kentucky. He spoke up for the rights of the individual against corporations when he was elected to the state House of Representatives, the United States House of Representatives, and the United States Senate, where he served for the greater part of his adult life. He never forgot who sent him to Washington, and Kentuckians loved him for it. He was bold and bravely defended the democratic principles of his party that championed the common man. He never shied away from a fight on their behalf. He was quick-witted and had a way of disagreeing with another person's opinion without attacking the person. Essentially, he was a man's man who understood the ways of the world, and everyone loved him. He was "Our Joe," the man who did not suffer fools lightly but who was tenderhearted enough to adopt his six-year-old granddaughter Terese when her parents died tragically young. He raised her like his daughter. She always called him "Daddy."

He is my great-great grandfather. I never met him but heard stories about him all my life from Terese, the granddaughter he raised and my grandmother. I wrote this book to get to know him and learn what he achieved in his political career. I hope you enjoy getting to know him while reading this as much as I have while researching this. His story is Kentucky's story and the country's story. His life encapsulates its growth from the time when Kentucky was the western frontier to the time the country fulfilled its "manifest destiny," spreading from the Atlantic Ocean to the Pacific Ocean and becoming an industrial, economic, and political nation-state and player on the world stage. He played key roles in America's successful development after the Civil War and helped lead the greatest work of modern time, the Panama Canal. He redeemed his earlier political passions when he oversaw the construction of the Lincoln Memorial and declared that President Lincoln was the greatest President of all time. By the end of his life, he was respected by leaders from both parties who placed him in positions of trust and power. He never betrayed that trust or his friends during his long and eventful life that ended September 12, 1918. As it reads on his gravestone, "He passed through life a friend to all."

Kentucky's Joseph C.S. Blackburn

Soldier, Statesman
and a
Friend of All

For Tom and Graham

Part One

Down on the Farm

Chapter One

Blackburn Family Entwined with Kentucky's History

"Through every chapter of Kentucky's history, from its admission into the Union to the turn of the present century, the name of Blackburn ran like an unbroken thread."

Joseph Blackburn's grandfather George moved to the lush rolling hills of Woodford County in western Virginia in 1783 before Kentucky was recognized as a state. The family brought their love of God, law, politics, and thoroughbreds to the previously unsettled region. As the Blackburn lawyers, politicians, preachers, and thoroughbred racehorse breeders flourished over the generations, they helped establish the very essence of what we know today as Kentucky. It was only natural that Joseph Blackburn would share those passions when he became a man in this new country that was defining itself. His future, like the country's, seemed to be open to endless possibilities for those determined and willing to work hard with a little luck along the way.

Settlers like the Blackburn's spilled over the Appalachian Mountain Range to head "West" for land and the opportunity to make a new life immediately after independence from Britain was declared. There was a tremendous rush to grab land. Since the 1770s, the British had refused to allow any westward expansion over the Appalachians, forcing the colonists to live in a narrow several-hundred-mile-wide strip between the mountains and the Atlantic Coastline, mainly because of the French and Spanish claims for the land. In twenty short years, the population of the British colonies had doubled from one million in 1750 to more than two million in 1770. It had become unbearably crowded. Farming practices had depleted the heavily farmed soil in the thirteen colonies, towns felt crowded, and young men ready to start their life could no longer acquire land. The colonies grew so fast that Benjamin Franklin predicted that the center of the British Empire would shift to America. Despite prohibitions, the western lands were too tempting to ignore. By 1759, speculators and settlers had moved into the area around Lake Champlain and westward along the Mohawk River into central New York. By the early 1760s, hunters and explorers like Daniel Boone began opening the way west through the Appalachians. The "West" became a place in the mind of golden opportunities and new beginnings. Indeed, this ban on land purchases was one of the key items that led to the colonists finally revolting against the British King, plus the other well-known accumulation of causes, such as unfair taxes, debtor issues, religious divisions, and persecutions, some of the same issues that had compelled them to leave the Old World. Land became a premium because it was so scarce. Once the young country threw off the yoke of British rule, settlers raced west to find land to start a new life.

Joseph's grandfather George joined the movement west. It was an understandable urge passed down from the line of Blackburns who had left England, seeking freedom of religion and a chance to build a stable life. The first of the English Blackburns was Gamaliel de Blackburn, who had been one of King William the Conqueror's lieutenants in the Norman Conquest of 1066. King William awarded to Gamaliel the Manor of Blackburn, which is located on the west coast of northern England. It was described as a ten thousand acre tract, including an eighteen hundred acre estate. The area is now the city of Blackburn, Lancashire. Gamaliel became Gamaliel de Blackburn, Lord of Blackburn Manor. The descendants of Gamaliel de Blackburn line are, first, William Blackburn, born in Newcastle on the Tyne in Yorkshire, England in 1653, who moved to Abingdon Parish, in Gloucester County, Virginia, where his fourth child William was born in 1682. This William later married Elizabeth Haynes, and they moved to Middlesex County, Virginia, where one of their sons William was born in 1711. This William married another Elizabeth and named their first son Edward, who was born on November 30, 1729. Edward married Anne Jones in Virginia, and one of their children was George, who was born January 16, 1746 in Gloucester County, Virginia. George married Prudence Berry on December 12, 1771. George is Joseph's grandfather. The Blackburns had been migrating west since the Norman Conquest.

George and Prudence Blackburn moved from Augusta County, Virginia, to the western portion of Virginia immediately following their marriage, to Middlesex, Greenbriar County, when he was twenty-six and she was seventeen. The family grew and prospered allowing them to expand their land holdings and move further west. George bought 625.5 acres of land in Woodford County from the "Virginia Public Treasury for £994, 10 shillings, paid to the Land Office for Land Office Treasury Warrant No. 20739 on November 13, 1783," which directed the "principal SURVEYOR of any County within the Commonwealth of VIRGINIA... to survey and lay off in one or more surveys for George Blackburn, his heirs or assigns."

They claimed the rich land near the Big Spring in Woodford County, where they built a sturdy log fort on his land by 1784, known as Blackburn's Fort, that sheltered family, friends, and neighbors from Native American attacks that still occurred, even though no tribes lived in the area. Very few people were brave enough to settle in the area at the time. The calm surrounding the fort today within Lane's End Farm, Fort Blackburn Division on Old Frankfort Pike gives no hint of the dramatic scenes these early settlers endured. The fort's four rooms now serve as an office for Lane's End: two rooms on the ground level and two rooms up a narrow staircase, each with a fireplace. Major George and Prudence Blackburn had twelve children, seven of whom were born in Middlesex, Greenbriar County, Virginia, before they moved further west, where the remaining five were born in Woodford County, Virginia (later Kentucky), including Joseph's father, Edward M. Blackburn, who was born on February 10, 1787 in the fort.

Once settled, Joseph's grandparents joined the Forks of Elkhorn Baptist Church that was founded in 1788, located near Duckers Station, very close to the Blackburn estate. By 1810, they built what would become the second-oldest Baptist church west of the Allegheny Mountains, the Baptist Church of Christ at Big Spring on their land. The ruins remain visible today on the Blackburn land now owned by Rick and Carol Pope, the latter a Blackburn descendant. Within the next fifty years, a railroad company built a water stop along the road of rails for the water-consuming engines and named it "Spring Station" after the Big Spring.

The Big Spring was considered sacred by the Native Americans, where they buried their dead. The highest point to the east of the Springs on the farm contains two burial mounds. Arrowheads were regularly found when later farmers plowed the fields. The Blackburn horse farm at Spring Station would become the epicenter of Kentucky's thoroughbred industry, first created by Joseph's grandfather George and later expanded with an additional 1,550 acres by his father Edward at *Equira*. It became one of the six Bluegrass thoroughbred farms that formed the foundation for the thoroughbred industry: Edward Blackburn's *Equira*, Frank Harper's *Nantura*, A. J. Alexander's *Woodburn*, General W. Buford's *Bosque Bonita*, Warren Viley's *Stonewall Farm*, and Daniel Swigert's *Stockwood Farm*. The thoroughbred industry in the inner Bluegrass region of central Kentucky owes its start to these men and the legends they created. Some of the famous horses raised by Edward were Blackburn's Whip, Gray Eagle and Buzzard Superior. Among the most celebrated horses that stood at stud at *Equira* were Boston, sire of the immortal Lexington; and Eclipse, both champions of their day. Boston and Eclipse are buried at *Equira*. Years later, Joseph recalled when the famous thoroughbred Eclipse stood at *Equira*:

> While Eclipse was in my father's stable my father received one day an unexpected visit from Henry Clay, who was accompanied by several gentlemen from Fayette and Woodford Counties. They had been fox-hunting in the immediate neighborhood. Mr. Clay was a connoisseur of thoroughbreds and a breeder of them, and was anxious to see the horse that had won world-wide fame on the turf. My father was peculiar in that every horse he owned or had charge of was a trifle better than his predecessor. And as he was a fluent talker and could describe all the good points of a horse, Mr. Clay, it appears, for the amusement of the gathered company, called to draw out 'Uncle Ned,' as my father was called. After Eclipse had been viewed and admired, the guests adjourned to dinner. Mr. Clay was in excellent spirits. While the wine passed he raised his glass to his lips and proposed the health of my father and the health of Eclipse, 'the greatest horse on the continent.' My father was not to be outdone. Filling his glass and rising slowly from his seat and bowing to Mr. Clay, he responded, 'Eclipse is among horses, but Henry Clay is among men.'

Joseph's father Edward grew up on the farm and married Lavinia Bell. They moved into another brick home built by Edward on the Blackburn land, where they raised their thirteen children. The home still stands today, known as Blackburn Farm, *Equira,* in Midway, Kentucky (currently owned by Michael and Gay Barnett at the time of publication).

Joseph Blackburn was Edward and Lavinia's thirteenth and last child, born on October 1, 1838. Their first child George was born in 1810, twenty-eight years before Joseph. Joseph's older brothers and sisters became accomplished lawyers, doctors, and political leaders, including Kentucky Governor Dr. Luke P. Blackburn and Kentucky Secretary of State James W. Blackburn. Edward and Lavinia hoped to inspire their last son to become a minister and lead men in the paths of righteousness. They named him after the first minister of their church, the Reverend Joseph Clay Stiles of the Midway Presbyterian Church who was highly respected by everyone in the area. The Blackburns thought he was an excellent role model to inspire their youngest son.

Edward and Lavinia had great faith in Reverend Stiles, who is on record stating that he felt that slaveholding was not essentially sinful in and of itself because it depended on the goodness of the master and the servant and that the conversion to Christianity of many of these forced laborers had helped improve the slavery situation. The Reverend believed that the further education of slaves would allow the freed slave to be able to support himself and his family in our society. He believed that everyone should be prepared for freedom before being released from servitude, but that freedom should be granted to all ultimately. Edward owned about six slaves and presumably shared these feelings. While there is no absolutely no defense for slavery, the feeling sheds some light on the prevailing attitudes in young Joseph's family life.

Joseph's childhood was spent on the family's farm in Woodford County in the heart of the rich Inner Bluegrass Region, where he heard the calls of redwing blackbirds from the fields, the buzzing of bugs, and the soft whishing sounds of the long bluegrass swaying under the breezes. The front lane was lined with native dogwood, redbud, maple, and oak trees. Thoroughbreds flicked flies from their shimmering coats while they grazed in the green grass, followed cautiously by foals flicking their short tails. Joseph's father kept two of the best thoroughbreds in Kentucky's history on the farm: Boston and Eclipse, along with many others. The farm bustled with the activity of the large family, the frequent visitors, the half dozen slaves, and the horses.

When friends like John Breckinridge or Henry Clay rode up the long lane to the brick home in their horse carriages to visit, Joseph's father would have one of the slaves bring up the famous thoroughbreds one-at-a-time from the barn, where they were tied to two iron rings imbedded in a tree close to the house. There, the men studied the horse's racing and breeding record and conformation and discussed his bloodlines, which are essential to good breeding. Visitors to *Equira* enjoyed the best of the Bluegrass: fine horses and good food and conversation. They talked about the hot topics of the day, including the issues of slavery; the expansion of the country into the west, fulfilling its "Manifest Destiny;" and the future of the nation; and of course, thoroughbreds. They discussed ways agricultural states like Kentucky could achieve economic parity with Northern manufacturing states. The questions were unresolved and open-ended. Their decisions determined the actions that they would undertake, consciously defining the direction of their new country. They were building their community and a democratic way of life. It was a brand-new world of their making. They understood and accepted this responsibility. If something was not satisfactory, it was up to them to find a solution. If something was lacking, it was up to them to provide it. They did not wait for someone else to take care of their problems. They worked to make their world as they envisioned it, one likely to be based on the lofty ideals of John Locke and Jean-Jacques Rousseau, the famous philosophers of the Enlightenment. Racing their thoroughbreds against their neighbor's horses provided recreational outlets to stand out in their community. Their life on the land framed their world view at a time when there were few machines of any type and work was mostly done by hand—yours, your children's, or your slaves'.

Before Joseph was born, a religious fervor had swept the young country in the early 1800s. Religious revivals were frequent and lasted for a week at a time, drawing people from miles around to camp by the revival tent to listen to the country's traveling evangelists. Many believed that it was the manifest destiny of the country to dominate the continent from ocean to ocean and create a society that would serve as the beacon of hope and democracy to the world. This view was combined with a Protestant view that the new country was the place to prepare for the Second Coming of Jesus, but it relied on each individual to help make that vision come to pass. There was great work to be done by the citizens of this democratic experiment. It would require doctors, lawyers, architects, bankers, and businessmen, along with brave explorers, farmers, and mechanics to get the job done. The settlers felt united in the country's purpose, embracing similar values.

Education was extremely important, not only as a tool to meet the responsibility of creating this new ideal country but also to enable each person with the skills to make a new life and provide for their families.

Kentucky was the bright star of education and arts in the 'West,' providing the growing democracy with a long line of illustrious leaders, men like Henry Clay, John Crittenden, John Breckinridge, Jefferson Davis (before he was reviled), and Abraham Lincoln. It was the new intellectual center, and the Blackburn farm was located in the center of it, just eighteen miles west of Lexington, the "Athens of the West." It was called this in part because Lexington was the home of the first college west of the Appalachians, Transylvania, founded in 1780. Transylvania provided one of only two medical schools in the country. The other medical school was located in Philadelphia on the other side of the Allegheny Mountains, which is not a significant barrier today, but in the early days of the country, the mountains were a prohibitive barricade. Transylvania's medical school on the west side of the Alleghenies meant that education and opportunity could be found in the frontier, giving equal opportunities to frontiersmen. Education was admired and respected by the leading families like the Blackburns. Most of the Blackburn children attended Transylvania or Centre College in Danville, founded in 1819. The land, law, education, thoroughbred racing, politics, and duty to God were dominant in the lives of the large Blackburn family.

While the Blackburns settled into the heart of the Inner Bluegrass, new American settlers continued to pour over the Appalachian Mountain Range into the western frontier lands spreading ever westward. Over time the residents in western Virginia came to rely on the Mississippi River for trade to ship goods downriver, like tobacco, corn, and hemp, the major crops of the time. When it became more dangerous to travel back to the capital of Virginia for business and after Virginia forbade trade with the Spanish colony of New Orleans, which controlled the mouth of the Mississippi River, these new settlers became restless and wanted to become a separate state. These facts combined with the incredible population growth compelled Colonel Benjamin Logan to call a constitutional convention in Danville in 1784. Over the next six years, nine conventions were held in Danville, where they discussed many ways to achieve independence from Virginia. Finally, on June 1, 1792, with Virginia consenting to separation, the United

States Congress accepted the Kentucky Constitution and Kentucky was granted statehood, making it the fifteenth state and the first U.S. state west of the Appalachian Mountains. All the while, settlers continued to push west looking for land to start a new life. By the middle of the nineteenth century, America had expanded across the entire continent from the Atlantic to the Pacific within three short generations, a staggeringly rapid expanse westward once the Appalachian Mountains were breached.

The Blackburn family pride in the new country ran back to its very founding. Joseph Blackburn's maternal grandfather, Major John Bell, was one of the select members of the Commander-In-Chief's Guard for General George Washington during the Revolutionary War, guarding the general and his personal papers and effects. The Guard was made up of soldiers specially selected for their patriotism and fidelity to duty. John Bell had enlisted in the Continental Army in 1776 for three years as a private in the Virginia Line and was transferred to Morristown, New Jersey, on May 1, 1777 to join the Commander-in-Chief's Guard commanded by Captain Caleb Gibbs. The Guard remained in Morristown with the main army in the winter quarters until four o'clock in the morning on May 31, 1777, when they moved to Middlebrook to new headquarters. The main army prevented the British from capturing Philadelphia. Joseph's grandfather John Bell fought in the battle of Brandywine, Delaware, on September 11, 1777; the battle of Germantown, Pennsylvania, on October 4, 1777; and the battle of Monmouth, New Jersey, on June 28, 1778. John Bell was discharged at West Point, New York, on July 28, 1779. He moved to Pisgah, Woodford County, Kentucky, and was later one of the delegates to the 1799 Kentucky Constitutional Convention. His daughter, Lavinia St. Clair Bell, married Joseph's father.

Joseph Blackburn is also linked to the founders of the state of Kentucky by his marriage to Terese Graham, daughter of Dr. Christopher Columbus Graham, who was, in turn, the son of James Graham, one of the famous Long Hunters with Colonel James Knox who explored the western frontiers lands that became Kentucky. James Graham was a Revolutionary War soldier who served under the command of General George Rogers Clark in 1788 and one of the forty-nine settlers of Corn Island, along with his wife and son, C.C. Graham, that formed the basis for the city of Louisville. C. C. Graham was part of the second generation of Long Hunters in Kentucky and later wrote about the many famous Long Hunters he had known who had helped discover and settle the state. Later in his life, Dr. Graham was the developer and owner of the famous Graham Springs in Harrodsburg. Graham Springs was known as the "Saratoga of the South" and was at its peak of popularity when Joseph was a young man. It is likely that Joseph met his wife Terese Graham there.

Dr. Graham was a family friend of the Lincolns and attended the wedding of Thomas Lincoln and Nancy Hanks on June 12, 1806. He helped to influence their young son Abraham's early education by giving him his first book and exposing Lincoln to a world of science, travel, and philosophy during his frequent visits to the Lincolns' home near Hodgenville, Kentucky. While it is not known exactly which book Dr. Graham gave to Abe Lincoln, it was precious. Dr. Graham's influence over young Abe Lincoln is memorialized in one of the five carved limestone panels of the Lincoln Boyhood National Memorial in Lincoln City, Indiana. Each panel depicts an important phase in Abe Lincoln's life. The first panel depicts Kentucky and the other four show the highlights of Lincoln's time in Indiana, Illinois, and Washington, D.C., and then the fifth panel shows the essence of Lincoln's life. The Kentucky panel shows a young Lincoln as the central figure, leaning on a staff, symbolic of the work of the backwoods boy. Lincoln is shown listening to a story told by Dr. Christopher C. Graham, whom the artist described as "a traveling philosopher and Lincoln's first contact with a glittering outside world." Standing behind Lincoln are his mother Nancy Hanks Lincoln, his sister Sarah, and his second schoolteacher Caleb Hazel. Standing behind Dr. Graham are Lincon's father Thomas Lincoln and neighbor Jesse La Follette.

Dr. Graham, like many a Scotsman, was an emphatic story-teller, as well. Joseph Blackburn heard his father-in-law's stories of the Abraham Lincoln family, Corn Island, and settling the state. Dr. Graham's grandson, Dr. William T. Davis, vividly recalled the stories of Lincoln while he lived for a time with Joseph Blackburn and his wife, Terese Graham Blackburn, and their children in Versailles, Kentucky, in their home located at 215 Rose Hill:

> But the stories that made the deepest impression on my boyhood mind were about the Lincolns, the boy Abe and his

parents, Tom and Nancy Lincoln. He told how delighted little Abe was to receive his first book, when grandfather fished it out of his saddle-bags where he had it for him. He often stopped at the Lincoln cabin—on Knob Creek I believe it was—on his journeys. I remember he described the Lincoln house as being a small log cabin pen with a loft and earthen floor.

He was very fond of the boy Lincoln, and in Grandfather's younger days, equipped with his hammer and specimen sack, he took Abe with him over the Lincoln farm, searching for interesting geological and ethnological specimens and in this way the young Lincoln mind was turned away from lowly home influence into the realms of history, natural and political.

I have often thought since that Grandfather's teachings and character had much to do with the mould and trend of Abraham Lincoln's mind and after-life. As I recall him, Grandfather was so positive and determined that his influence must have been very powerful. Anyone coming into his presence immediately felt that power. His personality was indomitable; he was very decided in his likes and dislikes and never forgot an injury. Dr. Graham's family remained friends with the Lincoln family. The last letter Dr. Graham wrote before he died on February 3, 1885 at the age of 101 was to Robert Lincoln, then U.S. Secretary of War. Dr. Graham died after catching a deep cold after one of his regular roundtrip walks from Louisville to Versailles to visit his daughter Terese and son-in-law, then U.S. Senator Joseph Blackburn.

Chapter Two

BLACKBURN POLITICIANS

"Whenever you say "Blackburn" to a Kentuckian, he pricks up his ears in joyful anticipation of horse racing or political oratory or both."

Joseph's father was a lawyer and horseman. Although he declined to pursue politics, he remained current in political affairs. He was rather short and portly and was well-regarded in his community for his frank manner that was "decisive without dogmatism." He read law with George Nicholas, who was best known as one of the most noted thoroughbred horse breeders and turfmen of his day, a trait they shared. Edward taught Joseph and all his children to become moral and/or political leaders, just as he had been taught. Joseph's uncles became leaders: Uncle George Blackburn was a respected minister; his Uncle Dr. Flournoy Blackburn was a prominent physician; and Uncle Colonel William B. Blackburn was an eminent lawyer of Versailles and state politician, serving twenty-four years in the Kentucky house or senate and once as acting Lieutenant Governor from 1818–1819 to Governor Gabriel Slaughter.

Each generation was raised to be a leader in their chosen field, a tradition that Joseph's father continued. Joseph's brother William Blackburn was elected Lieutenant Governor of the state under Governor James Turner Morehead (February 21, 1834–August 31, 1836). William also served as President Pro Tempore of the Kentucky Senate. Joseph's brother William had the Blackburn "silver tongue" and was a persuasive speaker. William married Miss Watkins, a half-sister of Henry Clay, the daughter of Henry Clay's mother by her second marriage.

Joseph's brother George was a successful planter in Mississippi in partnership with the former Democratic governor of that state, Charles

Clark, although he died young. Two older brothers died in childhood before Joseph was born: John Bell and Edward Lewis. Joseph's next oldest brother, Dr. Luke Pryor Blackburn, was twenty-two years old when Joseph was born and went on to make a name for himself with his untiring "personal ministrations and counsel" when yellow fever broke out in Memphis, Tennessee and Hickman, Kentucky, in 1878. Dr. Luke Blackburn regularly refused to accept any compensation for his services and became known as the "Hero of Hickman." As a result of these many selfless acts, he was propelled into the governor's office in Kentucky in 1879, where he succeeded in passing several reforms in the state regarding state finances, internal improvements, and prison reform. Today, the Blackburn Correctional Complex, named in 1970, stands in honor of the first physician Governor of Kentucky, who sought to improve prisoners' lives and assist them in reintegrating into the community as functioning citizens.

Joseph's brother William fought in the Mexican War and survived it, but was unfortunately shot by Mr. Steele almost immediately after his return to Kentucky. Joseph's brothers Henry and Churchill were both well-known physicians: Henry in Woodford County and Churchill in Desha, Arkansas. Joseph's brother Breckenridge was a captain in the Confederate Army but died two years after the Civil War ended. Former Confederate Captain James served as Kentucky's Secretary of State for brother Governor Dr. Luke P. Blackburn. When Joseph Blackburn went to the U.S. Senate for the first time, his certificate was signed by his brothers, Governor Dr. Luke P. Blackburn, and Secretary of State James W. Blackburn.

While women were not given opportunities to excel like men in those days, Joseph's older sisters achieved political expression in their marriages and activities. Mary married Judge Buckner Stith Morris, who became the first lawyer practicing in Chicago and later the second mayor of Chicago. Frances died before he was born, but her widower, Thomas B. Flournoy, remarried another of Joseph's sisters: Elizabeth. Flournoy was a lawyer who owned a large cotton plantation in Desha County, Arkansas, and was elected to the Arkansas state legislature in 1848 and 1850, where he was chosen Speaker of the House. Flournoy was a devoted and political friend of Judge Stephen A. Douglas and campaigned for him at the Cincinnati Convention in 1856. He also served as a delegate to the Democratic National Convention in

Charleston, South Carolina, on April 23, 1860 and was named the temporary Chairman of the Democratic National Convention. He died in August 1861 while on a trip to Kentucky. At the time of his death, he had been authorized by Confederate President Jefferson Davis to organize an Arkansas regiment for Confederate service. He was a prewar militia general.

It was only natural that Joseph would look to medicine or law and politics as a way to make his mark in the new world.

Chapter Three

Spring Station, the Epicenter of Kentucky Thoroughbreds

Near the end of his life, Joseph Blackburn gave an interview, quoted below, to a journalist during one of his stays in Woodford County. He was wearing yellow shoes, gray slacks, a pink shirt, a tobacco-colored vest, a blue tie and a white Panama Hat. He said:

> 'Yes, it gives me a thrill of pure delight to be back in Kentucky once more,' he said with a broad smile which was more expressive of his feelings than words, 'it's home to me, you know. As my train sped through the rolling Bluegrass into Lexington, I was reminded of the classic lines of Sir Walter Scott, which I learned when I was a school boy and which you doubtless recall.' And he rattled 'em off with an oratorical flourish of his old stump-speaking days:
>
> "Breathes there a man with soul so dead,
> Whose never to himself has said,
> This is my own, my native land
> Whose heart has ne'er within him burned,
> As home his footsteps he has turned
> From wandering on a foreign strand."
>
> That's just the way I feel—my heart's burning with an exquisite pleasure at being back once more on my native Bluegrass.' And he again gave a chuckle of delight.

Later in his life, Joseph recalled another story of one of his father's famous thoroughbreds:

> My father was among the first citizens of Kentucky who bred, trained, and raced horses. *Blackburn's Whip*, whose

blood has blended so kindly with trotters and thoroughbreds, was his property. *Boston*, sire of the immortal *Lexington*, died in my father's stable, and the great and unbeaten *Eclipse* was in my father's possession in the years 1837 and 1838. These horses were the champions of their day and the greatest horses of their generation; they were not furlong sprinters, but four-milers. It will hardly be believed in these days of palatial stables, that while these valuable horses were in my father's care they occupied a very ordinary log stable, through which the winds whistled on Wintry nights, and through which the snow drifted on occasions. When *Boston* and *Eclipse* were brought to Kentucky they did not make the trip in palace cars, as do the costly thoroughbreds of to-day; walking was good enough for them, and it was by walking every inch of the route that they reached their destination.

Boston caught cold on the way to Kentucky and went blind soon after his arrival. I was a small lad at the time, and used to visit *Boston's* stable every morning to see him cared for and walked by the colored groom. In the Fall of 1849, then 17 years old, he began to grow decrepit from the effect of severe racing and duties in the stud, and frequently had to be helped to rise. When on his feet he seemed to be all right again and able to take his morning exercise. Early one morning in the year named, I slipped out of the house and down to *Boston's* stable. The door was closed and fastened within. I hammered on it and clamored for admittance. The door was cautiously opened far enough to admit the passage of my body, when a black hand seized me by the hand and dragged me inside. I was no sooner in than the groom was out and the door fastened. I took the matter good-naturedly until my eyes became accustomed to the light, when I saw something that curdled the blood in my young veins: *Boston* was lying on his side in a corner of the stall, lifeless, and great splashes of blood were on the wall. In his dying struggles he had beaten his head against the logs. I screamed lustily for the groom, and seeing he had carried the joke far enough, he came to my rescue. My life has been in danger a score of times since on battlefields and elsewhere, but I was never quite so badly scared.

Boston was a chestnut horse, a little over fifteen and a half hands, with both hind legs white up to the hocks and a white stripe down the face over his "nose" giving him the nickname of "Old Whitenose." He was not named for the city in Massachusetts, as is often believed, but for the card game during which he was acquired by Nathaniel Rives. As a colt, Boston was so hard to handle that Colonel L. White, a well-known breeder in the Richmond, Virginia, area, suggested that he be "either castrated or shot, preferably the latter." Fortunately no one followed the recommendations. Surprisingly, he liked to run.

He began his seasons at stud in 1841, covering forty-two mares at one hundred dollars each. He stood at stud in Virginia in 1843, at Washington City in 1844, and after the seasons of 1845 and 1846, he came to Kentucky in very bad weather in late winter or early spring. When he arrived at Mr. Blackburn's *Equira*, he was suffering from a very severe cold, "from the effects of which Mr. B. states he never entirely recovered."

Boston was the winner of thirty four-mile heat races and nine three-mile heat races, and was one of the most famous long-distance race horses ever produced in America. He stood at stud at E. M. Blackburn's *Equira* the seasons of 1847, 1848, and 1849. Boston died on January 31, 1950 in his seventeenth year, "the greatest loss to breeders since the days of Sir Archy, and Diomed." Lexington was foaled in 1850 and was one of the last crop of foals out of Boston. Lexington went on to become the leading winner and sire of his time. He was great on the turf and wonderfully potent in the stud. Today an image of Lexington is used as the logo for the city of Lexington.

While Joseph was growing up, Spring Station was a telegraph center and the epicenter of thoroughbred racing in Kentucky. Since 1833, the train stopped at Spring Station, well before there was a train to Versailles and provided the main means of shipping horses around the country. Some of the horses sent from Spring Station to gain world-wide fame were Lexington, Longfellow, and Ten Broeck. Longfellow was so famous that he traveled to race tracks in New York and New Jersey in a train boxcar with his name emblazoned on the side. "No horse of his day was a greater object of public notice. His entire career was sensational.... People seemed to regard him as a superhorse." People would snatch long hairs from his tail as keepsakes. Many famous people, too, have left the train at Spring Station to visit the Blackburns,

Alexanders, Harpers, and other prominent families surrounding Spring Station. In 1900 then-New York Governor Theodore Roosevelt had his private car cut off a train at Spring Station while he visited the Alexander family. Other notable visitors include: Twenty-eighth U.S. President Woodrow Wilson, General George Armstrong Custer, author Charlee Dudley Warner, the 9th Duke of Marlborough, author John Burroughs, financier and thoroughbred owner and breeder August Belmont, businessmen Frank and William Rockefeller, lawyer and American writer Thomas Nelson Page, author James Whitcomb Riley. They wanted to see the greatest race horses in Kentucky, the United States, and some would say the world.

Joseph followed thoroughbred racing throughout his long life. He attended the first Kentucky Derby that was held in 1875, won by Aristides, who was ridden by a black jockey named Oliver Lewis. Aristides was owned by Price McGrath, a gambler of humble origins who had won $105,000 in a single night in New York and returned to Kentucky, where he founded McGrathian Farm and lived like a Bluegrass prince. He continued to gamble and lighten the pockets of the Bluegrass "sporting brotherhood" right up to his death in 1881. In 1876 McGrath was challenged to race Aristides against the famous Ten Broeck of Woodford County at Lexington's racetrack, "Chittlin' Switch." All Woodford County turned out, ready to bet heavily on Frank Harper's Ten Broeck, who had reduced the horse Lexington's four-mile record to 7:15.5, and the mile record to 1:30.75. Both Ten Broeck and Longfellow were bred and died on *Nantura*, Frank Harper's famed farm. Lawrence Thompson retells the legendary event:

> McGrath stood in the track taking all [...] bets that the Woodford County boys would place. [...It is claimed he] bet between $12,000 and $20,000, and he made no record of his wagers. A friend advised McGrath to jot down some of the names of the bettors, warning that every man at the track would claim a bet with McGrath if Ten Broeck won. "Don't you worry, sonny," the veteran gambler calmly replied, "The red hoss will keep the books." [...] All turfdom knows how "the red hoss" [(Aristides) finished] a full forty yards ahead of Ten Broeck. Kentucky Legend has it that all Woodford County

> went bankrupt and that the day after the race, the line to the local home finance company's doors in Versailles stretched around the block.

Joseph Blackburn attended the great race. His April 27, 1877 journal entry reads: "met Lewis Clark at Frank Harper's & took him to Lexington in buggy where we chased race between Ten Broeck & Aristides. Came home at night." Later that year on October 19, 1877, Joseph Blackburn met "McGrath and Sam Harper in Baltimore at racecourse and all come back to DC." Then on October 24, 1877, he "attend[ed] races and witnessed Ten Broeck's humiliation. Came back to Washington at night." One benefit of working as a Congressman in Washington, D.C. was the access to the race track in Baltimore, just a short drive or train ride away. Enjoying horse racing did not interfere with his national political career.

The association of Blackburns and thoroughbreds was recognized by other horse breeders, as well. Frank Harper of *Nantura Stud* named a thoroughbred for the Joseph Blackburn's mother, Lavinia Bell. In the 1880s, the famous Belle Meade stables in Nashville, Tennessee, named a colt for his older brother, Luke Blackburn, and the colt's brother was named Joe Blackburn. During the 1881 Belle Meade Yearling Sale, the colt Joe Blackburn brought seventy-five hundred dollars, when any price above five hundred dollars was extraordinary. Joe Blackburn was the highest-priced colt sold at the sale. It was a high compliment to the horse and foreshadowed the man's successful political career.

Chapter Four

Caught Between Lofty Ideals and Cruel Reality

Joseph's early family life in Woodford County was comfortable and cruel at the same time because it was powered by the work of enslaved hands. The impact that slavery has had on our country cannot be overstated. When the thirteen colonies were established in the late 1600s and early 1700s, slavery was legal, our nation's "original sin." The first shipload of African captives to North America arrived at Jamestown, Virginia, in August of 1619. Even though there were more European indentured servants than African slaves in the colonies for most of the seventeenth century, after 1680, the African slave trade exploded. By the middle of the eighteenth century, slavery was found in all thirteen colonies and already served as the engine that drove the Southern colonies' economy when there were no machines and all work was done by hand. By the time of the American Revolution, the English importers alone had brought some three million captive Africans to the Americas.

The colonial frontier was settled primarily from about 1717 to 1775 by mostly Presbyterian settlers from northern England border lands, Scotland, and Northern Ireland who were escaping religious persecution and financially hard times. The Scotch-Irish and Scots and others from the northern England border lands, like the persecuted Baptists in England, escaped and chose to settle in the region around the Appalachian Mountains from Pennsylvania to Georgia and soon dominated the population there and in the interior of the South. Between two hundred fifty thousand and four hundred thousand Scotch-Irish migrated to the colonies in the eighteenth century.

Settlers who were mostly from central England and the London area chose the agricultural Southern English colonies. At first, the large plantations were mostly owned by friends of the British-appointed governors and would have been considered "minor aristocrats." Indentured servants from Europe who chose to settle in the South worked off their terms of indentures, usually five to seven years, to repay the cost of their passage to the New World, thus helping the colonies with their free manpower to settle the wilderness. Once they were free, these formerly indentured servants chose to settle on small farms in the Southern colonies, where about fifty-five percent of the population were British, thirty-eight percent were African slaves, and seven percent were German. Over half of all new British immigrants in the South initially arrived as indentured servants, who were mostly poor young people who could not find work in England and who could not afford the cost of passage to the colonies, exchanging the promise of manual labor in the colonies for passage to the New World. Some indentured servants were wrongfully forced into manual labor, even though they had paid their passage to the New World.

The American Revolution brought the promise, if not the reality, of freedom for all men. Slavery issues were debated in Philadelphia from May 25 to September 17, 1787 during the Constitutional Convention. From the beginning, Southerner Charles Cotesworthy Pinckney of South Carolina had warned the Convention of dire consequences if protections for slavery and Southern agricultural exports (by not taxing them with tariffs) were not included in a new Constitution. Three provisions were included that explicitly restricted Congress' powers that favored the Southern interests: one proposal barred Congress from ever interfering with the slave trade; another prohibited taxation of exports; and the third required the support of two-thirds majorities of both houses of Congress for any legislation that regulated foreign trade through tariffs or quotas. These three proposals provoked outrage from Northern delegates to the Constitutional Convention and from slavery opponents. Eventually a compromise between Northern and Southern delegates was reached in the final version of the new Constitution that empowered Congress to end the slave trade beginning in 1808 while it simultaneously strengthened the Fugitive Slave Clause in exchange for removing the two-thirds requirements of both Houses of Congress to pass laws regulating international commerce. The Southern delegates had wanted the two-thirds requirement because they feared that laws regulating international commerce would economically hurt Southern slaveholding states' interests. The Fugitive Slave Clause was written in the new Constitution in Article Four, Section 2, Clause 3:

> No person held to service or labour in one state, under the laws therof, escaping into another, shall, in consequence of any law or regulation therein, be discharged from such service or labour, but shall be delivered up on claim of the party to whom such service or labour may be due.

These terms were adopted in the new Constitution of the United States, although the signers would openly doubt whether the United States would remain a single, unified nation for longer than 150 years. Benjamin Franklin said:

> I confess that There are several parts of this Constitution which I do not at present approve, but I am not sure I shall never approve them.... I doubt too whether any other Convention we can obtain, may be able to make a better Constitution.... It therefore astonishes me, Sir, to find this system approaching so near to perfection as it does; and I think it will astonish our enemies....

The battle lines over slavery and tariffs on international trade were drawn from the very moment the country was formed, but in the beginning, pro-slavery states outweighed free states. The Northwest Ordinance of 1787, passed just before the U.S. Constitution was ratified, prohibited slavery in the federal Northwest Territory and seemed to indicate a future without slavery. But by 1789, only five of the Northern states had adopted policies to at least gradually abolish slavery: Pennsylvania, New Hampshire, Massachusetts, Connecticut, and Rhode Island, while eight states endorsed slavery: New York, New Jersey, Delaware, Maryland, Virginia, North Carolina, South Carolina, and Georgia. The year after Kentucky was granted statehood in 1792, the Fugitive Slave Act of 1793 was passed to give effect to the Fugitive Slave Clause of the U.S. Constitution. The trend seemed to favor the continuation of slavery.

Slavery continued as a problem in the country with no easy solution. By the time Joseph was born in 1838, Southern Rights Clubs (SRCs) had formed in several Southern states that followed the philosophies of John C. Calhoun, advocating the re-establishment of the African slave trade, including a little-known group called the Order of the Lone Star, which helped orchestrate the successful Texas revolution that resulted in the independence of Texas from Mexico in 1836. The SRCs believed that the U.S. Constitution was a tyrannical document because it prohibited slave trade after 1808. The members of the SRCs secretly fitted out, manned, and equipped slaver ships that were to cruise around the African coast and kidnap men whenever possible. Between 1834 and 1840, the SRCs had at least six slaver vessels, some of which were successful in their dire mission. Fortunately, some were captured by the British and thwarted. These private independent invasions of foreign countries created a diplomatic problem for the new country, which had to be addressed by its leaders.

The U.S. President was Democrat Martin Van Buren, who was elected for the 1838 term. Soon after taking office, President Van Buren issued a proclamation against filibusters (or the unauthorized invasions of foreign lands) that was pursued by the SRCs. There was a Democratic majority in both Houses of Congress. There were twenty-six states represented in the Twenty-Fifth Congress, equally balanced between thirteen free states and thirteen slave states, a tenuous balance at best. Kentucky's Governor from 1836 to 1840 was the Whig James Clark. Henry Clay and John J. Crittenden were Kentucky's Whig Senators, who struggled to maintain that balance and avert civil war. The recognized territories were the Florida Territory, Iowa Territory, and Wisconsin Territory. The recognized states in 1838 were all east of the Mississippi River excluding the southern tip of the continent in the Florida Territory, not yet a state. The then most-northwestern lands west of the Mississippi River contained the territories of Wisconsin and Iowa.

When Joseph was born, America covered the North American continent almost halfway from the Atlantic coast to the Mississippi River. The Western lands that extended from the Mississippi River to the Pacific were ripe for conquest while Cuba lay tantalizingly close to the Florida Territory. Would the new states formed on these Western lands support slavery or oppose it? That was the main question in the country. Who would have the most power in the Halls of Congress: free states or slave states? Even with a "balance" of power between the two types of ideologies, how would the two cooperate or would there be cooperation?

Events in Europe brought changes to life in Kentucky. In Ireland, the Great Potato Famine in the 1840s and 1850s resulted in many Irish people immigrating to the United States. Some of the Irish immigrants became jockeys, hot walkers, or stable hands alongside the enslaved men, many in Woodford County. Meanwhile Kentuckian John Jordan Crittenden served as the fifteenth U.S. Attorney General in 1841 and then again later as the twenty-second U.S. Attorney General from 1850 to 1853 under U.S. President Millard Fillmore. Crittenden's regular visits to Woodford County and *Equira* kept the Blackburn family abreast of the latest national developments and new laws.

The U.S. Supreme Court ruled in *Prigg v. Pennsylvania* in 1842 that states did not have to offer aid in the hunting or recapture of slaves, basically rendering The Fugitive Slave Act meaningless. Southern slave owners lost money on escaped slaves. Many financed their slave purchases by borrowing money from banks for chattel mortgages on humans, as unthinkable as that sounds today. If the collateral escaped, the borrower still had to repay the bank loan. Borrowers were highly motivated to seek the return of their investment to save them from financial ruin, even if it was morally bankrupt. By 1843, several hundred slaves were escaping to the North each year. Some towns passed "personal liberty laws" that required a jury trial before any slave could be moved, while others passed "personal liberty laws" that forbade the use of local jails for runaway slaves or the assistance of their state's officials in returning runaway slaves. Southerners began to demand the passage of a Fugitive Slave Act with provisions that would be enforced. Eventually this movement would result in The Fugitive Slave Act of 1850.

Slavery was a locally pressing issue for families like the Blackburns in Kentucky. Joseph's namesake, Reverend Stiles, believed in the gradual emancipation of slaves combined with a continuing Christian education. Joseph's cousin, attorney George Blackburn Kinkead, believed in emancipation and created a subdivision for freed families from his family's farm in north Lexington called "Kinkead-town," where freed slaves could buy land and build a new life as free families. Statesman Henry Clay believed in emancipation, but Clay thought that it would be best to re-colonize them in Africa. He was a supporter of the Kentucky Colonization Society and was at one time its president. This was a benevolent group of Kentuckians who were willing to free their slaves but who were afraid that if too many slaves were freed at once, it would bring about a state of social and political chaos in slaveholding Kentucky. They agreed to fund the cost of re-colonizing former slaves in a new country established in Africa for that purpose: Liberia.

Unfortunately, slave owners could make a profit selling slaves on the market while re-colonizing former slaves to Liberia cost them money that many of them could not or would not pay for it. It is not clear if the former slaves wanted to be re-colonized in Africa, though a few undertook the challenge in order to be free. The Kentucky Colonization Society had limited success and was only able to send a few former slaves to Liberia. By 1845, the effort was fighting an uphill battle as the demand for help in Southern cotton fields and sugar cane fields increased. Britain began to buy more cotton from Southern producers, so states in the Deep South increased the number of slaves to feed the growing cotton market. Slavery was very profitable for a few plantation owners in the South growing cotton or sugar cane, creating massive amounts of wealth for a few, while costing many slaves his or her life.

Meanwhile the population was pouring into the west relentlessly. Not long after President Thomas Jefferson sealed the Louisiana Purchase, trains began crossing the continent on the new railroad lines along with the new telegraph lines that opened the way for the new country to dominate the North American continent. Thomas Jefferson declared the United States "an empire for liberty." People flowed into the open lands seeking a new chance for a better life and liberty. By 1845, John L. O'Sullivan wrote in the *Democratic Review*, then one of America's most popular magazines, that the desire to occupy more land was the fulfillment of America's "Manifest Destiny," a term that soon became as important as "empire" to describe American nationhood.

The phrase "Manifest Destiny" was meant to define and justify the country's expansionist policies, barely concealing the ideology of white supremacy, ignoring the interests of Native Americans or others who stood in the way of that "destiny." It was and continues to be a shocking assumption. U.S. political leaders simply did not consider any claim made by a non-white or a racially mixed society as serious or worthy of consideration, especially if it impeded progress towards creating an "empire for liberty." Early Americans then combined this idea of political liberty and Protestantism so that expanding the country across the continent became a goal for liberty and the Christian God. Expansion into Mexico became a type of crusade to liberate America from Catholic Mexico. Land speculators, railroad promoters, and small farmers eager for a chance to start over favored "manifest destiny." The United States could envision its potential reach, stretching from sea to sea with railroad lines and electric telegraph lines crossing the land integrating the new continental empire. Martial manhood dominated American imperialism and expansion before the Civil War. It fostered unstoppable and rapid growth across the continent. The balance of power between slave states and free states became more critical to the stability of the new country.

Senators debated proposed bills in Congress in terms of the sections of the country rather than considering the general welfare of all, pulling at the fragile fabric of the flag that waved over the entire country. While debating a tariff compromise proposed by Kentucky Senator Henry Clay in 1845, South Carolina Senator John C. Calhoun objected to the proposed compromise on tariffs, saying it would betray the South. He said Northerners would have to agree to federal protection of slavery for the South to feel comfortable remaining in the Union. The North did not agree to federal protection of slavery. While the national leaders failed to resolve the issue, the country continued to expand westward to the Pacific, increasing the tension.

The following year the country removed the barriers to the final expansion of the remainder of the continent. In 1846, the British claims to the Oregon Territory were ended. This vast territory encompassed land that would later become parts of the states of Washington, Oregon, Idaho, Iowa, and Montana. On January 24, 1848, when Joseph was nine-years-old, gold nuggets were discovered in the Sacramento Valley in the California territory at Sutter's Mill in the American River at the base of the Sierra Nevada Mountains. Days later the Treaty of Guadalupe Hidalgo was signed, ending the Mexican-American War and leaving California in the hands of the United States. As news spread of the discovery, thousands of prospectors traveled by sea or over land to San Francisco and the surrounding area to join in the mad gold rush. The Gold Rush led to the growth of the population in California and the necessity of admitting California as the thirty-first state on September 9, 1850. Southerners knew it would be admitted as a free state because Mexico had prohibited slavery. This meant that admitting California as the thirty-first state would be counted as the sixteenth free state in the Union, giving the non-slave-holding states an edge in the Senate with sixteen free states and fifteen slave states. Since the non-slave states already held the House of Representatives, the free states would then dominate legislation.

The U.S. Congress then passed the Fugitive Slave Act of 1850 as part of the Compromise of 1850 between Southern slave-holding states and Northern "Free-Soilers." As time passed, Northern citizens and leaders became convinced of a Southern slave power conspiracy, while Southern citizens and leaders defiantly defended the institution of slavery. Each section of the country was taking a stand on the issue of slavery, which was becoming intractable.

Zachary Taylor was elected as the President of the United States from 1849 to 1850, and the Blackburn family friend John C. Breckinridge was elected to the Kentucky state legislature. In 1850, the Whig Millard Fillmore became President with no U.S. Vice President, and the Whig John L. Helm became Kentucky Governor, with no Kentucky Lieutenant Governor. These men would not be the leaders who could maintain calm between the wary sections of the country or within the state of Kentucky. Tensions continued to build between the pro-slavery and the anti-slavery proponents. There was no clear resolution at hand, and no great leader stepped up to alleviate the crisis.

In 1850, Kentucky passed its pro-slavery constitution. The tracks for the state's future destination seemed to be leading in one direction. Abraham Lincoln pleaded for patient confidence in the justice of the people over time. Daniel Webster pleaded with the North to accept Southern demands for the sake of the Union. Things remained calm for a time, but by 1852, Clay of the West, Calhoun of the South, and Webster of the North had all passed away. No one was left standing to maintain balance between the anti-slavery and the pro-slavery factions. The generation that followed did not produce any "father-figure" leaders that could unite the country without the force of arms. Less than a decade later, Senator Calhoun's warning came to pass with the outbreak of the Civil War.

By 1851, the Kentucky Colonization Society was fighting a losing battle. Only 297 freed people had been transported from Kentucky to Liberia, and there were still ten thousand freed slaves in the state.

Kentucky residents were uncomfortable. When Joseph was twelve-years-old, the Kentucky legislature passed an act on March 24, 1851 that required all freed slaves to leave the state immediately upon securing their freedom and at the same time forbade free persons from other states from entering Kentucky. This was meant to encourage the colonization effort, but it did not succeed. The situation was deteriorating for slaves and freed slaves. Solutions to the slavery issue were desperately needed. More and more slaves escaped using the "Underground Railroad" to seek freedom in the North. Harriet Beecher Stowe wrote *Uncle Tom's Cabin; or Life Among the Lowly* and published it in 1851. It was the story of long-suffering slave Uncle Tom enduring the harsh realities of slavery while asserting that Christian love could overcome something as destructive as enslavement of a fellow man.

Many slaves were sold from the country's large slave market in Lexington at Cheapside, separating families and compelling Stephen Foster to write "My Old Kentucky Home" in 1852 in protest of the cruelties of slavery and the havoc it wreaked on slave families. It is a mournful song sung from the perspective of a slave who has been sold down-river to New Orleans and from there to a sugar plantation in the Deep South, where life will be lonelier, more difficult, and probably fatal. While he waits to be shipped out, the slave sings of his life in Kentucky with his family and other slaves, sad that financial hard times in Kentucky had caused his owner to sell him and the others. He sings a lonely song grieving his fate on a plantation in the Deep South, where there was little regard for the slave's personal health or happiness. Once the song was published and released, it became extremely popular, selling thousands of copies. The first verse of the song was adopted as Kentucky's state song in 1928, and later in 1986, the phrase was changed from, "the darkies are gay" to "the people are gay."

Chapter Five

Coming of Age in a Time of National Political Unrest

The competing forces in the country continued as Joseph came of age. Southern dissatisfaction continued even though the Fugitive Slave Law had been strengthened by the (second) Missouri Compromise of 1850. This discontent led to the development of a plan to create a separate world to their liking: one that required slavery. Dr. C.C. Graham first revealed the grandiose scheme in his article on Bland Ballard in which he said that General Wilkinson had told him that he and other prominent leaders were paid by the Spanish Crown and that they were planning to create a new empire with Aaron Burr as their first Emperor, like the scheme pursued by a group known as the "Knights of the Golden Circle." The overarching plan of the Knights of the Golden Circle ("KGC") was to form a separate country that was to include the Southern Confederate States, Cuba, Central America, South America, and Mexico, forming a great golden circle of territories dependent on a slave-based economy. The slave-holding Southern Empire was envisioned as a great circle centered around the proposed capital at Havana, Cuba. Under the plan, Mexico would be acquired and divided into fifteen new slave-holding states that would then shift the balance of power in Congress in favor of slavery. The new states would form a crescent around the Gulf of Mexico and thrive on a strong economy based on cotton, sugar, tobacco, rice, coffee, indigo, and mining, with labor provided by slaves.

Tensions simmered in 1853. Then the Kansas-Nebraska Act of 1854 was enacted as "an act to organize the territories of Nebraska and Kansas." It repealed the Missouri Compromise and *reopened* the national struggle over slavery in the Western territories. Pro-slavery and anti-slavery settlers rushed to Kansas, each side hoping to decide the issue in their favor by votes or force. The Republican Party evolved after the Kansas-Nebraska Act of 1854, formed by those who opposed the spread of slavery into the territories. People chose sides, and they were ready to fight in Kansas over the issue of slavery under the guise of the right of a state to choose to support slavery upon its admittance to the Union.

The Kansas-Nebraska Act of 1854 led to corruption, hatred, anger, and violence. Men from the neighboring pro-slavery state of Missouri crossed the border and voted illegally to ensure a vote for slavery. Stuffed ballot boxes in Kansas ensured that a legislature friendly to slavery would be elected. Anti-slavery or "free-soil" settlers reacted and formed a legislature of their own in Topeka. Within two years, there was armed conflict between the proponents of slavery and those who opposed it. Kansas became known as "Bloody Kansas." It is fair to say that the Kansas-Nebraska Act of 1854 was the catalytic event that led civilians into bloody conflicts, a precursor to the Civil War. By the end of 1856, over two hundred people had been gunned down in cold blood.

The violence spilled over onto the U.S. Congressional floor when Representative Preston Brooks of South Carolina beat Massachusetts Senator Charles Sumner over his head with a gold-tipped cane for Sumner's bitter speech in the Senate called "The Crime against Kansas," in which Sumner blasted the murderers in Kansas and indulged in a personal tirade against South Carolina Senator Andrew Butler. Sumner declared Butler an imbecile and said, "Senator Butler has chosen a mistress. I mean the harlot, slavery." Representative Brooks brutally caned Sumner for these words. It took Sumner many years to recover from the physical and psychological injuries that resulted from the caning. The situation was out of control.

The KGC increased its numbers, rituals, regalia, goals, and money and sought to extend its vision of a southern slave-based government. This vision was represented by the emblem of a crescent in the KGC regalia. Skull and crossbones represented *death* to all abolitionists and those who opposed Southern independence. The focus shifted to the disruption of the United States, which they considered an "accursed Union" whose continuance would only degrade and oppress the South. The KGC gave up the expensive kidnapping business and turned to the development of castles in the Southern states to increase their membership and political strength. Even the architecture of the day in Kentucky reflected the image of castles in fence rows, buildings, and distilleries—many of which remain visible today—in a pervasive spread of the underlying message.

Between 1856 and 1860, there was more violence and the political process continued to break down. This flood of violence hurried the country toward civil war. The Supreme Court offered the last hope to put the burning issue of slavery in the territories to rest with the *Dred Scott v. Sanford* case, 60 U.S. 393 (1857), but the decision failed to resolve it. The Supreme Court decided that a slave who had lived in a free territory was not free when he returned to a slave state and that neither a state nor Congress had the right to outlaw slavery. Abolitionists could not accept this. Debates were held all over the country about the issue. The national debate drew the young lawyer Abraham Lincoln from Illinois to return to politics, seeking Stephen Douglas's seat in Congress. Their series of debates summarized the most pressing issues of the presidential election of 1860. Northern leaders could never accept a President who planned to protect or extend slavery, and Southern leaders would never accept a President who refused to do so.

During this period of political unrest, Joseph attended Centre College in Danville, graduating in 1857 at the age of nineteen. He then "read law" in Lexington with the abolitionist George Blackburn Kinkead (1849-1940), his second cousin, who was willing to help him as a family member. They may have shared a belief in the education and eventual emancipation of slaves. George Kinkead had served as Lincoln's lawyer in the settlement of an estate case against a claim that he had not disbursed collected funds, an allegation disputed by an indignant Lincoln in a letter to Kinkead discussing the claims. Kinkead represented Lincoln and was a Whig, but later when Lincoln became President, Kinkead was unable to support all the actions of the Lincoln administration, even though he too opposed secession. Joseph would have been well aware of his cousin's abolitionist views. By the time Joseph was admitted to the bar in 1858, around the age of twenty, there were seventeen free states and fifteen slave states in the Union. The tensions between the anti-slavery and pro-slavery factions were building.

The country continued in a state of political tension when Joseph married Terese Graham in 1859. The newlyweds moved to Chicago, Illinois, after Joseph was admitted to the bar. He practiced with his brother-in-law Judge B. S. Morris, who was married to Joseph's older sister Mary. It was there in Chicago that Joseph had the good fortune to be helped by Abraham Lincoln in his first case when he appeared before the U.S. District Court in Chicago. Joseph's opposing counsel was the prominent attorney Isaac N. Arnold. Arnold was the lead counsel for the Chicago bar and would later serve as a U.S. Congressman and become Lincoln's first biographer. Years later Joseph recalled the case:

> I was a very young man, beginning the practice of law, and, for the first time, I was appearing in a United States court in Chicago. The opposing [counsel] was Isaac N. Arnold, one of the most distinguished men of Chicago. When the case was reached, I was so nervous that I became bewildered and made only a feeble effort. I was about to sit down and let the case go by default, as it were, when a tall, homely, loose-jointed man sitting in the bar, who I had noticed giving close attention to the case, arose and addressed the court in behalf of the position I had assumed in my feeble argument, making the points so clear that when he closed the court sustained my demurrer.
>
> I didn't know who my volunteer friend was, but Mr. Arnold got up and attempted to rebuke him for interfering in the matter, when I for the first time, heard that he was Abraham Lincoln of Springfield.
>
> Mr. Lincoln, in his good-natured reply to Mr. Arnold's strictures on his interference, said that he claimed the privilege of giving a young Kentucky lawyer from the State of his birth a boost when struggling with his first case, especially if he was pitted against an experienced practitioner.
>
> Of course, I thanked him, and departed from the court as proud as a young field marshal. I never saw Mr. Lincoln again, and he probably never recalled the young struggling lawyer that he so kindly assisted and rescued from defeat in his maiden effort before a United States tribunal.

Chapter Six

Joseph Campaigns for Breckinridge Against Lincoln

In 1860 at the age of twenty-one, Joseph left his job in his brother-in-law's Chicago law practice and returned to Kentucky with his wife and their newborn son, Joseph Clay Stiles Blackburn, Jr., born in June 1859 in Chicago. Once home, he turned to politics, assisting John Breckinridge in his bid for the U.S. Presidency in the 1860 campaign. Joseph's work probably consisted of attracting supporters and voters, much like campaign workers today. The Democratic Party in the 1860 campaign had split into two seemingly irreconcilable different parties: Breckinridge ran as the candidate for the Southern Democrats against the Northern Democratic candidate Stephen Douglas. The split in the Democratic Party did not resolve all of the contentious issues over slavery and state's rights. There were dissensions within the faction of the Southern Democrats. The Southern Democratic Party held a convention in Charleston, South Carolina, on April 23, 1860. Joseph's brother-in-law Thompson Breckinridge Flournoy was elected chairman. Unfortunately, the Southern Democrats in Charleston could not agree upon a candidate, and they adjourned without nominating anyone. They met again in Baltimore in June but again failed to nominate a candidate.

The problems could be traced to the KGC, which sought to divide the Democratic national ticket from Stephen Douglas, whose platform was not as pro-slavery as they wanted. The Democrats sought to adopt a former platform called "the old Cincinnati Platform" and merely add that the slavery question in the territories should be settled by the U.S. Supreme Court, presuming it would provide Southern Democrats sufficient protection and guarantee to the rights of property and slaves everywhere and protect the institution of slavery. However, the Knights, like Breckinridge and, presumably, Joseph, would not agree to this because they wanted a full and explicit acknowledgment that "neither Congress or a Territorial Legislature" could impair the rights of property in slaves and that it was "the duty of the Federal Government, in all its departments, to protect the rights of persons and property in the territories, *and wherever else its authority extends.*" The KGC knew this would not be acceptable to the proponents of the Northern Democrats. Their goal was to divide the Democratic National platform, which they were able to accomplish.

Unable to agree, the Democratic National Party separated into the Northern Democrats and the Southern Democrats, and the two parts of the Democratic Party each nominated a candidate. Senator Stephen Douglas of Illinois was nominated by friends of the doctrine of "Popular Sovereignty." Herschel Johnson of Georgia was chosen for Vice President.

A rebel "rump" convention representing the conservative or "states-rights" wing of the Southern Democratic Party unanimously nominated then-U.S. Vice President John C. Breckinridge of Kentucky for U.S. President and unanimously nominated Senator Joseph Lane of Oregon for Vice President. Each Democratic Party convention, however, denounced the Abolition Party as "subversive of the Constitution, and revolutionary" in its tendency.

To add to the confusion, a third convention was held in Baltimore by the old Whig Party with delegates from all states, saying that they were the party who declared it to be "both the party of patriotism and of duty to recognize no political principle other than the Constitution of the country, the Union of the States, and the enforcement of the laws." The Whig Party nominated John Bell of Tennessee and Edward Everett of Massachusetts.

This meant that there were four rival national tickets in 1860:

1. The Constitutional-Union Party led by Bell and Everett, which ignored the territorial controversy altogether. (Whig Party)
2. The Party of Popular Sovereignty headed by Douglas and Johnson, which affirmed the right of the people of the territories to decide about slavery. (Northern Democratic Party)
3. The States-Rights Party supporting Breckinridge and Lane, which stated that the territories were open to citizens with slaves. (Southern Democratic Party)

4. The Republicans supporting Lincoln and Hannibal Hamlin, which asserted the right and duty of Congress to exclude the slaves from the territories.

Lincoln's views on the slavery issue had evolved from his Quaker-like roots into an anti-slavery view that would be called the Northern view. When President Lincoln said the issue was one of limiting "the extension of slavery" into territories, Southern leaders proclaimed that "the only true Republic is an absolute slave Republic." Lincoln announced that the Union "could not permanently endure, half slave and half free." Each side in the 1860 Presidential campaign dug into its position on slavery.

The Republican convention assembled in Chicago on May 16, 1860 to nominate a candidate for Presidency. At this Republican convention, there were no Southern delegates present who came from below the latitude of thirty-six degrees, thirty minutes (or the southern border of Missouri as it was described in the Missouri Compromise). For the first time, instead of nominating one candidate from a state in the North and one from a state in the South for President and Vice President, as had been done traditionally, the Republican convention nominated two men from Northern states: Lincoln of Illinois and Hannibal Hamlin of Maine.

Lincoln's Republican platform opposed slavery in any territory of the United States and supported the power of Congress to prohibit slavery in the territories. The Southern Democratic Breckinridge "secession ticket" divided the vote from the Northern Democratic Douglas ticket, preventing either Democrat from receiving a majority of the votes. The divide in the Democratic Party split the votes, and the ineffectiveness of the Whig Party allowed the Republican Party to win the general election. Republican Abraham Lincoln became the sixteenth President of the United States. Even though the KGC secession ticket of the Southern Democrats lost, the election enabled members of the KGC to learn which Northerners might support them in the event of a revolution. This could be valuable information if a revolution took place in 1861 when soldiers supporting the Southern cause would be needed. During this time, many letters were exchanged among members, assuring the KGC of Northern support. There were then thirty-three states that made up the United States of America in 1860.

If the Whig Party and Democratic Party delegates, both Northern and Southern, had cooperated with one another and united their forces, choosing one nominee to best represent their position, they might have carried the election and been able to avert the secession of the Southern states and the eventual Civil War. That is the tragedy, that the Northern Democrats, the Southern Democrats, and the Whigs did not unite and save the country from the terrible Civil War. However, the radical force of the KGC successfully disrupted any chance of the three parties uniting in a compromise because it was determined to force the Southern states to secede. Compromise among the three parties could have saved many lives and much suffering.

Attempts were made by Bell, the Whig candidate, and Breckinridge, the Southern Democratic candidate, who were each "willing to withdraw" from the Presidential campaign if a generally acceptable candidate could be selected besides the three presented. But the Northern Democratic candidate Douglas refused to withdraw, saying that if he withdrew, his mostly Northern Democratic friends would join in support of Lincoln, rather than any new candidate who might be promoted instead of him. The split in the Democratic Party helped to deliver a victory to the Republicans. With the election of Lincoln, the political divide between the Democratic and Republican parties expanded. The KGC had successfully split the Democratic Party and driven Southern slave states into secession.

When Lincoln was elected, the leaders from the Southern slave states thought it represented the end of slavery. Kentucky Senator Crittenden attempted to smooth tensions and introduced a joint resolution proposing amendments to the Constitution, including restoring and incorporating the geographical line of the Missouri Compromise, or the "Crittenden Compromise," with other provisions. Then another Kentuckian, Mr. Powell, tried to resolve the tensions in Congress and introduced a proposition to refer the problem to a special committee, which was adopted but to no avail. Another resolution was introduced by Senator Green of Missouri, but it was not adopted because it called for setting up armed police forces on the borders, which would have escalated tensions rapidly. This idea shocked many. In desperation, the House of Representatives tried to appoint a committee of thirty-three members, one for each state of the Union, to match the Senate's committee of thirteen, to "inquire into the present condition of the country," but they were unable to reach any agreement. Eventually they produced a majority report, which was adopted, but it failed to provide or suggest any solution of the territorial question, which was the vital point of the controversy. Things looked bleak at the end of the year. Southern states began to prepare their defenses by assembling arms and preparing for the battle that seemed imminent to them. They began to think of themselves as a separate entity against the U.S. Government.

On December 20, 1860, South Carolina adopted an ordinance that revoked the state's delegated powers and withdrew from the Union. The band had played "Dixie" in celebration after each vote for secession at St. Andrew's Hall in Charleston, South Carolina. The next day, all of South Carolina's representatives retired from their seats in Congress. The U.S. Senate and House had not acted to avert the coming catastrophe.

After Lincoln's election as the sixteenth U.S. President, seven Southern slave states seceded from the United States and joined the Confederate States of America: Mississippi on January 9, 1861; Florida on January 10, 1861; Alabama on January 11, 1861; Georgia on January 19, 1861; and Louisiana on January 26, 1861. Texas seceded on February 1, 1861, the last of the Deep South states, which were then joined by the four states of the Upper South: Virginia, which seceded on April 17, 1861 (except for its northwestern counties, which broke away and formed the Union-loyal free state of West Virginia); Arkansas on May 6, 1861; North Carolina on May 20, 1861; and Tennessee on June 8, 1861. The constitutionally recognized government of Kentucky and Missouri did not officially secede, however, and failed to join the Confederate cause, choosing to remain neutral.

On February 18, 1861, Jefferson Davis was inaugurated as the President of the newly formed Confederate States of America at the first Confederate capital in Montgomery, Alabama, where the song "Dixie" became something of a Confederate anthem. Like Kentucky, it was a complicated situation in Missouri, and though Missouri later seceded, Kentucky still remained a part of the Union. An unofficial Kentucky government formed and seceded and then dissolved, meaning Kentucky basically remained in the Union, although by force under Union military rule. This meant twenty-two free states defended the Union against eleven Confederate slave states. Sadly, the leaders of the states in each section of the Union had failed to recognize their economic interdependence on the other section and suffered economically after the secession and during and after the Civil War. Fighting soon erupted after the Southern states seceded.

Additional efforts had been made to avoid the war. In February, more than one hundred of the country's leading politicians held the "Peace Conference of 1861" to prevent the coming war. It failed. President Lincoln did everything he could to prevent a Civil War, but the Confederates were determined to protect the lucrative slave business. The Confederates had amassed a stock-pile of weapons and large sums of money to fund the war from numerous and various supporters all over the country. They had established a secret, extensive network of like-minded visionaries in their "brotherhood" of the KGC, who were determined to establish an empire with an economy based on slavery.

The election of Lincoln brought rejoicing among the KGC, who saw that the hour of *"Southern deliverance had come."* Shockingly, there were "a majority of genuine Knights in the Cabinet," including U.S. Secretary of War John B. Floyd, allowing the KGC ample time and facilities to drag six more states out of the Union, occupy forts, steal arms, "as much as three hundred thousand of the best arms of the Federal Government, to fortify themselves," and generally defy the U.S. Government. Peace was never a serious option. The Civil War soon followed these dismal efforts. Kentucky's own Governor Magoffin was said to be one of the Knights. Even though Kentucky was populated with Southern sympathizers, the Union military presence maintained the state's official neutrality during the Civil War.

In *The Private Journal and Diary of John H. Surratt, The Conspirator,* Surratt details his introduction to the KGC in the summer of 1860 by another Knight, John Wilkes Booth, and his induction on July 2, 1860 at a castle in Baltimore, Maryland. He describes the elaborate and secret induction ceremony and its rituals and revealed that cabinet members, congressmen, judges, actors, and other politicians attended the ceremony. He wrote in his diary that the KGC began plotting to kidnap Lincoln in 1860 before he was inaugurated in 1861, and when that failed, the plots continued throughout the Civil War, ultimately resulting in the misguided Knight John Wilkes Booth assassinating President Lincoln on April 14, 1865. It was a treacherous and powerful group that worked aggressively and secretly to impose their business and political model on others that ultimately failed.

Before the KGC's treachery took his life, Lincoln could not understand why the South thought that his Republican administration would interfere with their slaves. In his first inaugural address given on March 4, 1861, he tried to assure the Southern states that his administration did not intend to end slavery in the slave states where it existed when he was elected. He affirmed that under his administration the government would not forcefully cross any state or territory line. He also declared the Union perpetual and incapable of being terminated, meaning the secession of the Southern states did not terminate the Union because, he reasoned, any resolves or ordinances to secede were legally void. Furthermore, he reasoned that acts of violence against the Union were insurrectionary or revolutionary.

Lincoln declared that it was his job and duty to see that the laws of the Union were faithfully executed in all of the states, which he vowed to do as long as the American people supported it. He made it clear that the Union "will constitutionally defend and maintain itself." The Union would not instigate the fighting but, if attacked, would defend itself. Secession, he said, was anarchy. "A majority, held in restraint by constitutional checks, and limitations, and always changing easily, with the deliberate changes of popular opinions and sentiments, is the only true sovereign of a free people." Those who rejected the American constitutional form of government balanced by checks and limitations chose anarchy or despotism in some form.

Lincoln knew that there was only one dispute at the heart of the threat to the Union: slavery. "One section of the country believes slavery is *right*, and ought to be extended, while the other believes it is *wrong*, and ought not to be extended. This is the only substantial dispute." Lincoln knew that secession would not solve the dispute of slavery simply because, physically speaking, the Northern and Southern sections of the country could not separate or remove their respective sections from one another. Slavery would continue to be disputed between the two sections, even if each section attempted to operate independently. As he said, the different parts of the country "cannot but remain face to face; and intercourse, either amicable or hostile, must continue between them." The questions of slavery would continue. He pleaded for faith in the U.S. Constitution:

> Why should there not be a patient confidence in the ultimate justice of the people? Is there any better, or equal hope, in the world?...
>
> In *your* hands, my dissatisfied fellow countrymen, and not in *mine*, is the momentous issue of civil war. The government will not assail *you*. You can have no conflict, without being yourselves the aggressors. *You* have no oath registered in Heaven to destroy the government, while *I* shall have the most solemn one to "preserve, protect and defend" it.
>
> I am loath to close. We are not enemies, but friends. We must not be enemies. Though passion may have strained, it must not break our bonds of affection. The mystic chords of memory, stretching from every battle-field, and patriot grave, to every living heart and hearthstone, all over this broad land, will yet swell the chorus of the Union, when again touched, as surely they will be, by the better angels of our nature.

It is difficult today from our anti-slavery perspective to understand or begin to explain how well-educated men could fight to the death for an immoral cause, except to say that it was driven by greed. We know that people will fight to the death when their source of income and way of life are challenged, especially when they can see no other way to make a living for their families, but it is difficult to believe that no one thought of another way to make a living, given the abundant resources in the state. It could have been cheaper for the government to have bought every slave's freedom rather than fight the Civil War. It serves as a cautionary tale of limiting one's perspective in life to thinking that what is familiar and habitual is the only option. The cruelty and suffering to all the enslaved people, first in the colonies and then in the United States, and its impact on the people involved in this country's macabre time of slavery ultimately weighs on each of us today. As President Obama said in a speech on December 9, 2015, "The scars of our nation's original sin are with us now."

Part Two

Wearing the Gray

Chapter Seven

Joseph Follows Kentucky's Star

Just eighty-five years after the United States of America was founded, many of its Southern citizens did not trust that young system to protect their interests and turned to arms to resolve differences of political opinions over the legality and morality of slavery. The great experiment of democracy faced its most serious challenge from its unhappy citizens, who were unwilling to wait for the political process to address their grievances. War erupted at Fort Sumter, South Carolina, when Confederate forces bombarded Union soldiers on April 12, 1861. Lincoln's pleas to trust in the government's system of checks and balances had gone unheeded. It is a wonder that our form of government continues today after this crisis. But that is now. Then, state leaders and citizens struggled with the moral, political, and military choices that had to be made. Tough choices had to be made and made quickly. Joseph Blackburn was a twenty-two-year old lawyer, married, with an infant son, living in Kentucky in his parents' home at *Equira,* where he had returned when he joined John Breckinridge's unsuccessful 1860 U.S. presidential campaign.

With Lincoln as President, the young lawyer was drawn into the inevitable conflict between the Union and the Southern states that chose to form into the Confederacy. Not surprisingly, he chose to follow his family, friends, community, and political mentor and joined the Confederate cause. He joined, even though Kentucky chose to remain neutral and refused to arm, outfit, pay, feed, or otherwise care for those who wished to fight for the South. Kentucky men who chose to wear the gray uniform of the Confederacy had to fund their fight quickly by providing their own horses, weapons, gear, and clothing and whatever else they could provide, while Union soldiers were outfitted by the U.S. government, armed, trained, paid, and fed. It was a commitment either way.

What follows is a brief review of some of the local events in Kentucky after the election of Lincoln and the outbreak of the Civil War, briefly tracking the state's neutrality followed by its formal plea for Union aid, bringing the state under Union control while a shadow state government chose to join the Confederacy. Kentucky was represented simultaneously by a star in the Union flag and one in the Confederate flag. Joseph followed Kentucky's star in the Confederate flag in the footsteps of Confederate commanders John Breckinridge and William Preston. While there are few records of Joseph Blackburn's individual actions during his military service as aide-de-camp to General William Preston, the records of General Preston's actions during the Civil War provide a comprehensive description of his military action.

Kentucky's Neutrality

Kentucky Governor Beriah Magoffin believed that the rights of the Southern States had been violated, and he favored the right of secession but avoided it as much as possible. On April 15, 1861, President Lincoln sent a telegram to Governor Magoffin requesting that the Commonwealth supply part of the initial troops to put down the rebellion, which the Governor refused: "President Lincoln, Washington, D.C. I will send not a man nor a dollar for the wicked purpose of subduing my sister Southern states. B. Magoffin."

Most Kentuckians opposed secession and favored Kentucky's U.S. Senator John J. Crittenden's position that the state should act as a mediator between the two sides. Indeed, soon thereafter, both houses of the Kentucky General Assembly passed the "declarations of neutrality," officially declared by Governor Magoffin in May of 1861. The Kentucky legislature passed the resolution in an effort to prevent Kentucky from seceding and becoming a battleground. Confronted with Kentucky's neutral stance, Lincoln had to act with care towards the state and wait "for the population's latent Unionism to assert itself." He avoided forcing the issue like he had done in Maryland because it would have been easy to drive the state into the Confederacy. Lincoln made no threats and used conciliatory language, even though many Republican governors, newspaper editors, and military leaders begged him to take control of the state by invading it. Lincoln did not think that Kentucky could remain neutral for long. He forbade the army to recruit volunteers in the state, declined to prohibit trade with the Confederacy, and promised Garrett Davis, a prominent Unionist, that the Union would not use force against the state if it did not resist the laws and authority of the United States. Lincoln repeated this pledge in another meeting with state leaders in July but did not commit to future action, even though he had begun shipping arms to Kentucky Unionists and by early summer had authorized recruiting Union troops in the state. The soft touch paid off in a special Congressional election held in June when Union candidates won nine of ten seats, including the election of U.S. Representative John J. Crittenden, the symbol of border state Unionism.

By February 1, 1861, the seven states of the Deep South had seceded, and by June 8, 1861 the four states of the Upper South had also seceded, forming the new ill-fated republic of the Confederate States of America dedicated to preserving slavery under the argument of states' rights and political liberty for whites. The capital of the Confederacy was at first in Montgomery, but by May 1861, the summer's humid heat and mosquitoes changed the minds of the Confederate leaders about the suitability of Montgomery. When the recently seceded Virginia offered their own state and capital as the seat of the Confederacy, the Confederate leaders accepted, and on May 29, 1861, Jefferson Davis arrived in Virginia to cheering crowds.

Albert Sidney Johnston, who had been the Commander of the U.S. Army Department of the Pacific in California, resigned his federal position when he heard that his adopted state of Texas had seceded from the Union on February 1 , 1861. Johnston's resignation was accepted on May 6, 1861. Johnston became one of the key leaders in the Confederacy and the fight in Kentucky.

While U. S. Army soldiers resigned and then joined the Confederate cause, an astonishing number of citizens helped the Confederates early in 1861 and throughout the war, and many would be arrested for "disloyalty" to the U.S. Government. (See the *Record Book, State Department, "Arrests for Disloyalty."*) So many people aided the Confederates that life seemed chaotic. Order needed to be restored during war time. As one Loyalist wrote in a letter:

> It is a melancholy fact that hundreds of men who before this rebellion were above reproach, who were ornaments in society

and high perhaps in public station, are now acting the traitor's part and in this our hour of needs are joining hands to strike down the best Government in and the hope of the world."

U.S. Secretary of State William H. Seward described the treasonous situation in the country in a March 25, 1862 letter to a North Carolina friend, he wrote regarding a person adjudged to be guilty of violating the emergency laws President Lincoln enacted to provide order in the time of the national crisis at Wilmington, North Carolina, and Halifax, Nova Scotia:

> You are but too well aware, sir, that a party of seditious persons early in the last year [1861] organized an insurrection and attempted by civil war to set up a revolutionary government under the name of the Confederate States of America upon the ruins of the constitutional government of the United States of America....
>
> You hardly need to be reminded that as early as the month of March last [1861] the insurgents laid siege around this capital which siege has only been fully raised within the past month; nor are you a stranger to the fact that agents of the revolutionary authorities have for more than a year [1861–1862] been engaged in different parts of the United States endeavoring to extend the insurrection while others being political agents were abroad, some seeking direct intervention by the European states to subvert the American Union, and still others who were commercial agents were engaged in those states obtaining ships, ordnance, ammunition, military stores and supplies for the revolutionary army.... You are also aware that on the breaking out of this attempted revolution the President of the United States having issued his proclamation declaring the existence of the insurrection assumed the extraordinary powers vested in him by the Constitution for such emergencies and proceeded to suppress it by prohibiting commercial intercourse and treasonable correspondence with the then insurrectionary portion of the country and the other parts of the United States, and arresting and detaining temporarily when necessary without judicial process parties

> who were found or suspected on probable grounds to be engaged in contraband trade or treasonable combination and conspiracies against the Government.....

As a part of the extraordinary power that Lincoln assumed, on April 27, 1861, Lieutenant General Winfield Scott, U.S. Army, was authorized to suspend the writ of habeas corpus in his discretion on any military line between Washington and Philadelphia. Suspending the privilege of the writ of habeas corpus meant that the commanding general was authorized to arrest and detain individuals as he determined might be dangerous to the public safety, a precedent dating back to the common law and England. President Lincoln soon thereafter issued a second proclamation to suspend the privilege of the writ of habeas corpus in Florida.

President Lincoln searched for ways to control the Southern spies and sympathizers within the Union. On July 2, 1861, President Lincoln instructed the U.S. General-in-Chief Winfield Scott:

> You are engaged in repressing an insurrection against the laws of the United States. If at any point on or in the vicinity of any military line which is now or which shall be used between the city of New York and the city of Washington, you find resistance which renders it necessary to suspend the writ of habeas corpus for public safety you personally or through the office in command at the point where resistance occurs are authorized to suspend the writ."

The suspension of the write of habeas corpus was later approved by Congress.

Throughout the spring and summer of 1861, both sides recruited in Kentucky, but Lincoln continued to ignore Confederate activities in the state. In the next special election in August to elect a new state legislature, Unionists won seventy-six of one hundred seats in the Kentucky House, combined with the previously elected holdovers in twenty-seven of thirty-eight seats in the Senate. Unionists were firmly in control of the state legislature and the Congressional delegation. Lincoln had been correct to handle the state carefully. It was only a matter of time until Kentucky's policy of neutrality was discarded.

Remaining neutral is a difficult business. There were events of military and political action taking place within its borders. Many Kentuckians wanted to remain above the fray, but as events took place on their soil, their hearts began to turn. Kentucky slaveholders were divided in their support between the Union and the Confederacy because the Lincoln administration had not made the abolition of slavery a war aim. Many slaveholders wanted both the Union and slavery. But Kentucky men began to choose their sides. By August 1861, both the Union Army and the Confederate States Army were openly recruiting soldiers in the state.

Kentucky was critical to the Civil War effort. As Lincoln said, "I hope to have God on my side, but I must have Kentucky." In a September 1861 letter to Orville Browning, who was appointed to fill the U.S. Senate seat of Stephen A. Douglas after Douglas' untimely death, Lincoln wrote, "I think to lose Kentucky is nearly the same as to lose the whole game.... We would as well consent to separation at once, including the surrender of the capital." Kentucky was important to both the North and the South. It had the ninth-largest population in the Union in 1860 and was a major producer of tobacco, corn, wheat, hemp, and flax. The South wanted Kentucky for her border along the Ohio River, which would provide the South a defensible boundary. Kentucky became a central battleground with its key strategic position bordering the Northern Union States and the Southern Confederate States. Joseph Blackburn was caught up in the swirl of political and military events of the day. He chose the Confederate cause and served directly under William Preston.

The Orphan Brigade

The decisive event that drove Kentucky out of neutrality was the Confederate Army's invasion of the state on September 3, 1861 when Confederate General Leonidas Polk ordered Brigadier General Gideon J. Pillow to occupy Columbus without Jefferson Davis' approval. It was a major blunder. In quick order, U.S. forces under the command of Ulysses S. Grant, the 21st Illinois Volunteer Regiment, occupied Paducah, Kentucky, followed by the state legislature demanding the withdrawal of the Confederate forces. Governor Magoffin denounced both sides for violating Kentucky's neutrality. When the Confederacy refused to withdraw from the state, Kentucky's legislature requested federal aid to expel them from the neutral state. Lincoln promptly responded by sending additional troops to occupy the state and the Confederate forces were soon driven out of Kentucky. As a result of the failed attempt to establish a Confederate government and despite General Braxton Bragg's subsequent invasion in 1862, Kentucky thereafter became firmly under Union control during the war.

Military action within the state followed quickly thereafter. By early September 1861, the Kentucky legislature had voted to side with the Union. The Kentucky legislature, controlled by the Unionists, immediately requested John Breckinridge's resignation from the U.S. Senate. More military movements rapidly covered the state. By the first week of September, Union forces appeared in the state to take control. On September 6, 1861, Brigadier General U.S. Grant, commanding the federal forces in Southern Illinois and Southeastern Missouri, took Paducah, Kentucky unopposed where he issued a proclamation advising its citizens that the U.S. Army was there to protect and defend them against their common enemy in rebellion and would continue to do so until the state was able to defend itself. On September 13, 1861, Confederate General Albert Sidney Johnston ordered Brigadier General Felix Zollicoffer with the four thousand men under his command to occupy Cumberland Gap in Kentucky and block Union troops from coming into eastern Tennessee. More men chose sides. The situation grew more serious daily.

Kentucky men who had been respected leaders in the state were declared traitors by the state legislature when they joined the Confederate side, men like former U.S. Vice President and Kentucky U.S. Senator John Breckinridge, future Kentucky Governor Simon Buckner, and former Kentucky Governor Charles S. Morehead. Simon Buckner had been Kentucky's State Adjutant General and Major General in charge of the sixty-one companies that he had raised, but he resigned on July 20, 1861 when the state board that controlled the militias considered them secessionist and ordered them to store their arms. He accepted a commission as a brigadier general in the Confederate Army on September 14, 1861 and was followed by many of the men he had formerly commanded in the state militia. As soon as Buckner's Confederate commission was approved, Union officials in Louisville indicted him for treason and seized his property. By September 18, 1861, the Justice of the Peace of Jefferson County issued the warrant to arrest former Governor Charles S. Morehead. Events were moving rapidly in the state as the Union forces sought to establish order over the unruly supporters of the Southern position.

Many Southern Confederate supporters in Kentucky felt abandoned and orphaned by the state's decision to remain neutral and had no state organized military unit to join the fight. They looked to John C. Breckinridge as their natural leader. Breckinridge was the son of a prominent political family in Kentucky, whose grandfather had served in the U.S. Senate and as Attorney General under President Thomas Jefferson. John C. Breckinridge was the former Vice President of the United States and former candidate for U.S. President in the 1860 presidential election against Lincoln and Douglas. He was the former Kentucky statesman who had represented Kentucky in the U.S. House of Representatives and the U.S. Senate. He had served as Speaker of the Kentucky House of Representatives. Naturally Joseph, who had campaigned for Breckinridge during the 1860 U.S. Presidential campaign, joined Breckinridge in the First Kentucky Brigade. Other Kentuckians quickly and willingly volunteered to join and follow Breckinridge. They loved him. They paid for their military training and provisioning from private funds. It was an extraordinary act for 1861, one that was not that uncommon in the days of the American Revolution, the War of 1812 or even during the Mexican-American War of 1848 when men had to make decisions, choose a side, and act with whatever means they had at their disposal. But it was extraordinary in 1861 when other states had dutifully formed their own militias. It was an unusual, unsettled time. The First Kentucky Brigade, also known as The Orphan Brigade, trained as best they could and later became known nationally as the fiercest fighting brigade and for never quitting a fight. As historian Kent Masterson Brown noted in *Johnny Green of the Orphan Brigade:*

> The Orphan Brigade campaigned over more territory (eight states), suffered higher casualties, and lost more brigade commanders than any other comparable unit in the war. And as if those trials were not enough, the brigade was never able to return to fight for its native state of Kentucky after February of 1862.

One of the flags of the First Kentucky Brigade Flag heralded the motto "Kentucky Shall Be Free," which presumably meant that Kentucky shall be free of the "tyrannical" U.S. Constitution and "free" to choose as a state whether to support the economic institution of slavery or to reject the morally bankrupt institution of slavery. The choice was a foregone conclusion in the minds of the members of the Orphan Brigade.

Twenty-two-year old Joseph enlisted in Kentucky's Orphan Brigade to help the Confederate cause. He was brash, confident, and felt that his life was charmed. He volunteered as aide-de-camp to Breckinridge's cousin, Colonel William Preston. Blackburn served with Colonel Preston during the Kentucky campaign when the Confederate forces retreated from Bowling Green, Kentucky, through Nashville and central Tennessee to the town of Corinth, Mississippi. Colonel Preston and Blackburn were at the decisive Confederate loss in the Battle of Fort Donelson in Tennessee that took place from February 11–16, 1861. More battles followed throughout the year. One major battle they fought was the Siege of Corinth in Mississippi in late April 1861, but it paled in comparison to the Battle of Shiloh that took place the following year.

In late March 1862, Confederate forces from Louisiana under General Daniel Ruggles and from the Gulf Coast under General Braxton Bragg joined General Johnston's troops at Corinth, Mississippi, which was just a railway junction in northeast Mississippi. The Confederate Army of forty thousand recently trained soldiers was just twenty-three miles south of General Grant's force of about forty thousand encamped around the Pittsburgh Landing on the Tennessee River north of the Mississippi-Tennessee line. Another thirty thousand under General Buell's command of Union Army soldiers were marching from Nashville to join Grant, but Confederate General Johnston attacked on April 3rd before the reinforcements arrived, which could have been a strategic plan if confusion, errors, and logistical problems had not delayed the Confederate troops' planned movements. On April 5, 1862, Johnston's second-in-command, Louisiana General Beauregard, argued for retreat since the advantages of time and surprise were gone, but Colonel Preston argued that there should be no delay, an opinion supported by John Breckinridge and Major General Leonidas Polk. General Johnston was determined to prove his worth in the battle and said as much to Colonel Preston, his brother-in-law. Joseph saw action in the ensuing battle.

The battle started the next morning, April 6, at 5:30 a.m. when a Union patrol came upon a Rebel patrol. The Battle of Shiloh would prove to be one of the hardest-fought battles in American military records. The small log Shiloh Church stood next to the bluff above Pittsburgh Landing, where most of the fighting took place. Colonel Preston noted the bucolic countryside in his note the night before the battle and during the battle noted the "sharp skirmishing," "loud cheers and handsome advance of our troops." By noon, he noted that the "camp carried and firing stopping." But Joseph Blackburn, along with the other Confederates, met unyielding resistance along a wooded wagon trail called "the Hornet's Nest" that kept them from advancing around the enemy line towards Pittsburgh Landing. Around 2:00 p.m., Colonel Preston urged his men, including Blackburn, to use their bayonets to advance and remove the Union troops. While the Colonel rode to the rear, one of his boots was ripped by a musket ball and his horse was wounded twice. Three hours later the Confederates broke the Union line, using two cannons firing in a fierce artillery barrage that forced Union General Benjamin M. Prentiss to surrender.

Confederate General Johnston thought he had proved himself with a victory that day. He sent a messenger with orders to a brigade to change position, but just at that moment, General Johnston was struck by a musket ball and was seriously wounded. The messenger returned to the general's side and led the general's horse to a protected ravine, where he could lay the general on the ground. Colonel Preston and the rest of his staff were called to his side. Joseph was likely there, as well. Kneeling down, Colonel Preston held his brother-in-law's head in his arms and "cried passionately, 'Johnston, do you know me?'" The general smiled faintly but gave no other sign of recognition. No one thought to staunch the bleeding from his right leg with a tourniquet. Preston called for whiskey, and Captain Haydon tried to pour it down the general's throat, but he was unable to swallow. He died from blood loss from a minie ball that had pierced an artery below his right knee. His son later said that the wound was not fatal, and if the doctor could have been found to attend to his father, his father could have lived. It was said that this was the first time in American history that such a high-ranking officer had been killed at the head of his troops, "at the moment of victory, after routing the enemy at every point." Colonel Preston notified Beauregard that he was now in command and said, "the completion of the victory would devolve on him." In Richmond, President Davis sent word of the death of his "long and close" friend to the Confederate Congress. Colonel Preston and five other members of the General's staff went with Johnston's body to New Orleans for burial, leaving his trusted aide-de-camp Joseph Blackburn in charge in Preston's absence, along with other trusted aides.

General Beauregard decided not to continue a sustained attack in the late afternoon of April 6, 1862 because his men were exhausted, but by early evening, General Grant had gathered fifty-three cannons above Pittsburgh Landing to protect his Union Army men. The next morning, Grant had seventeen thousand fresh troops to support him, which allowed him to re-take the Union's lost ground and force the Confederates to withdraw to Corinth. It was a victory for the Union. Joseph Blackburn had fought in one of the toughest battles and suffered the defeat with the Confederates. Naturally there was much debate over the wisdom of General Beauregard's decision, but the South lost one of the most crucial battles of the war at Shiloh, which resulted in the loss of control of the vital transportation routes in Western Tennessee and the lower Mississippi.

Of the seven thousand troops under Breckinridge's command at the battle, 386 were killed and 1,628 were wounded, including Breckinridge. Joseph Blackburn was not injured. John Breckinridge was then promoted to Major General on April 14, 1862. Major General Breckinridge was close to Confederate commanders Joseph E. Johnston, Wade Hampton, John B. Floyd, and William Preston, all of whom were related to him.

For his loyal service to the deceased General Johnston, General Beauregard and President Davis nominated William Preston for the rank of Brigadier General, which was approved by the Confederate Senate on April 18, 1862. Once he returned from New Orleans, Preston reported to the Louisiana commander and was assigned to General Breckinridge, who was reorganizing the First Kentucky Brigade or the "Orphan Brigade." Breckinridge placed Brigadier General Preston in charge of a new brigade made up of three regiments of the "Orphan Brigade" that included Blackburn and an Alabama battery. Preston wrote of his new unit, "I have... got to be popular among the men and getting them under my control and in better organization," relying on the aid of Joseph Blackburn to execute his orders.

In late May 1862, the Union troops forced the Confederates to retreat from Corinth, Mississippi. Joseph served with Preston as the rear guard, a fearsome task. While Breckinridge was on leave in Louisiana, the new Brigadier General Preston was placed in temporary command of the reserve corps with ten thousand soldiers, three thousand animals and 250 wagons and oversaw the removal of the government supplies from Oxford and Grenada, Mississippi, as they moved southward, placing more responsibilities on his aide Blackburn. Preston, Blackburn, and their men went to Abbeville, where they guarded a nearby railroad bridge over the small Tallahatchie River.

Preston was in poor health as they withdrew. He complained that they had been "on duty every day… since Bowling Green," and was confined to his quarters for nine days for his liver and digestive problems. His major complaint was against General Braxton Bragg's execution of the retreat that included six weeks of indecision and delay, plus the fact that he sent "the provision wagons . . . thirty miles in advance." The troops could not eat without the food on the supply wagons. They were hungry and demoralized, and desertions increased. Preston estimated that "we lost a fifth of the army… by sickness, straggling and desertion. We cannot show more than 40,000 to 45,000 effectives here now as against 50,000 to 55,000 effectives at Corinth." Preston criticized the leadership of both Beauregard and Bragg and felt that Bragg's abrasive personality and punitive military discipline of the soldiers resulted in resentment in the ranks. Preston continued to complain about General Bragg as the war progressed.

On June 23, 1862, Brigadier General Preston was ordered to bring his men by train to Vicksburg to help Major General Earl Van Dorn fight a fleet of Union gunboats that had been sent there from the Union-occupied cities of Memphis and New Orleans. Blackburn helped Preston's wagon train gather supplies as they traveled. Soon Breckinridge returned from Louisiana and resumed command of his troops, which were then camped along the river. Near Vicksburg, Preston developed a high fever in the midst of the heat, mosquitoes and malaria that surrounded them and was unable to lead the men further south. Many of the men fell ill, but Blackburn seems to have escaped the worst of it. This meant more leadership responsibilities were placed on his shoulders during Preston's illness, and Blackburn continued with General Breckinridge and the men southwards, where they attempted to remove the Union forces at Baton Rouge without success. Later Preston recovered and was able to rejoin the men and help reorganize the division on its return to Mississippi.

General Bragg replaced General Beauregard in June 1862 as commander of the Army of Tennessee. The General of the Army of East Tennessee, Major General Edmund Kirby Smith, supported a planned Confederate invasion of Kentucky in the fall of 1862, and General Preston concurred with him. In fact, Preston sent word to Confederate President Davis through his nephew William Preston Johnston, who served as aide-de-camp to Davis, to urge Davis to support the plan and asked that Davis require General Bragg to consult with President Davis and other Kentuckians familiar with the local political playing field before undertaking any invasion. General Bragg wrote to General Breckinridge that "it would please me to see General Preston along," so while Breckinridge's troops were sent to retake Corinth, Brigadier General Preston and his staff, including Blackburn, were relieved of their duties at their request to participate in the Kentucky campaign. The thought of fighting for Kentucky thrilled Preston and, no doubt, Blackburn. Preston wrote, "I wish to help secure Kentucky forever for the South. The hope makes me well and excites my every energy. I wish on returning to get the men of influence to espouse our cause and enlist their children in our own ranks."

September 1862 was when the Confederacy had its greatest success in Kentucky: General Bragg's forces marched into Tompkinsville until they were east of Bowling Green, while General Kirby invaded the state from the southeast. General Kirby Smith marched eleven thousand men into Lexington on September 2, 1862, with bands playing and colors flying and crowds cheering, applauding, and tossing flowers to the street to welcome them. Two days later, General John Hunt Morgan and his nine hundred men were cheered wildly as they paraded in columns of four down Limestone Street to Main Street and then to the ["Old"] Courthouse. "Dixie" and the "Bonnie Blue Flag" were played repeatedly for several weeks afterwards in Lexington. By the end of September, the Confederates controlled a line that ran from Bardstown in the west to Frankfort, Lexington, and Mount Sterling in the east. Preston and a few cavalrymen, including his trusted aide-de-camp Blackburn, then traveled from Mississippi through Chattanooga and Knoxville and joined General Kirby Smith's command in Kentucky.

General Bragg was glad to see the Kentuckians, noting that General Preston "has great influence here and will forward our recruiting." While the Confederates had control of Lexington, Preston stayed in his luxurious home, Wickliffe Place, in Louisville, with his family who were well, except for his wife, who had suffered a broken ankle. They entertained General Bragg with "brilliant festivities" at Wickliffe Place, as well. This home can no longer be seen because it was demolished many years after the war. No doubt, Joseph was able to return home to *Equira* to see his family for a brief respite from the fighting. It is likely that was the last time he saw his mother and father alive. His mother died just a few months later on June 3, 1863, and his father died in 1867 before Joseph was pardoned and allowed to return to Kentucky.

On October 8, 1862, the Confederate and Union forces met at Perryville outside of Danville, Kentucky, to finally determine who would control Kentucky. There, fifteen thousand of Bragg's men fought against Union Major General Don Carlos Buell's Federals. More Federal troops flowed into Kentucky from Tennessee, but each side avoided a major battle. In the end, Perryville would be considered an inconclusive but deadly afternoon of battle, where approximately seventy-six hundred men were killed on the rolling hills surrounded by hardwood trees. Over the next few days, the outnumbered Confederates slowly retreated to Tennessee. Brigadier General Preston and his aide Blackburn missed the Battle of Perryville because they were with Kirby Smith's army blocking the Federal troops that were expected to cross the Kentucky River at Frankfort. After the Confederates withdrew from Kentucky, Preston and Kirby Smith no longer trusted Bragg, and Bragg no longer trusted them because they had told him that thousands of volunteers would join them when they invaded Kentucky but instead only a few hundred joined in the fighting.

After the Kentucky campaign, Preston assumed command of an Alabama brigade until its wounded leader General Sterling Wood was able to resume his command in late November1862. Joseph Blackburn was promoted to the rank of Captain. The defeated Confederates regrouped around Murfreesboro in middle Tennessee. On December 12, 1862, Confederate President Davis ordered the formation of a new division of four brigades under Breckinridge's command, with Preston in charge of one of the units and Captain Blackburn by his side. The units were made up of five regiments of soldiers from Tennessee,

North Carolina, and Florida as well as an Alabama contingent. In late November, General Bragg told Preston and the other commanding officers to prepare the Army of Tennessee for a well-ordered engagement between the two forces to determine who would control middle Tennessee. Desertions had been a problem with Bragg's men since the summer, and the day after Christmas of 1862, four men from Preston's unit were shot for taking flight. The next major battle took place from December 31, 1862 to January 2, 1863 at Stones River. General Bragg led thirty-five thousand Confederates and confronted forty-two thousand Federals marching south from Nashville under General William S. Rosecrans' command. They met just outside of Murfreesboro at Stones River in an area that was bounded by limestone hills and thick overgrowth, typical of Tennessee, and further out, corn and cotton fields. It rained the cold pelting rain of December the night before the battle. The Union troops sang "Hail Columbia" and the Southern men sang "Bonnie Blue Flag."

On New Year's Eve, General Bragg struck first, surprising some of the Federal soldiers, gaining a momentary advantage, but Union General Rosecrans was ready with a solid defense line and strong artillery at the ready that stopped the Confederates, inflicting heavy losses. On seeing the losses, Breckinridge cried out, "My poor Orphans! My poor Orphans." Even though Breckinridge did not capture the Union battery, Brigadier General Preston's brigade, including Captain Blackburn, fought fiercely with its four artillery pieces and was able to take a northern position on the battlefield. Preston achieved this victory by sending one of his units to the far right of his main troops, forcing the Federals to shoot to their left and straight ahead, which allowed Preston's men to charge across an open field and flush out Union soldiers from their hold-out in a grove of cedar trees. At one point when his men became confused, Preston fearlessly "seized the colors and rode before the line toward the enemy," encouraging his soldiers to charge into the woods. Confederate Major John T. Lesley said in amazement that after that heroic act, "with a joyous shout our boys sprang forward, and were soon in possession of the wood that had lately covered the enemy." Most of General Preston's staff survived, including Captain Blackburn, but one member of the staff was killed at the General's side and another member who was riding General Albert Sidney Johnston's horse "Nelson" fell across General

Preston's horse, covering Preston with blood. During the battle, the visor of Preston's cap was hit by a shell fragment. When the battle began on New Year's Eve, General Preston had 1,951 men in his brigade, but by the end of the day, fifty-four men had died and 384 were wounded.

General Bragg thought he had won the battle and prematurely announced the victory to President Davis, but the Union troops were not done yet. They held their ground. New Year's Day was spent burying the dead. Then on January 2, 1863, Bragg ordered Breckinridge to take a ridge occupied by a Federal division on the east bank of Stone's River, defended with fifty-seven pieces of artillery on high ground. Breckinridge protested that it would end in defeat and many men would be killed, but Bragg insisted. When Breckinridge delivered this order to General Preston, he pointed out that this was Bragg's plan and not his. Captain Blackburn followed General Preston as he gave up his hard-fought position in the cedars that they had taken the day before and crossed the river to join Breckinridge as ordered. The troops advanced across an open field in a close-ordered, successive-lines formation, with Preston's men making up the second row of soldiers about two hundred yards from the first. The Confederates were able to capture the ridge on the east side of the stream and take some two hundred prisoners. Then they chased the Federals down the rugged banks toward the river, but just then, Union General Rosecrans moved up fresh batteries on the opposite bank, and "they poured a withering and continual fire on our men on the hill-side, converting the momentary victory into bloody defeat." Everything was chaos and confusing. General Preston grabbed the first flag he saw and "beat all fugitive men and officers over the head with my sabre till I got a handful of men around me." Then he rallied the men with a rousing speech, regrouped them, and established a new line of defense, but the assault failed and Preston's brigade had forty-one men killed and 245 wounded. Preston was bitter:

> During the battle both men and officers displayed great intrepidity, and I attribute the repulse Friday January 2 to the manifest hopelessness of the attempt to hurl a single division, without support, against the cardinal position of the whole hostile army. This was apparent to the least intelligent officer.

Preston concluded that Murfreesboro was a "concentrated Shiloh," differing in that it had "shorter rushes and bloodier struggles, and the same results." Preston was recognized for his bravery at Stones River. No doubt, Captain Blackburn experienced harrowing moments in the fighting, as well.

General Bragg retired his troops from Murfreesboro on January 3, 1863 and headed southwest towards Tullahoma, about thirty miles north of the Alabama line. Brigadier General Preston assumed command of Breckinridge's division of fifty-five hundred men to allow General Breckinridge a short leave of absence to be with his wife, who was following the troops, and Captain Blackburn continued to assist him in these expanded duties.

Preston's dissatisfaction with General Bragg grew. He was joined in this distaste by Breckinridge and other officers. The two cousins were considered the leaders of the "Kentucky block" of officers who opposed Bragg. President Davis sent William Preston Johnston to Tennessee to investigate the accusations against Bragg, but nothing came of it and Bragg remained in command. His men however lost respect for him after Stones River, and to stop the fighting among his officers, Davis removed Breckinridge and Preston from Bragg's command: Breckinridge and his division were sent to Mississippi, and Preston with Captain Blackburn and their men were sent to Virginia. Breckinridge was eventually reassigned to Joseph E. Johnston in May 1863, but after Vicksburg fell to Grant's forces, Breckinridge returned to Bragg's command on August 28, 1863.

On April 24, 1863, Preston and his men, including Captain Blackburn, were ordered to southwestern Virginia to replace Brigadier General Humphrey Marshall. Preston, however, was very ill with a high fever and spent a week in Columbia, South Carolina, with his cousin General John. S. Preston, who found him in very poor health and in need of a long rest. Captain Blackburn again stepped up to lead the men during Preston's illness. After General William Preston recovered, he went to Richmond, Virginia, to meet with the Confederate President and Mrs. Davis and rest. Preston then traveled to Knoxville, Tennessee, with General Buckner before he took up his new post in Virginia on May 14, 1863, joined by Captain Blackburn and his staff.

Southwestern Virginia was important to the Confederacy because of the salt works that supplied most of the Confederacy east of the

Mississippi River. William Preston's uncle, General Francis Preston, had settled in Abingdon, Virginia, and had started manufacturing salt in nearby Saltville in the 1790s. The mined salt was transported by the Virginia and Tennessee Railroad and had become a prime target of the Union forces by 1863, but it was not until May 1864 that they were able to shut down the Confederate railroad.

Preston established his headquarters in Abingdon, just north of Bristol, Tennessee. He realized that the brigade was poorly organized and quickly relocated the positions of many of the dispersed troops so that they could be re-assembled quickly when needed. "Preston relied on his aides, Captains Joe Blackburn and Harris Johnston, and on George B. Hodge, a dedicated cavalry officer who carefully carried out the general's orders." Preston was now in command of 2,416 men that guarded the saltworks and the ten thousand bushels of salt produced there daily, plus an ill-defined two hundred miles of mountain frontier dividing the Union and Confederate forces in Kentucky, Tennessee, and Virginia. Impressed by Brigadier General John Hunt Morgan's raids against the surprised Union forces, Preston organized similar excursions from his base in Virginia.

Some of the battles where Captain Blackburn fought were recorded briefly in private diaries of some of the soldiers. The diary of Edward O. Guerrant reported that his old college mate Joe Blackburn participated in "harrowing fights." On June 23, 1863, two hundred men advanced on Abingdon, Virginia, where they met Major Timothy Williams of the Union army's Fourteenth Kentucky Cavalry, just beyond the Oly Springs of Bath County, Kentucky. From Guerrant's diary:

> [The] advance guard of 30 pistol men attacked and killed 13 of the Fed's and captured some 20 or 30 and routed the rest, pursuing them on towards Mt. Sterling—Occasionally they made a stand—the strongest when reinforced by Trim W. himself—but were routed and pursued to near Gatewood's. Trim. Williams was shot and severely wounded in a hand to hand rencontre with James T. Rogers. 23 of the Enemy were killed and 25 captured and 3 or 4 wounded. Remarkable.
>
> In this *running* fight, not one of our men was wounded. Peter [Everett] had two horses wounded under him, Jim Rogers one, Joe Blackburn one, etc., etc., etc."

Brigadier General Preston ordered a small group of his men that likely included Captain Blackburn to conduct another raid from the Virginia base in July 1863 into Kentucky, first raiding Mount Sterling and then reaching all the way up north to Maysville on the Ohio River. His men reported fighting Federal soldiers four times on their "very exciting and somewhat hazardous trip." They intended to keep the Federals on the defensive.

Preston used his connections to secure supplies for his men. Mrs. Jefferson Davis had persuaded the Confederate Government to send two thousand pounds of cured pork and fifteen or twenty hams to Preston's unit the week after the Battle of Stones River. When Preston requested arms, Mrs. Davis helped him secure five hundred rifles, and in August he accepted a new major to his Abingdon division at Mrs. Davis' request.

In late summer 1863, the Confederates decided to stop the advance of General Rosecrans' units towards Chattanooga, a crucial rail center. This effort led to the Battle of Chickamauga in September. Preston was ordered to bring most of his four thousand men in three brigades, one artillery battalion, and one group of reserves, south by train from Virginia through eastern Tennessee to form one of the two divisions of General Buckner's corps. Naturally, Captain Blackburn was by his side. Another twelve thousand men from General Lee's army in Virginia were sent to reinforce the western Confederates, but they were forced to travel through Charlotte, Wilmington, and Atlanta after the Union forces captured Knoxville on September 6, 1863.The battle began when Union General Rosecrans' troops crossed the Tennessee River below Chattanooga. Confederate General Bragg evacuated the city, taking his army into northern Georgia. Ten days later, the combined Confederate forces met at Chickamauga Creek, just twelve miles south of the state line. It was a heavily wooded area mixed with cultivated fields full of cornstalks and pumpkins along the six-mile front. Approximately sixty-six thousand Confederates faced towards the setting sun, while several hundred yards apart fifty-eight thousand Union soldiers faced towards them to the east. September 18, the night before the battle, the first frost coated the ground, shimmering before the onslaught over the next days that would be called the bloodiest battle of the war in the west. During the daylight hours of September 19, 1863, Bragg ordered massive assaults on the Union forces, trying to outflank them and cut them off from Chattanooga, but the Union troops did not yield. Preston's division, which made up the left wing of Bragg's army, took orders from General Buckner that day. Only one of Preston's brigades saw battle that day in support of another unit in the late afternoon. By dusk, 150 men had been killed. Breckinridge led a division of D. H. Hill's corps in an attack on the second morning of the Battle of Chickamauga on September 20, 1863 against the Union forces, where he succeeded in breaking the Union line but failed to destroy the main army.

Preston and Blackburn's men quickly constructed defenses during the night while Confederate General Longstreet arrived with his troops. Longstreet was given command of the left flank and brought a burst of confidence with him not usually felt among Bragg's men. Longstreet led his forces in a charge through a gap in the Union lines that sent the Union soldiers scattering, running for Chattanooga, until Union General George Thomas organized the men into a defensive position to prevent a rout. His efforts would earn him the nickname, the "Rock of Chickamauga." General Thomas formed a line on top of a ridge called Snodgrass Hill that basically could not be broken and protected the Federal retreat to the north. Longstreet was determined to break this stronghold and launched heavy attacks on Thomas's right side while General Polk's men attacked Thomas's left side. The battle of Snodgrass Hill was one of the fiercest battles in the war and has been compared to the fury of Gettysburg. But Snodgrass Hill could not be taken despite the furious effort. Three divisions had failed by the middle of the afternoon when Longstreet ordered Preston's brigades to make an all-out effort to break the position that was protected by artillery, rocks, and logs.

Brigadier General Archibald Gracie's and Colonel John H. Kelly's brigades moved up the cleared southern slope of Snodgrass Hill in two lines until only forty paces from the crest. There they stood in the open and traded volleys with the entrenched enemy. The bravery of these troops under fire has encomia from both contemporaries and later military historians. "Nothing in this battle, marked with gallantry so frequent that it became commonplace, surpassed the courage of these two brigades as they watched their ranks thin minute by minute and still doggedly refused to yield an inch of ground." But glory that day had its price. Gracie's unit suffered the worst losses—698 men killed or wounded out of 2,003. When General Preston presented President Davis with the flag of the brigade's Second Alabama Battalion, it had been pierced in eighty-three places by enemy balls. After more than an hour of combat, the remaining exhausted troops retreated down the slope. After the Confederates retreated, Union General Thomas was ordered by General James A. Garfield, future President of the United States, to withdraw "immediately," but General Thomas refused to do so because he did not want to demoralize the men who had just fought so brilliantly and instead waited until sunset to begin organizing his withdrawal.

General Preston gained his greatest military success that day. General Buckner praised him:

> The gallant manner in which he conducted his division to the assault, contributed in a manner second to none to the winning of the key point of the field and thus deciding the fate of the day....
>
> Upon Brigadier General Preston, and his brigade commanders.... I cannot bestow higher praise than to say, that their conduct and example were such as to convert a body of troops, but few of whom had been before under fire, into a division of veterans in their first battle.

Confederate General Longstreet said "Preston dashed gallantly at the hills," and added that the Kentuckian's attack "crippled the enemy so badly that his ranks were badly broken, and by a flank movement and another advance the heights were gained."

A *London Times* correspondent who witnessed Preston's attack on Snodgrass Hill wrote that Preston's "bearing on the slope of Missionary Ridge, under the setting sun of the 20 September, will ... rank ... with any other famous deeds of arms ever witnessed on earth."

Captain Blackburn fought with a distinction during the Battle of Chickamauga that has been regarded by many as providing the best illustration, given by any battle of the war, of the military prowess of the American Confederate and Union soldier. It was the two hundredth battle fought in the long Civil War and was decisively won by Confederate General Braxton Bragg when he defeated Union General Rosecrans, but it was not enough to win the war.

Naturally there were some dissenters after the fact in typical "Monday Morning Quarter-backing," as they say, but Preston's victory stood. He and Blackburn had seen fearsome fighting. Many good and brave men had been lost. When General Breckinridge looked upon his dead men after the Battle of Chickamauga, there were tears in his eyes.

Chickamauga was General Preston's last battle. Generals Buckner and Longstreet nominated Preston for promotion to Major General to command the division now under his command, but Confederate President Davis never agreed to the requests. One of the main reasons Davis did not promote Preston was because of Preston's prickly relationship with General Bragg. When Bragg did not follow the success at Chickamauga with a rapid attack on Chattanooga, Preston and several others wrote to President Davis complaining, asking that Bragg be removed from command, saying he was not a good field commander. Over time, historians have agreed with this assessment of his leadership ability, but President Davis supported Bragg. It seemed that Davis took criticisms of Bragg personally and defensively, emblematic of Davis' shortcomings as a leader.

After the Battle of Chickamauga, Preston remained a brigadier in the Army of Tennessee, but he was removed from command of his division. Preston then asked General Buckner to reassign him, and on October 18, 1863, Preston was reassigned to his former post in southwestern Virginia by General Buckner, and Captain Blackburn went with him to Virginia. But Bragg and Buckner were involved in an argument over Buckner's East Tennessee command, and Bragg denied that Buckner had the authority to offer Preston an appointment and Jefferson Davis agreed with him but said to Bragg that he was going to let Preston keep his Virginia post because "it is for the best."

President Abraham Lincoln delivered his second Gettysburg Address on November 19, 1863, in which he dedicated the country to the principles of nationalism, republicanism, equal rights, liberty, and democracy. It became the most quoted speech in American history. In 272 words and three minutes, Lincoln asserted the nation was born not in 1789 but in 1776 "conceived in Liberty, and dedicated to the proposition that all men are created equal." He defined the war as an effort dedicated to the principles of liberty and equality for all. The emancipation of slaves became part of the national war effort. He declared that the deaths of so many brave soldiers would not be in vain, that slavery would end as a result of the losses and the future of democracy would be assured, that "government of the people, by the people, for the people, shall not perish from the earth." Lincoln concluded that the Civil War had a profound objective: a new birth of freedom in the nation. Lincoln had a patient confidence in the U.S. Constitution and the ultimate justice of the people and believed there was no better, or equal hope, in the world.

Meanwhile, Brigadier General Preston and Captain Blackburn resumed their Virginia post for three months through the end of the year, but Preston was disgruntled. On January 7, 1864, Preston was relieved of his appointment to Virginia and ordered to go to Shreveport, Louisiana, to serve General Kirby Smith in the Trans-Mississippi Department, but the same day, the Richmond government countermanded these military instructions and offered Preston a diplomatic post instead, after remembering his prior diplomatic experience as the American ambassador to Spain under President Buchanan. During Preston's twenty-seven months of military service in the Confederate army from 1861 to 1864, Preston had traveled thousands of miles through Kentucky, Tennessee, Mississippi, Alabama, Georgia, the Carolinas, and Virginia on horseback and by rail, and Captain Joseph Blackburn had traveled almost every mile with him. Even though Preston left this command, Captain Blackburn remained on, leading the men until his next promotion to Lieutenant Colonel under Confederate General Leonidas Polk along the Mississippi River in 1863. The following story of Blackburn's new assignment was recalled:

> In 1863, while Blackburn was a captain wearing a Confederate uniform, he was ordered to the Red River Bottoms, and all of his friends objected to that destination for popular 'Young Joe,' as he was then called.
>
> One old friend of the family, who had known Joe Blackburn from his babyhood, rushed off after Joe's elder brother Doctor, later Governor Blackburn, and urged him to use his influence to have the order rescinded.

> 'What for?' asked the Doctor.
>
> 'Why, Doc., haven't you heard how the yaller fever's a-ragin' down there?' 'Oh, well, Yellow Jack won't hurt Joe.' The family friend then became diplomatic, and, instead of arguing any more about the yellow fever, he said: 'But, Doc, there's the swamp fever carryin' off our Johnnies like flies. A man wakes up well in the morning and is dead by noon. It would be a downright shame to expose Joe to such danger.' But Doctor Blackburn still shook his head and said: I will not interfere with Joe's orders on any such trivial grounds."Trivial grounds!" shouted the angry friend. Do you call absolutely fatal diseases "trivial grounds?"' '"Fatal diseases!" sneered Doctor Blackburn. "You ought to know as well as I do, man, that no disease could possibly prove fatal to Joe Blackburn, except lockjaw."'

Doctor Luke Blackburn must have been right. His brother survived. As the war continued, the advantage continued to favor the Union, but the fighting did not stop. The war went on for four long years from April 1861 to April 1865. Lieutenant Colonel Joseph Blackburn fought in many more battles in Mississippi under General Polk. On June 22, 1864, Special Order Number Forty-Eight was issued from Meridian, Mississippi, by the Head Quarters Department for Alabama, Mississippi, and Louisiana, directing that:

> Captain Harry [sic] H. Johnston and Captain J.C.S. Blackburn, both acting under orders from the War Department, to raise Companies respectively for special service on the Mississippi, are hereby authorized to organize such Company and to enlist therefore any men in this Department, not belonging to other command, who may desire to join them. Capts. Johnston and Blackburn will report direct to these Head Quarters, and in addition to the special duty entrusted to them will give any information with reference to the movements of the enemy that they may deem important, and will take action in any other case where they consider it to the interest of the service to do so.

It directed the Quarter Master and Commissioner in this Department to give Captains Johnson and Blackburn (who had been promoted to lieutenant colonel, but records were not carefully coordinated, apparently) "any assistance that they may need, in conformity with instructions given by the War Department." It was given "By the Command of Major General Lee" and signed by Acting Assistant Adjutant General William Elliott.

In essence, Captains Blackburn and Johnston were ordered to raise their own command and serve as scouts and spies for the Confederate States of America War Department in Alabama, Mississippi, and Louisiana. Because their assignment was to act independently and discreetly, it is difficult to tell which battles they fought in the area.

On July 21, 1864, the Confederate States of America, War Department at Richmond, Virginia, belatedly issued the appointment of J. C. S. Blackburn as captain in the Provisional Army in the service of the Confederate States under the Act approved February 17, 1861, pending the next Senate session of the Confederate Senate, to confirm and advise of his permanent commission. This letter of appointment directed J. C. S. Blackburn to:

> Immediately on receipt hereof, please to communicate to this Department, through the Adjutant and Inspector General's office, your acceptance or non-acceptance of said appointment: and with your letter of acceptance, return to the Adjutant and Inspector General the OATH, herewith enclosed, properly filled up, SUBSCRIBED and ATTESTED, reporting at the same time your AGE, RESIDENCE, when appointed, and the STATE in which you were BORN.
>
> Should you accept, you will report for duty to ____________ [left blank].

It was signed by James A. [Alexander] Seddon, Provisional Army of the Confederate States Secretary of War. Seddon managed to hold this position for over two years, but resigned when the Confederate Congress turned against him as the war effort crumbled.

After the surprising death of John Hunt Morgan on September 4, 1864 in Greeneville, Tennessee, during a Union raid of the town, Breckinridge resumed command of the Department of East Tennessee and West Virginia, where he reorganized the department. In October 1864, at the First Battle of Saltville, Breckinridge protected the critical Confederate salt works from Union forces under Stephen Burbridge. Breckinridge then fought in northeastern Tennessee in mid-November 1864 and again in December in Virginia in the Battle of Marion.

In January 1865, Jefferson Davis appointed Breckinridge the Confederate Secretary of War to replace James A. Seddon after he had resigned. His first act as secretary was to promote Robert E. Lee to general-in-chief of all Confederate forces. But by the end of February 1865, Breckinridge concluded that the Confederate cause was hopeless. Jefferson Davis wanted to keep fighting, but Breckinridge said: "This has been a magnificent epic. In God's name let it not terminate in farce."

On April 2, 1865, Lee sent a telegram to Breckinridge, informing him that he would have to withdraw from his position that night and evacuate Richmond, the Confederate capital, which he did, ensuring that the Confederate records were kept intact. At first, Richmond had thrived as the capital of the Confederacy, but by the end of the war, it suffered. Richmond's residents were blockaded and starved, then the city was burned, and at last, Robert E. Lee's forces were forced to retreat, leaving the city defenseless. Lee surrendered on April 9th, and the Confederate cabinet fled to Greensboro, North Carolina. Eventually, Breckinridge met up with Davis in Abbeville, South Carolina, with Basil Duke, where they finally convinced Davis that the war was hopelessly over. Breckinridge was put in charge of 150 thousand dollars in gold bullion and coins left in the Confederate treasury, which he took, escorted by some of his soldiers, to Washington and deposited and then left instructions to disband the War Department.

Breckinridge and Davis went on the run now, with a small group of Kentuckians under the command of his cousin, William Campbell Preston Breckinridge. Breckinridge and Davis split up. Davis was captured, but Breckinridge made it to Florida and then to Cuba and then to Britain, arriving there in late July 1865. He remained out of the country until President Andrew Johnson's pardon on February 10, 1866, and later on December 25, 1868, Johnson proclaimed all former Confederates pardoned. Breckinridge never entered politics again, saying "I no more feel the political excitements that marked the scenes of my former years than if I were an extinct volcano."

Although he resided in Kentucky for the rest of his life, Breckinridge never bought a home there after the war, living first in hotels and then renting a home on West Second Street in Lexington, Kentucky.

During the Civil War, many changes took place at Blackburn's home as well. Captain Blackburn's mother Lavinia died on June 3, 1863. At her death, two of her sons were actively fighting in the Civil War: Captains Joseph and James Blackburn, and a third son, Dr. Luke, was engaged supporting the war effort as a civilian while practicing medicine and saving hundreds of lives from yellow fever. There were changes in Kentucky, as well. In September 1863, Kentucky elected a new governor by a commanding majority: the Union candidate former Judge and Colonel Thomas Bramlette. Governor Bramlette served until September 1867. By September 1863, most homes in the state had fallen under the shadow of death, whether from the loss of a Union soldier or a Confederate soldier or death by the hand of a raider or punishment meted out by citizens against supposed criminals or by federal officers against suspected Southern sympathizers. It was a dark time.

After the Civil War, Dr. Luke Blackburn was acquitted of all charges of violating Canada's neutrality laws. On September 19, 1867, Dr. Blackburn left Canada for New Orleans, having obtained permission to return under the amnesty proclamation. He would eventually return to Kentucky once all of the former Confederates were pardoned. Dr. Luke redeemed his life by continuing to volunteer his efforts in the fight against yellow fever around the country and in Kentucky in places like Versailles and Hickman. In gratitude for his service and sacrifices, Kentuckians elected Dr. Luke Governor of Kentucky in 1879.

After the Civil War during Reconstruction, Kentucky felt her way through the new relationships between the men of the North and South and the newly freed former slaves. On May 23, 1865, both Houses of the Kentucky legislature met, and the House adopted a resolution directing the Committee on the Condition of Slavery to revise the slave code. A committee was appointed to prepare resolutions about the assassination of Lincoln. On May 31, 1865, it was reported that the recruiting of slaves into the U.S. Army in Kentucky was going briskly and that "a few months more of negro enlistments will settle the question of slavery in Kentucky, independently of the constitutional amendment."

It was going to be difficult to reassemble the sliced-up country after the close of the war. Usually the victor writes the story of a war, but in this case, it could be said that the North won this sad war on the battlefields, but for the next 150 years, the South won the war on the pages of history. Only now is that history under closer scrutiny.

Part Three

Political Career

Chapter Eight

Rebuilding After the Civil War

When the war finally came to an end, each former Confederate officer had to sign an oath of allegiance to regain status as a citizen of the United States. On December 8, 1863 in the 88th year of the independence of the United States of America and again on March 24, 1864, President Lincoln issued proclamations to grant pardons for former Confederates that addressed three concerns:

> First, it allowed for a full pardon for and restoration of property to all engaged in the rebellion, with the exception of the highest-ranking Confederate officials and military leaders. Second, it allowed for a new state government to be formed when ten percent of the eligible voters had taken an oath of allegiance to the United States. Third, the Southern states admitted in this fashion were encouraged to enact plans to deal with freed slaves so long as their freedom was not compromised.

Even though this meant that Joseph, James and Dr. Luke could not be restored as full citizens because they were former "civil or diplomatic officers or agents" or "military or naval officers of the so-called Confederate government," overall, Lincoln's plan for postwar Reconstruction was very charitable, particularly in light of the enormous financial, emotional, moral, and political costs of the war. Many Radical Republicans in Congress thought it was too easy.

The first results of Lincoln's Reconstruction Plans produced anger and disbelief in both Northerners and Southerners. The Northern Radical Republicans were shocked when they witnessed three states, Louisiana, Arkansas and Tennessee, "reconstructed" in early 1864 under Lincoln's Ten Percent Plan. In their outrage, they immediately caused Congress to refuse to recognize the governments or seat their elected federal representatives.

Instead, in July 1864, Congress passed its own Reconstruction Plan, the Wade-Davis bill, which required a majority of voters to take the loyalty oath in any state. Only those who swore an "ironclad" oath of having *never* fought against the Union could participate in reconstructing their state's government. Congress required the state constitutions to include bans on slavery, disenfranchised former Confederate political and military leaders, and repudiated debts to the former Confederate states. Lincoln refused to sign it, so it was not implemented. Both sides were inflamed. Lincoln took the long view on Reconstruction, but other members of his party and many Southerners took a different view.

Then, Congress created the Bureau of Refugees, Freedmen, and Abandoned Lands, commonly known as the Freedmen's Bureau, within the U.S. War Department in March 1865. It provided temporary relief to the freed people with basic shelter and services like medical care, assistance in labor-contract negotiation, and the establishment of schools, etc. The conflicting plans to reconstruct the country were drafted even before the Civil War ended. The plans were a continuing source of tension in Congress after Lincoln's assassination in April 1865, generating heated debates.

If President Lincoln had not been assassinated, it is likely that Reconstruction could have evolved more closely according to his vision of restoring the Union by embracing the former Confederate States as quickly as possible, but Reconstruction suffered without his compassionate guiding presence. When Vice President Andrew Johnson became president, he took up the task begrudgingly. While Johnson presented a Reconstruction Plan that was essentially the same as Lincoln's, he did not feel kindly towards the South. Now, the fate of reuniting Southern states "lately in rebellion" back into the Union rested on the shoulders of men who lacked Lincoln's charitable convictions and compassion and who wanted to punish them instead.

During the summer of 1865, President Johnson implemented a Reconstruction plan that included an amnesty proclamation issued on May 29, 1865 for former Confederates who had not been pardoned in 1863 or 1864, if they took an oath to defend the Union and Constitution and obey federal laws and proclamations regarding slavery, similar to the 1863 and 1864 proclamations. This oath also included the following:

> I, ______ , declaring that I do, freely and forever, disclaim, and that I will never assert, right or title to slaves, and that I will never hereafter own a slave, or any interest therein, pursuant to the President's proclamation of date — day of —, 1865, do solemnly swear (or affirm) in the presence of Almighty God that I will henceforth faithfully protect and defend the Constitution of the United States, and the union of the State thereunder.

Civil or diplomatic officers or agents of the former Confederate government were excluded from the pardon, along with all military or naval officers above the rank of colonel in the army or lieutenant in the navy, among others. As a result, in 1865 Joseph and his young family moved to Desha, Arkansas to be closer to his sister and two brothers: Elizabeth, the widow of Confederate General Thompson Flournoy, and James and Dr. Churchill Blackburn. While Joseph and James waited in Arkansas for their rights as citizens to be restored, Joseph practiced law with his partner Judge R. H. Thompson and farmed in Desha County, raising cotton near the same areas he had patrolled during the Civil War. On December 18, 1865, the Thirteenth Amendment to the United States Constitution was ratified by Congress, formally abolishing slavery throughout the United States:

> Section 1. Neither slavery nor involuntary servitude, except as a punishment for crime whereof the party shall have been duly convicted, shall exist within the United States or any place subject to their jurisdiction.
>
> Section 2. Congress shall have the power to enforce this article by appropriate legislation.

Still, Congress refused to recognize the state governments that had been reconstructed under Johnson's plan. The Republicans in Congress were upset that white Southerners were reluctant to ratify the Thirteenth Amendment.

While the two border states of Maryland and Missouri had abolished slavery during the Civil War, Kentucky had failed to do so. Slaves secured their own freedom by escaping north. It is estimated that during the war about seventy-five percent of the slaves were freed or escaped to Union lines.

Achieving civil liberty for all after the war did not come easily. The tension around the idea of civil rights had shifted by the end of the Civil War. Initially, former Confederates had gone to the war to fight for the idea of the state's power to choose its own laws, particularly those authorizing slavery, and for the right of a state to secede from the Union at will; while Union soldiers had gone to war to fight against slavery and against the idea that a state could choose to secede from a perfect and perpetual Union after it was formed. During the war, the fight became about slavery only. After the Civil War, the idea of civil rights shifted from the rights of a separate state to the rights of the men in the reconstituted Union. Now the idea placed Southern whites and former slaves as equal citizens of a state in the Union. Rather than looking at this transformation as a victory for all in the Union, Southern whites felt a bitter loss once male slaves were raised up to the status of free citizens in a state within the Union with an equal right to vote. There was dangerous dissatisfaction on all sides.

In April 1866, the Radical Republican Congress passed the Civil Rights Act over President Johnson's veto. The President feared Southerners would resist it, which would result in more bloodshed because the Act allowed, in essence, more former slaves to have the right to seek and hold state and national offices and vote than former Confederates who were barred from office. Congress plowed forward regardless and approved the Fourteenth Amendment to the U.S. Constitution in June.

The Fourteenth Amendment stated plainly in Section Three:

> No person shall be a Senator or Representative in Congress, or elector of President and Vice President, or hold any office, civil or military, under the United States, or under any State, who, having previously taken an oath, as a member of Congress, or as an officer of the United States, or as a member of any State legislature, or as a[n] executive or judicial officer of any State, to support the Constitution of the United States, shall

> have engaged in insurrection or rebellion against the same, or given aid or comfort to the enemies thereof. But Congress may by a vote of two-thirds of each House remove such disability.

Johnson's fears came to pass. Race riots and massacres took place in Memphis on May 1, 1866 and in New Orleans on July 30, 1866. While Congress sought to punish the rebels and to protect freed Southern black men, white Southerners sought to limit the rights of black freedmen socially, politically, and economically in an effort to sustain their false sense of superiority. The battle over civil rights left the fields of arms and clashed in debate in Congress, the courts, and on the streets of cities. Southern cities and state legislatures enacted so called "Black Codes" in several Southern states, basically to regain control over the freed slaves, maintain white supremacy, and ensure the continued supply of cheap labor, while protecting themselves from a feared retaliation for the years of slavery.

The Black Codes enacted by Southern states in 1865 and 1866 were based on the so-called slave codes from colonial times that prohibited free blacks from voting, bearing arms, gathering in groups of worship, and learning to read and write, mainly as a way to preserve slavery. Black Codes were modeled on the broad vagrancy laws that allowed authorities to arrest freed blacks for minor infractions and commit them to involuntary labor. In other words, slavery continued under a different guise. The Black Codes were not the only tool used to keep former slaves enslaved. "Jim Crow" laws were enacted between 1874 and 1975 that were meant to separate the white and black races in America based on the theory that it would enable the creation of "separate but equal" treatment of whites and blacks. In reality, for the next hundred years, the Jim Crow laws condemned black citizens to inferior treatment in segregated schools and public facilities like hotels and restaurants. The term "Jim Crow" originally referred to a black character in an old song and was the name of a popular dance in the 1820s that became engrained in the culture when the actor Thomas "Daddy" Rice developed a routine in which he blacked his face, dressed in old clothes, and sang and danced in imitation of an old and decrepit black man.

Former slaves mourned their treatment under Black Codes and Jim Crow Laws while former Confederates resented their treatment under Republican Reconstruction laws. After the Civil War, the black population lacked a public forum to object to the injustice, but Southerners were able to voice their dissatisfactions openly in Congress. As former seven-term U.S. Representative and former Vice President of the Confederate State Alexander Hamilton Stephens said on the House floor:

> Whatever may be said of the loyalty or disloyalty of any in the late most lamentable conflict of arms, I think I may venture safely to say that there was on the part of the great mass of the people of Georgia and of the entire South, *no disloyalty* to the principles of the Constitution of the United States.... Our only alternative now is either to give up all hope of Constitutional liberty, or retrace our steps, and to look for its vindication and maintenance in the forums of reason and justice, instead of the arena of arms. In the court and halls of legislation, instead of on the field of battle.

It would take a long time for former Confederates to achieve constitutional liberty. In 1867 Radical Republicans in Congress passed three Reconstruction Acts geared to keeping the Southern states out of the Congress. Each passed over President Johnson's veto. The First Reconstruction Act was an act that divided the rebel states of Virginia, North Carolina, South Carolina, Georgia, Mississippi, Alabama, Louisiana, Florida, Texas, and Arkansas into military districts under the military authority of the United States. The Second Reconstruction Act of March 23, 1867 gave the military commanders total control over registering voters and holding elections and required that every voter swear an oath to support the Constitution and obey the military law. The Third Reconstruction Act of July 19, 1867 gave "supreme power to the five Union generals overseeing Reconstruction in the five districts of the South." The five generals could remove any official, elected or otherwise, from office if they thought that official was hurting rather than helping the process of Reconstruction.

Then in 1868, a Fourth Reconstruction Act was passed and the Fourteenth Amendment was ratified, entitling all persons born or naturalized in the United States to citizenship and equal protection under the laws of the United States, while excluding former Confederate civil or military officers from holding any office or participating in the government. The new order was confirmed in 1869 when the United States Supreme Court agreed with Lincoln's analysis of the U.S. Constitution. In *Texas v White*, 74 U.S. 700 (1869), the Supreme Court wrote that the Constitution intended the perpetuity of the Union to survive from the Articles of Confederation; therefore, states could not secede and destroy the Union.

Joseph Blackburn's family remained on the farm in Arkansas until 1868, when President Johnson extended amnesty to all former Confederates, including officers in the Confederate government and its military. Joseph and James were finally able to return to the family farm in Woodford County, but by then, both of their parents had passed away.

When Joseph returned to Kentucky in 1868 with his family, he was a thirty-year-old pardoned former Confederate. His first child, Joseph, Jr. ("Josey"), was nearly ten years old at this time, with no brothers or sisters. Now, Joseph was back in Kentucky, defeated, heart-broken, with no clear path to the future. He was not allowed to hold any state or national office as a former Confederate officer, but he could earn a living in his state as a free man. This marked the end of an era and the beginning of a new one, a time to move from fighting battles to a time of seeking justice and civil liberty. He opened a law office in Versailles. A daughter, Terese Blackburn, was born on June 29, 1868 at Spring Station, followed by another daughter, Corinne Blackburn, born on June 10, 1869 at the Cottage Home on the farm, and finally their youngest daughter, Lucile ("Dottie") Blackburn, was born there too, on April 4, 1871.

At the same time, Republican and former Union General Ulysses S. Grant was elected President of the United States in 1868 and took office in 1869. Former Confederate soldiers could not forget General Grant's relentless determination and military push through the South that ended the Civil War. To the victor, go the spoils, and the highest office in the land was one of the choicest. Once Grant was elected president, the Radical Republicans in Congress now had the political majority to enact legislation that would attempt to remove all traces of the shame of slavery.

President Grant agreed to enforce the protection of the freed slaves, using the U.S. military to suppress white insurgency in the South while reconstructing their state governments. He gave no quarter, just as he had done during the war. Black voters seeking civil liberty and equal justice under the law supported a growing Republican Party in the South. For a time, Southern blacks enjoyed political representation, but by the time Grant left office in 1877, the Democrats in the South had regained control of state governments, and most blacks lost whatever political power they had gained. It would be another one hundred years before blacks would experience political powers again. During Grant's Presidency, the Fifteenth Amendment was ratified in 1870, which granted voting rights to all male citizens, regardless of color or previous condition of servitude. The next year, 1871, the Act to Enforce the Fourteenth Amendment was passed, known as the Ku Klux Klan Act. In 1872, the Freedmen's Bureau was abolished. In 1875, the Civil Rights Act was enacted by Congress, providing blacks with the right to equal treatment in public places and transportation, but it was later declared unconstitutional by the U.S. Supreme Court.

Finally, all "political disabilities" that had been enacted in the Fourteenth Amendment was later removed by Congress by a series of three bills enacted on May 22, 1872. This opened the gates for former officers like Joseph Blackburn to hold political office, but Republicans were not receptive to former Confederates. The Republican press openly expressed their misgivings, distrust, and distaste of a "united and sectional South," who they feared would seek to elect a President who, "first failing to destroy the Union, now seek to rule it to the same end."

As Southern Democrats regained political power, allegations of widespread corruption in the Republican administration of the federal government rose. By contrast, the defeated former Confederate veterans were honored in their home states. Kentucky veterans from the "Orphan Brigade" became idols to their fellow Kentuckians, who accorded them a kind of nobility. Ultimately, this helped Joseph Blackburn launch his political career, a career that would span fifty years. Men like Blackburn who were elected to national office during these years charged many Republican's in office with foul play, likely as a way to inflict some pain on their conquerors while regaining power. Battles between the sections of the country were now fought in the halls of Congress and in the election booth.

Some of the Northern victors declared their willingness to embrace members of the conquered South if each former rebel would acknowledge that slavery was wrong and that liberty, union, and justice for all remained the true, great, and just cause of this nation. Southerners, however, did not admit defeat nor that the Southern cause was wrong. Instead, Southerners claimed that they had been right and that their cause would be able to triumph even after losing the war, if not directly, then indirectly. Hatred for freed blacks seethed in the South, often maintained under a veneer of excruciating politeness among whites. Somehow, Southerners began to win the collective war memory. Overall, many agreed with the saying, "The North won the war, but the South won the peace." Mark Twain added that "In the South the war is what A.D. is elsewhere; they date from it." The stage was set in Kentucky for Southern Democrat Joseph Blackburn to take a prominent role on the political stage.

Chapter Nine

The Rise of Democrats in Kentucky

In 1871, during Grant's Presidency, thirty-three-year-old Joseph C. S. Blackburn was elected to the Kentucky House of Representatives to represent the Democracy of the famed Ashland District, succeeding James B. Beck. Democrat Preston H. Leslie was governor of the state with fellow Democrats Lieutenant Governor John G. Carlisle, Speaker of the House James B. McCreary, and Blackburn's fellow House members "Cerro Gordo" Williams (so nicknamed in the Mexican-American War) and William Sweeney. Blackburn managed to defeat worthy opponents in his first campaign.

In June 1871, two Democrats, Blackburn and former Major J. W. Gillespie, both from Midway in Woodford County, were each interested in running for the state legislature. They agreed to test their relative merits before the Midway voters with the understanding that the one falling short would withdraw. The test in this precinct came out in Blackburn's favor, and Gillespie withdrew from the contest and supported Blackburn. By the second week of June 1871, E.C. Marshall announced that he had withdrawn from the race for the legislature, stating that he could not give his support to Congressman James Beck for the Senatorship. This left the field to Blackburn, who was supported by Midway and opposed to the railroad tax, and former acting Lieutenant Governor Thomas Porter, leader of the Democratic Party in Woodford County, who was supported by Versailles and in favor of a heavy railroad tax. Most of the Democratic delegates had been instructed to vote for former Lieutenant Governor Porter. Blackburn's gave his first speech in politics, and while it was moving, it was not enough to win. On July 28, 1871, Thomas P. Porter was nominated narrowly over Blackburn for the legislature by the Democratic County Convention.

This was immediately followed by a "rump" convention that nominated Blackburn, which would seem to only ensure a victory by the Republican or Radical candidate if the Democrats split their votes. After much talk among their supporters, both Porter and Blackburn agreed to remove themselves from the race and search for a compromise candidate. Then, surprisingly, Blackburn's name was put forth again, but Porter, no doubt surprised by the move, refused to put his name up. Running unopposed, Blackburn was easily nominated in a called primary where he received the popular vote. In the general election, he was opposed by Major J. E. Hoskins. Blackburn won.

Joseph and his family moved into a rented a house in Versailles. He and a local Versailles lawyer, Mr. Fryman, formed a partnership to practice law together. When the legislature was in session, Blackburn would leave the law partnership temporarily, and Fryman would find associate counsel as needed. Not long afterwards, his brother James returned to Kentucky and joined the firm. Home again in Woodford County with a larger family now, the future looked brighter. At last, Dr. Luke was able to return to Kentucky from Canada in 1872 after the Fourteenth Amendment's "political disabilities" were removed and after he was acquitted of violating Canada's neutrality law while there. All the Blackburn brothers were home and ready to make a difference. While Joseph worked in the state legislature, Dr. Luke aided victims of yellow fever during the 1873 epidemic in Memphis and in the 1877 outbreak in Florida and Kentucky. Joseph's political career as a Southern Democrat flourished in the post-Civil War Reconstruction era.

Blackburn's private journals in 1871 reflect his frequent travel to Frankfort. Some of the legislative actions he undertook included an amendment to the Lexington city charter, defeating a resolution that sought to repeal the library lottery, removing the railroad tonnage tax, passing a bill for the benefit of school district Number Twelve in Woodford County, addressing threats of open elections in Lexington and the presence of state military troops at the election booths, and addressing local taxation of railroad, among many others.

His journals from this time serving as a state representative reflect his busy political activity. When he was not serving in the state legislature, he was practicing law in Versailles. In one case, his law practice proved to be life-threatening when he agreed to defend the cousin of his long-time friend and neighbor, John Harper, Sr., of the famed *Nantura* farm. The case arose from a disgraceful family situation. A nephew, who was also named John Harper, was suspected of trying to murder all of the heirs to the farm, apparently hoping to be the sole survivor, and a cousin said as much publicly. The suspected nephew, John, sued the cousin for defamation. John Sr. asked Joseph and James Blackburn to defend the cousin, J. Wallace Harper, in court. The Blackburn brothers took the case and won it. Joseph's 1871 journal notes that the suspect John Harper attempted to assassinate him the day after the trial by "*drawing his pistol on him*" in a hotel in Georgetown. Fortunately, nothing came of it, and Blackburn simply carried on about his business. While the case was reversed on appeal, the ultimate resolution is not known, though it likely settled out of court. Unfortunately, the murderer was never discovered, although the nephew, John, continued to be suspected. John, Sr., willed the farm to the suspect's brother, Frank Harper, who continued the thoroughbred farm and expanded it by purchasing Joseph Blackburn's farm when it was sold. Frank Harper remained grateful to Joseph for his legal expertise defending the Harper family. In 1905 Harper's will left the 160 acre farm that formerly belonged to Joseph Blackburn to Blackburn's granddaughter, Terese Blackburn Lane and her heirs.

Blackburn's busy law practice prevented him from actively seeking the state representative nomination in 1873, but the Democrats in the state pressed him to run. They were girding for the next election fight since President Grant had carried the county for the Republican Party in 1872, but Blackburn won. Southern Democrats were on the rise in Kentucky, and Blackburn rose with them into the national arena.

Chapter Ten

"Drink It, Sir, and Give Up Your Soul to the Lord."

- J.C.S. Blackburn

U.S. Representative Blackburn Elected to the Forty-Fourth U.S. Congress

Blackburn's election to the U.S. Congress moved him from the state House to the U.S. House of Representatives for the Seventh Congressional District of Kentucky. He took his seat in the Capitol in Washington, D.C. for the first time in the Forty-Fourth Congress in March 1875. Joseph Blackburn would make his name in U.S. House debates concerning the major issues of the day, which included corruption in the Grant Administration's War Department and postal service, the use of silver for money, and the rules governing the Congress. His new position and responsibilities compelled him to sell his parcel of the family farm to Frank Harper in 1874 and move full-time into his federal home at 215 Rose Hill in nearby Versailles, Kentucky, the county seat for Woodford County. A Kentucky Historical Marker has been placed in front of this home where he lived during most of his national political life. The move from the state legislature to the national Congress evolved from a change in political circumstances. In 1874 near the close of the Forty-Third Congress, James B. Beck, the Democratic representative to Congress from the "Ashland District," as the Seventh District was known, announced that he would not seek re-election after serving eight years in office from 1867 to 1875. Representative Beck's withdrawal from the race meant that Colonel Trabue, an old-fashioned conservative or a so-called "mossback Democrat," was the only man in the race. It is reported that friends of Blackburn "besieged him to run," and he reluctantly consented to do so.

Living in Versailles on Rose Hill and freed from the daily demands of farming life, Blackburn agreed to run for Congress as the regular nominee against Ed C. Marshall, the independent candidate. A citizen's letter to the *Louisville Ledger* in July of 1874 reads:

> Capt. Blackburn, the regular nominee, familiarly known among his friends as "Jo" is now in Bourbon, I believe in his line of business as a lawyer. He is regarded by many the ablest young lawyer and the finest debater of his age in Kentucky. The people here idolize Blackburn, and it is believed that when he meets the brilliant humor-loving Marshall, he will make the sparks fly more fiercely than a sledge does from a tire iron at white heat. It will be another case of Grecian contact, with the odds largely in favor of Capt. Blackburn. Marshall will find a foeman worthy of his steel in the regular nominee, and he may select the peg now upon which to hang his battered armor in August.

In late August 1874, Blackburn and Marshall spoke to a very large crowd in Versailles in the Odd Fellows hall, chosen because it was larger than the courthouse. The hall was packed, with many people not able to get inside the hall.

> Both gentlemen, we believe, made better speeches than we had heard them make before during the canvass; Marshall in his opening speech made some oratorical flights, and Blackburn also, although always eloquent and logical, far surpassed his ordinary efforts, and in his closing speech he gave Mr. Marshall such a castigation as we have seldom heard; in fact he did exactly what some of Mr. Marshall's friends were expecting of Marshall before the canvass opened. He chewed Marshall up completely, and scarcely left a grease spot of him. His remarks were decidedly spicy, and kept the crowd in a roar. There is no denying the fact, whatever Marshall's ability may be, that in this race Mr. Blackburn gets the better of him upon the stump. There was very little sympathy in the crowd for Mr. Marshall, and so far as we could see, although the Hall was so densely packed we could see but a small part of the crowd, nearly all the applause Marshall got came from the Radicals.

Blackburn and Marshall had "over 100 joint discussions on the stump. It was one of the most exciting races ever made in the Blue Grass region of Kentucky." One farmer who heard Blackburn's magnificent speech sized it up: "Gosh! How he shook the apples off the tree." He ran a brilliant campaign that resulted in making "Blackburn a Congressman, and since that time his history is part and parcel of the public records of this country." In 1874 Blackburn was nominated and elected to the Forty-Fourth Congress by a majority of over six thousand votes to represent the Ashland District, succeeding James B. Beck. The *Woodford Sun* noted the following:

> The nomination for Congress from the proud old Ashland District of Capt. J.C.S. Blackburn without a dissenting voice, is a compliment of which he may well feel proud. It is an honor of which any man may feel proud. Capt. Blackburn is a young man of decided ability, strong will, a brilliant speaker, and an indomitable worker; he certainly has a bright future before him. We predict that he will carry the banner of Democracy aloft both in the canvass and in Congress, and that his friends will never have cause to regret zeal in his behalf.

When Blackburn was elected to Congress, he carried Woodford County and every other county in the district by large margins. Blackburn received a larger tally in every precinct than Beck did in 1872 and even more than Marshall had received in his loss to Beck in 1870. Kentucky elected only Democrats to Congress that year.

> It is impossible to describe the joy of the South over the election news. The cities are blazing with torchlites [sic] and bonfires while the cannon are shaking the Earth. Everybody rejoices that the mailed hand of the government has been stricken from these prostrate states, and that we are now to be great and wealthy like the North. Men are so crazed with joy that business is neglected. Never, since the surrender of Cornwallis, has anything been seen like it.

The Democratic star was rising in the South, pinned on the lapels of former Confederate soldiers and officers. Indeed, the Blackburn brothers were rising up with the Southern political tide as the *Woodford Sun* reported:

> We have heretofore noticed that the Blackburn brothers were looming up. Joe being our Congressman, Jim nominated (equivalent to election) for State Senator in Woodford, Dr. Luke up for State Senator in Louisville and some friends urged his claims for Governor. Well, they are worthy and capable and there can't be too many of them. Old Uncle Ned didn't breed any but No. 1 stock, horses or men. True Kentuckian.

Bourbon may have played a role in Blackburn's 1875 election. The distillation and consumption of bourbon was a time-honored practice in Kentucky. Even though he was not a highly-educated man, Kentucky's early hero, Davy Crockett, had succeeded in politics with a little help from the amber liquid. It was said that Crockett was sent to Congress three times despite his shortcomings. In one of his campaigns, when a political opponent offered to lead the electorate to the cannon's mouth, Crockett countered with a proposal to lead them to the "mouth of a barrel of whiskey." He was ushered to Congress by a three-to-one majority. Blackburn took a page from Crockett's playbook with a little help from Dr. Crow.

Dr. Crow had arrived from Scotland in Kentucky in 1823 and introduced the sour mash process of bourbon making, stressing quality over quantity. Dr. Crow died in 1856, which meant that by the 1870s, only a fortunate few people had bourbon made by the scientist, although subsequent producers would follow his whiskey-making method and keep his name alive. Jim Crow's whiskey was some of the very best of its time. Gerald Carson, in his *Social History of Bourbon,* tells the story of Blackburn's masterful use of the amber liquid to support his campaign:

> Joseph C.S. Blackburn used the last decanter of Jim Crow's whiskey known to exist on earth. Blackburn of Versailles, KY, used the last of the whiskey in the hot political campaign for Representative he made against Ed Marshall in 1875. Marshall was a brilliant campaigner, but Joe Blackburn had one advantage: a ten-gallon cask of Old Crow in his cellar. With his political career at stake, Blackburn decanted the precious fluid into small cruets. He would take a stubborn Marshall supporter aside and tell him all about Crow and his wonderful

> whiskey and then, as an old account puts it, 'he poured the liquor into his soul.'
>
> 'As you drink that, sir,' Blackburn would say, 'I want you to remember that you are helping to destroy the most precious heirloom of my family. It is the last bit of genuine Crow whiskey in the world. Observe, sir that you do not need to gulp down a tumbler of water after swallowing the liquor to keep it from burning your gullet. On the contrary, you know instinctively that to drink water with it would be a crime. All I ask of you is to remember that you are getting something in this liquor that all the money of an Indian prince cannot buy. Drink it, sir, and give up your soul to the Lord. Then if you can vote for Ed Marshall I cannot complain, because it will be the Lord's act!'

Blackburn beat Marshall handsomely. Blackburn was famous as a connoisseur of Kentucky's famous bourbon, as was his closest personal and political friend, Colonel Jack Chinn of Mercer County. "Both were generally recognized by the people as unswerving Democrats of the militant-type, always ready to do battle in season and out of season for the party nominee against Republicans." These two Kentucky gentlemen appreciated "Old Bourbon," as the best brands of Kentucky whiskey were called then.

A well-known liquor dealer of Frankfort, who desired expert testimony on the quality of a barrel of old Kentucky whisky he had bought for the delectation of his patrons, invited Senator Blackburn and Colonel Chinn to sample the liquor and pass judgment on its quality and flavor, according to the story.

> Accepting the invitation, the two met by appointment at the dealer's place and were each given a glass of the beady beverage drawn from the barrel in their presence. Each sipped the liquor appraisingly, and when they had drained their glasses, their host asked them for an opinion. 'That's good whisky,' said Blackburn, 'but it seems to have a slight flavor of iron.' 'Yes, that's first-class whisky,' retorted Chinn, 'but instead of iron, I detected a flavor of leather in it.' Their contention about their respective differences in the flavor of the liquor puzzled the

> dealer, who said he could not account for either in the whisky, and to settle the argument, he announced that he would have the barrel emptied of its contents to ascertain what, if anything, was the matter with it to call forth such criticism from these two acknowledged experts. The cask was accordingly drained and lo! To the surprise of all, on the bottom of the barrel was found a small iron carpet tack, with a leather collar around its head, which was pointed to as a solution to the mystery. Whether this incident actually occurred or not, the writer will not vouch, but it serves to illustrate the delicate taste and unerring judgment attributed to these two distinguished sons of Kentucky in their estimate of one of the state's most famous products, of which tradition says they were quite fond of as an inspiring beverage.

After all that Old Bourbon had done to help Blackburn's campaigns, it was fitting that during the next Congress, Blackburn was able to support legislation that favored distilled spirits during his second term as U.S. Representative for Kentucky in the second session of the Forty-Fifth Congress (December 3, 1877–June 20, 1878).

Chapter Twelve

The Belknap Scandal

"A Man Who Still Cherishes the Courage of His Convictions"
– J. C. S. Blackburn

Joseph Blackburn was seated among Republican and Democratic U.S. Congressmen who held strong opinions about the right and wrong sides in the Civil War. Neither side was willing to change its views or give in to the other side for years after the close of the war. The former Confederacy may have lost the battles on the field, but once the U.S. Government restored former Confederates to U.S. citizenship and allowed them to rejoin the U.S. political process in Congress, Southern Democrats did not apologize for their interpretation of the U.S. Constitution. Instead, Southern Democrats aligned in a "Solid South" that allowed them to flex political power by the time Reconstruction ended in 1877.

In response, Northern Republicans resorted to a by-now familiar tactic of fear-mongering, projecting the image that Southern Democrats were "atheists and unbelievers," who pretended to be for the general welfare of the people, while they could not "comprehend the character of the nation they now in part misrepresent." Not surprisingly, Southern Democrats were accused of being "reactionary," "the decided enemy of national education," "in league with the dark forces of Vaticanism." Republicans accused the Democratic Party of denying the American nationality and saying the word 'Nation' only with disgust and placing the sovereign states *above* the nation in "continued rebellion against the achievements of the late bloody war of secession;" and accurately stated that "the equal political and civil rights guaranteed to all citizens" had been brought to "naught in the Southern States by the Democratic Party;" that the ballot-box had been "defiled by it with many thousands of Republicans murdered" including freed slaves, and lastly that "the honor and credit of the nation is threatened and endangered by a Democratic inflation of rag money."

Things were clearly not going well. Republicans accused Democrats of spurting out the poison of sectional hate at the Union and charged them with a type of "Southern Judicial Ku-Kluxism" worse than in the times of slavery when there was no pretense of civil rights. Now slaves who had thought they were freed found themselves targeted by punitive laws. Southern legislation made petty crimes like theft, regardless of the value of the item stolen, a felony, and once convicted of a felony, freedmen were not allowed to vote or to serve on a jury nor did they have the right to testify as a witness in any of the courts. Only if a felony was pardoned or removed by act of the legislature could these civil rights be regained and that was not likely to happen to a former slave. Freedmen were not able to make a living in the South, particularly if they were tenant farmers, and were generally distrusted and despised. Freedmen were easily suspected, caught, convicted, and forced to serve out long terms of imprisonment at hard labor in the state prisons, and then hired out to private plantations. Conviction rates were high because Democratic sheriffs and jurors did not want to risk the release of one guilty party, no matter how many innocent men were convicted. It was alleged that, by contrast, "Any wealthy white man who is known to be a good Democrat can commit crime with impunity." Midnight murders were frequent, as well. It was a horrible state of affairs that continued for far too long in the South.

First Session, Forty-Fourth Congress (March 4, 1875–March 4, 1877)

These circumstances made Blackburn's rise in Congress all the more improbable. It is a rare thing for a U.S. Representative to secure a chairmanship of a committee or even positions on desirable or important committees during his first term in Congress, but Blackburn was accorded respect when he was placed third on the Committee on Elections and third on the Committee on Expenditures in the War Department. He was also appointed to a special committee of five to impeach Secretary of War Belknap and made the second member on the important committee to investigate federal offices in Louisiana. He was placed on joint committees to attend the funeral of Kentucky Representative Parsons. Furthermore, he was called upon to act as the Chairman of the Committee of the Whole many times during this Session.

The Chairman of the Committee of the Whole is often, under the House Rules, called upon by the Speaker of the House, who was then Michael C. Kerr, when he was in good health, and when Kerr was not, Samuel J. Randall, to preside over the House when it was considering general appropriation bills, revenue, and other bills of great national importance. The Chairman of the Committee of the Whole had to be a knowledgeable parliamentarian and a good presiding officer, with a thorough knowledge of the rules and practice. Speakers Kerr and Randall discovered early on in Blackburn's first Session that he was particularly gifted in that capacity and called on him no less than thirty times. In addition to this, Blackburn worked dutifully for his constituents. He introduced several bills for the relief of individual Kentuckians and offered several resolutions that were passed, including one regarding the manner in which the committee investigating the Louisiana elections should take the testimony regarding the elections and balloting and another one requesting the President to inform the House if any executive duties had been performed at a distance from the seat of government, and if so, what were the reasons that required the executive duties at that location and to what result, and other questions like that. The amount of work that he accomplished was fairly extraordinary.

The 1874 elections put Democrats in control of the House for the first time since the eve of the Civil War, and they focused on cleaning up the corruption in the Republican administration. The Forty-Fourth Congress impeached the Secretary of War William W. Belknap for bribery and his involvement in a trading post extortion scam, and investigated the President's private secretary for defrauding the government by reckless speculation that squandered the life savings of former slaves.

The Democratic majority, made up of former Confederate soldiers, controlled the House when former Union General Belknap, then Secretary of War, was charged with taking twenty thousand dollars, not government pay, from illegal profits from a military trading post at Fort Sill in Indian Territory. Belknap was widely known for his sumptuous Washington parties and his elegantly attired first and second wives, befitting what Mark Twain termed "the Gilded Age." Many began to wonder how Belknap was able to live so well on his annual eight thousand dollar government salary. By 1876, answers began to surface, thanks to the investigative work of a special committee that included Blackburn.

Early in the first Session, the War Department's Committee on Expenditures began an investigation into the administration of that department's affairs. This committee consisted of three Democrats—Representatives Hiester Clymer of Pennsylvania, Joseph C. S. Blackburn of Kentucky, and John Robbins, Jr. of Pennsylvania—and two Republicans—Lyman Bass of New York and Lorenzo Danford of Ohio. The committee uncovered evidence supporting a blatant pattern of corruption, even by the standards of the scandal-tarnished Grant administration.

The trail of evidence extended back to 1870 when Belknap's luxury-loving second wife, Carita, lobbied her husband to help an unscrupulous New York contractor by the name of Caleb Marsh, to get the job operating the profitable military trading post at Fort Sill in Indian Territory after Marsh agreed to send some of his profits her way. When Mrs. Belknap came up with the idea, the Fort Sill tradership post was held by John S. Evans, who refused to give it up. Instead, Evans came up with the idea of paying Caleb Marsh twelve thousand dollars annually if everyone agreed to let him keep his post at Fort Sill. Mr. Evans and Caleb Marsh made the deal, and Caleb Marsh then reciprocated and gave half of his yearly payments to Mrs. Belknap. After Mrs. Carita Belknap died of tuberculosis in 1870, the annual six thousand dollar payments were sent to Mr. Belknap directly. In all, he received nearly twenty-five thousand dollars in kick-backs on a regular quarterly basis. It was shocking. Resolutions for impeachment were proposed by the Committee. As soon as they were presented to the House, Republicans tried to keep the scandal quiet for damage control, but within one hour, the Democratic-controlled House adopted the resolutions by a unanimous vote, which would bring the articles of impeachment to the House for a vote. Things happened pretty quickly after the resolutions were adopted. Just minutes before the House was scheduled to vote on the articles of impeachment, Belknap raced to the White House and handed President Grant his resignation and burst into tears. This did not stop the House. Later that day, they voted *unanimously* to send the Senate five articles of impeachment, charging Belknap with "criminally disregarding his duty as Secretary of War and basely prostituting his high office to his lust for private gain."

While the House debated the proper procedure, the House Judiciary Committee, which has the duty to prepare the articles of impeachment, held back any report of its action, and Caleb Marsh, the accusing witness, fled the country. The Democrats then worked to pass an act to protect any informant who would come forward. Even the editor of the pro-Republican *Republic* admitted Belknap's wrongdoing and gave credit to the House members, both majority and minority, for handling the impeachment proceedings with dignity.

On Monday, April 17, 1876, the Senate was constituted as a High Court of Impeachment and the parties appeared before a large crowd of spectators. The proceedings were opened and General Belknap was called to respond to the charges exhibited against him. He answered by his counsel that he was a private citizen and denied the jurisdiction of the Senate. The House then asked for an adjournment of the court until April 19 to prepare the answer of the House. The question then before the Senate, sitting in its high judicial character, was whether a citizen could escape trial by impeachment by resigning an office while the examination into the charges of alleged corruption and malfeasance was ongoing. We now know that this is an effective way to escape impeachment. At the time, however, it was a question of "first impression" for the Senate.

In spite of the drama, work in the legislative halls in Washington, D.C. continued. The Democratic House launched sixty or seventy investigations, some prominent, that occupied the national press and the country for many months. The editor of *The Republic* wrote that loyal Union supporters in government would rise and band together, much like the Southern Democrats and ex-Confederates, whenever there was a "reasonable fear" that Southern Democrats would take over the government and that they never would be led into "the criminal folly of surrendering the country into the hands of those who would destroy it." The memories from the Civil War were too fresh to be forgotten by either side. This would define American politics and the divide in the political parties thereafter. The more the Southern Democrats crowed over their successes, the more the Northern Republicans banded together to ensure their defeat.

Nevertheless, among Southern Democrats and those Northern Republicans embarrassed by the unethical corruption within the Republican Grant Administration, Blackburn gained respect for his work on the special committee. He was seen as the leader who pursued the right cause of anti-corruption in our government, showing a love for the U.S. Constitution that rose above one party. Belknap quietly returned to his law practice in Iowa, while Blackburn became a national political hero for revealing Belknap's fraud.

Blackburn was celebrated at home in the local newspapers as a hero for restoring the South to honor and glory in August 1876:

> On last Friday evening Hon. J.C.S. Blackburn, the distinguished representative of the Ashland District, returned to his home in this place after an absence of 8 months, during which time he has made a national reputation and laid the foundation of an enduring fame. This event was the occasion of a spontaneous demonstration of welcome, approbation and affection by the people of this county. When the carriage containing Capt. Blackburn and several friends reached the head of Main Street, it was met by a procession of citizens, bearing torches and transparencies, and escorted through the town to his residence, preceded by a band of music. As they marched down Main Street cheer after cheer rent the air, and as they neared the residence the voice of the anvil cannon commenced to thunder forth its welcome. Over the piazza in front of the house was a large transparency bearing the words, 'Welcome Home' and the motto 'Our friend at home or abroad,' sparkled in letters of fire from the house top. Sky rockets and other fire works filled the air. The address of welcome delivered by Hon. John A. Steele was, as the Yeoman declared, 'singularly eloquent, classical, feeling and appropriate.' Capt. Blackburn responded in his own happy, inimitable manner. His tribute to his predecessors as representatives of the Ashland District, Clay, Crittenden, Marshall, Breckinridge and Beck was full of beauty, pathos and eloquence. He again and again expressed his gratitude to his friends and constituents for their repeated favors and for this last ovation, always in different form of speech, and as if struggling for some more ample mode of utterance for the deep emotion with which his big heart was bursting. The man shone out in his true simplicity and devotion when he laid all his honors at the feet of his friends and said, 'To you I owe all....'

Chapter Thirteen

Blackburn Stands Strong

"Whether the Spirit and the Genius of the Government Shall Be Reversed and Whether the Civil Shall Be Made Subordinate to the Military Power ...It is This Question, and It is None Other, That I Insist Shall Be Kept Before This House." – J. C. S. Blackburn

Forty-Fourth Congress (March 4, 1875–March 4, 1877) (Continued)

After cleaning up the corruption in Grant's Cabinet, Congress then debated the Electoral Commission bill following the voter fraud in the 1876 Hayes-Tilden U.S. Presidential Election, and Blackburn played a prominent and aggressive role in those debates. Elections are not the simple straight-forward counting of the popular vote for President and Vice-President. When the Founding Fathers wrote the U. S. Constitution, there was a conflicting desire to elect the President and Vice-President by a vote in Congress and to elect them by a popular vote of qualified citizens. As a compromise, a process called the Electoral College was adopted that purports to combine the two. The process consists of selecting electors and directing where they meet to vote for the President and Vice President and the counting of the electoral votes by Congress. Each state has its process for selecting electors, but generally, the political parties nominate electors at their state party conventions or by a vote of the party's central committee in each state. No Senator or Representative or any person holding a U.S. office or trust or profit could be selected as an elector. Electors are usually chosen in recognition of their service and dedication to their political party.

On election day, the voters in each state choose the electors by casting votes for the presidential candidate for their choice. In some states, the winning candidate in each state is awarded all of the state's electors; however, some states allow the electors the freedom to vote as they choose without following the direction of the popular vote in their state. There is no Constitutional provision or Federal law that requires electors to vote according to the results of the popular votes in their states, although some states require this. Generally, then, electors are bound by state law or pledges to political parties. Kentucky does not have a state law requiring electors to vote for the winning candidate.

The U.S. Presidential election of 1876 was one of the most contentious in American history, similar to the controversial Bush-Gore presidential election of 2000. The results of the 1876 (and arguably the 2000) election remain among the most disputed ever. There was no question that New York Democrat Samuel J. Tilden and his running mate Thomas Hendricks won the popular vote over Ohio Republican Rutherford B. Hayes and his running mate William A. Wheeler. This was the first Presidential election in twenty years in which the Democratic candidate won the popular vote and the first since the Civil War. After a first count of votes, Democrat Tilden won 184 Electoral votes to Republican Hayes's 165 Electoral votes, with twenty unresolved votes in South Carolina, Louisiana, and Florida. The fight in Congress was over the twenty unresolved votes. If Hayes won all of those twenty disputed votes, he would win the election by one electoral vote: 185 to 184. A special committee began to investigate.

Second Session, Forty-Fourth Congress (1875–1877)

Blackburn was appointed fifth on a special committee of fifteen to investigate the recent elections in Louisiana. The work on this committee consumed most of Blackburn's time in the Second Session, but he spoke about many subjects, including the deficiency appropriation bill, the withdrawal of witnesses involved in the committee's investigations, and the printing of the testimony from the state of Louisiana regarding the 1876 U.S. presidential elections charged with fraud and abuse. He spoke frequently about the disputed electoral votes during the Congressional recount. He strongly defended the American voters when he placed the responsibility upon Congress for giving the election to Republican Hayes in a rousing speech on the House floor that was applauded on the floor and in the gallery by the guests.

Congress appointed a special Electoral Commission to divvy up the disputed Electoral College votes from the states of Florida, Louisiana, and South Carolina. The fifteen members of the Electoral Commission were made up of five members from each House and five Supreme Court Justices. There were two Republican and two Democratic Supreme Court justices, and these four chose the fifth. At first, they chose a political independent Justice David Davis, but he was elected by the Illinois legislature to the Senate while the Electoral Commission Bill was passing Congress, so he resigned as a Supreme Court Justice to take his Senate seat. His departure from the high court left only Republican justices to choose from, so the four justices already selected chose Justice Joseph P. Bradley of New York, who they thought would be the most impartial. It turned out to be a crucial decision. It is believed that they knew that this final justice would provide the deciding vote on the commission because all fourteen of the other members were strictly partisan. Bradley had been nominated to the Supreme Court by Republican President Grant and ultimately sided with his party.

The Electoral Commission decided not to question any returns that were lawful on their face (prima facie) and then voted. The final eight-to-seven vote split along partisan lines and effectively made the Republican candidate Hayes President. Justice Joseph P. Bradley was the tie-breaker vote, giving Hayes a 185 to 184 electoral vote victory over the Democrat Tilden. Justice Bradley was heavily criticized and even received death threats. There were allegations that he had originally planned to vote for Tilden but was persuaded to vote for Hayes the night before the final decision. Nothing substantive came of these charges. Bradley always denied any undue or improper influence. Nationally, Blackburn gained notoriety for his filibuster against accepting the decision of the Electoral Commission until after the Inauguration Day in 1877.

The Electoral Commission Bill was simultaneously widely disliked and widely supported. Republican President-Elect Hayes, meanwhile, believed that by creating the Commission, Congress had unconstitutionally usurped the president's power of appointment but kept it to himself and his close friends. Joseph Blackburn opposed it because it gave away the House's specific power to determine the vote and took away the "popular right" in selecting "the people's rulers" as he said on the House floor on January 26, 1877:

> I object to it because if passed it robs this House of the constitutional prerogative to protect a popular right. I hold that under the provisions of the Constitution (in common with majority of the members of this House, and in accordance with the expression of the Senate as illustrated in its vote upon this bill yesterday morning) the President of the Senate has no authority in the count to settle anything as regards the validity of any vote; that this power is lodged with the Houses of Congress, and that nothing coming here as the vote of a State can be received if this House enters its protest against it.... To agree to this is, in my judgment, an abandonment of the rights that the people have committed to our keeping. Not one atom of popular right in the matter of the selection of the people's rulers will I ever surrender; not one prerogative of this House that looks to the protection of that popular right will I ever consent to abandon. If this needs to be arbitrated, we require another tribunal.

Blackburn's journal in 1877 reflects the dark days of the struggles in the House. On Saturday, February 10, 1877, he wrote; "Spent day in the House; Electoral Commission Reported vote of Florida for Hayes—We seem to be lost before that partisan tribunal." Then on February 22, 1877, he wrote: "Went to the House for an hour & came back to my rooms. My God: how dark everything in the future looks." Later, he wrote: "Made speech on electoral count at 2:00 AM in House session on March 1, 1877."

After the Electoral Commission awarded all twenty disputed votes to Hayes to give him the Election, the episode became known as the Compromise of 1877. Many former slaves referred to it, however, as the "Great Betrayal." It was a purported informal, unwritten deal that settled the Hayes-Tilden Presidential Election dispute by accepting the election of Hayes in exchange for withdrawing federal troops out of state politics in the South, with the following conditions: that Hayes appoint at least one Southern Democrat to the Hayes Cabinet (David M. Key of Tennessee as Postmaster General), that another transcontinental railroad use the Texas and Pacific routes in the South, and that legislation be provided to help industrialize the South and get them back on their feet after their defeat in the Civil War. The Reconstruction Era was finally over.

Blackburn wrote one of his constituents a letter explaining his opposition to the Compromise of 1877:

> Washington, Feb. 10, 1877
> My Dear Sir:
>
> I have yours of the 24th, and thank you for it. 'Twas a good strong argument against the bill, though you conclude we had best take it. Well, we have it, and I sincerely hope that we are not to be swindled under its operation. I could not support it. That it was in plain conflict with the Constitution is too manifest to need argument. As a matter of policy, 'twas the greatest of blunders. Under it we may get Tilden; without it we had him, after the Senate eliminated the only danger we were ever in, that of the presiding officer of the Senate exercising any power. I have hopes, but also fears. There never was any danger of war or of Hayes' inauguration, if the House simply protested against the wrong.
>
> Your friend,
> J.C.S. Blackburn

But the Compromise of 1877 was the result. Outgoing President Ulysses S. Grant removed the soldiers from Florida, and newly-elected President Hayes removed the remaining troops from South Carolina and Louisiana. As soon as the troops left, many white Republicans left and "Redeemer" Democrats took control. Redeemers were a white political coalition in the South during Reconstruction who wanted to eliminate Radical Republicans, along with their coalition of freedmen, carpetbaggers, and scalawags in the South. Redeemer Democrats were not willing to admit defeat or allow black political activity of any kind. White and black relations in the South during and after Reconstruction were horrifically violent. It is a shame to say that the planter class, corrupted by their vast wealth earned on the backs of slaves, supported violence against freedmen and Republicans and let other whites, like those in the Ku Klux Klan, perform the dirty work.

"Jim Crow" laws and segregation also worked to keep poor blacks and poor whites from reaping the benefits of the Thirteenth, Fourteenth, and Fifteenth Amendments to the Constitution that ended slavery, provided equal rights to all, and prohibited denying voting rights on account of race, color, or previous servitude. Jim Crow laws effectively continued the pre-Civil War "Black Codes" that kept civil rights and civil liberties from former slaves. However, the Compromise of 1877 relieved the South from the presence of the federal military under Reconstruction.

Blackburn wrote in his journal for March 10, 1877, "Reached home at night. People gave me a reception at Court House. Artillery out and crowd enthusiastic." Blackburn was a local and national hero for revealing the corruption in Grant's Reconstruction Cabinet, for defending the popular right to choose the people's rulers in the Hayes-Tilden Presidential election, and—most of all—for ending Reconstruction. The South could now regain citizenship and political power in the country, but only for its white residents.

Upon his return to Congress, Blackburn was appointed a member of the committee to revise the rules of the House of Representatives, composed of Samuel J. Randall, Alexander H. Stevens, William P. Frye, and James A. Garfield. The rules committee appointed Blackburn to present its findings to the House.

Two years later in 1879, Blackburn, then Minority Chair, was asked about the Hayes-Tilden election by a street car conductor in Washington, D.C. This conversation was overheard by Thomas C. Donaldson, a personal friend of President Hayes. Donaldson wrote about the overheard conversation in his memoirs:

> *Washington, D.C., [Sunday] March 2, 1879.*—I came up to the Capitol to-day at 11 A.M. on a street car. Standing on the rear platform was Joseph C. S. Blackburn, M.C. of Kentucky. The car conductor said 'Who is going to be Speaker of the next House?' Blackburn answered, 'Well, I don't know that I should answer that; but it will be either General Garfield or myself, provided we organize the next House. It will not be Mr. Randall.' The conductor said, 'Are you afraid of the greenbackers [those

> who supported non-gold backed money]?' 'Oh, no; they don't mean us any harm.' The conductor said, 'I don't think there will be any greenbackers next year.' 'No,' said Blackburn, 'we will sit down on them the first chance we get.' The conductor said, 'Mr. Blackburn, if you had been Speaker at the time of the Electoral Commission, things would not have happened as they did.' 'No, sir,' Blackburn replied, and pointing towards the White House, 'there would have been a different set of officers there, and Hayes would not have been in office.'
>
> The conductor continued, 'Randall is just as much a fraud as Hayes, and never should have been Speaker.' Blackburn said, 'If Randall had kept his word at the time of the Electoral count, Hayes would not have been President. On Tuesday, before the Friday of the final action, eighteen of us met Randall in the afternoon in a private room under the House, and he agreed with us that we should have the advantage of the rules, and should be permitted to filibuster beyond the 4th of March, so as to put Tilden in, and agreed to hold out to the end of Congress. This was a solemn agreement. On Thursday after noon at five o'clock he went back on us and on his pledges, by voting against us. If he had kept his word, Mr. Tilden would have been President. Of course, there would have been a little revolution in that building (pointing to the Capitol) for a few hours; but I have such an abiding faith in the good sense of the people, that they would have hailed the result (Tilden) with shouts and asserted their rights.'
>
> We left the car. I walked into the Capitol and to Mr. Randall's room, wrote the above out and handed it to him to read. He replied sharply that it was an entire falsehood in every word that related to him.

Despite the political outcomes, Blackburn earned the respect for his work and dedication to Democratic principles in office, as reflected in the local newspaper years later:

> We always believed that Capt. Blackburn to be a brave, gallant, true man, devoted to principle and unflinching in his adherence to the Democratic faith as understood by the

> fathers. We now give him credit for a capacity and ability equal to the task of making these qualities as useful as the field on which he had been called to act is broad. He richly deserves a reelection and ought to have it without challenge.

Blackburn was admired at home and in Washington, D.C. In 1878, a Washington correspondent wrote:

> This gallant Kentuckian is one of the finest orators on the continent. He is about six feet in height, looks like a knight of old, stepping into the lists, ready for any comer. Blackburn has a voice a little stagey in its tone, but full, round and ringing.... A kinglier looking man you never saw. A bolder and braver one you will never see. He is perfect in his physique... and delivered one of the most sensible, one of the chastest and most pungent speeches I ever heard. It cut to the red every lick. It was pronounced by the Northern Democrats as a perfect gem.

Blackburn gained a national reputation for his debates with James G. Blaine of Maine, James A. Garfield of Ohio, Benjamin F. Butler of Massachusetts, William P. Frye of Maine, and Eugene Hale of Maine. Blaine became the Twenty-Eighth and Thirty-First U.S. Secretary of War; Garfield became the Twentieth President of the United States; Butler became Governor of Massachusetts; and Frye served five terms in the U.S. Senate, the headliners of their day.

Chapter Fourteen

Promoting the General Interests of the Country

Forty-Fifth Congress (March 4, 1877–March 4, 1879)

The Forty-Fifth Congress continued to be politically divided between a Democratic House and Republican Senate. There were 155 Democrats and 136 Republicans and two Independent Democrats in the House. All ten of the U.S. Representatives from Kentucky, including Blackburn, were Democrats, as were both Senators (Thomas C. McCreary and James B. Beck).

House Speaker Randall appointed a Ways and Means Committee of eleven members with seven Democrats and four Republicans. Five of the seven Democrats and three of the four Republicans were in favor of a high protective tariff, and as a result, no measure of a tariff reform was reported to the House. This created a bitter feeling in the Democratic ranks, who wanted a tariff reform to remove the protective tariffs that benefited the industrial sections of the country found mainly in the Northern section of the country without benefitting the agrarian sections of the country found mainly in the Western and Southern sections of the country. Arguably, the existing protective tariffs hurt the agrarian sections, because farmers had to sell their produce to buy manufactured goods that cost more as a result of the protective tariffs. This dissatisfaction among the leaders of the Democratic agrarian states, including Blackburn, led to an organized movement against Randall's re-election as Speaker of the next Congress.

"Sunset" Cox became a candidate for Speaker of the House, though the New York delegation, under the inspiration of Samuel J. Tilden, was solidly for Randall. In Ohio, Randall only had one vote out of a delegation of eleven, and that was cast by the brilliant Frank Hurd of Toledo, an open and avowed free trader but the devoted friend of Tilden, who was himself a devoted friend of Randall.

The Democratic members led by William R. Morrison, of Illinois, chose Joseph Blackburn as their candidate. However, several events evolved that turned the support away from Blackburn: the influence of the recently defeated Democratic Presidential Candidate Tilden, the defection of the Alabama delegation (who threw their support behind their candidate for clerk, John McMahon), and the action of the Ohio delegation. These developments split the votes between Cox, John A. McMahon, Randall, and Blackburn to result in the ultimate defeat of Blackburn for the Speakership. Randall received seventy-five votes, Blackburn fifty-seven votes, and the rest received just a few votes. Apparently, Randall had promised about a dozen Southern members good committee places if they voted for Randall. These Southern members had been Blackburn's companions-in-arms in the Confederate Army whom he had relied upon. The split in the caucus caused it to break up in a bitter and revengeful mood, in spite of Blackburn's eloquent appeal to every member who voted for him to sustain the action of the caucus and vote for its nominee.

In moving to make Randall's nomination unanimous, Blackburn steered his supporters away from the nomination of Hendrick B. Wright, a Democrat from Pennsylvania who was nominated by the independent party known as the Greenbacks.

In 1879 Blackburn gave a stirring speech in his motion to make the nomination of Mr. Randall unanimous:

> MR. BLACKBURN: Mr. Chairman, It is not in my power to express to the gentlemen who supported me in this contest those sentiments to which I hold this evidence of their friendship. I will in candor say that I had hoped that it might be the pleasure of this House to have imposed the responsibilities and duties of the Speakership upon one from the section and people with whom I am identified; for I felt assured that, had such been done, the result would have proved to the people of this country that the South might safely be charged with the formation of these Committees and to shape the legislation of the land. Had I been selected for this service, it would have been my duty, as it certainly

> would have been my pleasure, to wield the great powers that pertain to this station in such a way as to put all sections and factions behind me, and to promote the general interests of a common country in which citizens all hold equal rights, and to which each citizen should tender a common allegiance. I would have endeavored to prove to those generous friends from the North who stood by me in this contest, that their confidence was not misplaced; for I should earnestly have endeavored to bury the melancholy memories of the terrible past in those trenches where the moldering remains of those who gave their lives to those struggles, to-day are resting. I am a party man—I am a partisan—not for the sake of the party, but because I honestly and earnestly believe the best interests of my country are to be subserved by the triumph of my party's principles. I have but this to say: The edict of the caucus is to me final and conclusive, and if there be any among the fifty-seven gentlemen whose partial friendship has given me their votes that hesitate or doubt to give him their votes, I now appeal to them to make the verdict of this caucus effective when to-morrow's roll is called. I move you, sir, that the nomination of the gentleman from Pennsylvania (Randall) for the Speakership of the House of Representatives of the Forty-Sixth Congress be made unanimous.
> [The nomination was accordingly made unanimous.]

It was said afterwards that Blackburn's "manly and patriotic action in this regard… saved a bolt and the immediate disintegration of the Democratic party." As soon as the Speaker had been elected, Blackburn was appointed one of a committee of three Senators and three Representatives to notify the President that a quorum of Congress had assembled and was ready to do business, a tribute to Blackburn's fair leadership in the contest for Speaker. His concern for the greater good of the country continued in his next work, building up the country's capitol city.

Blackburn spoke on all District of Columbia bills and introduced a bill to revise and amend the laws of the District of Columbia, which came to be known as The Organic Act. In 1878, Congressman Blackburn's Organic Act provided a permanent and stable form of local government in the nation's capital. Blackburn's plan organized the District of Columbia as a municipal corporation governed by three civilian commissioners, one of whom was from the U.S. Army Corps of Engineers. "[Blackburn] brought to the study of the question all the energies of a powerful and an honest mind. He studied it profoundly, and now, forty years later, that organization yet maintains and Washington is the best governed city in America."

The Organic Act was needed after Washington suffered for three years under a corrupted form of the territorial government that had been set up by the Congress in 1871. This territorial government had been made up of a governor, an eleven-member council appointed by the president, and a popularly elected twenty-two-member House of Delegates. Washington was also allowed one non-voting delegate to the House of Representatives. The territorial government combined Georgetown, the city of Washington, and the county of Washington. The territorial government of Washington failed after a series of financial crises that revealed the corruption in its administration. Blackburn's Organic Act provided the needed corrections to create a solid National Capital.

Blackburn remained proud of his work on the act for the rest of his life. In 1918, Senator Blackburn said in an interview near the end of his life, "I am proud of writing the Organic Act" and that he wanted to be remembered as its author. He had spent days drafting the bill and weeks fighting for its enactment. Thanks to Blackburn's Organic Act, the capital prospered. It took him four month's hard work to frame that bill and several days on the floor speaking in support of it. The 1918 *Washington Herald* article reported:

> [T]he fight 'Joe' Blackburn put up was characteristic of the man. He never went into a fight to lose. He usually won. And with the passing of the Organic Act in 1878 an era of prosperity started in Washington.
>
> According to Senator Blackburn, the average constituent has little good-will toward the city of Washington. This results in the majority of Congressmen coming to Washington with the determination of keeping down appropriations for the upbuilding of the Capital city.

Blackburn had taken the job seriously, as he recalled it years later to a reporter from the newspaper, *The Washington Herald,* when he was U.S. Senator:

> [A] man accepting the chairmanship of the District Committee takes it with one of two views, or prejudices: that of being a friend of the District or an antagonist. If he is a friend, the District can expect good treatment. On the other hand, the District cannot expect much.

The act when first written stated one of the Commissioners must be a Democrat, another a Republican. This was to give Washington a nonpartisan government. President Hayes objected to this particular phrase of the bill and through Republican leaders in the Congress asked Mr. Blackburn to strike out that part of it. He silently consented, however, to name one Democrat and one Republican as the civilian Commissioners. President Hayes lived up to his promise appointing one from each political faith. Since then each successive President has followed the precedent, but does not have to unless he desires."

Senator Blackburn says Washington should be the most beautiful city in the world in every respect. He says the people of the United States, instead of being prejudiced against the National Capital, should fight for it, and not instill in their Representatives a feeling of ill will toward it.

I could want no greater monument to my memory than the Organic Act," said Senator Blackburn. "I am proud I am the author of that bill."

The government for the District of Columbia established by the Organic Act provided permanence and stability and allowed the construction of monuments to reflect the history and ideals of the nation in the city that serves as a host to the world. Blackburn's plan remained in place for nearly another one hundred years. Then the changing times and needs of the late 1960s brought change to Blackburn's three-member Board of Commissioners when it was replaced in 1967 under President Lyndon B. Johnson with a mayor-commissioner form of government with a nine-member council. This modified form of Blackburn's government in the district continues today.

On February 13, 1884, an evening serenade was given to Senator-elect Blackburn at the National Hotel by the citizens of the District of Columbia in recognition of his services on behalf of the interests of the Capital. The citizens of the District knew he had written The Organic Act that had given their District a stable government and provided for improving the city with national landmark buildings and statues suitable for the nation's capital before the world stage. No other national leader before or after Blackburn had been so kind, protective, and supportive of the nation's capital, but Blackburn understood the importance of creating a dignified capital to represent our growing nation to its citizens and other world leaders. The Reception Committee met at the Riggs House accompanied by a band and marched to the National Hotel, where they paid their respects to Blackburn. A large crowd assembled in the street in front of the hotel. Blackburn received the committee and others in the parlor and then went out on the balcony and gave a speech to the crowd, thanking them for their confidence in him.

Chapter Fifteen

Standing Upon His Convictions

"He Must Stand Upon His Conviction, and There We Will All Stand. He Who Dallies is a Dastard, and He Who Doubts is Damned."
–J.C.S. Blackburn

Special Session, Forty-Fifth Congress (March 5, 1877–March 17, 1877)

President Hayes called a Special Session, because the army appropriation bill failed to pass in the preceding Session. Blackburn was appointed Chairman of the Committee on Expenditures in the War Department and second on the Committee on the District of Columbia, one of the most important committees of the House. He was Chairman of the Committee of the Whole during the discussion on the naval deficiency bill. Blackburn spoke frequently during the three days of debate on the army appropriation bill, joined by the leaders of the House, such as Garfield and Foster of Ohio, Conger of Michigan, Hewitt of New York, Atkins of Tennessee, Mills and Culberson of Texas, and others. Mr. Blackburn was strongly opposed to any increase of the army and offered and then urged an amendment limiting the total number to fifteen thousand men in the various branches of the army and no more. Crowds watched these debates from the gallery overlooking the House floor and applauded when they strongly agreed with the speaker.

> MR. BLACKBURN: I have heard no argument adduced, no suggestion offered, either from that side of the House or from this side of the House, in favor of an increase of the army or in favor of a continuance of the army at its present standard of strength, except it was for the protection of the

Texas Indian frontier, as claimed by citizens of that State and the Representatives of that State, or, as asserted by our friends on the other side, an increase in the army should be given in order that laws should be enforced, order maintained and peace governed within the borders of the sovereign States. It had as well be understood and tested now as hereafter that there are those of us upon this floor who deny the theory advanced by our friends on the other side.

We deny that the proper method for preventing disorders that have disgraced the country for the last twelve months is to be found in the increase of the standing army. We deny that the proper method to amend those evils under which this people is now suffering, that the proper remedy to be offered for those sufferings that we are now enduring, is to be found in an increase in the army, in an increase of soldiers, in giving more batteries, in furnishing more guns, in supplying more canister and more grape shot to shoot down the impoverished laborers of the land who dare to complain of the robbery of which they are the victims by reason of the persistent class financial legislation of the dominant party for the last fifteen years. [Applause]. We are not willing to admit that this process of repression, coupled with the wholesale murder of starving millions, is either safe policy, fair dealing or manhood properly illustrated.

I would not reduce the army beneath a standard that will give ample and complete protection to both the Texan and Indian border. I believe that 15,000 men are more, after making a proper reduction for your arsenals and sea-coast defenses, than ever have as yet been employed for the protection of those two border sections. I am perfectly willing to see the cavalry force of the army increased at the expense of the infantry and artillery; for I believe the exposed frontiers of the country warrant and require it. But I desire to notify this Committee of the Whole that in the event of the amendment just presented being lost I will ask in the House for a vote, and I give notice that I will demand yeas and nays, to test the sense of this House as to whether it is proposed to remedy the rights and redress the wrongs of the impoverished citizens scattered throughout our borders by an increase of military power for their subjugation and their slaughter. [Applause on the floor and in the galleries].

Forty-Sixth Congress (March 4, 1879–March 4, 1881)

For the first time in nearly two decades, the Senate had a Democratic majority and the House had more Democrats who were willing to cooperate and compromise with the other party members. As a result, the Democrats were able to control the House with the help of the independent politicians who caucused with them in a coalition. Hayes was the Republican President and Vice President William Wheeler was the Republican President of the Senate.

Special Session, Forty-Sixth Congress (March 18, 1879–July 1, 1879)

Blackburn again presided over the Committee of the Whole during the Special Session while the army appropriation bill was under consideration a second time. The debates on the floor between Blackburn and Republican James Garfield of Ohio were regularly featured in the national headlines of papers like the *New York Times* and the *Washington Post*. In this particular speech about the army appropriation bill, Blackburn staunchly defended the right of the people to vote freely without the presence of the military at the voting booth and argued against an increase in the army in a speech that includes the phrase for which he would become known: "He who dallies is a dastard, and he who doubts is damned."

Republicans wanted to fund an increase of the army fund and Democrats wanted to reduce funding and the size of the army, primarily as a way to limit the army's ability to act in Southern states, especially at the voting booths. In the speech, Blackburn explained that the proposed amendment that limited army supplies and removed the army from the polling place was not revolutionary. He summarized his argument as follows:

> MR. BLACKBURN: There is but one issue here, and I insist that neither this House nor the people of this country shall be allowed to wander from it. It is but this, and nothing more:

whether the military power shall be allowed at your polls; whether the elections shall be guarded by the mailed hand of military power; whether the ballot-box, that last and safest shield of the freeman's liberties, shall be turned over to the tender mercies of the armies of your land. Or to state it yet more tersely and probably more fairly, it is simply whether the spirit and the genius of the government shall be reversed and whether the civil shall be made subordinate to the military power.

It is this question, and it is none other, that I insist shall be kept before this House. We are declaring that the ballot shall be free. We are denying that it is either constitutional, legal, just, fair, or decent, to subject the sovereign to the surveillance of the soldier....

I am willing, and those with whom I stand are willing, to accept this issue, and we go further, we tender it. We are the ones to make the issue and we are ready for you to accept it. Planting ourselves upon this broad ground, we welcome controversy. *We seek no quarrel with you, but for the first time in eighteen years past the Democracy is back in power in both branches of this Legislature, and she proposes to signalize her return to power, she proposes to celebrate her recovery of her long-lost heritage, by tearing off these degrading badges of servitude and destroying the machinery of a corrupt and partisan legislation.* [Emphasis Added].

We do not intend to stop until we have stricken the last vestige of your war measures from the statute-book, which, like these, were born of the passions incident to civil strife, and looked to the abridgment of the liberty of the citizen.

We demand an untrammeled election; no supervising of the ballot by the army. Free, absolutely free right to the citizen in the deposit of his ballot as a condition-precedent to the passage of your bills....I do not mean to issue a threat. Unlike the gentleman from Ohio I disclaim any authority to threaten. But I do mean to say that it is my deliberate conviction that there is not to be found in the majority a single man who will ever consent to abandon one jot or tittle of the faith that is in him. He cannot surrender if he would. I beg you to believe he will not be coerced by threats nor intimidated by parade of power. He must stand upon his conviction, and there we will all stand. *He who dallies is a dastard, and he who doubts is damned.* [Emphasis added].

Forty-Sixth Congress (March 4, 1879–March 4, 1881)

Blackburn had additional debates with Garfield and McKinley over the army appropriation bill when it was under consideration in the House, but none captured the public's imagination like his Special Session speech quoted above.

Chapter Sixteen

Champion of Free Silver

By 1878, it had been five years since Congress passed the Fourth Coinage Act of 1873 that removed the silver dollar from the list of authorized coins. As a result, owners of silver bullion were no longer allowed to deposit their silver bullion and have their metal struck into legal tender dollar coins. It ended bimetallism in the United States and eliminated three smaller-denomination coins. It was enacted after the 1859 discovery of the large lode of silver ore known as the Comstock Lode in a part of the western Utah Territory (later Nevada), that, if coined, could lower gold prices and "endanger the gold standard." When silver prices dropped in 1876, many silver ore producers tried to have their bullion struck into silver dollars at the U.S. Mint but found out that it was no longer possible. It was a shock and became a major national political controversy that lasted for the rest of the nineteenth century. The Act became known as "the Crime of '73," and it would play a central role in Blackburn's political life. By now, Blackburn's political perspective had broadened to embrace policies that affected the entire country and not just his home state of Kentucky.

Free silver meant the return to using unrestricted quantities of silver as currency in the country, along with gold as currency or as the backing for currency, and returning the country to using two metals for money or bimetallism. Supporters of free silver, as it was called, included Western silver mine owners and farmers who thought it would increase their crop prices. Many believed silver would raise prices. Debtors supported free silver because they thought it would ease their debt payments because silver's value tended to change more rapidly in response to market demands than gold. Blackburn believed that supporting the return to bimetallism as the national money standard would help the farmers and debtors in Kentucky and across the country. Silver became the symbol of economic justice for the mass of American people and a rallying cry for a developing populist movement, one that tends to flourish in this country whenever many suffer financially.

Silver was produced from Western mines free of Northeastern Wall Street control and became a symbol of Southern and Western agrarian values. Free silver advocates, "Silverites," were in favor of an inflationary monetary policy using the "free coinage of silver" and against the more stable gold standard. Silverites promoted bimetallism at the ratio of sixteen to one, or sixteen ounces of silver equal to one ounce of gold. Because the actual ratio was about thirty-two-to-one at the time, most economists warned that the cheaper silver would drive the more expensive gold out of circulation. Everyone agreed that free silver would raise prices; the question was whether or not this inflationary measure would be beneficial.

The bimetal currency issue peaked during the severe depression known as the Panic of 1893. Prices fell, unemployment rose in the industrial areas of the country, and farmers across the land suffered severe distress. Blackburn firmly supported the Free Silver Movement. It was clear to him that the Populist role championing the free coinage of silver in national politics was his calling. A bill was proposed in the House to return silver to the list of authorized coins. On February 21, 1878, Representative Blackburn openly objected to one House amendment to the bill for re-monetization of silver because it limited the amount of silver that could be coined, but otherwise supported it because, as he said on the House floor:

> MR. BLACKBURN: Mr. Speaker, I have ever favored what is known as the silver bill; first, because it was right to restore that metal to the place and to give it back the power it has ever held until stricken down, not at the demand, but without the knowledge of the people....
>
> But the measure, even as it stands, is not to be accounted valueless. It does not restore silver to the coinage. It does make it a legal tender for all debts, public and private, without limit. It does give us a bimetallic instead of a single standard. Aye, sir, it does more; it opens up the way for other and further legislation in this direction, which should, and I doubt not will,

Joseph Clay Stiles Blackburn (Image courtesy of the author, Blackburn Collection)

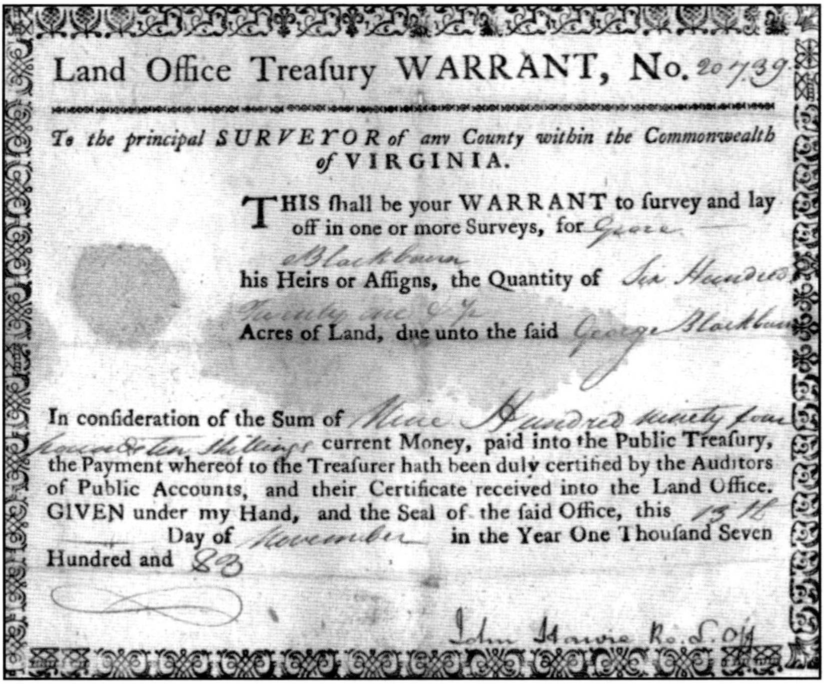

Land Office Treaſury WARRANT, No. 20739

To the principal SURVEYOR of any County within the Commonwealth of VIRGINIA.

THIS ſhall be your WARRANT to ſurvey and lay off in one or more Surveys, for George Blackburn his Heirs or Aſſigns, the Quantity of Six Hundred Twenty one & ½ Acres of Land, due unto the ſaid George Blackburn

In conſideration of the Sum of Nine Hundred ninety four pounds & Ten Shillings current Money, paid into the Public Treaſury, the Payment whereof to the Treaſurer hath been duly certified by the Auditors of Public Accounts, and their Certificate received into the Land Office. GIVEN under my Hand, and the Seal of the ſaid Office, this 13th Day of November in the Year One Thouſand Seven Hundred and 83

John Harvie R. L. Off

George Blackburn, Joseph Blackburn's grandfather, Virginia Land Office Treasury Warrant for 625.5 acres of land in Woodford County, Virginia, on November 13, 1783, within Woodford County, Kentucky.

In 1811, George Blackburn built second oldest Baptist Church west of the Alleghenies: Baptist Church of Christ at Big Spring, Woodford County that burned August 21, 1962. (Photo by J. Winston Coleman, Jr. courtesy of the author).

Joseph's father, Edward Mitchell Blackburn (Image courtesy of the author, now on display at the Kentucky History Center, Frankfort, Kentucky)

Joseph's mother, Lavinia Bell Blackburn (Image courtesy of the author, now on display at the Kentucky History Center, Frankfort, Kentucky)

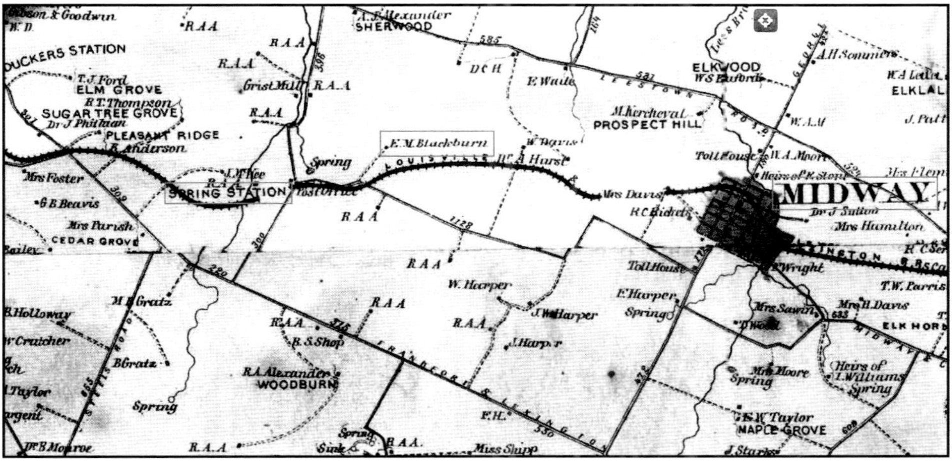

A 1861 map of Spring Station, Woodford County, Kentucky showing location of E.M. Blackburn horse farm owned by Joseph's father, Edward Mitchell Blackburn. (Library of Congress)

Gravesites for Kentucky Governor Dr. Luke Blackburn, Kentucky's first physician governor, center; to the right are the monuments to his parents, Edward M. Blackburn and Lavinia Bell Blackburn; to the left are the monuments to the Governor's wife Ella, son Dr. Cary B., and sister Mary, in the Frankfort Cemetery. (Image courtesy of the author)

Kentucky panel of the Lincoln Boyhood National Monument, Lincoln City, Indiana. Dr. C.C. Graham (in hat) is depicted tutoring young Abraham Lincoln. Dr. Graham is Joseph Blackburn's father-in-law. E.H. Daniels sculptor. (Image courtesy of the author's husband, Thomas E. Fielder)

Dr. Luke Pryor Blackburn (Image courtesy of the Kentucky History Center)

James Weir Blackburn (Image courtesy of Kentucky History Center)

Lincoln's First Inaugural Address, March 4, 1861

American Eclipse, by Edward Troye (1814-1847)

Boston, from the painting by Edward Troye (1833-1850)

Luke Blackburn (Image courtesy of Kentucky History Center)

President Lincoln and his Cabinet in 1861

First Kentucky Brigade Flag or "The Orphan Brigade." Captain Joseph C. S. Blackburn was an early member of The Orphan Brigade. (Wikipedia)

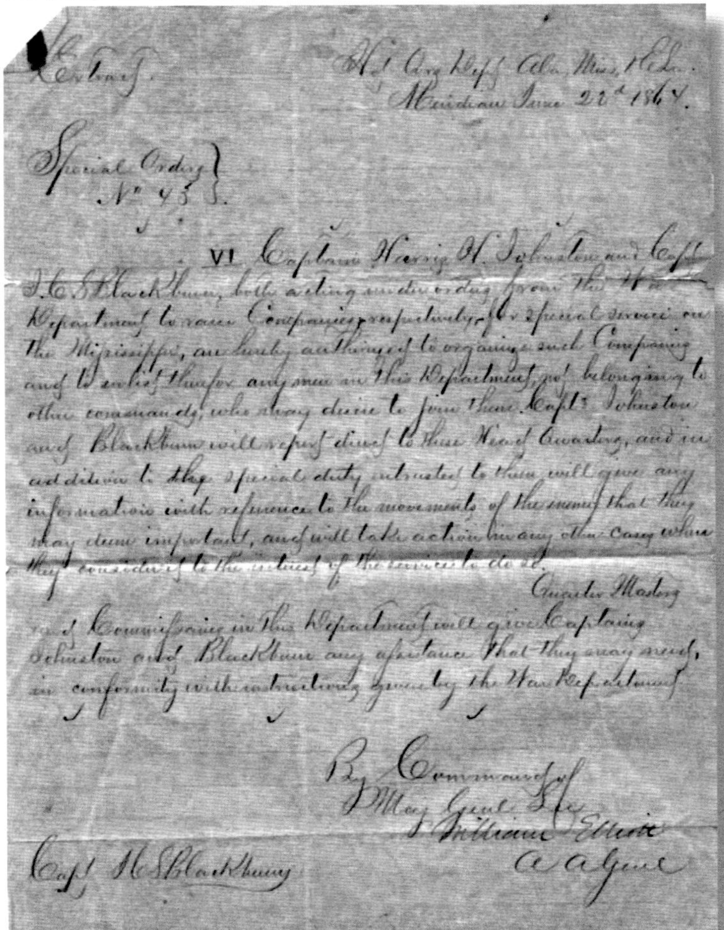

Extract.

Hd Qrs Dept Ala, Miss, & La.
Meridian June 22d 1864.

Special Orders
No. 45

VI Captain Harry H. Johnston and Capt J.C.S. Blackburn, both acting under orders from the War Department to raise Companies respectively for special service on the Mississippi, are hereby authorized to organize such Company and to enlist therefor any men in this Department not belonging to other commands, who may desire to join them. Capts. Johnston and Blackburn will report direct to these Head Quarters, and in addition to the special duty entrusted to them will give any information with reference to the movements of the enemy that they may deem important, and will take action in any other case where they consider it to the interest of the service to do it.

Quarter Masters and Commissaries in this Department will give Captains Johnston and Blackburn any assistance that they may need, in conformity with instructions given by the War Department.

By Command of
Maj Genl Lee
William Elliott
A A Genl

Capt J.C.S. Blackburn

Letter authorizing Captain Joseph C.S. Blackburn to raise an independent cavalry company that reads:
Hd Qtrs Dept. Ala, Miss, & Lou.
Meridian, June 22, 1864
Special Order No. 45

"VI. Captain Harry H. Johnston and Captain J.C.S. Blackburn, both acting under orders from the War Department, to raise Companies respectively for special service on the Mississippi, are hereby authorized to organize such Company and to enlist therefore any men in this Department, not belonging to other command, who may desire to join them. Capts. Johnston and Blackburn will report direct to these Head Quarters, and in addition to the special duty entrusted to them will give any information with reference to the movements of the enemy that they may deem important, and will take action in any other case where they consider it to the interest of the service to do so.

By Command of
Maj Genl Lee
William Elliott
A A Genl
Capt J.C.S. Blackburn
(Image courtesy of the author, Blackburn Collection)

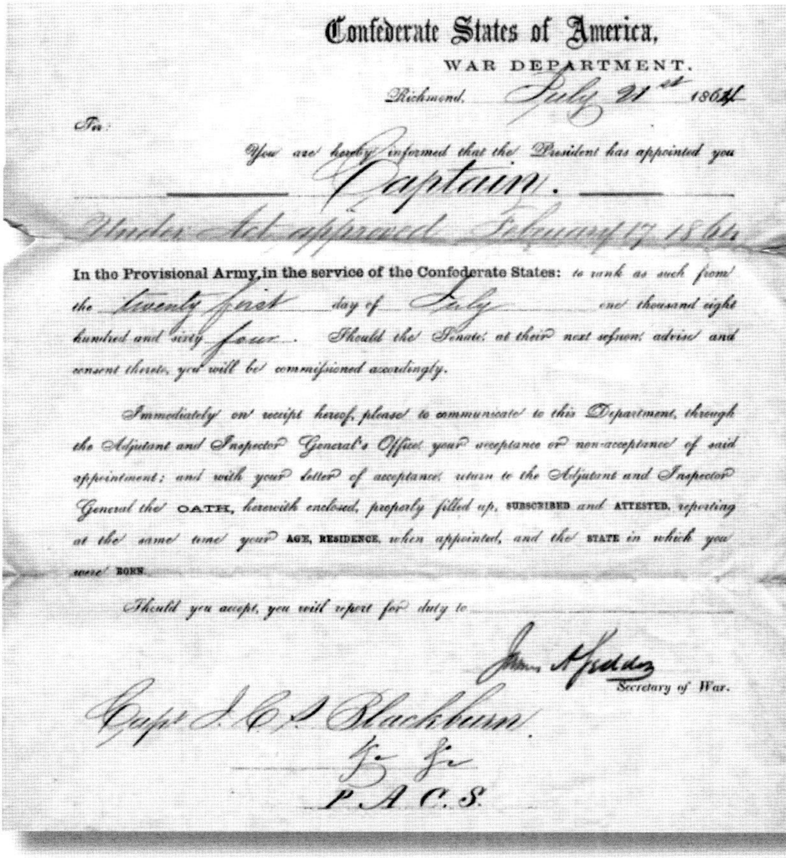
Confederate States of America,
WAR DEPARTMENT.
Richmond, July 21st 1864
To:

You are hereby informed that the President has appointed you
Captain.
Under Act approved February 17 1864

In the Provisional Army, in the service of the Confederate States: to rank as such from the twenty first day of July one thousand eight hundred and sixty four. Should the Senate at their next session advise and consent thereto, you will be commissioned accordingly.

Immediately on receipt hereof, please to communicate to this Department, through the Adjutant and Inspector General's Office your acceptance or non-acceptance of said appointment; and with your letter of acceptance, return to the Adjutant and Inspector General the OATH, herewith enclosed, properly filled up, SUBSCRIBED and ATTESTED, reporting at the same time your AGE, RESIDENCE, when appointed, and the STATE in which you were BORN.

Should you accept, you will report for duty to

James A Seddon
Secretary of War.

Capt J C S Blackburn.
P.A.C.S.

CSA Secretary of War letter appointing Captain Joseph C. S. Blackburn that reads:
Confederate States of America
War Department
Richmond, July 21st, 1864
To:

You are hereby informed that the President has appointed you Captain Under Act approved February 17, 1864

In the Provisional Army, in the services of the Confederate States: to rank as such from the twenty-first day of July one thousand eight hundred and sixty-four. Should the Senate at their next session, advise and consent thereto, you will be commissioned accordingly.

Immediately on receipt hereof, please to communicate to this Department, through the Adjutant and Inspector General's Office your acceptance or non-acceptance of said appointment: and with your letter of acceptance, return to the Adjutant and Inspector General the OATH, herewith enclosed, properly filled up, SUBSCRIBED and ATTESTED, reporting at the same time with your AGE, RESIDENCE, when appointed, and the STATE in which you were BORN.

Should you accept, you will report for duty to _________ [left blank].

James A. Seddon
Secretary of War
Capt. J.C.S. Blackburn.
G.G [?]
P.A.C.S.
(Image courtesy of the author, Blackburn Collection)

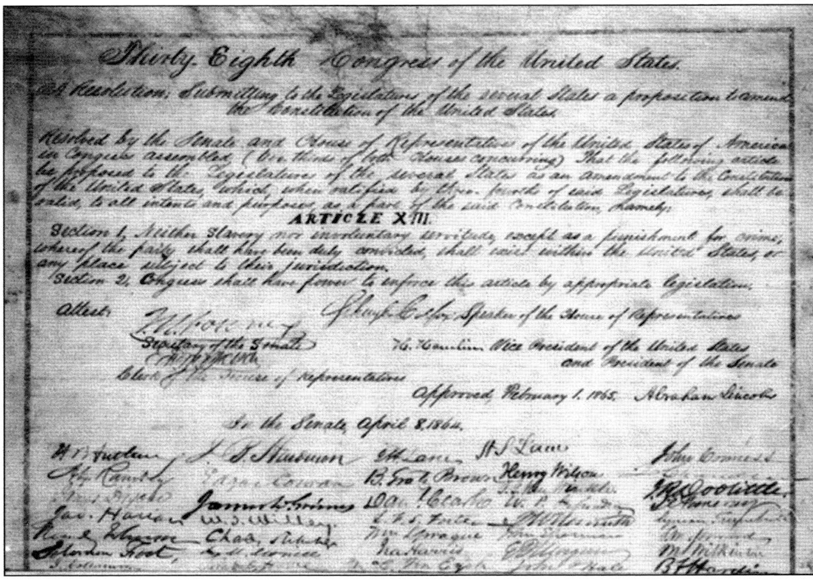

Thirty-Eighth Congress of the United States.

A Resolution: Submitting to the Legislatures of the several States a proposition to amend the Constitution of the United States.

Resolved by the Senate and House of Representatives of the United States of America in Congress assembled (two-thirds of both Houses concurring) That the following article be proposed to the Legislatures of the several States as an amendment to the Constitution of the United States, which, when ratified by three-fourths of said Legislatures, shall be valid, to all intents and purposes, as a part of the said Constitution, namely:

ARTICLE XIII.

Section 1. Neither slavery nor involuntary servitude, except as a punishment for crime, whereof the party shall have been duly convicted, shall exist within the United States, or any place subject to their jurisdiction.

Section 2. Congress shall have power to enforce this article by appropriate legislation.

Attest: Schuyler Colfax Speaker of the House of Representatives

J.W. Forney Secretary of the Senate — H. Hamlin Vice President of the United States and President of the Senate

Edw. McPherson Clerk of the House of Representatives

Approved, February 1. 1865. Abraham Lincoln

In the Senate April 8. 1864.

Thirteenth Amendment to the U.S. Constitution

Residence of U.S. Senator Joseph C. S. Blackburn, 215 Rose Hill, Versailles, Woodford County, Kentucky, 1871-1899. (Image courtesy of the author's husband, Thomas E. Fielder)

Joseph Clay Stiles Blackburn by Matthew Brady

THE DAYS' DOINGS

Illustrating Extraordinary Events of the Day.

Vol. XVI. NEW YORK, MARCH 18, 1876. PRICE, 10 CENTS

THE NATIONAL DISGRACE.

Above: Wife of Secretary William Belknap Pleading for Mercy from Mr. Blackburn (Mark Grossman, Political Corruption in America, An Encyclopedia of Scandals, Power, and Greed [ABC CLIO, 2003]).

Left: William W. Belknap, Secretary of War, 1869-1876. (Wikipedia)

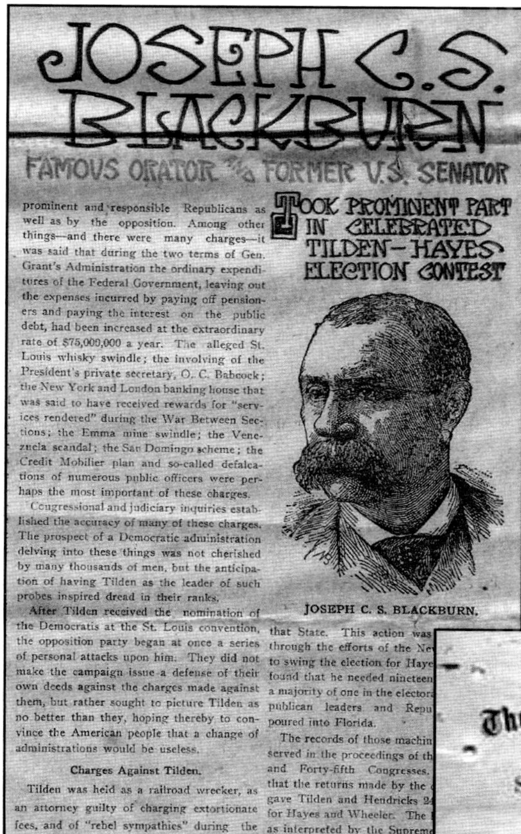

JOSEPH C.S. BLACKBURN

FAMOUS ORATOR and FORMER U.S. SENATOR

TOOK PROMINENT PART IN CELEBRATED TILDEN-HAYES ELECTION CONTEST

prominent and responsible Republicans as well as by the opposition. Among other things—and there were many charges—it was said that during the two terms of Gen. Grant's Administration the ordinary expenditures of the Federal Government, leaving out the expenses incurred by paying off pensioners and paying the interest on the public debt, had been increased at the extraordinary rate of $75,000,000 a year. The alleged St. Louis whisky swindle; the involving of the President's private secretary, O. C. Babcock; the New York and London banking house that was said to have received rewards for "services rendered" during the War Between Sections; the Emma mine swindle; the Venezuela scandal; the San Domingo scheme; the Credit Mobilier plan and so-called defalcations of numerous public officers were perhaps the most important of these charges.

Congressional and judiciary inquiries established the accuracy of many of these charges. The prospect of a Democratic administration delving into these things was not cherished by many thousands of men, but the anticipation of having Tilden as the leader of such probes inspired dread in their ranks.

After Tilden received the nomination of the Democrats at the St. Louis convention, the opposition party began at once a series of personal attacks upon him. They did not make the campaign issue a defense of their own deeds against the charges made against them, but rather sought to picture Tilden as no better than they, hoping thereby to convince the American people that a change of administrations would be useless.

Charges Against Tilden.

Tilden was held as a railroad wrecker, as an attorney guilty of charging extortionate fees, and of "rebel sympathies" during the

JOSEPH C. S. BLACKBURN.

that State. This action was through the efforts of the Ne to swing the election for Haye found that he needed nineteen a majority of one in the elector publican leaders and Repu poured into Florida.

The records of those machin served in the proceedings of th and Forty-fifth Congresses. that the returns made by the gave Tilden and Hendricks 2 for Hayes and Wheeler. The as interpreted by the Suprem

"Joseph C.S. Blackburn, famous orator and former U.S. Senator, took prominent part in celebrated Tilden-Hayes election contest" (Image courtesy of the author, Blackburn Collection)

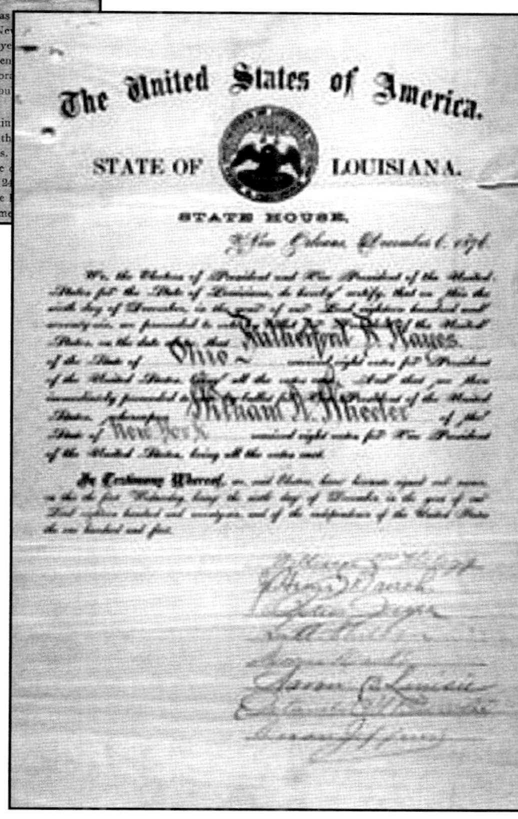

The United States of America.

STATE OF LOUISIANA.

STATE HOUSE,

New Orleans, December 6, 1876.

Rutherford B. Hayes

Ohio

William A. Wheeler

New York

In Testimony Whereof,

Certificate for the Electoral Vote for U.S. President Rutherford B. Hayes and for Vice President William A. Wheeler issued by the State of Louisiana in the intensely disputed 1876 U.S. presidential election. (Wikipedia)

Union Major General Stephen G. Burbridge had military control of Kentucky during the Civil War, unjustly executing four guerillas for every Union citizen killed, a wrong that Joseph Blackburn worked to correct years later in 1882.

Senator Joseph Clay Stiles Blackburn (Library of Congress)

Our Protection Levee, published April 26, 1890, depicted the fierce debate raging in Congress over raising rates on imported goods. The Tariff Act of 1890, commonly known as the McKinley tariff bill for its main sponsor, faced stiff opposition in the Senate from "free trade" Democrats like Joseph Blackburn of Kentucky, George Vest of Missouri, and Arthur Pue Gorman of Maryland. They argued that it would create monopolies and cause significant inflation. In his cartoon, F. Victor Gillam drew the supporters of free trade as dark waters threatening to breech the nation's levee. (United States Senate, Art & History)

Joseph "Josey" Clay Stiles Blackburn, Jr., oldest child and only son of Senator Joseph C. S. Blackburn and Terese Graham Blackburn. (Image courtesy of the author, Blackburn Collection)

Terese Blackburn Hall, oldest daughter of Senator Joseph C. S. Blackburn and Terese Graham Blackburn, shown with the youngest of her two children with General William Preble Hall. (Image courtesy of the author, Blackburn Collection)

Mrs. Corinne Blackburn Gale, wife of Consul General William Holt Gale and second daughter of Senator Joseph C. S. Blackburn and Terese Graham Blackburn. (Image courtesy of the author, Blackburn Collection)

Lucile Blackburn Lane, wife of Thomas F. Lane, and youngest daughter of Senator Joseph C. S. Blackburn and Terese Graham Blackburn. Lucile is the author's Great Grandmother. (Image courtesy of the author, Blackburn Collection)

Opening ceremonies of the U.S. 59th Congress, 2nd Session, 1906, with Speaker Joseph Cannon presiding. This image views the Republican side of the Congress so Democrats like Blackburn are not visible. (Library of Congress)

"IN BATTLE ARRAY, - AND THERE'S NOT MUCH DOUBT ABOUT THE RESULT." This cartoon by Louis Dalrymple shows Joseph Blackburn among others aligned behind William J. Bryan fighting for Free Silver at sixteen ounces of silver to one ounce of gold. (Library of Congress)

> speedily follow. For these reasons this bill should not be lost. It has passed both houses by more than a two-thirds vote. We are and have been threatened by a presidential veto [by President Hayes]....If the act declaring silver money a legal tender for all debts shall safely pass without Executive interference, a veto need not be feared in the case of a bill which simply authorizes its issue to a larger amount.

The bill passed in the House.

Forty-Sixth Congress (March 4, 1879–March 4, 1881)

There were thirty-eight states in the Union and eight non-voting delegates from the territories in the House. All ten U.S. Representatives from Kentucky, including Blackburn (and J. Proctor Knott and John G. Carlisle) were Democrats, as were both U.S. Senators (James B. Beck and John Williams). Democrats ramped up their efforts to undercut Reconstruction legislation protecting African-American voting rights in this Congress. Congress continued to challenge President Rutherford B. Hayes by attaching "riders" or substantive amendments to Army appropriations bills that prohibited federal funding being used to protect voting places in the former Confederacy. Democrats tried this tactic seven times, and Hayes vetoed each attempt before Congress abandoned its efforts.

In March 1879, Blackburn again challenged Samuel J. Randall of Pennsylvania for Speaker of the House in the Forty-Sixth Congress, but conceded it when it became clear that the North was still not ready for a leader from the South. Randall was elected Speaker of the House for the Forty-Fourth, Forty-Fifth, and the Forty-Sixth Congresses, but this was his last.

Blackburn had demonstrated his ability as a parliamentarian and debater in the former Congresses and was made the third member of the Committee on Rules, made up of Speaker Samuel J. Randall of Pennsylvania, Alexander H. Stephens of Georgia, Joseph C. S. Blackburn of Kentucky, James A. Garfield of Ohio, and William P. Frye of Maine. This committee worked under the Chairmanship of the Speaker and substantially controlled the legislation of the House, making it one of the most important committees of the House. Blackburn was also made

Chairman of the Committee on Expenditures in the War Department, the committee where he had made his name, and was placed fifth on the important Committee on Appropriations. Somehow, he found time during this busy Session to deliver the oration at the Confederate Decoration ceremonies in Frederick, Maryland, on June 5, 1879. But while he honored the past, even though filled with mistaken choices, regret, and loss, Blackburn's perspective embraced the entire country now. He was ready to move beyond the former positions on the battlefields to support a unified country and to do what was best for the nation.

On June 25, 1879, Blackburn reported a resolution from the Committee on Rules authorizing that committee to sit during the next recess "for the purpose of revising, codifying and simplifying the rules of the House." It was long overdue. Blackburn stated that of the 166 rules of the House at the time, sixty-three were adopted in whole or in part before 1800 and that the only revision since that time had been made in 1860 for over thirty of the rules. Many of the standing rules of the House were practically obsolete, either in whole or in part. The House debated the necessity of a revision. It was supported strongly by Garfield, Mills, and others. The resolution was adopted.

The committee then met in a hotel at Elberon, New Jersey, on August 5, 1879 during the summer recess from regular Congressional sessions. The Committee on Rules worked there in session for two weeks until some of the committee members had to leave to honor campaign appearances. Unable to finish during the summer recess, the committee resumed its work in Washington at the beginning of the Second Session.

Second Session, Forty-Sixth Congress (Dec 1, 1879–June 16, 1880)

Once the Second Session began, the Committee on Rules was able to resume its work begun during the previous summer recess. The committee was subdivided into two subcommittees, one consisting of Speaker Randall and Frye and the other of Blackburn, Garfield and Stephens. The subcommittees met until they were ready to report to the full committee. Blackburn worked diligently and zealously on the work assigned to him and carefully read the reports of the former Committees on Rules, Questions of Order and Decision of Speakers, and the debates regarding the rules. The final revision of the work of the committee, on motion of Stephens of Georgia, was committed to Blackburn and Frye for what Stephens called the "Committee on Style," following the precedent of the convention that stylized the Constitution.

Blackburn submitted the final report to the House on December 19, 1879, and the proposed "code" was held over until after the holiday recess, because it was a long and exhaustive report with a complete history of the rules and the changes proposed. The debate over the new rules was long and made longer by Speaker Randall, who extended the debate in order to shut out revenue and other legislation. During the debate, Blackburn had charge of the floor with the assistance of Speaker Randall. While the report was being considered in the Committee of the Whole, with Carlisle of Kentucky serving as its Chairman, Blackburn had the duty to explain and defend the many changes made by the Committee on Rules, to resist the many amendments offered by the Democrats and Republicans, and, above all, to keep in line his discontented party friends who thought the changes did not go far enough. Blackburn again demonstrated his ability to look beyond partisan claims and provide leadership that benefitted all parties, not just the Democrats or the Republicans, a trait that would continue to grow during his time in office and lead him to be selected by future Presidents to lead projects of significant national and international importance. It was not an easy task. The debate on the new "code" took nearly two months. Representative Adlai E. Stevenson, the future vice president to President Cleveland, was known as a good parliamentarian. Stevenson often expressed his admiration for the skill and versatility with which Representative Blackburn defended the report and resisted obnoxious amendments.

Finally, on March 2, 1880, the Code as amended was adopted. Its passage in the House was saved at a critical period by the support of Frye of Maine, who joined with a few other Republicans to vote for its adoption, while several Democrats voted against it. Even Republican Garfield at the last minute voted against it as soon as he realized that his party was substantially solidly against it. Blackburn later stated in an interview that while not ideal, the new Code was a vast improvement over the Old Code. He also noted that until the Democratic Party was able to elect a Speaker in harmony and sympathy with its position on tariff reform, they must be content with what they could get. As he put it:

> In view of the fact that the Ways and Means Committee is constituted expressly not to report a measure of tariff reform, and the Appropriations Committee is constituted to block the way to any real legislative or executive reforms, the Southern Democracy must wait for "Randallism" and "Holmanism" to run its race. The Republicans will win the next House, but after that will come the "Democratic deluge," which will sweep the Republican Party from power for many years.

Blackburn's prediction came to pass in the succeeding Congressional elections.

Chapter Seventeen

"Let There Be One Permanently Great Man Furnished From Among Us"

- J.C.S. Blackburn

Second Session, Forty-Sixth Congress (Dec 1, 1879–June 16, 1880)

Blackburn was appointed twice on conference committees. Blackburn was also called seven or eight times to preside over the Committee of the Whole House. In addition, Blackburn introduced several bills during this session, including a bill to amend the act for an additional Associate Justice of the Supreme Court of the District of Columbia; a bill for relief for various individuals; a bill to provide for a register of enrollment for any vessel built in a foreign country; a bill for a public building in Frankfort, Kentucky; a bill to amend the Revised Statutes; a bill to amend the act to incorporate the National Fair Ground Association; a bill to abolish the tax on tobacco; a bill to reduce the tax on distilled spirits to fifty cents on each proof gallon; and a bill from the committee providing for a general post office appropriations bill. The bill for a general post office appropriations bill was part of the effort to enact legislation to allow the government's postal service to continue to operate without the corruption that had been discovered in some of the postal routes, like the Star Route Service that delivered mail along Western routes.

Blackburn played an important role in the investigation into the frauds and deficiencies of the Star Route service concerning the U.S. postal service and the contracting of mail delivery services. He spoke ten times during the Star Route discussions during the Second Session. The Star Route Scandal involved a lucrative nineteenth century scheme that allowed U.S. postal officials to receive bribes in exchange for awarding postal delivery contracts in Southern and Western areas of the expanding United States and its territories, especially where they were not economically justifiable.

After the Civil War, the three inland mail routes created by Congress in 1845 carried more and more traffic as the population expanded into the west and southwest regions of the country. Government contracts were bid by supposed disinterested parties to avoid fraud and kickbacks, but fake or "straw" bidders would make very low bids for the routes and would then "win" the contract at an exorbitantly high price. The scandals first happened in 1872 and 1876 during the Grant administration. The 1872 investigations were tainted by bribery, while the 1876 investigation managed to shut down the Star Route frauds temporarily. However, a resurgence of greed and corruption appeared in 1878 during the Hayes Administration that continued into the Garfield Administration. Blackburn was involved with investigating the 1878 incidents. Democrat Blackburn's role in the on-going investigations revealed the fraudulent scheme and resulted in the schemes being finally shut down in 1882–1883 under President Arthur's Administration. Blackburn was a bitter and uncompromising opponent of public officials using their office for personal gain throughout his public life. He introduced a resolution instructing the Committee on Appropriations to inquire into the cause and extent of the financial losses to the U.S. Treasury for the government's Star Route Service.

Blackburn introduced several other resolutions this Session including a resolution for the printing of five thousand copies of the new rules that he had helped author, which was passed. Blackburn spoke frequently each day during the consideration of the report of the Committee on Rules, over the two months that the House considered it, because he was in charge of that report. Blackburn spoke as often as necessary to discuss all of the various appropriation bills and the solutions to the Star Route Scandal. The investigations found that there were multiple frauds committed in the Post-Office Department, which were collectively called the "Star-Route Scandal." Congress was able to clean up the Post Office Department and save the U.S. Treasury millions of dollars "in money," as Blackburn would say. Congressional neglect and lack of oversight was largely to blame for the wasteful and criminal extravagance.

By 1879, though, Blackburn's view of the life of the politician was changing. He still wished for a member of his political family to achieve the political prominence that had been instilled in them since birth, but the political consequences resulting from the side he had chosen in the Civil War and the stance as a Southern Democrat during Reconstruction battling corruption in office had taken a toll on him personally and politically, as reflected in a letter he wrote to his brother James at Frankfort on February 26, 1880 while James was serving as the Secretary of State to their older brother Governor Dr. Luke Blackburn:

> My dear Brother—I have delayed writing from time to time because of an indisposition to write at all and pressure of work. I was never so busy—I have no reason to complain. I have my way as much as one man probably could do. Your telegram just received, makes me easy as to the report of your trouble, as given in the papers, I still fail to understand why you didn't telegraph me. I will do all I can to aid poor Old Mr. Shotwell, but I think the time has passed for obtaining anything upon Claims growing out of the War, however just they may be. I will do everything in my power—Now my Dear Brother: a word for your private ear. I shall not trouble you by repeating what I now say to you. This is the only appeal I shall make & it shall be put as tersely as I may—Dr. Luke is getting old. His work will end with his term. What little there is left in my life is fixed irrevocably. I am the victim of Surroundings that may not be controlled. There is no need of regrets. I have none. I have about finished my work, however imperfect it may be. I will be elected to another term, but will not serve it out. I do not want to prolong this thing. I am without a future. There is nothing for me to look forward to except the excitement incident to political wrangle and the vapory prominence it gives. Of this I have had enough. I take no gangrened view but soberly consider the inevitable. You can & if you will it so, will be the most valuable of the name. You can come & take the place I have, & go beyond. I appeal to you, for but one thing. Never take another drink. If I knew this was to be I would have no fear nor anxiety about the rest. If my own course, has been, is now, or shall be amenable to criticism in this regard, 'tis not from weakness or want of purpose, upon my part, but simply because I do not wish to shun the consequences. My hope is in you. I am not at fault in my view—This is the only

thing I have to ask of you. If there be any saved from the wreck, it must be you, & you alone must do it. Ten years will find you the front man of your section. The road is not as long or difficult as it seems. I have tried it. Take the testimony of every one here, & it will tell you that I today touch that point, that there is no man in the American Congress holding & wielding as much power, but I can't hold it, not because of any trouble in front, but for the difficulties that lie behind. Don't promise me, but make this promise to yourself and let our ambitions all be realized—Let there be one permanently great man, furnished from among us. I started with good faith & fixed purpose, to win that place. I thought I had it. Surely no man ever had better reason for belief. I fail & fall under a blow that could not be anticipated & cannot be parried. Take this work up manfully. You will win. If you will come here on a visit after your adjournment, I will have RR passes sent you & the trip will cost neither you nor me, anything. Love to all

Your brother, J.C.S.B.

Chapter Eighteen

"Let Us Stand Together, Having Assumed the People's Cause, and Keep the Faith That We Plighted to That People"

—J.C.S. Blackburn

Joseph Blackburn aspired to be a permanently great man from among his family but found his way blocked. Nevertheless, he continued to champion the people's cause. His career was far from over, and there was much work to be done.

Third Session, Forty-Sixth Congress (Dec 6, 1880–March 3, 1881)

Blackburn was made Chairman of the Committee of the Whole and was twice appointed on conference committees. He introduced several bills for the benefit of various individuals, for refunding tax illegally collected under the Internal Revenue Law, for a general post office appropriation bill, for a bill making an appropriation for flooring the National Museum (part of the Smithsonian), and for a bill for a public building at Lexington, Kentucky. He introduced a joint resolution for retiring as a Brigadier-General Colonel Thomas L. Crittenden, Seventh United States Infantry. He introduced a concurrent resolution for the printing of six thousand copies each of volumes six, seven, eight, nine and ten of the North American Ethnology and fifteen thousand copies each of the second and third annual report of the Director of the Bureau of Ethnology, both of which were passed by both Chambers and became laws. Blackburn also introduced a resolution for an additional Clerk for the remainder of the Session for the Clerk of the House, another for a similar Clerk for the Doorkeeper, and still another for the appointment of a select committee of five to examine the charges of abuse in the United States mail system, all of which were passed. He spoke many times on the post office, legislative, and civil appropriations bills and on the bill for the National (Smithsonian) Museum, among other subjects.

Forty-Seventh Congress (March 4, 1881–March 4, 1883)

As Blackburn predicted, the Republicans won the House and the Presidency while the Senate was evenly divided between Republicans and Democrats after the 1880 elections. There were still thirty-eight states represented in Congress and eight non-voting members representing the territories in the House. Nine of the ten U.S. Representatives from Kentucky, including Blackburn, were Democrats, as were both U.S. Senators. The Forty-Seventh Congress focused on immigration: approving a treaty with China to slow the flow of Chinese laborers, passing a Chinese Exclusion Act, and sending a general immigration act to President Hayes. Congress also appropriated funds for river and harbor projects and for modernizing the U.S. Navy, work generated by Blackburn's committees.

Republican President James A. Garfield was assassinated on July 2, 1881, less than four months after his election and died seventy-nine days later on September 19, 1881. He had been shot in the back by Charles J. Guiteau at the Baltimore and Potomac Railroad Station in Washington, D.C., because Guiteau thought that Garfield would not have won the election without his support. Guiteau believed President Garfield owed him a diplomatic appointment and took this cowardly "revenge" when he was not appointed to any administrative post. The nation was shocked and enraged by the assassination. After the trial and execution of Garfield's assassin, Congress replaced the patronage system with a Civil Service program to hire government workers.

First Session, Forty-Seventh Congress (Dec 5, 1881–Aug 8, 1882)

Republicans had control of the House. Speaker Randall was replaced by Speaker Keifer, and Blackburn did not fare as well in his committee assignments as he had in former Democratic Congresses, losing his Chairmanship. He was, however, placed first on the minority of the Committee on Appropriations and Expenditures in the War Department, fifth and next to Randall on the Committee on Rules, and second on the Committee on Public Expenditures, a new committee chaired by Randall. Later, he was appointed the seventh member of a special committee of eleven on the expenses resulting from attending to the sickness and death of the late President Garfield. Blackburn was twice appointed on conference committees and was five times chosen Teller on important votes. A Teller is a person who counts votes in the House either when a voice vote is challenged or when a two-thirds vote is required. Towards the close of the session, Blackburn was appointed by Speaker Keifer as one of the House visitors to the United States Military Academy at West Point, New York. Blackburn introduced several bills during the First Session, including relief for various individuals and various civil appropriation bills for a public building in Frankfort, Kentucky and for a public building at Lexington, Kentucky, among others. In fact, there was a dispute between U.S. Representative Blackburn and Senator Williams over who deserved the credit for securing the passage of the bill appropriating one hundred thousand dollars for the public building at Frankfort. Stoddard Johnson, the editor of the Frankfort *Yeoman* and an enthusiastic friend of Blackburn, gave Blackburn the credit for the measure. Words were presumably exchanged, and there were whispers around the Capitol for several days of a possible duel, but Kentucky's Senator Beck and Representative Carlisle intervened and helped settle the dispute between the two men.

The Williams drama had no impact on Blackburn's work during the First Session of the Forty-Seventh Congress. He made speeches on many important public questions, such as on the bill to make the Agricultural Bureau an Executive Department, as shown by the following excerpts from one of his speeches on the House floor:

> MR. BLACKBURN: The Committee on Agriculture has reported a bill to this House which, in my judgment, meets the demand of the agricultural interests, and which makes suitable provision for them.
>
> I am not desirous of entering the lists for the championship of the agricultural people of the land, but I am extremely desirous of seeing the interest at least receive some recognition at the hands of this Government. From the very nature of the farmer's avocation, the agriculturists of the country are more widely scattered, and their opportunities for interchange of views or for dissemination of information are less by all odds than belong to any other class of our industrial population.

> I find that the bill presented by the committee proposes to create a Department of Agriculture, to consist of four bureaus; the first to be termed the Bureau of Agricultural Products; the second to be termed the Bureau of Animal Industry, which reaches and covers all the stock rearing interests of this country; the third is the Bureau of Lands; the fourth and last is the Bureau of Statistics for the dissemination, as well as the collection of all information that may be of service to the growers of cereals, to the cotton planter and stock rearer of the country. We find, then, that every agricultural interest of this country is comprehended and embraced in the provisions of this bill.
>
> I believe that it ought to be passed.

It was passed. Blackburn also spoke on a bill to investigate alleged abuses in the adjudication of claims, on a Senate bill for a public building at Frankfort when it passed the House, on the proposition to enlarge the committees, on the appropriations to pay for the medical attendance to President Garfield, on the removal of official reporters by the Speaker, on a Senate bill to amend the law relative to polygamy, on the right of the Speaker to vote, on a bill for the appointment of a Tariff Commission, on the adjudication of war claims, and on various other appropriation bills. He was quick to defend a wrong even when asserted by a fellow Kentucky Congressman.

Second Session, Forty-Seventh Congress (Dec 4, 1882–March 3, 1883)

Blackburn was appointed a conferee on two appropriation bills, was appointed a Teller three times, and was appointed on a commission to adjust the salaries of Congressional employees. He spoke on several bills, including a bill relating to distilled spirits, an Internal Revenue bill, and a bill for a public building at Paducah, Kentucky, as well as on the tariff question, on the constitutionality of the Senate action on the tariff bill, on a tariff bill rule, and on pension adjudications.

House debates continued to focus on the tariff that Blackburn believed unfairly oppressed the agricultural and laboring classes. The issues of the tariff bill and changes in the tax laws must have displaced more practical concerns from Blackburn's mind. A journalist heard a story that Mr. Blackburn had left home for Washington in such a hurry that he did not take enough clothes with him for the summer of 1883. When Mr. Blackburn wired home to have his summer wardrobe sent to him, Mr. Blackburn's youngest daughter Lucile sent a few unusual items that she thought he would need. The journalist asked Mr. Blackburn if the story was true and then published Blackburn's response in the paper as follows:

> He laughed, and said it had a grain of truth in it. He said he had left home for a day or two only, and took only a small bag with him. The consolidation of internal revenue districts brought him unexpectedly to Washington. He telegraphed home to have a trunk of clothes sent to him here. His little daughter [Lucile, age 10], in the absence of her mother, opened the dispatch, and thought it was her duty to obey it. So, she packed a trunk and put a note in it, as follows:
>
> Versailles, Ky.
> Dear Papa: I send you all the clothes I can find, and I hope you are well.
>
> Mr. Blackburn said that the trunk contained the following: Seven white shirts, 6 Winter scarfs, 1 tooth-brush, 1 bowie-knife, 2 revolvers. This is what a Kentucky girl regards as a suitable Summer wardrobe for a gentleman.

Forty-Eighth Congress (March 4, 1883–March 4, 1885)

Kentucky's representation had grown based on the Tenth Census of the United States. There were thirty-eight states represented in Congress in 1883 and eight non-voting members representing the territories. Nine of the now eleven U.S. Representatives from Kentucky, including Blackburn, were Democrats, along with the Thirty-First Speaker of the House Carlisle, as were both U.S. Senators. The Forty-Eighth Congress replaced Alaska's military rule with a civil territorial government, passed the Second Chinese Exclusion Act, and stiffened penalties for violating immigration policy. Congress continued to shift away from the civil rights legislation of the Reconstruction Era in favor of addressing America's emerging industrial economy. Congress established bureaus of labor and of animal industry and modified tariff rates to encourage American shipbuilding, all work that came out of Blackburn's committees.

First Session, Forty-Eighth Congress (Dec 3, 1883–July 7, 1884)

As Blackburn predicted, the Democrats had again returned to power in the House during the last two years of President Chester A. Arthur's term. Blackburn had announced himself a candidate for Speaker of the House for his third try against Randall, but withdrew after his Kentucky colleague Carlisle entered the race. Blackburn threw his support to Carlisle, who ultimately won and became Speaker of the House in the First Session.

Blackburn was made one of the committee to notify the President that the House was organized and ready to do business, considered a high honor by the members of Congress. He was also given fourth place on the important Committee on Ways and Means and second place on the more important Committee on Rules and was its Chairman. As the Chairman of the Committee on Rules, Blackburn was thus made the acting Chairman, for the second man always acts as spokesman for the committee when any matter from that committee is before the House. He was twice made Chairman of the Committee of the Whole, was on two different days designated by the Speaker as Speaker *pro tem* for the day, and on the last day of the session, on motion of ex-Speaker Randall, was formally elected Speaker *pro tem* for the day.

Blackburn introduced several bills, including bills for the relief of several individuals; for pensions for individuals; to fix the salaries of the Capitol police; to amend the laws relative to land titles in the District of Columbia; to provide for a wharf and marine way at Jeffersonville, Indiana; to regulate the jurisdiction of the United States Courts in Kentucky; for a public building at Lexington, Kentucky; for relief of the Masonic Lodge at Cynthiana, Kentucky; to incorporate the National Academy of Dental Science; and for the joint resolution providing for the printing of the report of the Health officer of the District of Columbia, among several others. He made several speeches including on the appointment of a Committee on Alcoholic Traffic, on the appointment of a Committee on American shipping, on the increase of committee membership, on the extension of the tax on distilled spirits, on the appointment of a Committee on Rivers and Harbors, on the case of a contested Congressional seat, on the naval appropriation bill, and on the post office appropriation bill, among others, including speeches on the tariff.

On May 6, 1884, Blackburn gave one of his famous speeches on the Tariff in the House meeting as Committee of the Whole. Tariffs were important to Blackburn, who believed that it was important to balance their effect so that all parts of the country benefitted, not just the Northeastern manufacturing states at the expense of the agrarian states of the South and West. This speech continues to evidence Blackburn's desire to move beyond the injuries of the Civil War days and focus on the future of the country. The House debated the bill to reduce import duties and war-tariff taxes. Blackburn argued that the Republicans could easily agree with this proposed tariff reductions in 1883, because in 1882 the Republicans had asked for a deeper cut of twenty to twenty-five percent. In reality, the tariff rates were reduced by a mere 1.75 percentage, according to the census records. Furthermore, he argued that this proposal guaranteed it would not fall below the war-tariff taxation rates put in place on goods in 1861 when the country was raising money for the Civil War. Blackburn argued that the savings clause in the bill should be enough to "commend it to the support of every protectionist."

> The tariff bill of 1861 was passed in the face of the greatest civil war of modern times, when the necessities of this country forced Congress to exaggerated attempts upon the tax-paying people of the land, when producers by the millions were turned into consumers in the persons of soldiers; when armies and fleets and navies were to be raised and builded [sic] and maintained; when war was to have all of its frightful exactions met. The tariff that was deemed sufficient for that purpose constitutes the minimum rate of protection contemplated in the bill before you.

At this point, other representatives including Randall of Pennsylvania, began to interrupt and argue their positions during

Blackburn's speech. Representative Blackburn responded to the various points presented as he continued with his speech, noting in particular that the previous year, the Republicans sought to reduce the tariff and internal-revenue taxation in 1882 because there was an excess overflowing the Treasury. As Blackburn spoke the audience in the gallery listened carefully, breaking into applause when they agreed with his points:

> If it was necessary to combat the surplus revenue in 1882 by the reduction of the tariff taxation, tell me why it is not more necessary now? You heard [Randall] say that if you would abolish the internal-revenue system of taxation, there would be no surplus of revenue that would amount to anything. I ask you, sir, in common candor, to tell me how close did that avowal approximate to a confession that the war now waged upon the internal-revenue system of taxation is for the single and ill-disguised purpose of maintaining high protective-tariff rates?….Gentlemen, we ask you what is it you mean by your opposition to the bill? Is it revenue that you want? If so, we tell you to take it. Take all you need. Take until you yourselves admit that you have all that you can use. Take what the necessities of the Government demand, but when you have obtained that, say "halt" to the tax-gatherer, for whenever you go one inch beyond the limit, the tax-gatherer's hand becomes a robber's hand. [Applause.]
>
> What is your estimate of the people with whom you are dealing? Do you think the people will think you sincere when you tell them that a tariff is a tax, and in the same breath assure them the laying of that tax upon a certain article will cheapen its cost to the man who buys and consumes it? What is your estimate of popular intelligence, if you expect the people to believe you, when you tell them that your policy is either fair or friendly to the laborer while you force him to sell the coinage of his sweat in the cheapest market known among men, the free-trade market of the world, and at the same time compel him to buy that upon which he lives in the dearest market that either human or devilish ingenuity can construct through the agency of protective arbitrary tariff laws like this?

Mr. Chairman, I do not believe that the victims of this deception so long practiced will continue to endure it. The time will come when they will grow weary. The time, I believe, is not far distant when they will repudiate such bald political hypocrisy and refuse to submit to such political jugglery.

The people are aroused for the first time in our lives upon this tariff issue. It is the issue of American politics to-day. It will not down. Cunning and insincerity have for years been able to evade the issue. It can not be longer deferred. Parties are ranging themselves upon this line, and whether we will or no we must fight the battle out in that direction. I do not care what gentlemen may say about free trade and the ultimate purposes of the party here. That is not the issue. It is not the question presented. Their effort is not sincere when they seek to evade it through such a subterfuge. There is no man proposing free trade. I do not know a man who wants to put under the ban of proscription the great manufacturing interest of this country. For my part I want to see that interest put upon a normal and natural footing. I want to see it kept alive, and I want to see it promoted and expanded, moving on and keeping pace with other honest industrial interests of the land. [Applause.]

Mr. Chairman, protection is an enemy to barter and trade. Its only purpose is to choke those channels which commerce has fashioned and opened for itself. The commerce of this country or any other can not be carried on with a foreign nation upon a gold and silver basis. There is not coin enough among the civilized nations of the earth as a basis of transaction to support the trade of this country or England for a single twelvemonth. It can only be conducted on the basis of exchange of commodities....If I lacked the faith in the people I could hold no confidence in popular government. My trust in the ultimate triumphs of my party and the maintenance of our institutions rests deeply rooted in my unwavering and unfaltering faith in the intelligence, patriotism, and the manhood of the American people. The end of this conflict must come, and when it comes the people will stand for the right.

Let us broaden our policies. Let us liberalize our laws. Let us give a free American register to which each citizen may go and under its aegis may fly the America's flag from the masthead of every American-owned vessel, whether built here at home, or upon the Thames, the Mersey, or the Clyde. Do this; repeal your cramping statutes, release your throttling grasp from the strangling trade of a struggling people, rebuild your shattered and wasted merchant marine. And when you have done that, put our country upon the high road of that destiny for which her location, her power, her advantages, and the genius and the manhood of her people have fairly entitled her. Unhand this young commercial giant and leave him to work out his own grand destiny among the nations of the earth, unfettered by the shackles with which folly and selfishness would bind him....But upon a measure as broad and as fair as this, as clearly defensible and as easily maintained, having for its object these beneficial results which no man dares to oppose, I do appeal to those who sit around me to let us stand together, having assumed the people's cause, and keep the faith that we plighted to that people. [Applause.]

We told them—the gentlemen know that I utter the truth—we told them in the last Congressional campaign that if we gained power in this country we would revise the tariff laws and make them equitable. We told them we would reduce their taxation that was burdensome and needless. Here in this House at least we hold the power to make that promise good. If we fail, then we will not be worthy to receive and will not receive the indorsement of the people.

It is a solemn contract that we have entered into. The conditions have been compiled with all the polls by the sovereigns of this land. The power has been vested in our hands, and let him who would strike down his party, its principles, its measures, and its policies, show by the record upon whose hands that blood is to be found.

As I stand here looking up I see over me the broad and grand wise motto of my own beloved Commonwealth. I can do no more than to emphasize that motto which is above us in an earnest, an honest, and a final appeal to those of my faith.

> If we stand united we will conquer; if we are divided disaster may likely come....
>
> Mr. Chairman, I will not go further, except to express the hope that in the near future we may be able to bring to this House enough of enlightenment, of patriotism, and progressive intelligence to repudiate the bigotry that disgraces politics in the shape of protection, as bigotry is a disgrace even to the cause of religion. No bigot, whether he be Christian, so called, or politician, ever contributed one atom to the advancement of humanity's cause. The bigotry in connection with this question is driveling in its tendencies; it curbs and restricts the natural course to greatness which commerce would bring. I ask at the hands of this House, with a firm reliance upon a favorable answer, that it shall never be said that a Democratic House in an American Congress refused even to consider a bill that proposed to reduce admitted excessive taxation and to revise to a degree an admittedly bad tariff. [Great applause.]

Despite Blackburn's earnest plea, the tariff bill was defeated in April by just four votes. In fact, a new tariff bill was not passed until the Fifty-First Congress, known as the McKinley Bill. Nevertheless, Blackburn captured the heart of the people during his five consecutive terms in Congress, spending the decade from 1875 to 1885 in the House, from the Forty-Fourth through to the Forty-Eighth Congress, until he was elected to the Senate, where he would continue to champion the people and the popular government. The sections that follow reflect his notable work in his remaining sessions in the House.

Second Session, Forty-Eighth Congress (Dec 1, 1884–March 3, 1885)

Blackburn was first appointed by Speaker Carlisle *pro tem* for a day, the most that a Speaker can appoint a person as Speaker *pro tem*, and later on January 31, when Speaker Carlisle returned from his visit to the seriously ill President-elect Cleveland at Albany, Blackburn, on motion of Mr. Randall, was elected Speaker *pro tempore* until the Speaker's recovery, twenty days later. When he stepped down, Mr. Poland, a Republican of Vermont, tendered a unanimous vote of thanks from the House. Blackburn was recognized from across the aisle for his selfless work for the benefit of the House and the nation. At the close of the Second Session, Blackburn returned to campaign in Kentucky.

Blackburn's constituents loved him. The people of the city of Lexington were proud of their Kentucky Congressman, and the city announced it would name one of its streets in honor of Blackburn. The local press adored him.

Exuberant predictions were made of Blackburn's future:

> No news of any consequence this week, in the absence of which I have concluded to express some of the sentiments of this section in regard to one of Woodford's distinguished sons. The subject of conversation down this way for some time past has been the probability, if not the certainty, of the Hon. J.C.S. Blackburn's future career, as indicated by his past record. Some say that he will be our next U.S. Senator while others go so far as to say, your correspondent for one, that he will be the next Vice President of the U.S. But no matter what his next stop may be, he is a man destined to rise, and the people, not only of Woodford, but of the state at large, will never be slow to elevate him to the position that he feels called upon to serve them in....
>
> Though Capt. Blackburn has had honors heaped upon him in rapid succession, a thing that would spoil some of the least presumptuous, Joseph is himself today and ever the same, socially, all of the time. While his stateliness might remind one of the "Knights of Old," he is with the peasant as with the Lord, holding that man is but a man be he elevated or humble in rank.

Blackburn continued as a conspicuous figure on the floor of the House and was recognized as one of the strongest and readiest debaters in that body, fighting against extravagance and corruption. His natural ability to lead and sense of fairness continued to earn him the respect of his peers in Congress for his "promptness, clearness and correctness of his decisions and by his love of fair play." His powerful presence on the House floor was described by the local paper:

> As a popular orator he has few superiors in the country. His full and powerful voice easily reaches every part of the hall of

> the House, so hard to fill; his measured but vehement manner and exact articulation put the attention on inquiry; and that indefinable magnetism which differentiates the orator from the mere speaker hushes the galleries. His personal appearance too adds to his effectiveness. Tall, square-shouldered, sinewy, he has a certain alertness and springiness of action which must give the adversary... the uncomfortable feeling which a hippopotamus feels in the presence of a tiger. His features are handsome and a heavy brown mustache shades a jaw of unusual length, strength and evident grip. His face is rather haggard, with the worn look of late hours and incessant intellectual activity. His blue-gray eyes are not restless, but vigilant, and with a concentrated fixedness of attention which takes in every possible element or incident of the situation. Blackburn owes much of his influence to a genuine sympathy and tenderness underlying his otherwise aggressive and combative nature. He never turned his back on friend or foe. Entirely loyal in his friendship, dangerous in controversy or quarrel, he is yet as placable as a boy. Ardent, generous, magnanimous, skillful and eloquent, he possesses many of the highest requisites for a party leader.

Not surprisingly, then, Blackburn carried every county in the district, except Scott County, the home of his opponent, W.C. Owens, in the primary for the Forty-Eighth Congress. Blackburn's majority was nearly four thousand votes. On October 26, 1882, the official count for Blackburn shows that he received 7,051 votes and W.C. Owens 3,251 of his congressional district. The vote in Woodford favored Blackburn by 1,014 to 43. On November 23, 1882, Congressman Blackburn defeated Asbury, the Republican, in the general election by 6,619 votes in the district. He was recognized as a:

> Democrat of the old school who ... during his day was considered one of the greatest orators in Congress. He will be looked upon as one of the greatest Democrats since the time of Thomas Jefferson. Everybody knew "Joe" Blackburn. Everybody loved him.

Chapter Nineteen

GALLANT JOE BLACKBURN ELECTED TO THE U.S. SENATE

"To Say That He Has Covered Himself With Glory and Nobly Served His Constituents is to Do Him a Simple Justice"

Forty-Ninth Congress (March 4, 1885–March 4, 1887)

"Gallant Joe Blackburn," began his service in the U.S. Senate in the Forty-Ninth Congress on March 4, 1885, succeeding General John Stuart "Cerro Gordo" Williams, the old hero of two wars who had served in the Senate for one term. Blackburn had not announced his candidacy until after the August election, nearly too late to win. He had remained at his post in Washington almost up to the day of the assembling of the Democratic caucus in the Kentucky legislature and did not spend a dollar or ask one man to vote for him before then. "Never was a following more of a spontaneous and of the lift-me-up-and-put-me-there kind of growth than that which boosted Blackburn into the Senatorship." Blackburn entered the senatorial canvass with but twelve votes pledged for him, while Senator Williams had fifty. Then Carlisle and Sweeney withdrew, and Blackburn's votes increased to forty-five. At one point, a Mr. P. Kimball of Fayette County changed his vote from Williams to Blackburn. When Williams found out, "he chartered a special train, one engine and coach, to go to Lexington to see Mr. Kimball's father and bring him to Frankfort to try and influence P. Kimball and bring him back to Williams, but it was a flat failure" because Williams could not find the elder Kimball when his train reached Lexington. Blackburn never lost a vote and finally succeeded in carrying off the prize by superior management. The longer the struggle lasted, the more certain he was of success. His confidence that he would win the race never faltered. He believed that it was his destiny. There seemed to be about him an irresistible personal magnetism.

The struggle that lasted over three weeks was finally settled in the Kentucky legislature on the seventy-third ballot when Blackburn received sixty-three votes to fifty-seven for General Williams. It was called the most exciting contest in the annals of the state. Some called it the "Dead Lock of 1884." Nearly everyone seemed to be pleased with his election to the Senate, even though one newspaper article noted that he was "a trifle too hot-headed and free in the use of his really eloquent tongue," but it also added that he would calm down with age. "In all the qualities of true statesmanship, he is unspeakably the superior of his predecessor."

His prominence in the House of Representatives for the past decade had shown him to be an honest man and a good fellow, a man of his word, frank and honest in all his acts. His role in uncovering the Cabinet Minister Belknap's post-tradership scandal in the Grant administration launched his national career. When Mr. Hayes' administration began, Mr. Blackburn dealt with the Republican rascals openly. He was widely known as an orator of national reputation and a favorite of the Democrats of Baltimore, where he had made several addresses in behalf of his party.

He was an acknowledged leader of the Southern wing of his party in Congress, "and needs no more emphatic testimonial of his faithful and efficient services as a member of that body than the repeated endorsements which his constituency has continued to give him at the polls." "It's not often that greatness is thrust upon a man." Blackburn had never been defeated in a political contest and was said to be "a universal favorite" in Washington, and "the most popular man in Congress." He was described as "brave, generous, sunny-hearted and companionable—there is nothing of the demagogue about him; he is plain Joe Blackburn, the friend of the friendless, the champion of the weak." His long experience in public life enabled him to stand equal in rank as a Senator, even if he was a comparatively poor man, unlike most of the Senators of his day. His election as Senator served as "proof that, at least in the Southern States, candidates for the United States Senate do not buy their way into that body, for Blackburn is happy not to be possessed of that surplus of cash needed on such occasions."

> In these days when Congresses, Legislatures and courts are said to be packed by the money bags and monopolies of the

> country, it is refreshing to know that after many days of hard work Blackburn was elected to the United States Senate. No scent of coal oil lingers around the Legislature, for his victory came to him as the unbought token of Kentucky's love for a brave and bold tariff reformer and friend of the people. He got his seat in that august body as Clay, Crittenden and Beck got theirs.
>
> Critics complained very severely about the protracted contest, that preceded the election, but when it is properly considered, that was all right. It showed that the Kentucky Legislature is still the home of unterrified and unpurchasable and nominated gentlemen, and that the odors of corruption dare not blow from that quarter.

Senator Blackburn was well known as an "earnest champion of the Southern interests." "He has refused to adopt the policy of apology, and has always insisted that the south should assert itself and claim the rights and privileges as any other section of the country." He proved himself "the earnest friend and advocate of Louisiana when it appealed to the Congress for justice," bravely defending their cause. "He advocated every democratic measure of consequence and opposed republican corruption and extravagance."

> In those dark days, when the future fate of the Democratic party hung trembling in the balance of existence, the South and West stood greatly in need of the invaluable services of just such a debater as Blackburn, and never in a single instance has he proved recreant to a nation's trust in his courage, his intelligence, or his fidelity. The Republican Party had grown arrogant and aggressive, and it was eminently necessary that they should be met in national councils with such valor and logic as Blackburn—and Blackburn alone—possessed. To say that he has covered himself with glory and nobly served his constituents is to do him a simple justice.

In accepting the Democratic nomination for the United States Senator from Kentucky, Congressman Blackburn said:

> As your Senator, I shall insist that the inequalities of national legislation in the past shall not be perpetuated. I shall insist upon a revision of the navigation laws which have sunk our American tonnage to only 11 per cent of the volume once attained. It is a mistake to say that the war destroyed our foreign tonnage. Our tonnage was as great when the gallant Lee surrendered at Appomattox as when the war was first begun. The existing shipping laws must be repealed in order that American citizens can buy vessels in any ship-yards in the world, if this great element of our prosperity is to be restored. The tariff laws need revision. God helping us, with the star of Democracy again in the ascendant, the tariff law will be revised until the basis of the tariff shall be the needed revenue for the Government, which is a just tax, and not protection, which is robbery. I shall never rest satisfied until every American citizen is free to sell his products in that market which will bring him the greatest returns, and can buy in the cheapest markets the wide world over. I feel sure of one thing—that I understand the needs and wants of the great State of Kentucky, and I pledge myself to devote the same energy toward meeting these wants as a member of the Senate as I have tried to devote to them in the lower house of Congress.

Not surprisingly, Northern Republican papers thought the election of Blackburn showed evidence of the "old rebel spirit," and "proof of the hostility of the Southern people." The Chicago Herald admitted begrudging admiration in a bit of back-handed compliments:

> The fiery and eloquent Blackburn walks off with the Senatorial honors from Kentucky. Blackburn has had a short but rather remarkable career. He first came under the national eye in the winter of 1873 when he went to Washington as a member of the Forty-fourth Congress, and a more ornery looking specimen never took a seat in the House. He was coarse-featured, with a red face and loud voice. He wore a huge mustache trained down from the corners of his mouth in the vulgar style then affected. But his most conspicuous feature

> was a huge green neck tie that fairly dazzled the multitude and drew every eye. A tendency to get on his feet all the time soon excited derision and people began to laugh and suggest that the wild Kentuckian was "fresh." But the celebrated Hill-Blaine debate gave him an opportunity to make a speech and he fairly electrified the House. From that day to this Blackburn has been a national figure, and his success in reaching the Senate is the reward of his ability and individuality.

The Hill-Blaine debate took place in 1876 when Congressmen Benjamin H. Hill of Georgia, a Southern former Confederate, and James G. Blaine of Maine, a strident Radical Republican, were the principal debaters regarding a bill that proposed amnesty to all former Confederates who had not yet received it. Blaine insisted on amending the bill so that Jefferson Davis would be excluded. The emotion-charged debate joined in by Blackburn recalled many of the horrors of the Civil War. The bill did not pass and the aftereffects from the debate lingered for many years among Congressmen from each section of the country, but the Hill-Blaine debate secured Blackburn's honored place in Congress that carried over to his new seat in the U.S. Senate. Newly elected U.S. Senator Blackburn took his seat as a respected equal of the other members of the Senate. He spoke openly in the Senate Chamber from his first day.

> In those days new members of the Senate were not tolerated for an instant, but the prestige of a brilliant service of ten years in the House almost at a stroke gave Blackburn a prominent place in the councils of that body. His first year had not expired before he wielded an influence far greater than belongs to most individual members of the Senate, and his re-election for another term followed.

The fact that Senator Blackburn was a former Confederate officer, however, was predominant in the press comments after his election. For example, the Alabama press defended his election, noting that Kentucky was as much a Southern state in sentiment and feeling as Alabama, excusing its failure to join the former Confederacy because of its border situation. The local press noted that a large majority of Kentuckians were opposed to the Republican Party and supported the election of a former Confederate soldier. The addition of Senator Blackburn strengthened the Democratic Party in debate, even though it seemed likely that the Republicans would continue to maintain a slim majority in the Senate. Blackburn came in on the rising tide of support for Democrats that had started to revolutionize the polls in several Northern and Western states the previous year. The *Nashville World* wrote:

> Blackburn is thoroughly a man of the people, as Clay was their great 'commoner.' He says that his restless nature shall know no respite until the burdens of taxation thrown upon the people by an infernal war tariff are reduced and until every American citizen can sell where he can get the highest market price and buy where he can get the cheapest articles. This declaration, in the hour of the most magnificent political victory in the history of Kentucky shows that his head is level and his heart is in the right place.

Another article said:

> He is a hero, this big-mouthed, plain-spoken, Kentuckian. He is frequently rash and unduly hasty in his public utterances; but vigor and life are as much a part of his existence, as the air he breathes. Joe Blackburn has ever been the faithful friend of every employee of either branch of Congress, standing up for what was due each in every instance. No wonder people love him; he deserves every one of the thousands of the kind words that have been spoken of him to-day. He will add weight and respectability to the Senate, for it cannot be said of him that he is a 'millionaire' or a 'nobody' or 'somebody's man.' He is Joe Blackburn, and may his shadow never grow less.

When he was elected to the U.S. Senate for the term beginning in 1885, his son Joseph was a grown man of twenty-six, and his three daughters, Terese, Corinne, and Lucile, were intelligent and beautiful young women. Corinne helped her father in his canvass for re-election when the Kentucky legislature was deadlocked in 1883. She heard about the struggle when she was in Belgium, and hurried back to the Blackburn home in Versailles to help her father in his great struggle for re-election.

> She received letters and telegrams, sent answers in his absence and wired him of any new developments in his canvass. She also received with captivating grace and tact the friends and constituents who called at the senator's house. Miss Corinne is of tall and commanding figure, her complexion is clear and beautiful. She is a thorough woman of the world, and her charming manners are equally well known in Kentucky, Washington and Brussels. She is a talented musician, a splendid conversationalist, and a politician from the ground up.... The Legislature was deadlocked and remained so for two weeks, during which time feeling at the state capitol was keyed to a high pitch of excitement. One day, after the seventy-second ballot, it was announced that a young bachelor senator had been won over to the Blackburn camp, and on the seventy-third ballot Blackburn was elected to the United States Senate. Miss Corinne was credited with having turned the deadlock into a victory for her father.

Immediately after he was elected to the Senate, Senator Blackburn went to Washington with his oldest daughter, Terese, traveling by the Chesapeake and Ohio Railroad. Senator Blackburn was known as one of the most entertaining of conversationalists, equally at home in the drawing-room of the millionaire or by the humble fireside of his lowliest constituent. He was a prominent Mason and Odd Fellow and was ever ready to lend his influence to anything that helped out the condition of the great human family.

> His nine years' service in Congress have added nothing to his worldly possessions, being now, as when he first began public life, a poor man. In his native county he is almost reverenced, his home people, irrespective of politics or color, have the feeling that he belongs to them. There he is simply called 'Joe,' and under no circumstances having bestowed upon him a higher title than 'Cap'n Joe'.... As a friend Joe Blackburn is a diamond of the first water. There is nothing within his power

> that he would withhold from any one having the least claim upon him. We are no prophet, or the son of a prophet, but we shall be much disappointed if in less than a score of years Joe Blackburn is not President of the United States.

Blackburn joined Senator Beck in the Senate, the latter who served in the Senate from 1876 to 1890, filling Kentucky with the hopeful promise that Kentucky would keep her prestige as the state of orators and statesmen, continuing the line begun with Clay, Crittenden, and Breckinridge. Senator Blackburn was the "plumed knight upon whose chivalrous shoulders has fallen the honored mantle of Henry Clay," and it was fully expected that he would not "allow even so much as the hem of that treasured vestment to trail the dust."

But some did not think of his election in such romantic terms, believing instead that he was elected U.S. Senator as a type of reward for getting out of the Speakership contest and allowing Carlisle to carry off that honor.

> And so 'Joe' gets his reward for keeping out of the Speakership contest and permitting his colleague CARLISLE to carry off that honor. There was unquestionably an agreement between the two on this point, it being understood that if BLACKBURN withdrew from the contest for Speaker, CARLISLE would not be a candidate against him for United States Senator. Uncommonly strong inducements have been held out to CARLISLE to go back on this agreement and consent to the use of his name for Senator, and there is little doubt that he would have been elected had he given his consent. It is very much to his credit that he did not yield to the temptation, but carried out in letter and spirit the agreement he had entered into.

After Blackburn was elected, he expressed in an eloquent and appropriate speech his thanks for and his appreciation of the high and coveted honor just conferred upon him. His election marked a new era for the young democracy of Kentucky and "the grandest of political parties." Blackburn was forty-five, only a junior senator, but he fully understood the "genius of our government" and most of all he understood the wants and needs of the people.

The newly elected Senator was congratulated all around. Even ex-Speaker of the House John W. Keifer sent him a telegram of congratulations, saying that Mr. Blackburn "had no warmer congratulations from personal or political friends" than from the ex-Speaker. It was to Blackburn's credit that even though he was "one of the strongest partisans of the House, his genial character and straightforward way of meeting every question" made him a "great favorite with the Republican members."

Chapter Twenty

U.S. Senator Joseph Blackburn's First Term in the Senate

Once Blackburn reached the Senate floor, it was evident that he was bringing his usual energy and determination to the job:

> At a meeting of a Senate special committee on Indian Traderships, of which Senator Chandler of New Hampshire, was the chairman and Senator Blackburn a member, Chandler made a bitter attack in a report on Secretary of Interior William F. Vilas and ex-Indian Commissioner Atkins. Blackburn, who was to make a minority report, protested against Chandler's report as unfair and unwarranted by the evidence. He demanded the names of the witnesses who had sworn to such things as were charged in Chandler's report. Chandler denied the right of Blackburn to question him. Blackburn retorted that he had the right to question an infamous lie and slander made upon innocent men.
>
> Hot words between the two senators followed. Senator Blackburn denounced the New Hampshire senator as a liar, a thief and a scoundrel and said if Chandler had his deserts he would be 'an inmate of a penitentiary.' Chandler replied that Blackburn was a coward to insult him and that he would not be 'bull-dozed by a slave-driver.' At this juncture, Blackburn walked to the end of the table where the man from New Hampshire was sitting, and told him if he would arise he would 'wear him out.' Chandler appealed to the others present for protection. It was here that Blackburn caught him by the right ear and jerked him from his chair. Another senator threw his arms about Blackburn and prevented his giving Chandler severer punishment.

Occasional high-tempered exchanges like these did not slow Blackburn's dedication to his committee work and official duties in the Senate. The Senate accomplishes its work by committees, where members can develop specialized knowledge on the matters studied. Senate committees are "little legislatures" that monitor ongoing governmental operations, identify issues that are suitable for legislative review, gather and evaluate information, and recommend courses of action to the Senate. Standing committees are permanent committees with specific responsibilities spelled out in the Senate's official rules. Since the Fourteenth Congress met in 1816, there have been eleven permanent standing committees: Foreign Relations, Finance, Commerce and Manufactures, Military Affairs, Militia, Naval Affairs, Public Lands, Claims, Judiciary, Post Offices and Post Road, and Pensions. Permanent committees can undertake long-term studies and investigations on issues in addition to regular legislative duties. Special and select committees are formed for particular purposes and are not initially considered permanent, though they may become permanent. Senate committees are divided according to relative importance into three categories, with limitations on how many of each type a Senator can serve. Members are assigned to committees by Senate party leaders who meet in a Senate party conference, or what Democrats call a "caucus," a process that allows the party leaders to promote party discipline through the granting or withholding of desired committee assignments. The percentage of a party's representation within the Senate determines the percentage of seats it will gain on each committee, although exact numbers are determined in negotiations between the party floor leaders. Since the work of the committees is essential to the legislative process, the chairmen of the committees assume great power, and the committees, in effect, set the agenda for the Senate.

First Session, Forty-Ninth Congress (Dec 7, 1885–Aug 5, 1886)

Democrats retained their House majority and won the White House in the 1884 Presidential Election with Grover Cleveland for the first time since the Civil War. Republicans maintained control of the Senate, where Blackburn served as a Democrat, along with fellow Democrat Senator Beck. There were thirty-eight states represented in Congress and eight non-voting members represented the territories. Ten of the eleven U.S. Representatives from Kentucky were Democrats. The divided Forty-Ninth Congress still managed to produce a substantial legislative record, however. It established presidential succession beyond the Vice President, authorized new space for the Library of Congress, reformed procedures for contested electoral votes, regulated railroad rates with the Interstate Commerce Act, replaced the Indian reservation system with citizenship in the Dawes General Allotment (Severalty) Act, repealed the Tenure of Office Act, and seized the Mormon Church's property until it disavowed polygamy.

The Democrats were able to pass many bills and achieve other goals during the Session, even though the party was in the minority in the Senate but in the majority in the House. The committees were reorganized and were called in to confirm President Cleveland's Cabinet. Senator Blackburn was made fifth on the Committee on Rules, ninth on Railroads, ninth on the District of Columbia, and ninth on Naval Affairs. Later in the Session, Blackburn was made a member of the committee to attend the funeral of Congressman Rankin of Wisconsin. Senator Blackburn was also appointed by the Vice President as one of the Senate visitors to the United States Naval Academy at Annapolis, Maryland. Senator Blackburn introduced several bills for the relief of individuals, for pensions for individuals, to allow the Covington and Cincinnati Elevated Railway to bridge the Ohio River, to amend the law relative to copies of papers in the General Land Office, to incorporate the Potomac and Chesapeake Steam Navigation Company, for the settlement of state war claims, and to make trade dollars legal tender, among many other bills.

Having been a Representative for ten years, Senator Blackburn did not feel called upon to preserve the traditional silence in the Senate for two or three years, but spoke as he had been accustomed to do in the House whenever the occasion required it. Senator Blackburn spoke on various issues such as on the authority of the Assistant Secretary of the Navy, on the Cumberland River improvement, on the Kentucky River improvement, on the relations existing between the Senate and the Executive, and on the admission of Washington Territory. Senator Blackburn also made six reports from the Committee on the District of Columbia, continuing his long-running interest and support of the nation's capital.

Senator Blackburn was a member of the Full Committee and Sub-Committee to investigate how the Custom House operates under the civil service law. The subcommittee took testimony that revealed the dysfunctions in the Custom House, including abuses of power, frivolous firings, extortion, drunkenness, and general corruption. Senator Blackburn's participation and questions helped to reveal the corruption in the Customs House while demonstrating Blackburn's legal skills, political acumen, and, more importantly, his sense of justice above party politics.

Second Session, Forty-Ninth Congress (Dec 6, 1886–March 3, 1887)

Senator Blackburn made several remarks on the Senate floor, including condemning the remarks made by Senator Hoar of Massachusetts about Speaker Carlisle's refusal to allow the rules to be suspended so as to allow the tariff revision to be brought up. Senator Beck responded quickly to the cowardly remarks made behind the Speaker's back and was about to say more but gave way to Senator Blackburn, "whose eye shone with a dangerous light and denounced his speech in words that cut to the quick." The Senate Chamber was as quiet as a church while Senator Blackburn spoke, and it broke into applause when he finished. "It was as severe a castigation as any man ever received in the Senate, and Mr. Hoar is not likely to forget it."

> MR. BLACKBURN: Mr. President: I am disposed to regret that my colleague found it necessary, in his own judgment, to make any reply to the unwarranted and inexcusable tirade the Senator from Massachusetts [George F. Hoar] has seen fit to indulge in. It may be true that the rules of the Senate have become moss-grown and old and effete to the Senator from Massachusetts, as he describes them, but it does occur to me that the universal rules of propriety and self-respect and common decency should yet prevail among us. I do not admit that the Speaker of the House of Representatives [John Carlisle] needs any defense from an attack like that, emanating from such a quarter. The idea of the Senator from Massachusetts assuming to stand on this floor and preach homilies on non-partisan legislation is more absurd than the devil prating about the scheme of universal redemption. [Laughter.]

> Whenever the name of the Speaker of the House of Representatives is known throughout the country, or the world, it is recognized as a synonym for all that is decent, for all that is fair, and for an immense deal that is able. His Republican colleagues in that House, outside of the more formal methods of attesting their appreciation of these great properties and qualities, as is known to every man in this land, by enduring mementoes and souvenirs, have given proof of their appreciation of the falsity of the charge that is here lodged against him. He needs no defense at the hands of my colleagues nor at my hands. Where he is known an assault like that will not hurt him, and I flatter myself that even in the State of Massachusetts, where the Senator is known and seems to be appreciated, it will not work a great deal of harm.

The debate between the men continued and eventually moved onto other matters. When Senator Blackburn returned to the Senate Chamber on the evening of March 3, 1887 from a dinner party in Baltimore given by President Garrett of the Baltimore and Ohio Railroad Company, he found on his desk a large package containing an Indian war club, presumably a memento of his attack that afternoon on Senator Hoar. Attached to the package was a card that read: "For Senator J.C.S. Blackburn; a Sioux war club, placed where it will do most good."

Fiftieth Congress (March 4, 1887–March 4, 1889)

The Senate had a Republican majority and the House had a Democratic majority. There were thirty-eight states represented in the Congress and eight non-voting members represented the territories. Kentucky's Senators were both Democrats and nine of the eleven Kentucky U.S. Representatives were Democrats, including Speaker of the House Carlisle. The Republican majority in the Senate eroded, and the Democratic majority in the House declined after the 1886 election. President Cleveland fought the Fiftieth Congress on a number of different legislative fronts and wound up vetoing more than two hundred bills (mostly private pensions). He got little help from fellow Democrats in lowering the tariff and none from the congressional

Republicans calling for higher protectionist rates. Congress established an independent Department of Labor in 1888 and a cabinet-like Department of Agriculture in 1889.

The country was continuing its white sweep of the land. The major legislation of this Congress involved the Chinese Exclusion Act of 1888, the Nelson Act of 1889, and the Enabling Act of 1889. The Chinese Exclusion Act was signed into law by President Chester A. Arthur on May 6, 1882 and represents one of the most significant restrictions on free immigration in the history of this country, prohibiting all immigration of Chinese laborers. It was the first law enacted in the country to prevent a specific ethnic group from immigrating to the United States and was not repealed until the end of 1943. Indeed, during this time, the Supreme Order of Caucasians, whose primary goal since it formed in April of 1876 was to run the Chinese out of the country, grew to sixty chapters in the state of California. The exclusionary tendencies appeared in the Nelson Act of 1889, too. Native Americans were consolidated on a Western reservation in Minnesota and communal lands were sold for subsistence farming as a way to resolve the growing tensions in the state between whites and American Indians. The Enabling Act of 1889 was a United States Statute that enabled North Dakota, South Dakota, Montana, and Washington to form state governments and to gain admission as states to the Union. All the states were subsequently admitted in November 1889.

First Session, Fiftieth Congress (Dec 7, 1887–Oct 20, 1888)

In the reorganization of the committees of this Congress, Senator Blackburn was assigned tenth place on the powerful Appropriations Committee, fifth place on the Committee on Rules, fifth on the Committee on Indian Traders, seventh on the Census, eighth on Naval Affairs, and tenth on Railroads. Later he was appointed on a select committee to examine the condition of the Civil Service. He was also appointed by Vice President Thomas A. Hendricks a Director on the part of the Senate for the Columbia Hospital for women and Lying-in Asylum to provide care for destitute but respectable women in confinement during maternity.

He was also named a conferee on the bill for relief of the wounded from the wreck of the United States steamer *Tallapoosa*. A conferee is a Senator who is appointed to serve on conference committees, and they are also called managers. They are usually appointed from the committee that reported the legislation to the Senate and are expected to work to uphold the Senate's position on measures when they negotiate with conferees from the House. The *USS Tallapoosa* was a wooden-hulled, double-ended steamer in the United States Navy during the American Civil War. However, once retired it served in various capacities, including a dispatch vessel. Shortly before midnight on August 24, 1884, the *Tallapoosa* collided with the schooner *J.S. Lowell* and sank about five miles from Vineyard Haven, Massachusetts. After the ship was raised and repaired, it was re-commissioned at the New York Navy Yard on January 11, 1886 and continued in service along the coast of South America until January 30, 1892 when it was condemned as unfit for service. On March 3, 1892, it was sold at public auction to Uruguay.

Senator Blackburn continued his work for the capitol city by introducing numerous bills, including a bill to grade the streets in the District of Columbia and a bill to amend the act to define the powers of the Supreme Court of the District of Columbia. He also introduced other bills, including those for pensions for various individuals, a bill to allow the Louisville Southern Railway to bridge the Kentucky River, a bill to purchase the portrait of General George H. Thomas, a bill to allow the Union Gas Company to lay pipes across the Ohio River, a bill to extend the streets and alleys in Washington, D.C., a bill to prohibit pool selling on races in Washington and Georgetown, D.C., and a bill to adjudicate the claim of an individual.

Senator Blackburn made remarks on the Civil Service investigation, on a monument to General George Rogers Clark, on a dependent pension bill, and on the Washington Cable Electric Railway, to name a few topics.

It was during the First Session that Senator Blackburn gave a rousing speech on the Senate floor in the "Vindication of the Country's Dead Heroes, Hancock and McClellan," on March 6, 1888. His speech was made in response to the false and derogatory remarks of Senator Ingalls of Kansas about the dependent pension bill, the U.S. President, former military heroes, and Senator Blackburn. Blackburn was offended by the inaccuracies in Senator Ingalls' speech and the injustice. He said, in part:

> MR. BLACKBURN: Mr. President, I am at a loss to account for the course that the Senator from Kansas [Mr. Ingalls] has seen fit to adopt in lugging me into the tirade in which he has just indulged, for I am sure that I had never made boast of identification with any military service in my life. I had never referred to the fact of having been a Confederate soldier. Unlike the Senator from Kansas, I thought my military record was too modest and too humble to prove a subject of interest to the galleries that have been assembled to listen to his political harangue.
>
> I did not need to be told by him that I stood here a representative from a State that had never seceded from the Union. I did not need to be reminded that Kentucky had always been loyal. I knew then, as he should know now, that I represent a constituency that are entitled to draw more pensions than the State so ably represented by the Senator who has just preceded me. The records of this country, I believe, show that the State of Kentucky furnished three men to the Union Army for every one that Kansas furnished; and in passing I may assure the Senator that it is not without pride that I recall the fact that of the thirty-odd States then in this Union the one from which I came is the only one that, without the application of a conscript law, furnished more than her quota of men to both sides during that struggle....
>
> I do not care to follow the Senator, for time forbids, through all of his inaccuracies of his utterances, but this much I do propose to say before I close. Mr. President, party man as I am, partisan as I confess myself to be, I do sincerely trust that I may never find my term of public service prolonged to that day, nor my life extended to that hour when, without warrant, without fact to support me, without truth at my back, I shall deliberately traduce and abuse the dead who whilst living were honored by all men. [Applause in the galleries.]

Blackburn's respect for former officers was appreciated by military men from both sides of the past Civil War. On March 8, 1888, the General Robert Patterson Post No. 275, G.A.R., Grand Army men thanked Blackburn for his remembrance of the services of "those tried and true patriots, Gens. George E. McClellan and Winfield S. Scott."

Blackburn took the floor many times, most notably in response to Senator William B. Allison, Republican of Iowa, who had called up the conference report on the Sundry Civil Appropriations bill and then made a speech that started a political debate. When Senator Allison sat down, Senator Eugene Hale, Republican of Maine, jumped up and talked about the ninety-five million dollars excess in the U.S. Treasury as proof of the hollowness of Democrat pretensions of economy, from the former "watch dogs" of the national budget. Senator Blackburn responded forcefully, as reported by the *New York Times*, in an exchange between Senators Blackburn and Hale that exposed Hale's cowardly behavior for all time by Blackburn until Senator Hale had nothing more to say.

> In language as strong as parliamentary law would permit and as scathing as it was earnest the Senator read Mr. Hale a lesson he will not soon forget and which will be long remembered by those who heard it. Mr. Blackburn declared a violation of every rule and precedent of parliamentary proceedings and common decency and an outrage on propriety for a Senator to quote testimony taken by a committee before it had been submitted to the Senate or a report made upon it, and then he declared that it had been concealed by Mr. Hale, who had never dared to call the committee to consider it. That committee was a mud-slinging committee, raised as such by Mr. Hale to try to find out that the President had not properly enforced 'the greatest and grandest political abortion that ever afflicted and cursed mankind in the shape of a civil-service law.' The committee's quest had been a failure, and Mr. Hale was skulking away from the failure. In a room in the Senate wing of the Capitol he had, without notice to a quorum of the committee, taken the testimony of a tramp without putting him on oath, and had put it in the record without giving it to the Senate.

It was a complete humiliation of Senator Hale.

In between the First and Second Session, Kentucky's State Democratic Convention was held on May 16, 1888 in the Lexington Opera House.

The Chairman of the State Committee made a stirring speech referring to President Grover Cleveland as the one man in the Union who could lead the Democracy to another victory in the State. The editor of the *Courier-Journal* Henry Watterson appeared on the platform and gave one of his well-known tariff speeches claiming that the Republican Party now had the tariff issue squarely laid down by President Cleveland's message to Congress and that the result of the Republican high protection could be seen in the many idle workmen and the kindness shown them by Pinkerton's armed detectives. Watterson went further and characterized the Republican Party as the enemy to progress and said that the Democratic Party was in favor of union and prosperity, while the Republicans wanted to disrupt the Government and was the party of destruction. The convention erupted into loud cheers and commotion. When it settled down, the Committee on Permanent Organization announced that Senator Joseph C. S. Blackburn was chosen unanimously as the permanent Chairman. Blackburn made a speech upon taking the Chair in which he commended President Cleveland for the noble work he had done and for placing himself on record in regard to the tariff issue. Other leading State Democrats spoke and the delegates for the State at Large were announced.

Many tariff debates took place outside of Congress, as well. That summer, the campaigning in Kentucky was fierce. Senator Blackburn and Speaker Carlisle gave speeches on the efforts and positive rationale for tariff reform at a large barbecue in Erlanger, Kentucky on September 19, 1888. It was estimated that about six thousand people attended. Senator Blackburn spoke first. The race was on. After campaigning in Kentucky, Blackburn returned to Washington for the Second Session of the Fiftieth Congress.

By the end of the summer of 1888, Senator Blackburn was discouraged by the political challenges the Democratic Party faced as he wrote on August 24, 1888 in a letter to his brother James, then at Spring Station, Kentucky:

> My dear Brother: —
>
> I would have written you before this, but it seems that I am kept constantly busy with bothers of one description or another. The tariff fight has been transferred to the Senate and it seems that we are to be here until October or even later.

It is my purpose to take part in it. I wish you would talk to Sam [James' son], Josie [his son] and John Graham [Joseph's brother-in-law]. I hesitate to write them for fear that they might indiscreetly repeat the advice that I would give them. Urge them to shape their matters so as to be prepared for whatever may come in November. I have just returned from New York where I met the State Committee and the leaders of our party in that State. The outlook is not encouraging. Unless some change occurs, which cannot now be foreseen, the chances are that we will lose this fight. Those who are in office now should look the facts in the face and prepare themselves as best they can for whatever is to come. The children who are with me are well. Love to all.
Your brother, Jo. C.S. Blackburn"

Time would tell if his misgivings were well-founded.

Second Session, Fiftieth Congress (Dec 3, 1888–March 3, 1889)

During the Second Session, Senator Blackburn was appointed to a conference committee, and introduced several bills including: relief for various individuals, a bill to allow the Kentucky Union Railway Company to bridge the Kentucky River, and a bill for printing the report of the Board of Health of the District of Columbia. He made several remarks during this session, but the session in general was an uneventful one.

Chapter Twenty-One

Senator Joseph Blackburn's Greatest Speech

"May the Youth of our State and Country Learn from a Study of His Life, Whom To-Day We Honor, the Lofty Patriotism, the Dignity, the Fidelity and Courage That Constitute the Worthy Citizen." – J.C.S. Blackburn

The most notable speech Senator Joseph Blackburn made was extemporaneous. It was the eulogy for former Vice President, Senator, and Confederate General John C. Breckinridge, which he gave in Lexington, substituting for former General William Preston, who had died unexpectedly before the unveiling. Blackburn's speech was included in "The World's Greatest Orations," recognized for its astonishing breadth and wisdom. Even though Blackburn's and Breckenridge's proslavery stance remains offensively heinous to this day, and thankfully Breckenridge's statue has been rightfully removed from it's former location by the old courthouse, the eloquence of the speech that Blackburn gave without any preparation or notes is worth reviewing.

On November 16, 1887, crowds gathered in Lexington outside the courthouse to unveil the monument of John C. Breckinridge that depicted him standing with his right hand extended as if addressing his fellow citizens at the bar. The sculptor, Edward Virginius Valentine of Richmond, Virginia, had been instructed to show Breckinridge this way. Breckinridge had been the youngest Vice President of the United States when he was elected with President James Buchanan in the 1856 election. Breckinridge had presided over the bitter Senate debates during the four years before Lincoln was elected in 1860. In fact Breckinridge had been the Southern Democrat candidate for President against Lincoln, while the Northern Democrats nominated Stephen Douglas. The split in the Democratic vote allowed the Republican Party candidate, Abraham Lincoln of Illinois, to win the election with less than a majority.

After Breckinridge lost the 1860 presidential election, the Kentucky legislature appointed him to the U.S. Senate, effective March 4th, 1861 after seven states had already seceded from the Union. Senator Breckinridge hoped to be able to steer the country away from civil war but failed. While he could not change the Southern course to secession, he urged Kentucky to remain neutral. He lost that plea, as well. Once Unionists took control of the Kentucky state legislature in a special election in June, Breckinridge was regarded as a traitor for his Confederate sympathies. In August 1861, Breckinridge resigned his Senate seat, and on September 19, 1861, he fled to Virginia before Union General Thomas E. Bramlette was able to arrest him. The state legislature immediately asked for his resignation. On October 8, 1861, he wrote an open letter to Kentuckians stating that the Union no longer existed and that Kentuckians were free to choose their own course, publicly resigning again. In early November 1861 Breckinridge joined the Confederate Army, first as a brigadier general and then as a major general. He led troops in battles and was later appointed the Confederate Secretary of War by Confederate President Jefferson Davis. Breckinridge was indicted for treason by the U.S. District Court in Frankfort on November 6, 1861, just days after he joined the Confederate army. On December 2nd, 1861, he was declared a traitor by the United States Senate. Ten southern U.S. Senators had been expelled earlier the same year. It was not until late 1868 that President Andrew Johnson extended amnesty to all former Confederates, and Breckinridge returned to the land of his birth, but as an exile without the right of citizenship.

Senator Blackburn made a masterly speech at the dedication of the statue in Lexington's courthouse square on November 16, 1887, filling in at the last minute for General Preston. Blackburn had served under both General Preston and Breckinridge in the Civil War. He was more than prepared to share his memories of John C. Breckinridge.

> 'Blackburn,' recalled Judge Charles Kerr years later when he was practicing law in Washington D.C., 'hurriedly substituted, spoke for about an hour "entirely extemporaneously and during its entire delivery he did not use a single note." His memory for names, dates and events was uncanny.' From among all Blackburn's speeches, that one was chosen for inclusion in "The World's Great Orations" because, in the

> opinion of the compiler, 'it was the only logical explanation he had ever heard for Kentucky's choosing neutrality, rather than an alliance with either North or South.'

By 1887 when the monument was unveiled, tensions had eased enough to encourage the committee to invite the Grand Army of the Republic of Yankee veterans, whose state commander replied cordially "that the GAR probably appreciated the invitation more than any other organization that had been asked." Consequently, the *Lexington Morning Transcript* of the time published the next day an estimate that there were more former soldiers, Union and Confederate, in Lexington that day than there had ever been at one time during the war.

> Address of Hon. J. C. S. Blackburn at the unveiling of the Statue of General John C. Breckinridge at Lexington, Kentucky, November 16, 1887
>
> By Hon. J.C.S. Blackburn
>
> *Mr. Chairman and fellow-citizens of Kentucky:*
>
> With doubt I come to the discharge of a service that belonged to another. Near four hundred years ago the French Knight died. When the life of the Chevalier Bayard went out, it was said that there was none left among the living to pronounce his eulogy. Kentucky was more fortunate when this, her modern Bayard, died, for she then numbered among her living sons one thoroughly equipped and fitted to the task that has fallen to me. Whether as a soldier, upholding upon foreign soil the flag of his country that he loved so faithfully and served so well, or in the council chambers of the Republic, or in that later, darker, bloodier period of that country's history, the illustrious names, the towering figures of Breckinridge and Preston are so indissolubly linked that fame will claim them a common heritage. Had Preston's honored life been spared until this hour, this monument would have been dedicated with an oration that would have endured in the memory of men as long as yonder bronze will defy the wasting of time.
>
> When a great man dies the living seek to perpetuate his memory. For this, monuments are builded [sic], mausoleums founded and statues erected. This is not done to appease the dead,

nor to render their sleep more peaceful or profound, but rather to inspire the living to nobler and better lives. No monuments that we may build, no honors that we may render, no eulogiums that we may utter, can reach into that far-off mysterious realm to which the spirit of the mighty dead has gone; but the living may be taught by great example, and ambition stirred in those who are to follow us by study of the lives of those who were truly great. Kentucky has selected a model to offer to her coming generations. She, the great Commonwealth, comes to-day with uncovered head to consecrate a statue that she has built with loving hands to the memory of an illustrious son whom 'she wisely nursed for fame.' John Cabell Breckinridge was born in this city on the 16 day of January, 1821. He came of a family that for generations had been distinguished for illustrious services rendered to the State and country. His father, John Cabell Breckinridge, died at 35, after having ranged himself among the leaders of his day and State. His grandfather, John Breckinridge, died at the early age of 45, but in that short life he crowded the honors that are scarcely ever gathered in a century. As the law officer of the government in the cabinet of Mr. Jefferson, as an expounder of the principles of Constitutional Government set forth in his immortal resolutions of 1798, defining the limitations fixed by the Constitution upon Federal power, he placed himself in the front rank of American statesmen, and became, as it were, the second father of a political system that stood, in its grand and well balanced proportions, the wonder and glory of the world. His maternal grandfather, Samuel Stanhope Smith, was President of Princeton College, and reckoned among the foremost men of letters of his generation; whilst his great grandfather, upon the mother's side, John Witherspoon, a direct descendant of John Knox, was a distinguished member of that convention of sages, statesmen, patriots and heroes who framed and issued to the world the immortal declaration of independence. Born of such an ancestry, bearing upon his youthful shoulders the responsibilities inseparable from such an illustrious lineage, much was expected of the young Kentuckian, when, with couched lance and visor down, he entered the fiercely heated arena of political strife, destined to a still fiercer, whiter heat, in which to prove his title to the name he bore, around which clustered so much hereditary glory. But high as was the standard of expectation, Breckinridge met and went far beyond its severest exactions.

Is it to be wondered that a man, bred like this, upon whom nature, with lavish hand, had bestowed more than a liberal share of intellectual power, of magnetism, of eloquence and courage, should play a conspicuous part in the most turbulent and perilous period of his country's history? Is it to be wondered that he became the nucleus upon which centered all the elements that sought to establish those same principles which had been so stoutly asserted and steadfastly maintained by all the ancestry that lay behind him? Born and reared, having lived and died here among you, it is not needed that I should trace, in detail, his development from boyhood to manhood, nor need I deal with those years that lie behind his entrance into public life.

Having graduated at Centre College, he studied law at Princeton, was admitted to the bar and located in the then sparsely settled State of Iowa. His love for his own State predominated and he soon returned to this, his native place, and began, with bright promise, the practice of his profession. From its peaceful paths he was soon called to enter the military service of his country.

As Major of the 3d Regiment of Kentucky Volunteers he served with gallantry and distinction through the Mexican War, and was with that portion of the army which terminated the contest by the occupation of the Mexican Capital. Returning to his home he was but starting anew upon the professional life that he had chosen when called upon to take his place in the arena of active politics. The conditions under which he made that appearance were peculiar, if not anomalous.

Breckinridge had inherited the creed of Democracy. His study of our system of Government had but strengthened and deepened his convictions of the soundness of that party's principles. His State, his Congressional District and this, his native county, were all Whig by overwhelming majorities. All had felt the influence and been permeated by the magnetic power of the great Whig leader. This was the home of the great Commoner, then and for many years the central figure of American politics.

Mr. Clay, in the ripened fullness of his great powers, stood the acknowledged leader of the Federal Senate. It required the exercise of sublimest faith to attempt to wrench either county, district or State from the close grasp of the great Captain, but defying conditions, with unfaltering faith in the creed that he cherished, Breckinridge entered the contest and in 1849, as the Democratic Representative from Fayette County, appeared in the lower house of the Kentucky Legislature. The part that he bore in the legislation and debates of that body soon marked him as a man reserved for no ordinary destiny. In 1851 he was nominated for Congress in this the Ashland District. Its loyalty to the Whig party had always been so constant and devoted that it was not thought possible that it could be loosed from its moorings, but, through abundant caution, the opposition, determined that Mr. Clay's own district should not be surrendered, selected as their candidate the scarred and honored veteran of the War of 1812. Gen'l Leslie Combs was immensely popular—one of the most captivating, humorous and inimitable campaigners that ever appeared upon the Kentucky hustings. The canvass was active, hot and sharp. Breckinridge won by a majority that surprised his supporters and staggered his opponents. Not overestimating, but conscious of his own great powers, he now felt that the future was his own. He had laid broad and deep the foundation of his strength at home.

The power of the Whig party was waning in Kentucky, its organization had crumbled under its own ponderous blows, its citadel had been stormed and carried, its mighty leader, in many respects the grandest that this continent has ever furnished, wasted by the labors of half a century, broken in health and bent with age, was rapidly passing to his honored and consecrated grave. When he was gone there would be none to take his place. His often-beaten but ever faithful legions were to be left headless, as were the Highland hosts when Roderick's bugle was no longer heard. The future opened before Breckinridge the grandest vista down which mortal vision ever swept to scan its own assured possessions. Without the sacrifice of modest dignity, Breckinridge moved promptly to the front rank in that council chamber of his country, and stood at least the peer of any who sat about him. Renominated in 1853, the Whig party made a last desperate rally to compass his defeat. It selected as its candidate Ex-Gov. Letcher, known as the invincible apostle of its faith when commissioned to preach it to the populace. The contest was even fiercer than the one preceding, but at its close Breckinridge emerged from the smoke and turmoil of the fray with a shield brighter than before, upon which was recorded another triumph splendidly achieved.

Of his brilliant service for four years in the National House of Representatives the imperishable records of the country furnish the best and most conclusive testimony. The Whig party was rapidly disintegrating. The day of its power and usefulness was past. New organizations were in process of construction. The masses of the Whig party in the Southern States drifted into what was soon known as the Know-Nothing organization, whilst in the North they affiliated with the Republican party, till then too weak to be considered a rival in the great struggle from National supremacy, while many of its most devoted adherents, unwilling or unable to adapt themselves to new and changed conditions, still held together and strove to preserve their old and honored form.

The Democracy seemed united and solid. It looked as though it held an unlimited lease on Federal power. Breckinridge, with a National reputation established, was now accepted as the ablest, most available and promising young leader of this vast, compact and dominant party. Here was threatened a break in his political career. Pressed by lack of fortune, like his great predecessor, Mr. Clay, he voluntarily retired from Congress to devote himself to the prosecution of his profession, but the country had already fixed its measure upon his value as a political leader. In 1856 the National Democratic Convention met in Cincinnati. After a sharp contest between Mr. Douglas, of Illinois, and Mr. Buchanan, of Pennsylvania, the latter was nominated for the Presidency. This was a recognition of the older class of leaders, who were rapidly passing away. Recognizing the necessity of such action, the Convention turned instinctively to the accepted leader of the more active and younger elements of the party, and against his urgent protest and amid scenes of wildest enthusiasm, that beggar description, the gifted young Kentuckian was given the second place upon the ticket. His nomination electrified the Democracy of the country, and the ticket was elected by an overwhelming majority. For four years he presided over the Senate with conspicuous ability and fairness. Evidences of discord now appeared in the ranks of the Democracy. Breckinridge stood without a rival for the Presidential nomination, except in the person of Douglas. The Charleston Convention of 1860 went to pieces without making a nomination, Breckinridge refusing to allow his name to go before it. Breckinridge received the nomination of the Baltimore Convention, representing one section of the party; Douglas became the candidate of the other. The organization was hopelessly divided, and defeat was inevitable. Breckinridge received 72 electoral votes, Douglas 12, demonstrating the former's strong hold upon his party. In 1859 Breckinridge had been elected to the Senate of the United States for six years, beginning March 4, 1861, to succeed Hon. John J. Crittenden. His term as Senator began in the hour that closed his term as Vice-President. He had scarcely passed the constitutional limit of age when he became a member of the Kentucky Legislature. He was five years beyond the constitutional requirement when elected to the Federal Congress. At 35 he was elected to the second office in the gift of the American people; while at 40 he was Senator-elect from Kentucky, Vice-President, and the candidate of the majority wing of his party for the Presidency of the United States. This records stands without a parallel in American history.

On the 4 of March, 1861, Mr. Lincoln was inaugurated President. The clouds that had been lowering since the disruption of the Charleston Convention gathered thickly and fast. Fanatics in the North elated over the first triumph of a sectional party, planted upon a single sectional issue, were deaf to every suggestion of a peaceable solution of the situation, whilst Southern leaders, taking hasty counsel of the chagrin brought by defeat, pushed the dread issue to a precipitate and fatal decision. Passion had thrust reason from her throne. State after State seceded from the Union. War, with all its attendant horrors, confronted us. Kentucky, conscious of the peril she must meet, earnestly strove to avert the conflict. None doubted, for all knew, that if coercion was attempted, her sympathies were with the South. Trusting to the promises made, only to be broken, by many of the most prominent leaders of the Union party in the State, Kentucky was beguiled into a sense of security. She relied upon the address published to the world over the signatures of James Speed, George D. Prentice, and others, and endorsed by Crittenden, declaring that no military force of government should be marched into or over the soil of Kentucky to wage war upon the people of the South. Her honest, but credulous people, believing that these promises were to be made good, still clamoring for the neutrality the State had proclaimed, were wakened from their dream, to find that the fraud that had been so successfully practiced, had given place to the force that, through military occupation, was ample for her enslavement. The Senate was convened in extraordinary session in March, '61. Breckinridge then assumed, for the first time, his great and grave responsibilities as a Senator. His position was trying in the extreme. With his inherited principles and well matured convictions, he could hold no sympathy with the policy adopted by the Federal administration. He did not believe that the power existed in the Federal government to coerce a sovereign State by force of arms. He did believe that the essential and fundamental principles of State's rights and local self-government were being ruthlessly violated, and the constitutional limitations upon Federal power were being trampled under foot. He knew that his heart and the hearts of his people were with the South, and yet he loved the Union with an unfaltering, a deathless devotion. Holding to the right of secession, he did not regard it as a wise or prudent remedy for existing conditions. He went to his great place as a Senator to plead with all his power for an adjustment of the issue. The supreme hour of trial had come. 'Twas like the approach of the hour of crucifixion. How earnestly he must have prayed 'if it be possible let this cup pass from me.' Never was patriotism, conscience and courage subjected to severer test. His love for and devotion to the Union of the States still burned as brightly as when he painted it in his own matchless eloquence in his memorable eulogy upon Mr. Clay and his never-to-be-forgotten oration upon the removal of the Senate from the old to the new chamber.

During the period preceding the inauguration of Mr. Lincoln, Breckinridge had, from his position as Vice-President, been barred from participation in debate. He had seen State after State withdraw its representation from the august chamber, over the deliberations of which he presided with impartial dignity, and was able only to exercise a mute influence in support of the Crittenden compromise resolutions with which he was heartily in sympathy. Those who knew him best were well aware that his great heart was filled with patriotic concern at the threatening storm which was fast gathering. A just inquiry into the sentiments which animated him at this trying period of his country's history will show that they were the same which had challenged the admiration of his countrymen, when he was the recipient of the highest popular favor. His utterances at a time long anterior to the critical period of which we speak, when read by the light of after events, will be received by those whose desire to do justice to his deserts as prophetic warnings of a great mind, anxious to avert public calamity, rather than as the arguments of one seeking, as his enemies claim, to overthrow the government of his choice. Within the mind and heart of John C. Breckinridge there dwelt the most profound love and admiration for the principles of the Constitution, and for a government administered under them. Fortunately, although no historian has yet formulated these views for the enlightenment of posterity, he has left in enduring print the record which vindicates his name. On the 4 of January, 1859, in the memorable address which he delivered as Vice-President in vacating the old Senate Chamber to occupy the new one, he said, in a burst of patriotic fervor, after reviewing the progress of the country to its then advanced position of national glory: 'Is there an American who regrets the past? Is there one who will deride his country's laws, pervert her Constitution or alienate her people? If there be such a man, let his memory descend to posterity, laden with the execration of all mankind.' Concluding, he placed upon record in imperishable words his estimate of that Constitution: 'And now Senators, we leave this memorable chamber, bearing with us unimpaired, the Constitution we received from our forefathers. Let us cherish it with grateful acknowledgements of the Divine Power who controls the destinies of empires, and whose goodness we adore. The structures, reared by men, yield to the corroding tooth of time. These marble walls must moulder into ruin; but the principles of constitutional liberty, guarded by wisdom and virtue, unlike material elements, do not decay. Let us devoutly trust that another Senate, in another age, shall bear to a new and larger chamber, this Constitution, vigorous and inviolate, and that the last generation of posterity shall witness the deliberations of Representatives of American States still united, prosperous and free.' Again, on December 21 , 1859, in an address delivered before the Legislature of his own State on the occasion of his election as Senator, treating of the threatened disruption of the States he said: 'When questioned I will say in your name, Kentucky will act in a manner answerable to her character and history. She will cling to the Constitution while a shred of it remains, and if, unhappily, madness and folly and wicked counsels succeed to destroy the fairest fabric ever erected to Liberty among men, she will conduct herself with so much wisdom, moderation and firmness as to stand justified before the tribunal of history and in the eye of Heaven for the part she will unwillingly play in the most disastrous drama ever enacted on the theatre of the world.' In further proof of my assertion as to the persistence of the great Kentuckian's patriotism I give the following exact extract from a speech delivered in the Senate after the inauguration of Mr. Lincoln, March 20 , 1861: 'I inherited and all my life have cherished a habitual and cordial attachment to a constitutional Union and now would be willing any day to die for it. But while I believe that, administered according to the true principles of the Constitution, it is the best government on earth, I also believe that, administered without the lines of the Constitution, by the simple power of majority, it becomes the worst on earth; and for myself, neither in public or private life, will I consent to sacrifice the principles of constitutional freedom, of municipal liberty and of State equality to the naked idea of Federal unity.'

War had come. The Southern Senators had gone. Deserted and abandoned, solitary and alone, treading in the footsteps of the immortal Clay, illustrating his statesmanship, his patriotism and his courage, pleading for a rational adjustment, an honorable peace, he will pass into history all the grander because he stood alone.

Suspected and mistrusted, upon his entrance into the Senate, he patiently braved and bore it all. The battle of Manassas was fought. A beaten and broken army sought refuge in the Capital, but this triumph of the South extorted no exultation from the grave and anxious Senator. His allegiance was still due to the government that he was seeking to serve. He had seen the political system of his forefathers shattered. His efforts were futile. His mission was ended. Amid the ruin that surrounded, in this same chamber over which he had so long presided, sadly surveying the wreck that had come both to the Union and himself, he sat like Caius Marius amid the ruins of Carthage. All was lost but honor. Brave words he spoke. Unawed by power, he dared to plead his convictions. He clung with a hope that defied despair. He came back to his people to find that they were shackled. His love of country, his hopes, his ambitions, his aspirations, were all at stake. Before him had stretched all that a trusting people could bestow. The goal for which American statesmen have ever struggled had been within easy reach, but only to be had by a forfeiture of principle and an abandonment of friends. He took counsel of his conscience and did not err. Caesar has been accredited with pushing aside a crown, but Caesar accepted imperial power. Washington refused to don the purple of permanent authority, but Washington accepted the rulership of a new born Republic, numbered with the foremost nations of the earth—a place that outranks crowns, if acquired not by fraud or accident, but as a tribute paid to ability and conspicuous service.

None who knew him doubted the decision he would make. Faithfully and fearlessly he had striven to avert war and save the Union of the States. His powers had all been exerted and exhausted. Nothing remained but to take his place where conscience pointed and meet the inevitable with lofty courage.

He knew that the voice of Kentucky was stifled by the methods already described. He knew that, with the mailed hand of military power at her throat, she could not voice the will of the people. He knew that the State could not go with him to the Confederacy, but that he must go alone, uncovered by her shield; but he knew that thousands of her intrepid sons would gather to his standard and follow where he led. He did not ask to place his action upon the ground of obedience to the edict of his State. He recognized, as the great issue involved in the struggle, the preservation or destruction of the whole system of Constitutional Government. He believed that the question to be determined was whether the government that survived should be one of limited powers under which the liberties of the citizens might find shelter, or one resting alone with arbitrary power. Every principle or conviction that he cherished was at stake. He did not hesitate. Refusing to recognize as a State government those who were overawed by a military power they dared not defy, on the 8th of October, 1861, he published an address from Bowling Green to the people of Kentucky, returned to them the great trust they had given, resigned his seat in the Senate, and, flinging away ambition, drew that sword that was never sheathed until the last army had melted from the earth, and the flag that he followed had gone down at last amid tears and blood. Viewed in the light of results personal to Breckinridge, the great mistake of his life would appear to consist in the persistency with which he clung to hope of a peaceful adjustment and in his failure to take his State with him into the Confederacy which he could have undoubtedly have done in the spring of 1861. The only explanation is to be found in the hope, to which he tenaciously clung, of a settlement without a resort to arms. With Kentucky as a member of the Confederacy Breckinridge would have stood on even terms with the other leaders of that great drama, but throughout this stormy period he seems never to have thought of self but only to take his place wherever assigned and discharge its duties as best he could. He never sought promotion, nor did he need to. Of his record as a soldier, let the history of that great struggle testify.

The fields of Shiloh, Stone River, Vicksburg, Baton Rouge, Chickamauga, Lookout Mountain, Missionary Ridge, Monocacy, New Market, Cold Harbor and Saltville hear ample testimony to his great abilities as a commander and his cool unfaltering courage. After his transfer from the western army to Virginia he came under the eye of the great commander. Lee here had the opportunity of measuring the man. So had the authorities at Richmond. As the result he was called to the head of the War Department of the Government. It was too late. With all his great powers as an Executive officer, he could not retrieve the losses nor restore the wastage of well nigh four years of incessant terrific strife. The resources of the Government were exhausted. The Confederacy was already tottering to its fall. Its doom was sealed, its hour about to strike.

No member of the Cabinet possessed the same degree of confidence in the Executive, the army and the country. His last official act was an attempt to negotiate a peace securing terms that were alike liberal to the vanquished and creditable to the victor. There was no longer a government or army left to the South. Breckinridge stood a proscribed man beyond the shelter of the law. In all the history of this Government the legislative authority has never, save in this one instance, usurped and exercised the odious power carried in a bill of attainder. The eruptions of that war period had flung into the Federal Senate a member who, moved by the greed of notoriety that possessed the aspiring youth who fired the Ephesian dome, offered a resolution, which the Senate in its made frenzy, adopted, declaring that Breckinridge, *the traitor,* be expelled from that chamber. No trial was had, no confession received, no testimony taken. Here to-day, in the presence of the world, in the sight of Almighty God, Kentucky files her imperishable answer to that libel. States do not build monuments to traitors. Breckinridge had already, by his own act, ceased to be a Senator.

The decree passed in open defiance of the Constitution was but a *brutum fulmen,* serving only to evidence the malignity of its authors. Breckinridge was left with no choice, no alternative. An alien in the land of his birth, denied the protection of the laws that he had borne so conspicuous a part in framing for the government of a country, any of the brightest pages of whose history were adorned with the names of his ancestry and his own, he determined to seek shelter in foreign lands from the tyranny that pursued him. Who will paint his emotions as he stood upon the shore looking out upon the sea in search of a sail that would carry him he knew not whither. His hopes were blighted, his ambitions were buried, his career was ended, his work was done, and his life lay behind him. He was bidding what seemed to be an eternal farewell to home and country, to family and friends. Calmly he surveyed the universal wreck that reigned around him. His great soul was unshaken. 'Though a broken orb should fall, fearless he would stand amid its ruins.' In an open boat he crossed to the Cuban shore. He remained abroad until bitterness and passion had sufficiently subsided to permit him to return to spend what little of life was left him and to die among those who loved him so fondly, but destined to wear into his grave the clanking shackles that a narrow, unwise and unmanly policy had riveted upon his limbs. His own dignity, in the light of his antecedents, precluded any slavish, unmanly appeal for pardon. He never asked and never received the right of citizenship. He came back with the consent of the Government to live and die an exile in the home of his fathers, to obey the law that had been made and to respect the authorities that had been established. Faithfully he observed the condition. Never obtruding himself upon public notice, taking no part in the controversies pending, in the quiet of home and friendship's circles he patiently waited the end that was so near. On the 17 day of May, 1875, the irrevocable mandate came. Conscious to the last, fully advised of the inevitable, calm and unmoved he faced, for the last time, the grim destroyer that he had so often confronted upon the field of battle. Conscious of the rectitude of his own life, feeling that he had done the right as God had given him power to see it, he surrendered back to his creator unspotted a life that had been given to the service of his fellows.

Breckinridge might have returned to public service had he desired. Had he asked for relief from political disabilities it would have been granted. There was no honor within Kentucky's gift that he would not have been tendered. The pathos that gathered about his life, the lofty dignity, the sublime courage that had marked his bearing in disaster, made him the idol of his people. But he saw no good, but only harm to result from his reappearance in the field of politics. Whether he proved himself worthy to be numbered among the great, history must determine. Its verdict will be traced with impartial pen. That verdict Kentucky, with unfaltering faith, abides. It would be unreasonable to expect justice at the hands of those who differed from his conclusions as to look for impartial judgment at our hands who fought by his side. Strive as we may, we cannot be fair. Confidently I surrender the right of judgment to posterity, assured that when the passions and prejudices of this generation have been buried and his name shall have be assigned to the place in history that he fairly won, it will be found among the brightest that this great Commonwealth has furnished to the shining list of the immortal. It may be true that he had his equals as orator, statesman and soldier, but in fairness it must be conceded that in all these characters combined he had no superior. Mr. Clay was probably the greatest popular leader this country has ever known, but it will be admitted that in that realm Clay, Breckinridge and Douglas constitute an immortal trio, whose like we have never seen. As a statesman, whilst he ranked with the first, it might not be fair to claim for him pre-eminence over all men of his day. As a soldier, his record, conspicuously brilliant, did not lift him above the well-earned plane attained by several of the great commanders on either side, but, measured in all these roles, he stands without a peer in all this country's annals. Tried everywhere—in the stormy House of Representatives, as presiding officer of the most august deliberative body upon the earth; in debate, as a member of the Senate; in the field, as a commander of division or corps, or as the chief war officer of a government struggling for its existence—anywhere, everywhere, he loomed up above those by whom he was surrounded as one who was born to rule. No success elated him, no disaster disheartened.

It is not to the soldier, but to the honored son that Kentucky dedicates this statue. In the Legislature that decreed him this honor many true and manly men united that held no sympathy with his views, and bitterly opposed the cause for which he fought. Despite political differences they united in doing honor to the memory of one who stood the embodiment of our civilization, representing all that was chivalrous, manly and true. Remembering this I would not stir the bitternesses of passions of the past. The war lies behind us. Would to God that it had carried with it its own sad and bitter memories. A majority of those who witnessed its coming are no longer on this earth. Most of its great captains have crossed the shadowy line that bounds the unknown realms. Grant and Lee, Johnston and Thomas, Jackson, McPherson, Breckinridge and others have long since met upon the other side, we hope in fraternity and good will.

A country, united not only in name but in purpose, in hope and in destiny, will cherish the memory of all its worthy sons, and teach posterity to hold it as a precious legacy. 'Tis true that no proud pantheon stood with eager opening gates to receive his honored ashes, but they rest in the soil that nourished his birth, whilst fame reposes in an ever enduring pantheon—the hearts of the people. Here, within the limits of your beautiful city, rise toward heaven the monument of Clay and the statue of Breckinridge. Well may you guard these treasures. Around them cluster a half century of glory. Westminster Abbey holds no more precious dust. Earth never gave sepulcher to grander men. But it is the lessons that these monuments teach that we would impress. The greatest historians told us nearly two thousand years ago 'the bodies of men are perishing and mortal, so likewise are their statues, but the form of the mind is eternal and can never be preserved by any foreign material or art, but only by the real character and behavior of the persons who imitate it.' May the youth of our State and country learn from a study of his life, whom to-day we honor, the lofty patriotism, the dignity, the fidelity and courage that constitute the worthy citizen.

Recalling the past and measuring her responsibilities to the future, in the presence of her sons and daughters, in the sight of the Omnipotent God, Kentucky dedicates this monument to her broad-brained, great-hearted, idol son. Orator, statesman, soldier, patriot, to thy immortal name and to thy deathless fame Kentucky consecrates this statue, and tenders it to posterity, as proof of the love she bore thee.

Chapter Twenty-Two

Our Joe: Champion of the Average Man

In the late 1800s America was perhaps the most protectionist nation on earth to the great profit of the so-called "Robber Barons" of the age. Robber barons were not interested in free trade and enjoyed the high tariffs on foreign goods which went as high as forty percent and fifty percent during the period from 1860 to 1914. America went from being an emerging economic power to an economic colossus, whose Gross Domestic Product (GDP) was as great as the GDPs of England, France and Germany combined. The tariff issue was one of the most hotly contested in the country, generating intense animosity between high tariff and low tariff advocates. Supporters of high tariffs said that if the tariff was lowered, then American goods would not be able to compete with European manufacturers. High duties had been imposed on everyday items like shoes, clothing, furniture, and steel, so American manufacturers could compete, but since the Civil War, American manufacturers had become competitive and were reaping huge profits. American manufacturers profited while American farmers and the common workers did not. The higher tariffs also allowed businesses to charge higher prices for goods in America that were least affordable to farmers and workers. The tariff issue became a type of class warfare. Western farmers and settlers resented Eastern bankers and businessmen profiting off the backs of their hard labor. Senator Blackburn championed the farmers and working men in his state and across the country.

Generally speaking, Democrats were opposed to high tariffs that hurt the farmer and worker, and Republicans supported high tariffs. While Congress had been deadlocked, the national surplus grew. By the Fifty-First Session, tariff battles were being won by protectionists who favored protecting American manufacturing, allowing the country to continue to grow.

Hand in hand with this condition, the Free Silver Movement dominated national politics before the 1896 Presidential campaign. Ever since the demonetization act of 1873, called "the Crime of '73," omitted the silver dollar from the list of authorized coins and tied the nation's monetary system to the gold standard, the issue had been debated in Congress and across the country. It was not resolved during Blackburn's decade in the House and continued while Blackburn served in the Senate. In 1878 while Blackburn served in the U.S. House, Congress passed the Bland-Allison Act, which restored the silver dollar as legal tender and required the U.S. Treasury to buy between two million dollars and four million dollars in silver each month and coin it into dollars. Farm prices improved for a while, but in 1887, land and farm prices collapsed again, and Congress responded by enacting the Sherman Silver Purchase Act of 1890, requiring the government to increase their monthly purchases by fifty percent. Unfortunately, in the years after 1890, the amount of gold in the U.S. Treasury dropped sharply, causing a panic in the spring of 1893. Conservatives said it was the Sherman Act that was the cause of the panic, and in 1893, Congress repealed it. It was debated extensively in the Senate and ultimately became the "cause célèbre" of the growing populist movement in the days leading up to the 1896 Presidential campaign.

Fifty-First Congress (March 4, 1889–March 3, 1891)

Senator Blackburn consistently championed Free Silver and other populist causes that he believed served the people. On December 30, 1895, a review of Senator Blackburn's career was published in the *Cincinnati Enquirer* in anticipation of the 1896 presidential election. The editor of the *Enquirer* asked the journalist Henry Smith to prepare it from the Congressional Record. It reflects the essential role Blackburn played in securing a soundly organized government for the District of Columbia that enabled the Capitol City to be "built up" to proudly represent the new country to the world. It reported that "Blackburn's long experience in public and political affairs, his intelligent judgment and wise counsel, combined with his great parliamentary knowledge and skill," were appreciated and fully recognized by Democratic leaders in caucuses and conferences. "The fact that Mr. Blackburn is, and for over six years has been, a member of the Democratic

'Steering Committee' of the Senate, is the most conclusive evidence of his standing in the councils of his party in that body," the report added. The review began near the end of what was called the "Gilded Age." The Gilded Age lasted from about 1870 to 1900. The term came from author Mark Twain's 1873 satire, *The Gilded Age: A Tale of Today*, which describes "the era of serious social problems masked by a thin gold gilding." The economic divide between the wealthy classes and the less fortunate was reflected in the divide in the political parties in the country, a divide that is seen again today.

The political deadlock in Congress that had lasted for several Congressional Sessions finally ended with the Fifty-First Congress. Republicans won control of both houses of Congress and the U.S. Presidency with Benjamin Harrison after the 1888 election. In 1889, there were forty-four states represented and nine non-voting members from the territories in the House, until six of those were admitted as states and a new territory was organized (Oklahoma). Both of Kentucky's U.S. Senators were Democrats: Blackburn and Beck. Senator Beck died in office, and on May 26, 1890, Democrat John G. Carlisle was elected by the state legislature to fill Beck's seat in the U.S. Senate. Nine of Kentucky's eleven U.S. Representatives were Democrats, including Carlisle until he moved over to the Senate when the Kentucky Legislature elected Democrat William P. Dickerson to fill his vacated seat.

The Speaker of the House, Thomas Reed of Maine, streamlined House rules and prevented the minority Republican Party from obstructing the legislative process. As a result of the rules changes and a unified government, the Fifty-First Congress became known as the "Billion Dollar Congress" that passed generous military pensions and approved long-stalled naval expansion. New economic pressures also resulted in the Sherman Silver Purchase Act and the Sherman Antitrust Act of 1890. The Fifty-First Congress met during the first two years of Republican U.S. President Benjamin Harrison's term. This Congress was based on the Tenth Census of the United States. The major legislation during this session included the Dependent Pension Act (1890), the Sherman Antitrust Act (1890), the Sherman Silver Purchase Act (1890), the Morrill Land-Grant Colleges Act (1890), the McKinley Tariff (1890), the Forest Reserve Act of 1891, the Land Revision Act of 1891, the Immigration Act of 1891, the Merchant

Marine Act of 1891 and the International Copyright Act (The Chace Act, 1891). In November 1889, North Dakota was admitted as the thirty-ninth state, South Dakota as the fortieth state, Montana as the forty-first state, and Washington as the forty-second state. On May 2, 1890, the new Oklahoma Territory was organized; on July 3, 1890, Idaho was admitted as the forty-third state; and on July 10, 1890, Wyoming was admitted as the forty-fourth state.

First Session, Fifty-First Congress (March 4, 1889–April 2, 1889)

Senator Blackburn was appointed fifth on Rules, seventh on Census, eighth on Naval Affairs, ninth on Railroads, and ninth on Territories. Later when a vacancy occurred on the Committee on Appropriations, Senator Blackburn was excused from the Committee on Territories and appointed to the better place on the Appropriations Committee, membership of which is considered an equivalent to the chairmanship of an ordinary committee. Blackburn was appointed conferee on the Post Office appropriation bill. He was reappointed Director to Columbia Hospital for Women and was appointed to the committee to attend the funeral of Kentucky Senator James B. Beck, with whom he had served in the Forty-Ninth, Fiftieth, and Fifty-First Congress until his death. He was also appointed as a Visitor to the Naval Academy. He introduced several bills, including one for the admission of Arizona into the Union; one relating to the Inspector General of the army; one for relief for various individuals; one to allow the Chesapeake & Ohio Railroad (C.O.) and Southwestern Railroad to maintain bridges; one relating to junk dealers and pawn brokers in the D.C.; one for a public building at Henderson, Kentucky; one for the relief of the Commissioner of the Sinking Fund of Louisville, Kentucky; one granting the use of the Louisville and Portland Canal Basin; one to protect the fish in the Potomac River; one for the settlement of accounts with railway companies; one to incorporate the St. Rose Industrial School; one granting land to the Vestry of Christ Church, in Washington, D.C.; and one for a public building at Winchester, Kentucky, among many others.

Senator Blackburn introduced joint resolutions, including one to print the eulogies on Senator Beck and the report of the Health Officer of the District of Columbia. He introduced bills, including one for a bridge across the Ohio River at Louisville, among others. He shared eulogies for Senator Beck and ex-Speaker Randall and spoke on the Potomac River Fisheries, on Senate Quorum, on Soldier's Home managers, on Washington Street Railroads, and on the Indian and Post Office Appropriation bills.

He was instrumental in causing the first electric lights to be installed in the White House at Washington.

> One hot night in the summer of 1890, Senator Blackburn called at the White House to see President Benjamin Harrison. He was ushered into a room used as a library, where the Republican President sat at a desk on which were drop-lights, fed by gas from a chandelier.
>
> 'Whew,' said Blackburn, as he fanned himself.
>
> It's the gas that makes it so hot, explained Mrs. Harrison.
>
> 'Wouldn't you rather have electric lights in the White House?' the gallant Senator asked.
>
> 'Yes, indeed,' replied the President's wife, 'but there is too much else that has to be done with the available appropriation.'
>
> 'Well, you shall have electric lights,' declared Blackburn emphatically.
>
> He offered a resolution in the Senate for wiring the executive mansion and for current for lighting to be supplied by 'the dynamo' that provided lights for the State, War and Navy building.
>
> At the same time Blackburn warned his colleagues not to oppose his resolution. It went through.

After the Session, Blackburn returned to his hometown of Versailles and spent the first week home in Lexington attending the race meeting. He was returning home with his friend Andrew Steele on October 22, 1890 when he was thrown from a buggy in his hometown of Versailles at three o'clock in the morning and suffered serious injuries. Both reported it was so dark that it was impossible to see where to drive when the horse passed Main Street and turned into a dark street back of Amsden's bank, close to Blackburn's home on Rose Hill, and the buggy hit something in the road and overturned. Blackburn suffered a broken collar bone, crushed right shoulder, and bruising, but he was able to recover in time to attend the marriage of his widowed daughter Terese Blackburn Stewart to Captain William Hall of the U.S. Army in Washington, D.C., on November 5, 1890.

Second Session, Fifty-First Congress (Dec 1, 1890–March 3, 1891)

Senator Blackburn was appointed conferee on four of the great appropriation bills. He was also appointed on the committee to attend the funeral of Admiral David D. Porter. After Senator Beck's death created a vacancy on one of the two most important committees of the Senate (Appropriation and Finance), Senator Blackburn was promoted to the Appropriation Committee, and Senator Carlisle was placed on the Finance Committee, showing the respect held for the Kentucky Senators.

Senator Blackburn introduced bills, including one to allow the Bowling Green & Northern Rail Road Company to bridge Green and Barren Rivers, one to incorporate the Mt. Pleasant & Rock Creek Park Railway Company, one to purchase a building for the use of the Senate, and other bills for relief of various individuals. Senator Blackburn spoke on army retired officers, on the Assistant Attorney-General for the Post Office Department, on a Bennington, Vermont battle monument. on the Civil Service Commission, on the pay of the District of Columbia Supreme Court Justices, on extra pay to employees, on the site location for the Government Printing Office, on silver coinage, on Utah legislative appointment, on points of order, on several appropriations bills, and for the relief of individuals.

On January 9, 1891, the Senate, as in Committee of the Whole, considered the bill to provide against the contraction of the currency, and Senator Blackburn made a long and elaborate speech in support of the amendment of Senator Stewart of Nevada that provided for the free coinage of silver, which was adopted. The speech was entitled "Free Coinage for the Masses," and was printed. Blackburn said, in part:

> MR. BLACKBURN: Mr. President: There has been so much said on behalf of the amendment which is pending before the Senate and so little in way of argument said against it, that it seems well nigh superfluous to continue this discussion, at least upon the part of the friends of the measure. And yet,

sir, I am not willing that this debate should close without bearing the testimony of my section and my people to the merits of the amendment that we are now considering. I am not willing to have it go to the country and to the world that this is simply an effort made by the representative from silver States, and that the rest of the country is indifferent to the result. There is not a silver mine within the limits of the great Commonwealth that sends me here, and yet I venture to assert that her people are as united, as earnest, as honest, and as clamorous in their demand for the free coinage of silver as are the people of Colorado, or California, or Idaho, or Nevada.

It would seem to an unprejudiced and fair-minded man that we, of all civilized countries in the world need a liberal per capita circulating medium when we come to consider the vast enterprises that are projected and are to-day and must for many years be in the process of completion, when we remember that we occupy a continent, and that the movement of its crops from ocean to ocean seeking seaboard transportation to the markets for which they are destined requires an outlay and an expenditure of money far in excess of that to which any pent up European country can possibly be subjected.

It would seem that these and many other considerations that may be submitted would entitle us to at least as large, as full a measure of per capita circulating medium as any of the countries of the Old World require or demand. And yet, sir, we have it not. These enterprises are required to go on, the crops of the country must be moved, its business must be maintained upon a relatively and comparatively small sum of money.

We are told by the official authorities of this Government that France, with a population of 38,250,000 people, is carrying in her circulation $900,000,000 of gold and $700,000,000 of silver and nearly $600,000,000 of outstanding notes, a total of metal and paper currency of $2,194,000,000 of money, which gives her 38,250,000 people a total per capita of $57.36. . . .

Great Britain carries to-day with her 38,000,000 people a gold circulation of $550,000,000, a silver circulation of $100,000,000, an outstanding note circulation of $190,000,000, a total of metallic and paper currency of $840,000,000, and a per capita of $22.01.

Germany carries with her 48,000,000 people $500,000,000 of gold to-day and $215,000,000 of silver. This, the single-standard country, this the nation that bows down in its fetish worship to gold, carries in her circulation to-day $500,000,000 of gold and $215,000,000 of silver, and she carries $275,000,000 of paper, and gives to her people a per capita of $20.63. Ours is $22.36. And yet, Mr. President, the gentlemen who oppose the passage of this amendment, they who see danger in the adoption of a free-coinage law, tell us that their apprehensions are based upon a flood of silver that is to pour in upon this country.

You have to-day in circulation but $116,000,000 of silver money. Of all these countries, Britain alone is below the silver circulation of the United States. Germany, which demonetized that metal, carries more than $2 of silver to our $1, whilst France carries well nigh $7 for every $1 that is in circulation in this country.

Mr. President, I have been listening and I have been reading the speeches made by those who oppose a free silver-coinage act. I have failed to find an argument or a suggestion that was entitled to serious consideration. . . .

The people demand free coinage and, what is more, they mean to have it. It is not in your power to deny it much longer. You have measured out your homeopathic doses of relief until they will no longer satisfy. . . .

The tillers of the soil throughout this land can endure no longer the burdens put upon their bowed, bent backs by injustice and partial legislation. They have at last determined to make their cause of grievance known and to demand that it be righted. . . .

During the sixteen years that I have been in Congress I have stood here as the earnest advocate of that metal's restoration to its old and honored place upon a fair, even plane of equality with gold. . . .

Mr. President, this debate has been so thoroughly exhaustive, so elaborate in detail, upon the part of the advocates of this

> amendment, that it would not only be unnecessary and out of taste, but smack of vanity for me to offer any additional suggestions. I trust, sir, that the day is not far distant, I trust that the time has come, and that ere the ides of March shall be ushered in the Senators who represent the sovereign States of the greatest Republic upon which the sun of God has ever shone, and the Representatives of the bravest, fairest, manliest, and most intelligent people upon this earth will unite in doing one act of justice—restoring silver to the place and to the position which it held and which it honored for more than three thousand years.

The bill passed, but not all agreed with him. An editorial in the *New York Times* chastised Senator Blackburn for his speech and argued that the Act of 1873 was not evil, corrupt, or secured for wrong or malicious reasons by members of Wall Street.

Fifty-Second Congress (March 4, 1891–March 3, 1893)

In the 1890 elections, Democrats won control of the House, but the Senate and presidency remained Republican. Both of Kentucky's Senators were Democrats: Blackburn and Carlisle. Forty-four states were represented in Congress and four non-voting members represented the four remaining territories in 1891. Ten of the eleven Kentucky U.S. Representatives were Democrats. Despite the divided Congress, cooperation enabled this Congress to enact several laws, including an eight-hour workday for federal blue-collar workers, laws that mandated new safety requirements on railway companies, and the renewal of the Chinese Exclusion Act for ten years. In foreign policy, Republican President Benjamin Harrison submitted a Hawaiian annexation treaty, but Congress adjourned before considering it. Despite the ambitious legislative record, this Congress failed to address the country's mounting financial crises, and as the economy teetered on the edge of recession, populist unrest began popping up across the country. Senator Blackburn continued to champion the populist causes of allowing the minting of silver into coins without limiting the amount of coins that could be minted and lowering the tariffs and taxes on imported foreign manufactured goods.

The United States Presidential election of 1892 was a rematch of the contest between former Democratic President Cleveland and incumbent Republican President Harrison when both ran for a second term. Cleveland won the popular and electoral vote and became the first person in American history to be elected to a second, non-consecutive presidential term. The country continued to grow rapidly, as did the need for Congress to issue legislation to manage the complex changes.

Senator Blackburn championed the causes of the working man on the Senate floors and in the public, giving speeches on the issues facing the country, but his extensive traveling and making speeches took a toll. During the summer recess from Congress, Senator Blackburn suffered a stroke of paralysis at the home of a friend on August 28, 1891. He was very sick for a while but recovered rapidly. Undaunted, as soon as he was well enough, he returned to delivering speeches championing the farmer, worker, and Democratic party principles.

Before the general election, Senator Blackburn spoke at the October 30, 1891 meeting of the New York Business Men's Democratic Association of the Ninth and Fifteenth Wards, which was held in Chickering Hall in New York City. The crowds were so large that it overflowed out onto Eighteenth Street and resulted in an outdoor meeting. Both meetings endorsed the Democratic New York State ticket enthusiastically.The tariff issue was paramount to the Democratic Party, even supplanting the silver issue. President Cleveland was the leader of the pro-business "Bourbon Democrats," the conservative Democrats who had supported Tilden in 1876 and who opposed high tariffs, Free Silver, inflation, imperialism, and subsidies to businesses, farmers, or veterans. Senator Blackburn agreed with some of the policies, but was a long-standing Free Silver advocate. However, he was conciliatory on the silver issue when he talked about the Presidential candidates and was willing to support Cleveland if the tariff was reduced.

Senator Blackburn supported Cleveland, who became the Twenty-fourth U.S. President. Unfortunately, Bourbon Democrats were hands-off capitalists who did not like to interfere with the competitive course of business. When the Panic of 1893 arrived, Cleveland did very little, and Bourbon Democrats were disliked in general thereafter. It would be difficult for Senator Blackburn to distinguish himself from the failed policies of the Bourbon Democrats in his campaigns after 1893.

First Session, Fifty-Second Congress (Dec 7, 1891–Aug 5, 1892)

At the opening of the First Session of the Fifty-Second Congress, Senator Blackburn was placed fifth on the Committee on Rules, seventh on Census, seventh on Railroads, eighth on Naval Affairs, ninth on Organization, ninth on Conduct and Expenditures of the Executive Departments, and tenth on Appropriations. A few weeks later when Senator Hill of New York recovered from his illness and returned to the Senate, Senator Blackburn resigned from the Committee on Expenditures of the Executive Departments in order to give him the place. Senator Blackburn was appointed six times on the conference committees on important appropriation bills.

Senator Blackburn continued his extensive work on re-organizing and improving Washington, D.C. as seen by the various bills introduced in this Session. He introduced many different bills, including a bill on the settlers in Arizona Territory; a bill to remit the penalties on the gunboats *Concord* and *Boatwright*; a bill to repeal the license tax on produce dealers in Washington, D.C. markets; a bill to fix the salaries of the Justices of the Supreme Court of the District of Columbia; a bill to amend the interstate commerce law; a bill for the relief of the citizens of Jefferson County, Kentucky; a bill granting the right of way to the Kentucky and Indiana Bridge Company; a bill to repeal the act to forfeit the charter of the Metropolitan Railroad Company in the District of Columbia; a bill to allow a bridge over the Hudson River in New York; a bill for the defense of the Pacific Coast; a bill for the removal of the Papago Indians; a bill to protect the fish in the Potomac River; a bill for the relief of settlers on the railroad land grants; a bill to settle accounts with railroad companies; a bill to amend the timber-culture act; a bill to establish an assay office at Tucson, Arizona [to determine the quantity of gold, silver or other metal in an ore, alloy, etc.]; a bill to remit the penalty of the dynamite cruiser *Vesuvius*; and a bill to allow war claims. Senator Blackburn offered a resolution on the removal of garbage in the District of Columbia. He spoke on the Senate floor about many of the aspects to promote and improve the Capital, including remarks he made on the District of Columbia appropriation bill, on garbage service, on street railroads, and on the sanitary condition of the capitol. Senator Blackburn made many reports from his committees, including reports on the Hudson River Bridge and a portrait of General Thomas, among others.

Second Session, Fifty-Second Congress (Dec 5, 1892–March 3, 1893)

During the Second Session Senator Blackburn was appointed by Republican Vice President Levi P. Morton as one of the Tellers on the part of the Senate to participate in the counting of the votes for President and Vice President in the joint convention held in the House. He was also appointed on the committee to attend the funeral of Senator Kenna of West Virginia and was appointed a conferee on one appropriation bill. Senator Blackburn introduced a bill to incorporate the East End Electric Railway Company and for the relief of two individuals. He introduced a resolution on the death of Senator Kenna. He spoke on the Senate floor about the Cincinnati Bridge, the election laws, the Geological Survey, the Hudson River Bridge, the post office appropriation bill, as well as on public land laws, various civil appropriation bills, and a eulogy for Representative Kendall and Senator Kenna.

Fifty-Third Congress (March 4, 1893–March 3, 1895)

Democrats won control of both the Fifty-Third Congress and the White House after the 1892 elections with President Cleveland and Vice President Adlai Stevenson. Kentucky's Senators Blackburn and William Lindsay were both Democrats, and ten of Kentucky's eleven U.S. Representatives were Democrats. Forty-four states were represented in Congress and four non-voting members represented the four remaining territories. The apportionment of seats in the House was based on the Eleventh Census of the United States. The Democratic control of both the Congress and the White House enabled the Democrats to repeal the Reconstruction-era Force Acts that mandated federal supervision of Southern elections. Party control, however, crumbled as the economy went into a sharp and deep downturn, and eight thousand businesses went bust in six months. This is when the champions of the gold standard were able to successfully repeal the Sherman Silver Purchase Act in response to the economic crisis, "The Panic of 1893."

It was a tumultuous time in the Democratic Party, and a disappointing contrast with the many lavish celebrations for the second election of President Cleveland. One of those lavish election events was held in the Pension Building, which was "transformed," with elaborate decorations at the inaugural ball for the thousands of people holding tickets for the social celebration of the change in the Administration. There was a large fountain in the center with a platform for the two bands that played. Mrs. Joseph Blackburn of Kentucky wore gold and blue brocade with duchesse lace, and their daughters Miss Corinne Blackburn wore white silk embroidered in pearls and Miss Lucile Blackburn wore pink silk and lace. Mrs. Luke Blackburn wore pearl satin, flounced with point lace.

Special Session, Fifty-Third Congress (Aug 7, 1893–Nov 3, 1893)

Committees were reorganized at the opening of the Session now that the Senate was controlled by the Democrats, and Blackburn was given better treatment than before. He was made Chairman of the important Committee on Rules and placed third on Naval Affairs, third on Territories, fourth on Appropriations, fifth on Women's Suffrage, and sixth on Railroads. He was also again appointed on the committee to notify the President that the Senate was organized and ready to business. In 1893, Delaware, Idaho, Montana, Nevada, and North Dakota had one "at-large" U.S. Representative, and South Dakota and Washington had two "at-large" Representatives elected from their new states. There were also four delegates from the Arizona Territory, New Mexico Territory, Oklahoma Territory and Utah Territory.

Senator Blackburn introduced several bills for the relief of various individuals and a bill to remit the penalties on the gunboats *Concord* and *Bennington*. He offered amendments to the bill to repeal the purchase of silver bullion act and offered a resolution on the amendment to the rules relating to the disposition of business. Blackburn made several remarks on the floor on the bond issue, the copies of the Senate archives, the officers of the Senate, and, of course, the silver issue.

On October 4, 1893, Senator Blackburn delivered a speech on the Senate floor urging the country to return to using silver for coin money, known as the "Remonetization of Silver" speech. It was made while the Senate was considering the bill to repeal a part of the act that had been approved July 14, 1890, entitled "An act directing the purchase of silver bullion and the issue of Treasury notes thereon, and for other purposes." Senator Blackburn spoke against the limiting terms in the bill and traced the history of silver up to 1893. He said that the Sherman Act of 1890 was a bad law that should have never been enacted and that it had another purpose of making "the silver metal ridiculous in the eyes of the world as a money metal by purchasing it in large quantities, refusing its mintage, and storing it as pig metal, not to be used even in the arts." While some Senators thought that Sherman Act was the cause of the country's financial troubles in 1893, Senator Blackburn did not, even though he agreed that it was part of the problem: "No financial disaster ever came upon a people save from over investments in the shape of speculation or from a contraction of the currency."

After condemning the act of 1873 and reading one of his former speeches that also condemned the demonetization of silver by the act of 1873 on the Senate floor, Senator Blackburn renewed his argument for the use of silver and gold for the nation's coin in a lengthy speech. He recited the history of the use of silver for money by other countries. Senator Blackburn said, "I protest against striking down the silver metal here, because of the burden that it will add to the debtor classes of this county, and not alone because of the unfair advantage it will give to the creditors."

Then Senator Blackburn outlined the national legislative changes that were needed to put the country back on sound financial and democratic footing as he continued his speech on the floor after many interruptions:

> MR. BLACKBURN: Mr. President, the repeal of the Sherman Law will not cure the troubles that we are under. We must go further. The treatment must be more thorough and it must be more heroic. You must revise your tariff system. You must strike out and eliminate its prohibitory feature and in many cases those that approximate so closely to prohibition. You must broaden your markets for the products of your labor. You must open up a wider trade. You must build up a demand for the productions of American labor. You must remember to feed the other nations with the surplus of our products. You must bring the tariff down to a strictly revenue basis. Your must strike from it the features of a class legislation which have enabled less than 25,000 of our people to put into

their pockets one-half of the aggregated wealth of the whole country, leaving the remaining 67,000,000 to divide among themselves the remainder.

The Sherman Law did not do that. It was a system of cunningly devised class legislation, not only in the taxing law and the tariff system, but in the monetary system as well. You must revise and you must remodel the financial system of your country. You must go back where the Constitution puts you and place your country upon the bimetallic basis, which the organic law of this land declares shall alone constitute the standard value in this country. You must adopt the gold and silver standard according to the provisions and the promises and the platforms of all the parties on even terms; and then the paper money that is issued to the people should be issued based upon that bimetallic standard, and it should be issued directly by the Government and not filtered to the people through the agency of petted and fostered national banks. . . .

You must reduce your expenditures to an economic and an honest basis. You must purge your pension roll, which now reaches one hundred and sixty-odd million dollars every year, of the heavy percentage of peculation and fraud by which we all know it is encumbered. You must enact an income tax law, forcing the wealth of the country to bear its just share of the burdens of Government.

When these things are done, if in God's providence they may ever be done, then financial disasters and panics will be supplanted by prosperity and progress; strikes will be heard of no more; tramps will give place to well paid and contented labor; we will then exchange hunger for happiness and tears for smiles amid the toiling millions of this land; every industry—agricultural, manufacturing, or mining—will gain new life; and then we may hope to attain the destiny to which we are entitled—that of the freest, the most prosperous, the happiest people upon the earth. . . .

The safest tribunal to which an appeal can be addressed is the sense of dignity, the sense of fairness, the conservatism, the manhood that constitutes this body. I appeal to those who sit around me, who have been trusted to guard the fortunes

> and to guide the destinies of the party to which we belong, lead us, I pray you, to a fair, a righteous, a speedy settlement of this vexed issue. [Applause in the galleries.]

Despite Senator Blackburn's pleas, the Senate and House passed President Cleveland's bill to repeal the purchasing clause of the Sherman Act. However, the partial legislation was too little and too late. President Cleveland and the Democratic Congress were unable to reverse the national depression, resulting in many Democrats losing their political office in the next elections.

Second Session, Fifty-Third Congress (Dec 4, 1893–Aug 28, 1894)

Senator Blackburn was appointed second member on a special committee on the Existing Public Distress, in addition to all the regular standing committees. He was appointed seven times a conferee on important appropriation bills and was twice appointed on committees to attend the funerals of Senator Vance of North Carolina and Representative Lisle of Kentucky. He introduced several bills during this session, including several for the relief of individuals and bills to suppress gambling in the District of Columbia. He introduced bills to amend the act for the protection of fish in the Potomac River, repeal the tax on State banks circulation, and amend the act to repeal the timber culture act. He introduced several resolutions, including one inquiring into the accounts of the Baltimore and Elk Ridge Railroad. He made several remarks on the Senate floor on various matters, including remarks about an amendment to the rules, on Bookmaking in the District of Columbia, on closing the Senate Chamber to the public, on Hawaiian affairs, on the death of Representative Lisle, on railroad stations in territories, on Senatorial investigation, on the District of Columbia post office, and on army, diplomatic and consular appropriations bills, as well as other matters. He also made remarks on Oklahoma town sites, which was so appreciated that the town of Blackburn, Oklahoma, was named for him. He submitted three reports to the Senate from the Conference Committees, three reports from the Appropriation Committee, three reports from the Naval Committee, two reports from the Committee on Rules, and two reports from the Committee on Territories.

Meanwhile, the Blackburn family was active socially. Some of the events were reported in the newspapers. On January 19, 1894, Lieutenant and Mrs. William Irwin gave a dinner in honor of the Secretary of the Navy and Miss Herbert [daughter of the Secretary of the Navy]. The guests attending the dinner included Secretary and Miss Herbert, Senator and Mrs. Blackburn, Mr. and Mrs. Benjamin Micou, General and Mrs. Adolph Meyer, Miss Barbour and Benton McMillin. Another entry in the paper noted that Mrs. Blackburn attended a luncheon given by Mrs. Albert A. Wilson in honor of the wife of the Vice President Adlai Stevenson on March 2, 1894. Guests included Mrs. Joseph C. S. Blackburn, Mrs. John G. Carlisle, and others. On March 16, 1894 Mrs. Blackburn and one of her daughters attended a breakfast given by Colonel and Mrs. Henry.

In the Senate, there was turmoil, with public allegations of the bribery of U.S. Senators, which led to an internal Senate investigation. On May 17, 1894, the Senate adopted a resolution to investigate each member of the Senate to appoint a committee to determine if there was any bribery or corruption of that body. All Senators were investigated, and two stated that they had been approached, but it appeared that the corruption rose higher up to the level of the Secretary of the Treasury Carlisle and the Finance Committee, but nothing ever came of it.

After the Panic of 1893, the country was unsettled and unhappy with the Democrats. This made it an unusually important year in the politics of the country. The elections gave the people of the country the opportunity to elect an entirely new House of Representatives to change the complexion of the legislative branch of the national government.

The local elections in Kentucky were held on November 6, 1894. They were less dramatic than the national elections because only four judges of the Court of Appeals needed to be elected after the new Kentucky Constitution increased the number of judges from four to seven, and three Railroad Commissioners needed to be elected for the first time. The state legislature still elected U.S. Senators, and it elected Democrat William Lindsay to a second term in the Senate. Lindsay's first six-year term expired on March 4, 1895. His second term ran from March 4, 1895 to March 4, 1901.

The general state election in Kentucky was held in early November 1895 to elect a Governor, Lieutenant Governor, Secretary of State, Treasurer, Auditor, Superintendent of Public Instruction,

Commissioner of Agriculture, Attorney General, and a Register of the Land Office. In addition, the newly elected state legislature elected the U.S. Senator to succeed J.C.S. Blackburn, whose term expired in 1897. It was an unusually important election year in Kentucky for Blackburn and the country.

Third Session, Fifty-Third Congress (Dec 3, 1894–March 3, 1895)

Blackburn was appointed nine times to important conference committees, and later in the session, he was added to the Committee on Printing. Significantly, he introduced a bill for the relief of Don Carlos Buell, who was a renowned U.S. Army officer who fought in the Seminole War, the Mexican-American War, and the Civil War, in which he led Union armies in the two great battles of Shiloh and Perryville. Senator Blackburn also introduced bills to sell burial sites to the Congressional Cemetery or the Washington Parish Burial Ground located at 1801 E Street, SE in Washington, D.C. on the west bank of the Anacostia River. Senator Blackburn also introduced a bill authorizing an examination of the Navy and Marine Corps officers and for a public building at Paris, Kentucky. He introduced a resolution to print the Senate Manual that was adopted. He made several remarks during this session on a wide variety of matters. For example, he spoke nine times on the army appropriation bill, seven times on the diplomatic appropriation bill, and six times on the naval appropriation bill. He also spoke on the fortification appropriation bill, on the post office appropriation bill, on sugar bounty, on distribution of documents, on navy court martial, on the Honduras Lottery Company, on public buildings at Paris, Kentucky, and other subjects. He gave two eulogies: one for Representative Lisle and another for Senator Vance. Senator Blackburn also made seven reports from Conference Committees, five reports from the Appropriation Committee, seven from the Naval Committee, and one from the Committee on Rules. During all of Senator Blackburn's twenty-eight years of service in the U.S. Senate and the U.S. House of Representatives, he presented every petition sent to him, running up into the thousands.

It was widely known that Senator Blackburn was not a wealthy man, but he was known as a generous man. His intimate friends agreed that at no time in his long Congressional career did he ever spare time or money in looking after the best interests of the people of the state of Kentucky. No deserving or worthy applicant from the Blue Grass State ever applied to him for aid or assistance in any direction that was not willingly and freely given, if it was in his power to do so.

On October 1, 1895 on Senator Blackburn's birthday, Lucile, his youngest daughter, and Thomas F. Lane of Summit, New Jersey, were married at noon in the St. Matthews Church. Lucile was given away by her father. She wore an imported bridal gown of black and green matelasse combined with a light brocade. She wore a large black hat, covered with plumes and faced with rose-pink velvet, and a short wrap of dark-green velvet and point lace. Lucile's bridal bouquet was made up of American beauty roses tied together with green ribbons and lilies of the valley.

The next morning, the wedding party held a breakfast at the Normandie Hotel, including Senator and Mrs. Blackburn; Miss Corinne Blackburn; Mr. Joseph Blackburn, Jr.; Major and Mrs. [Terese Blackburn Stewart] Hall; Miss Voorhees, Lucile's school friend; Captain and Mrs. Stephen Rand, Lucile's godmother; Lieutenant Niblack; Logan Carlisle; and Alfred Lane. Later in the afternoon, the newlyweds headed for New York, stopping in to visit with Mr. Lane's mother at her home in Summit, New Jersey, who had been unable to attend the wedding due to ill health. The couple spent most of the winter in southern France.

Thomas Lane gave Lucile a diamond sunburst as a bridal gift. He gave her a large collection of jewelry that had once belonged to Tsar Nicholas II of Russia as an engagement present. Senator and Mrs. Blackburn gave their daughter a string of pearls, a case of silver, and a set of duchess rose point flounces and bertha to enhance her fashionable wardrobe. After the wedding, Senator Blackburn's family returned to Kentucky, where the Senator faced a difficult campaign year.

Chapter Twenty-Three

1896 Presidential Election

"You Shall Not Crucify Mankind upon a Cross of Gold"
– William J. Bryan

Despite Senator Blackburn's clear warnings and pleas on the Senate floor, the purchasing clause of the Sherman law of 1890 was struck down, and the country returned to the previous policy demonetizing silver and using gold only for money. Farmers in the South and West protested loudly and blamed greedy East Coast bankers for the depression and resumed their demand for the unlimited coinage of silver. In 1893 Kentucky's new state constitution directed that elections be held in November. The Populists lost dramatically. By 1894 unemployment, labor conflict, and destitution were rampant. Many believed that an apocalypse was near.

With the 1894 Congressional elections, the Democratic Party collapsed in the West. The Republican Party did the same in the South. The People's Party became the main opponent to the dominant mainstream party in both sections, with William Jennings Bryan leading the charge for the Populists. A fluid three-way political struggle for power seemed probable for the all-important 1896 general election.

Senator Blackburn was a leader of the Free Silver wing of the Democratic party and took a conspicuous part in the memorable fight for Free Silver in the National Democratic Convention of 1896 in Chicago at the Coliseum. There, Senator Blackburn's name was presented by the Kentucky delegation under instructions of the Kentucky Democratic State Convention as its choice for President. He was one of four candidates receiving the highest number of votes in the balloting, having received forty-one votes. He was presented to the National Convention by J.S. Rhea of Kentucky, who spoke of his candidate as "Joe" Blackburn because to Kentuckians he was "Joe" Blackburn, and that meant everything:

> It was true that he was from the South, and had been a Confederate soldier, but his candidacy was not a sectional one. If nominated and elected, he would be no sectional President. His whole public career, covering a third of a century, had been a lifelong expression of his sympathy with labor. He had shown himself the peer of the ablest men in Congress. His voice had been heard in forty-five States in advocacy of Democratic principles. He was modest, but not wanting in that finer ambition which made men pure, his honor impregnable, and his simplicity sublime. [Cheers].
>
> Mr. Rhea added that if it was the will of this convention that Mr. Blackburn should remain in his present field of service, his voice would be raised in behalf of any other candidate that might be named.

Before the Democratic Convention in Chicago, a reporter for the June 28, 1896 edition of New York's *The Journal* said:

> Senator Joseph C. S. Blackburn, of Kentucky ...is a candidate for the Presidential nomination. His friends do not regard his chances as at all of the callow or pinfeather variety.
>
> 'Not that I expect to be named,' said Blackburn, as he leaned back in his chair and cast a bright and satisfied glance about the circle of Kentucky gentlemen who had met to do him honor. 'It is hardly to be expected that a time has come when a man who honestly wore the gray in the battle-shaken sixties can look for the White House. It's a trifle too much to expect from the North to ask it to name an old gray ex-Confederate President. And, as I said, I've no notion of the sort. But,' continued Blackburn, and his eye moistened with the energy of sentiment that possessed him, 'if the time has come, it would make thirteen States once in rebellion now as loyal as the most utterly loyal of the North swell with a pride and happiness to which they have been stranger for a third of a century.'

> 'So far as my candidacy is involved,' Blackburn went on, 'my State makes me her choice. I will have the twenty-six votes Kentucky takes to Chicago, and that is honor enough for any man.'

The reporter noted that Senator Blackburn said he would be pleased to run for Vice-President:

> 'While Blackburn is a candidate and the choice of Kentucky for a White House nomination, the Senator does not ape humility when he says he does not look to be named. However, if one were to get his honest hope in the business, one would find that he does see a Vice-Presidency among the possibilities of coming time. If the convention would name Blackburn for Vice-President, Kentucky's cup would overflow. A serious effort will be made to land Blackburn for second place. As to how Kentucky would go in November Blackburn had no fears.
>
> 'It will be Democratic by a tremendous majority,' he said. 'Every Southern State will be Democratic. McKinley can't win this fight....
>
> 'Finance is the overshadowing question,' he said. 'The West and South are in the saddle. It will be free silver. All else may as well stand aside and witness the glory of its coming.'

Senator Blackburn accepted the endorsement and told the four thousand delegates that "the gold standard has dominated for over twenty years until the masses are impoverished." He blamed the depression on the gold men in the Administration who had set the course for the American economy for the last two decades. He said, "Christ with a lash drove from the temple, a better set of men than those who for twenty years have shaped the financial policy of this country." The Democratic Party Platform of 1896 specifically supported the free and unlimited coinage of both silver and gold at the ratio of 16 to 1, the tariff for purposes of revenue only, stricter control of trusts and consolidated railways, Cuba's independence, improvements to the country's waterways, and the admission of the territories of New Mexico, Arizona, and Oklahoma in the Union as States. They also embraced the integrity of the dual scheme of government established by the founders and were opposed to interest-bearing bonds, the national banks, waste in government, government interference in local affairs, life-tenure in civil service, and the importation of pauper labor to compete with American labor. The convention was raucous and emotion-filled as conventions can be. At the convention, Senator George G. Vest Democrat from Missouri gave a speech in support of his nomination of Democrat Richard P. Bland, U.S. Representative from Missouri, known as "Silver Dick," as the so-called "logical candidate" that represented the sentiments of the convention. Bland had introduced the first free-coinage measure in Congress and was the author of the Seigniorage bill, which passed both houses but was vetoed by President Cleveland. Seigniorage is the difference between the value of money and the cost to produce and distribute it. For metal coins, it is basically a tax added to the total price of a coin to cover the costs of production of the coin. A customer with silver or gold had to pay the tax to the mint, which was then sent to the U.S. Treasury under then President Grover Cleveland.

By 1896, former U.S. Representative from Nebraska William Jennings Bryan, "the Boy Orator of the Platte," had become the star of the Free-Silver Populist movement. During the opening of the convention Bryan gave a rousing speech, and if nominations had been in order that day, Bryan would have swept the convention in the afternoon. He made his famous "Cross of Gold" speech in closing the debate on the party platform at the Democratic National Convention in Chicago and became the Democratic Party's nominee for President in 1896. "It is the issue of 1776 over again," he said as he came to the end of his speech. He said that America would not wait for permission from other countries to have Free Silver. "We shall restore bimetallism, and then let England have bimetallism because the United States have."

The last lines of that famous speech were:

> If they dare to come out in the open field and defend the gold standard as a good thing, we shall fight them to the uttermost, having behind us the producing masses of the nation and the world. Having behind us the commercial interests and the laboring interests and all the toiling masses, we shall answer their demands for a gold standard by saying to them, you shall not press down upon the brow of labor this

> crown of thorns. [Here 'he moved his hands down the sides of his head, his fingers slowly drawing invisible spikes about his temples, blood dripping from the scratches....'] You shall not crucify mankind upon a cross of gold.

With those famous lines, he thrust his "arms out at right angles, chest forward, and head back, the crucified man personified" and "held this pose for a few moments, then his arms fell to his sides, he stepped back, and his chin dropped. A second or so later, he straightened, turned, and walked off the stage, the hall in what the *Atlantic Constitution* called 'fearful silence.'"

The convention was quiet for a moment and then exploded. The floor was in a frenzy of emotion. Bryan had masterfully captured the political moment. There was some support for Senator Blackburn, who had votes in California, Virginia, and West Virginia, but there were not enough votes to launch Blackburn as the nominee. Out of the several nominees, there was "the dark horse William Jennings Bryan, who had long ago decided he should be president, though he may have been the only one to think so." Neither Blackburn nor Bryan was the obvious choice at the outset of the convention, but Bryan's closing speech made him the man for the hour. Voting began with several ballots, and when the clerks finished their tally, Bryan was in the lead.

After Bryan was nominated, Blackburn willingly campaigned for him and the Democratic Party on the Populist Platform of Free Silver. During the Bryan campaign, Senator Blackburn stumped in Kentucky "from Mill's Point to the Mouth of the Big Sandy," as he would say. He campaigned in other states to boost the Free Silver cause.

When it came to choosing a running mate for Bryan that could unite the divides in the Democratic Party, Senator Blackburn promoted Ohio newspaper publisher John McLean as Bryan's vice presidential candidate, whose fortune could underwrite the campaign. However, Ohio's Bimetallic Democratic National Committee man Allen W. Thurman said McLean was unreliable, and he was passed over in favor of Arthur Sewall. Sewall was a millionaire shipbuilder who owned banks and railroads and was reliably Free Silver but disturbingly wealthy, although his wealth could help with the campaign. It was decided. Bryan's Democratic running mate was Arthur M. Sewall, but it was a choice that Populists found unacceptable and one that gave undecided voters a reason to not vote Democratic. Even when the People's Party nominated Bryan for President and Populist Thomas E. Watson for Vice President, voters were not pleased.

The Democratic National Committee feared that New York would not vote for Bryan in the general election and sent Senator Blackburn to Tammany Hall to appeal to New York Democrats. As Senator Blackburn described the Democratic Platform in a speech in Tammany Hall in New York on September 29, 1896:

> The question that you have got to decide in this contest in November is not a question between parties. If it be a question between classes, God knows we didn't raise it. The issue that you are to determine, stripped [sic] of all its arguments [sic], presented nakedly, is simply whether the money power or [sic] the people are to rule this country.
>
> You will settle it one way or the other. It is a question between the plutocrat on the one side and the Democrat upon the other. (Applause.) It is a question between the bondholders on the one side and the plough holders on the other side. (Applause.)...I don't know what this narrow strip of earth between the Allegheny Mountains and the Atlantic Ocean means to do in November, but I think I do know what that great empire west of the Allegheny Mountains means to do. Across to the Mississippi and across the Mississippi to the Rockies, and from that to the Sierra Nevada, and from that to the Pacific seaboard, the West and the South, the great producing sections of the country, have determined that the day of ring rule has ended, and that the people of this country are the masters of their own destinies, and mean to make their laws under the guidance of a people's candidate. (Applause.)...Decide this question between the masses and the classes. Take no counsel of prejudice. Do not listen to pressure. Let your best and soberest judgment guide you in the premises and make that verdict, and make it right as an honest man, make it according to your consciences, and the great God who guides the destinies of nations and all men will approve it, and God will give victory to the right in this great contest. In fact, the Democratic National Committee sent Senator Blackburn all over the country, speaking on behalf of

> Bryan and the Democratic Party. He spoke in New York, New Mexico, Maryland, North Carolina, South Carolina, Georgia, Alabama, Kentucky, and Florida.

Despite his best efforts, the Democratic cause lost its momentum when the economic situation in the country started to shift, and farm prices rose by the end of the year, even as silver prices fell. This destroyed the Free Silver party's argument that linked Free Silver and higher farm prices. As farmers went to the market with their fall harvest, wheat prices were at a record high and corn prices were higher in December and again in March. Local prices for products were also strong for butter, eggs, and other products. It was the best year for farmers in decades. Bryan had said such a turnabout was possible only under Free Silver, which was completely at odds with the experience of farmers across the country in 1896. As a result the People's Party lost some of its relevance as the economy improved, and this—combined with a resurgence of patriotism after the Spanish-American War of 1898—played a role in destroying Populism.

Ultimately, the Republican candidate William McKinley defeated Democrat William Jennings Bryan in one of the most complex and dramatic races in American history. McKinley's well-organized campaign at the local levels proved to be critical. McKinley outspent Bryan by a factor of five with a 3.5 million dollar budget in the 1896 campaign. The Republicans continued to outspend Bryan over the coming campaigns. Although Bryan gave an astonishing number of speeches in his lifetime and ran for President three times (in 1896, 1900, and 1908), he was defeated each time. Republican McKinley won in 1896, Republican Theodore Roosevelt won in 1900, and Republican William Howard Taft won in 1908. Bryan was later the Forty-First U.S. Secretary of State for President Woodrow Wilson from 1913 until 1915, when he resigned. Bryan was a pacifist opposed to World War I. Throughout his life, he remained true to his beliefs: he was a devout Presbyterian and a populist who favored Free Silver because it reduced the power of money and gave more money to the people. He was opposed to banks and their gold standard, and he was a prohibitionist and an opponent to Darwinism on religious grounds.

In 1900, a Republican majority in Congress enacted the Gold Standard Act, which made gold the sole standard for all currency. This act required the U.S. Treasury to keep a minimum gold reserve of 150 million dollars and authorized the issuance of bonds to protect that minimum. The sound-money gold men of the two parties believed that the use of both silver and gold would cheat creditors by creating "cheap" money. In 1913 the Federal Reserve Act completely overhauled the U.S. monetary system and ended the silver debate when it created a new monetary system for the United States by setting up a new central banking system of the United States of America with authority to issue Federal Reserve Notes as legal tender or what we know as the U.S. Dollar. The Silver debate was over.

The defeat of the Free Silver cause at the national level was a blow to Blackburn's political career. It was going to be tough to keep his seat in the U.S. Senate.

Chapter Twenty-Four

Joe Blackburn Went Down with His Colors Flying

The split between the Free Silver Democrats and the Sound Money Democrats in Kentucky caused problems for the Party in selecting agreeable candidates for the 1896 elections for Governor and U.S. Senator to succeed Senator Blackburn. Early on, the battles showed that the Silverites were losing ground.

The Sound Money men in the Kentucky Democratic Convention won the first battle with the adoption of a Sound Money platform based on the gold standard. Surprisingly, in conciliation for winning this major achievement, the Sound Money men then allowed the Free Silver Democrats to name the candidates for Governor and Lieutenant Governor. Not surprisingly, they in turn nominated Free Silver Parker Watkins "Wat" Hardin for Governor. The editor of the *Evening Post* was so indignant by the choice that he refused to list Hardin as one of the candidates. The *Press-Transcript,* Lexington's paper, and the *Courier-Journal,* Louisville's paper, listed the name of P. Hardin but added nothing to support the candidate who did not support the Democratic Party platform. But this rebellion against the Democratic Party Platform was short-lived as other Free Silver candidates for treasurer and secretary of state were beaten at the convention. It was a painful reminder of the weakness of the Free Silver movement and nearly caused the Kentucky Democratic Convention to break out into open fighting.

The governor's race was decided by popular election in the fall of 1895. William Bradley won the governorship of Kentucky by nine thousand votes, the first Republican in the position for thirty years, since the end of the Civil War. The Senate named Democrat William Goebel president pro tem and Republican Charles Blandford speaker, which meant that Kentucky had a Republican Governor and a state legislature that was equally divided between the two parties. The stage was set in the state legislature to battle over the selection of the next U.S. Senator to succeed Senator Blackburn, beginning with the Fifty-Fifth Congress. In 1895 and continuing until the Seventeenth Amendment to the U.S. Constitution was adopted in 1913, the state legislature chose the two U.S. Senators from the state for a six-year term. The drafters of the Constitution thought that the state legislatures would align with the national government when voting for U.S. Senators. The selection of the U.S. Senator came up for vote early in the session. Silver Democrats were determined to return Joe Blackburn, but many Sound Money Democrats were strongly opposed to him. The Democratic caucus could not agree on the choice, which suited Republicans, who hoped to benefit from the split in Democratic Party. The chaos in the Democratic Party made the outcome of the election uncertain for Senator Blackburn.

At the beginning of the year 1895, the outlook for Senator Blackburn was rosy. It looked like he was going to be able to run unopposed for a third term in his Senate seat. Secretary Carlisle had announced early in January of 1895 that he would not run for the U.S. Senate seat until Wat Hardin disrupted the balance in the state Democratic Party. President Cleveland and Secretary Carlisle were watching the turn of events, and by the end of June, it seemed inevitable that Carlisle would be forced to run against Blackburn. Many felt that Sound Money Carlisle represented the state's true Democratic sentiment and that Free Silver Blackburn was on the wrong side of the issue. Most agreed that the situation would be different had Blackburn refrained from endorsing the silver idea.

> No self-seeking politician ever made a more fatal mistake than did Blackburn when he made the silver issue the chief factor in his candidacy.
>
> A surprising result of the recent events in Kentucky is the lack of sympathy shown here for Blackburn. A great many people who have watched his course in Congress will be pleased if he shall be retired to private life.

On August 28, 1895, it was announced that Secretary of the Treasury John G. Carlisle would go to Kentucky in the latter part of the campaign not later than October 15 and make several speeches in support of the Gold Democrats. These speeches would point out the evils of free and unlimited coinage of silver and generally oppose Blackburn's Free Silver stance. The Sound Money Democrats of Kentucky needed his help after their candidate for Governor, P. Wat Hardin, endorsed Free Silver and refused to stand on the party's gold standard platform. This divide within the state Democratic Party thrilled the Republican Party of Kentucky, who thought the days of Democratic power in the state were numbered.

Henry Watterson, the influential Democratic editor of the Louisville *Courier-Journal*, strongly supported any other Democrat for the Senate seat besides Blackburn and kept Carlisle and another Kentucky Democrat, Senator William Lindsay, in the headlines, giving them high praise. Watterson was a Sound Money man. He strongly supported Carlisle and Lindsay's break from the Free Silver platform of the Democratic National Convention.

Richard W. Knott, editor of the Louisville *Evening Post*, was "bitterly opposed to free silver and despised Joe Blackburn, whom he characterized as an "adventurous, noisy charlatan, who had brought his party to the verge of ruin." This opinion was aggravated by the comparison of Bryan's silver platform with the secession of the Confederate states in 1861. The balloting in the legislature for the Democrat who would fill Senator Blackburn's seat in the Senate was ready to begin.

By the time the Kentucky Legislature convened to decide the next U.S. Senator, the rivalry between Carlisle and Blackburn was intense. Carlisle refused to speak in support of Blackburn. Senator Blackburn's supporters were not surprised at Secretary Carlisle's response in declining to assist Blackburn, but they were angry over a cool and deliberate rebuff.

The time had come for the Democratic and Republican members of the Kentucky legislature to vote for the state's next U.S. Senator. The voting was going to be divided. Someone had to get a majority of the votes to win. In 1896, there were one hundred state Representatives and thirty-eight state Senators in the Kentucky legislature. At least seventy votes were needed for a nominee to be elected as the next U.S. Senator from Kentucky.

On March 2, 1896, the break in Senator Blackburn's lines appeared. The Sound Money Democrats who had been supporting the Silver

Senator decided, after a week of meetings, to vote for Blackburn on March 2 and March 3 , but after that, they would vote for some Sound Money Democrat in the hope of being met, in the spirit of compromise, by enough Sound Money Republicans to elect someone. Negotiations among the members were constant as they tried to resolve the issue of who would be the next U.S. Senator.

On March 6, 1896, the Kentucky joint assembly voted for the next Senator to succeed Senator Blackburn. The vote for senator was as follows: Blackburn, fifty-five; Deboe, forty; Carlisle, seven; Hunter, four; and a few others. There was no choice made. On March 7, 1896, two ballots were cast for United States Senator, but no one was elected.

On March 9, 1896, Senator Roswell Weissinger of Lousivlle, who had been the leader of the Sound Money Democrats in opposition to the re-election of Senator Blackburn, died of pneumonia, and the balloting for United States Senator was postponed. The joint session at noon was held only to formally comply with the law. When it was called to order, Mr. Carroll arose and explained that an agreement had been reached by which only two members, one for each side, was to vote. Senator Bennett voted for Boyle, and Senator Bronston voted for Blackburn. No one else answered the roll call, except Poor, who voted for Pettit, in order that the Populists might be represented and then the session was adjourned to the next day at noon. Kentucky State Representative Pence of Covington talked about the Senatorial deadlock:

> We are all getting tired of the long struggle between the Republicans and the Democrats. The Senatorial fight is blocking all legislation, and there are many legislators who want to adjourn now.
>
> I am still for Blackburn, and so are all of our delegation, but I am doubtful of his election. In the event that it becomes positive that Blackburn cannot be elected, I will vote for Carlisle. I believe the fight will end in Carlisle's election.

On March 10, 1896, nothing was done toward settling the senatorial contest. The joint session was called at noon, as required by law, with the agreement that only three members (Adams, Baird and Poor) should vote. These voted for Boyle, Blackburn, and Pettit, respectively. All other members sat in silence while their names were called. The President announced that there was no quorum for the vote and the session was adjourned until noon the next day. Then, on March 11, 1896, two Kentucky Senators were expelled from the Chamber, which caused a complete uproar. The unseating of Kaufman, Democrat, in the State House, was promptly followed by the unseating of Walton and James, Republicans, in the Senate. Some threatened bloodshed. Crowds of angry men surrounded the halls of both branches of the State Legislature and chaos reigned. Senator Blackburn led the crowd toward coolness. Order was barely but forcibly restored by the Lieutenant Governor.

On March 12, 1896, Kentucky Governor Bradley and Frankfort Mayor Julian conferred about keeping the peace, in case of trouble in the legislature that day. By ten o'clock in the morning, they had stationed six large policemen between the House and Senate Chambers.

On March 13, 1896, the Kentucky legislature balloted for a United States Senator to succeed Blackburn but again failed to make an election. Things then became very strange with multiple ballots that failed to elect a senator.

The Republican caucus selected Dr. W. Godfrey "Gum Shoe" Hunter of Cumberland County, and their balloting began. The Democratic caucus struggled to name a candidate. The Carlisle-Blackburn divide had become so wide that it was thought it would create support for someone else to run for Blackburn's Senate seat, like James B. McCreary, who had been Governor from 1875 to 1879. Local newspapers started promoting McCreary because he had experience in Washington, where he had served as U.S. Representative and had served as Chairman of the Committee on Foreign Affairs. The Sound Money Democrats put forward former Kentucky Governor James B. McCreary, who never received more than thirteen votes. By March 15th, Frankfort was in chaos. Governor Bradley recognized that local authorities could not control the situation, so he called out the state militia. Sound Money Democrats congratulated the governor, but some of Blackburn's supporters were reportedly furious. The state militia restored order. There was still no elected senator.

On March 16, 1896, there were four hundred soldiers encamped in the State House Square, but no senator was elected. The Legislature adjourned without choosing a successor to Senator Blackburn. The streets of Frankfort were crowded as early as eight o'clock, and every incoming train was loaded down with Blackburn sympathizers and curious people who had come to town expecting a fight. "Almost every man was armed, and pistols were very much in evidence." Governor William O. Bradley issued a proclamation that allowed soldiers to take possession of the State Capitol. But both Houses refused to consider any matter of legislation or to receive or consider any communication from the Governor, so long as the soldiers guarded the State Capitol.

On March 17, 1896, the Kentucky legislature adjourned again without electing a successor to United States Senator Blackburn. The last ballot was taken at noon on the 17th, and like the fifty ballots that preceded it, it was unsuccessful. By the middle of September 1896, the Gold Democrats were considering aligning with the Republicans to defeat Senator Blackburn. The men considering this unusual alliance said that they would "cast lots" to decide if the successor would be a Democrat or a Republican. At one point, Gold Democrat W.C.P. Breckinridge was considered as a possibility to run against Senator Blackburn in an effort to fuse the Gold Democrats with the Republicans, but nothing official came of it.

By October 1896, Kentuckians were bitter, and the intensity of the bitter feeling between Senator Blackburn and Secretary Carlisle made the local and national papers. By October 13, 1896, there were persons high in authority in Washington who were saying that Secretary Carlisle was likely to succeed Senator Blackburn:

> That a deal to that effect had been arranged between the sound-money Democrats of that State and the Republican leaders.
>
> The deal is understood to be that in return for sound-money Democratic votes for [Presidential candidate] McKinley and [Vice Presidential candidate] Hobart, Gov. Bradley will call a special session of the Legislature to elect a Senator, and the choice by prearrangement will be Carlisle.
>
> Senator Blackburn is said to be permanently broken down in health, and his re-election is among the impossibilities in any event.
>
> Secretary Carlisle will begin his stumping in a few days.

The divide between Silver Democrat Blackburn and Gold Democrat Carlisle increased to the point of dueling. Blackburn was interviewed by a reporter after he arrived in Lexington on October 17, 1896. The reporter wanted to find out if Senator Blackburn had recovered from a recent illness. He had recovered from his throat and lung trouble as a result of a cold contracted at Tammany Hall in New York during the first week of October and from a high fever that struck him on October 10th. His doctors had forbidden him from seeing anybody after he became ill at Mount Vernon, where he was scheduled to give a speech, and cancelled all of his appearances. His illness was so serious that his doctors had been afraid he would not recover in time to make any more speeches before the election, but he did. During the interview, the reporter asked him about the possibility of a duel between him and Logan Carlisle, one of U.S. Secretary of the Treasury John Carlisle's sons. Blackburn told the reporter:

> I never heard of that duel until after I got sick the other day. I saw it in a newspaper while in bed. As I am not in very good fighting trim, I honestly believe that duel story is a newspaper canard. If I have been considering entering into a duel, or have ever said anything about fighting young Carlisle I must have done it in my sleep. You may rest assured that if I wanted a fight out of the Carlisle family, I never would have sought to have it with one of the kids.

It was asserted later that the trouble came about because Logan Carlisle had dismissed some of Senator Blackburn's appointees for federal jobs, but nothing further was said about this, and no duel or fight ensued. It did not help to heal Blackburn's bitterness about Carlisle.

In mid-December 1896, Senator Blackburn's Free-Silver friends arranged to contest before the United States Senate the election of a Republican Senator if one was elected by the Kentucky legislature. They hoped to secure a Silver Democratic legislature at the next November election that would support Blackburn. They decided that if someone other than Blackburn was elected to take the U.S. Senate seat, then they would go before the United States Senate with a contest and ask the Senators to investigate the qualifications of those legislators who voted for and elected the new Senator. They would then claim that this new Senator was elected by the votes of four specific men—Lieberth,

Speed, Crumbaugh, and Stoll—or could not have been elected without their votes, and that these men were ineligible to hold their seats and were not, therefore, entitled to vote for the new Senator or to have their votes counted.

Apparently, Governor Bradley foresaw this eventuality and instead of allowing the Legislature to elect the new Senator, decided to appoint a Senator after the vacancy was created when Congress went into Session. Upon learning this, the Silver men decided that they would fight against the confirmation of any newly appointed Senator.

Governor Bradley then appointed Andrew T. Wood to serve if the legislature failed to make a choice for U.S. Senator. Governor Bradley then called a special session of the state legislature for March 1897. The old contest between Blackburn and Dr. Hunter was renewed in all its fury. Dr. Hunter withdrew from the race, replaced by Republican John Boyle, but he also withdrew later. The Republicans then put forward William J. Deboe, an imposing giant from Marion, who on the 112th ballot received a majority and election. William J. Deboe became Kentucky's first Republican United States Senator since the Civil War, and Joseph Blackburn suffered his first defeat in his long political career.

> After the official declaration of the election of Deboe there were such loud demonstrations that even the telegraph offices in the lobby of the House [in Frankfort] had to suspend business, and nothing but the bare ballot could be sent out. Senator Blackburn and his friends after fighting hard for over a year in the regular and extra sessions and went down with their colors flying. The silver Democrats conceded their disappointment and the gold Democrats joined in the jollification. There never was such a scene in the Kentucky State House. Senator Deboe will proceed to Washington at once with his credentials, to assist in reorganizing the United States Senate and in the passage of the tariff and other measures on which the lines are closely drawn.

Blackburn's loss was a blow to the Democratic Party in Kentucky. He had served in the Senate from 1885 to 1897. He represented:

> …two hundred and twenty-five thousand white men who voted for Bryan for President. They have looked to him as their leader, and he had not only been true to them, but he has stood loyally by every precept of his party. During the long struggle at Frankfort, Senator Blackburn has held his forces well in hand and has given the Republicans a battle that they will remember for all time. Any other candidate would have been beaten within a week. Blackburn for two years has battled against a rapacious army of Republicans on one side and a hand full of Democrats deserters on the other, who were willing at any time to bring about Republican success rather than see a free silver man go to the Senate.
>
> This defeat will not weaken Jo Blackburn in Kentucky. It will not take a single laurel from his brow. Like the noble Roman that he is, he has been borne from the field upon his shield. At no time did he waver or show the white feather. Bearing not only his personal fortunes but the fortunes of his party, he fought with unexampled skill and courage and went down with his face to the foe.
>
> THE CRITIC delights to honor Jo Blackburn because he represents so much that is manly and courageous. Whenever there is a fight to be made in Kentucky, the palm of leadership will be tendered him and wherever he goes thousands of true Democrats will be glad to follow, because they know that he will lead them only in straight paths.

Accepting defeat did not come so easily to others. The Democracy of Barren County met in Glasgow, Kentucky, at the courthouse and adopted a resolution calling for the resignation of Kentucky's other U.S. Senator, William Lindsay, because he had "violated the trust reposed in him by the Democracy of the State, and is now misrepresenting the constituency which gave him office," stating that "[b]efore his election to the Office of the United States senator he declared himself an advocate of the free coinage of both gold and silver, and has openly and frequently violated this declaration;" and "[h]e pledged himself to abide the action of the national Democratic convention, and afterwards bolted and defied the action of the Democratic national Democratic platform."

Indeed, one of the first actions of the state legislature was to pass a resolution calling upon Senator Lindsay to resign his seat in the United State Senate, on the grounds that he no longer represented his party.

Lindsay declared that he was not required to vote according to the wishes of a faction of one party. (Earlier Henry Clay had undergone the same experience.) Lindsay's statement did not fill Kentucky silverites with joy. Nevertheless, he remained United States Senator.

Blackburn was defeated, but he had not gone down without a fight. The local newspapers said:

> No man ever had a more faithful following and no set of men ever had a better leader. His fight to succeed to himself was the most remarkable in the history of politics. Though he was dealt a bad hand by the gold democrats, he played his cards with consummate skill and only quit when the last one was thrown. Those who claim that but for his selfishness he might have elected Martin to the Senate, are ignorant of the facts. At no time were the bolting republicans in earnest about voting for Martin and at no time could Blackburn have taken his strength to him. Senator Blackburn has fought a good fight, but he has not finished his course and will cut and come again as certain as his name is Joe.

Back in Versailles, Kentucky Joe Blackburn wrote to his trusted friend James C. Dedman of Cynthiana on November 11 , 1896:

> Yes! We are beaten this time, but we have just begun to fight. Next time we will win. I will be on hand, when legislature meets and will make the best fight we can.... Always your friend
> Jo. C.S. Blackburn"

By December 1898, former Senator Blackburn worked on his plans to return to the U.S. Senate. Through the friendship of State Senator William Goebel, who was the accepted Democratic candidate for Governor, Blackburn was able to organize the Election Commission in every Democratic county. He also dominated the County Committee, allowing him to ensure that nearly every legislative district in the state was ready to choose a man favorable to his re-election. The election of state senators who would participate in 1900 in the election of a United States Senator was of particular interest to Blackburn. State politics became even more raucous with the next election of Democratic Governor Goebel in 1900. The adopted party platforms helped set the stage for that battle.

The Democratic Party Platform of 1900 focused less on the gold and silver issue and more on the issue of imperialism, militarism, and monopolies, but reaffirmed and endorsed the principles of the National Democratic Platform adopted at Chicago in 1896, specifically the free and unlimited coinage of silver and gold at the present legal ratio of sixteen to one without waiting for the aid or consent of any other nation. It supported the development of the Nicaraguan Canal, denounced the Hay-Pauncefote Treaty which would become important to the subsequent development of the Panama Canal, and warned the American people against Executive or Legislative action in excess of the U.S. Constitution.

Chapter Twenty-Five

Blackburn and Goebel

In the aftermath of the election of Kentucky's first Republican Governor since the Civil War, a radical new act was passed by the state legislature called the Goebel Election Law of 1898. It seemed to have two goals: make Democrat William Goebel governor no matter what and give the Silverite Democrats control of the state.

> The act provided for the creation of a state election commission of three, for four year terms, to be appointed by the existing General Assembly. The state board was empowered to appoint annually three commissioners in each county, who, in turn, were to appoint all the elective and registration officers for their respective counties. Vacancies occurring on the state board, when the General Assembly was not in session, were to be filled optatively by the board's members. The measure empowered the state board to remove members of county boards at any time without showing cause. The state commission could be composed altogether of members of one party, although the county boards were required to select the election officers from the two leading parties. The county commissions were empowered to count the votes and issue certificates of election, said certificates to be sent to the state board, which, if satisfied, was to make duplicate certificates for those having the highest number of votes. In the event of a tie, the contest was to be settled by lot. Election contests were made impossible, because, it was advanced, going behind the returns of the county boards was not permitted.

It was passed by the Democrat-controlled state legislature in response to the alleged fraudulent Republican votes in the previous election, but it was outrageously bold. The Goebel election bill passed, and Republican Governor Bradley vetoed it. The Kentucky legislature re-passed it over the governor's veto. Goebel's election law was now the law of the state. Goebel then picked the three men to be the state election commissioners: Captain William T. Ellis, Charles B. Poyntz, and Judge Pryor, all Democrats, and the legislature adjourned.

State Senator Goebel defended the election law, but Edward A. Jonas, a Louisville reporter warned:

> What Senator Goebel proposed was that elections be held by officers to be selected by a partisan county board, that board to be appointed by, and therefore to become the creature and the servant of, a partisan state board. This last ... was to be named by one party in the Legislature and to be self-perpetuating. These canvass returns and decide contests. In practice, what is intended ... was that every election would be at the mercy, not of one party but of whatever faction of the party chanced to be on top. And so,... he not only destroyed self-government but party government in the broader sense.

As a result, there was revolution in the air. Republican Attorney General William S. Taylor said that the measure destroyed "the basic principles of republican government" and tended to "concentrate power so that one man might have full control." He charged that the law was "corrupt and dishonest in purpose" and held that it was unconstitutional. When the Republican State Auditor refused to honor the requisitions of the newly appointed commission, the measure went to the Appellate Court, where by a vote of four to three, it was decided that the Goebel law did not conflict with the state constitution and that the law would stand. Republicans were rightfully concerned about the section of the Goebel law about the election of governor or lieutenant governor in which a special board was to be selected by lot from the legislature to examine the contests and report to the General Assembly, because the Democrats usually controlled it.

Blackburn faced the difficult challenge of supporting a less than ideal Democratic candidate for Governor in William Goebel, who was a Sound Money Democrat and the author of the extreme election law. However, Goebel was Blackburn's only viable choice if he wanted to regain a seat in the U.S. Senate. Blackburn had paid his dues to the Democratic Party in the state while he was a U.S. Senator and while he was out of office and looked for party support in his bid to win re-election to the Senate. He had campaigned vigorously for William Jennings Bryan, who in turn campaigned in Kentucky for William Goebel for Governor and Joseph Blackburn for U.S. Senator. When Bryan spoke, an adoring crowd gathered and cheered enthusiastically.

Sadly, Blackburn faced personal grief now as well. On September 17, 1899, Blackburn's wife of forty years, Terese, died. She was sixty years old. Joseph and Terese had four children together who were still alive when she died. The oldest, Joseph Clay Stiles Blackburn, Jr. ("Josey") was thirty-nine and unmarried. He worked for his father as his secretary. Their oldest daughter, Terese Blackburn Hall, was thirty-one when her mother died. Terese had been married since 1893 to General William Preble Hall, with whom she had one child, Joe Blackburn Hall, aged eight (a daughter was born later). The second daughter, Corinne Blackburn Gale, was thirty when her mother died. In 1905, Corinne married General Consul William Holt Gale, who served all over the world. The youngest, Lucile Blackburn Lane, was twenty-eight when her mother died. Lucile was married to Thomas F. Lane of New Jersey. Together they had one daughter, three-year old Terese Blackburn Lane. After his wife's death, Senator Blackburn was left alone in his large Rose Hill home in Versailles. He sold the Rose Hill home that year. From then on, his primary residence was in Washington, D.C. although he spent time with his family at Spring Station in Woodford County, Kentucky. Blackburn had to deal with the loss of his wife while fighting to rebuild the Democratic Party in the state and to regain his U.S. Senate seat.

When Kentuckians went to the polls to elect the next Governor, the Democratic candidate for Governor Goebel and his running mate J.C.W. Beckham lost to Republican William Taylor and his running mate John Marshall. The new legislature, which was scheduled to meet in January 1900, was known to be safely Democratic, and upon the advice of Blackburn and other supporters, Goebel challenged the election results and won in the courts, but it wasn't easy.

The Goebel-Taylor and Beckham-Marshall contest committees met on Sunday, January 14, to prepare for the hearing. The Republican leaders said that a judgment for the state offices had to receive a majority in each branch of the legislature rather than a majority of a joint assembly. The Democrats claimed the outcome had to be backed by a majority of the joint assembly of the House and Senate and they were prepared to submit this question of procedure to the courts. If the Republican method was followed, Governor Taylor had a majority of supporters in the State Senate and would win. The House adjourned until Monday, January 15, 1900.

Senator Blackburn was one of the staunch Goebel supporters, along with his old friends Colonel Jack Chinn and Major Eph Lillard. It was rumored that it was Blackburn's idea to challenge the election. Some said that had it not been for him and Colonel Jack Chinn, Goebel would have abandoned the idea of challenging the election and would have quietly gone home to Covington. Blackburn is said to have discovered a one-hundred-year-old law on the Kentucky statute books that allowed a defeated candidate for governor to challenge it before the state legislature on final appeal, regardless of any decision of the state election commission or the state Court of Appeals, the highest court of the state. Under this law, it was possible that the state legislature could decide one way and the state court of appeals another way. If that happened, the state legislature's ruling would be the final ruling.

The Republicans, on the other hand, thought that if that happened, it would require the Federal military to intervene and settle the matter. Furthermore, the Republicans vowed that if the Democrats won, there would be a second appeal by them to the Court of Appeals, who might uphold the validity of the appointment of the Election Commissioners and the original election result for the Republicans. It would be a stand-off. This meant that if the Democrats were seated, the Republicans could refuse rightfully to give up their seats and choose to defend them with the military arm of the state, which the Republicans had conveniently assembled in Frankfort ready to answer the call, armed and in uniform. If the Democrats refused to accept that outcome, they might call for federal intervention on behalf of the Democrats to maintain order. A state political and military showdown seemed inevitable in Frankfort.

During this uproar, on January 2, 1900, a little over three months after his wife passed away and after four years out of the Senate, Joseph

Blackburn was chosen by the joint caucus of the Democratic members of the Kentucky legislature as the successor of William Lindsay in the United States Senate. Blackburn's nomination was presumed a foregone conclusion at this point, and some believed a moral certainty. The caucus was called to order at eight o'clock by Senator Goebel, acting as chairman of the joint caucus. It was reported that there was wild cheering in the galleries above the state legislature floor when Goebel came into the hall before calling the caucus to order. The cheering reportedly continued for several minutes. Goebel said that "the longest and bitterest fight ever waged for a Senator in this State began four years ago when Deboe defeated Blackburn and that it was about to reach its just termination tonight."

> The State Capitol rang with cheers as he placed Blackburn in nomination. Senator Harris made a seconding speech and was followed by other members who eulogized Blackburn and congratulated the party on the union of all of the Democratic members in returning him to the Senate. Senator Thomas asked that the roll be called so that every Democratic member might have an opportunity to go on record for Blackburn.

Two state Senators abstained from voting; otherwise, the vote was unanimous.

Republican Governor Taylor submitted a lengthy message, giving the reasons for the repeal of the Goebel Election Law, which he called the "infamy of 1898 that has demoralized, disturbed and disgraced the State." Many thought that Bradley would contest the seat of Senator Blackburn "on the ground that, owing to the fraud perpetrated under the Goebel law, Republicans were defrauded of their offices." By January 9, 1900, the Kentucky militia was prepared to answer the call if the Republican Governor declared that the state was under martial law. Under the provisions of the State Constitution, Governor Taylor could not call out the militia until trouble had actually begun, but the Republicans had the State Guard assembled in Frankfort, even though they were dressed in civilian clothes. Their guns and uniforms had been sent to Frankfort by express. Republicans denied any knowledge of the military guard, but it was not believable. On January 9, 1900, the House balloted for United States Senator with the following result:

Democrat Blackburn, fifty-seven; Republican Bradley, forty-two. In the Senate, the ballot for Senator stood: Blackburn, twenty-two; Bradley, twelve.

On January 16, 1900, the election of Blackburn was repeated to resolve any question of the legality of the election of the prior week. The proceedings and votes were practically the same as the first ballot. On January 20, 1900, the Republican legislators claimed Goebel had made a deal with leaders of the New York Democratic political organization known as Tammany Hall to help the Democrats win in the state. On January 25, 1900, a thousand or more armed men from the mountain counties of Taylor's home showed up in Frankfort in the morning. Nearly all of them were armed and openly carried rifles with two large revolvers strapped around their waists. They pretended to be witnesses for the Republicans before the Board, but it was generally believed that they had been brought to Frankfort to help the Republicans forcibly keep their offices if unseated by the legislature and the contest board. In addition, militia companies were assembled in Middlesboro, Pineville, Corbin, Barbourville, Mount Vernon, and other places. The men could not be controlled. They drank whiskey and brandished arms carelessly.

> There were fifteen coaches in the [L&N] train [on which the army arrived], and when it reached here [Frankfort] it was filled with a demonstrative crowd, many of whom had never been more than a few miles from their homes before. They had amused themselves on the way shooting from car windows, but as far as can be learned did no damage to any one.

When these men arrived in Frankfort, they marched in a line to the state House, where they met with Republican Commissioner of Agriculture Throckmorton, who allowed them to stash their weapons in his office, except for their revolvers, which they kept by their sides. The Republican Governor sent plenty of food and had state tents set up in the State House yard, but there were not enough tents, and many men were forced to sleep in the cold. On January 27, the Speaker of the House closed the galleries to visitors to avoid trouble. This meant that no citizen could be heard unless the House went into Committee of the Whole, which it refused to do. Fortunately, many of the armed men were convinced to leave that night, but because most had no money, a special train had to be provided by the L&N Railroad to allow them to ride home to Eastern Kentucky for free. This still left five hundred drunken, armed men camped out on the Capitol grounds overnight. One "cowboy" armed with his revolver took over the lobby between the House and Senate Chamber, forcing everyone out by firing his pistol. It was like the Wild West. No one had control over the men. Some were heard loudly threatening to assassinate Goebel, Chief Justice Hazelrigg, and others.

It was chaotic inside the state government buildings, as well. Republican Governor Taylor refused to sign Senator-elect Blackburn's certificate for Senator, despite the evidence presented to the Governor of its legality. Fortunately, the mountain men returned home on a special train that day, as well. After the mountain men left, the politicians took a day of rest, although rumors persisted that another detachment of men from the mountains would arrive in Frankfort within days.

On January 29, 1900, Governor Taylor said that if the gubernatorial contest decided that Governor Taylor had been elected illegally, then the legislators who elected Blackburn as the United States Senator-elect and who were declared elected at the same election at which he was a candidate for Governor had been illegally elected, too, and did not, therefore, have the power to choose a senator. January 29 was the last day for taking evidence in the gubernatorial contest, and a decision was expected to follow quickly. It did: the decision was in favor of the Democrats. Goebel was about to be officially named as the next Kentucky Governor by the legislature, when the proceedings were brought to an abrupt and tragic end. Goebel was walking over to the Senate Chamber when an assassin shot him in broad daylight on January 30, 1900, in front of the State Capitol, plunging Kentucky into a tense crisis bordering on civil war. Goebel was rushed to a room in the Capitol Hotel.

> While William Goebel lay at the point of death in his room as the result of an assassin's bullet, the contesting boards, which for two weeks had been listening to evidence in his contest for the Governor's chair, declared him entitled to the seat.

Then the Beckham-Marshall contest for Lieutenant Governor was decided in favor of Democrat Beckham, and the Boards prepared their reports for both that night. Unfortunately, only a few members of the legislature attended the session, so when they wished to act quickly, they could not because they were unable to gather a quorum. While the legislators hurried to Frankfort from Lexington and Louisville, it was certain that Goebel would be made Governor of Kentucky the next day if he lived through the night.

In the meantime, while they waited for all the members of the state legislature to gather, some of the assembled members and the military nearly broke out in fist fights or worse. Rumors kept everyone on edge. The Republicans vowed to seek injunctive relief from the United States Circuit Court at Cincinnati.

The Contest Board's report said:

> The undersigned, the board appointed and selected by the General Assembly to determine the contested election for the office of Governor for this Commonwealth between William Goebel, contestant, and William S. Taylor, contestee, beg leave to report that we have heard all the evidence offered by both parties, and we now respectfully report to the General Assembly of the Commonwealth of Kentucky that in our opinion William Goebel was legally elected Governor of the Commonwealth of Kentucky on the 7th day of November, 1899, and that he then and there received the highest number of legal votes cast for any one for the office of Governor of Kentucky at said election, and we therefore respectfully suggest that this report be approved, and a resolution adopted by this joint assembly declaring the said William Goebel Governor-elect of the Commonwealth of Kentucky for the term commencing the 12th day of December, 1899.
>
> We decide that the said William Goebel has received the highest number of legal votes, and is adjudged to be the person elected to said office of Governor for the term prescribed by law.

The report in the case of the contest between Beckham and Marshall for Lieutenant Governor yielded the same result.

On January 31, attorneys for the State Representatives advised them to leave Frankfort for their safety, and they did. Republican Governor Taylor refused to step down and ordered the legislature to meet in London, Kentucky, a shocking move.

Colonel Davis said that he was just outside Governor Taylor's door when he heard the shots and heard Governor Taylor say, "My God, what have they done?" He stated that he did not think Governor Taylor had assassinated Goebel. A full search of the building and grounds could not be conducted because several of the mountaineers held Winchesters and stood guard for several minutes, long enough for one to get away if he needed to make an escape. The shooting appeared to be the result of a carefully laid-out plan, with the assassin setting up well in advance to wait for the right moment. Ever since the mountaineers invaded Frankfort, a large number of them had been sleeping in the upper part of the State House, but no one knows who fired the shot, although it has been claimed by descendants of one Mr. Combs. There was no direct evidence pointing to any one man, and it was said that it was not likely that any would be found. A Mr. Combs was rumored to have been the assassin, but no evidence was found to implicate him or convict him. The case has never been solved to this day.

Republicans and Democrats denounced the shooting. Even before Goebel had been lifted from the ground and moved to the Capitol Hotel, General Collier had called the armory, half a mile away, and directed the local infantry company to take control of the Capitol grounds and prevent anyone from entering the gates. It was done within twenty minutes of the order. Other companies throughout the state were put on standby to come to Frankfort, along with the entire State Guard. Some feared the Democrats would swarm Frankfort once they learned Goebel has been shot, and others feared that the mountaineers would swarm the capital to protect the Republicans. Democrats, however, remained calm.

Three hundred men of the Second Kentucky Infantry camped around the Capitol building and 1,560 more men were expected to arrive during the night and before noon the next day. The Louisville Legion of the First Kentucky Infantry decided to bring its famous Gatling gun. Armed men filled the Executive office building. The Gatling gun of the Lexington company was posted just to the west of the Capitol steps. Senator-elect Blackburn of Kentucky, who was one of the first in Washington to receive word of the shooting of Mr. Goebel, made the following statement the night he heard the news:

> It is impossible for me to express the feelings produced by the news just received from Frankfort. The assassination of Goebel has been predicted for months, so that it would hardly be correct to say that it was altogether unexpected. The reorganization of the militia of the State by Bradley during the latter part of his administration, placing the military affairs of the State substantially on a Republican partisan basis; the importation of armed ruffians from the mountains into Frankfort within the last few days; their indefensible conduct while in the capital city, coupled with threats of resort to violence and force, all pointed to a culmination like this.
>
> Whether significant or not, it is peculiarly unfortunate that the shots of the assassin should have been fired from the building exclusively occupied by Gov. Taylor and other Republican State officials. Unless the assassin can be identified, the public will naturally conclude that it was prearranged and the building filled with those who would protect the perpetrator from identification. I doubt not that the greatest excitement prevails in the city of Frankfort, but sincerely trust that the supporters of Mr. Goebel will not allow themselves to be betrayed into any act of violence or any transgression of the law.
>
> The situation is, indeed, a serious one, but their course is perfectly plain. They should proceed with the contest for State officers until a final decision is reached by the tribunals established by law for its determination. The Democrats of Kentucky up to this time have kept themselves in the prosecution of this contest strictly within the limits of the law. This I hope and doubt not they will continue to do.
>
> It cannot be doubted that the attack upon Mr. Goebel's life was deliberately planned and attempted, because of the conviction in the public mind that the close of testimony in the contest case insured the award of the Governorship to him by the Legislature.

William Jennings Bryan was shocked when he heard the news. It was a first: on January 31, 1900, Kentucky had two Governors: Democrat William Goebel and Republican William Taylor. Taylor was entrenched in the State House, and the other lay on a bed in the Capitol Hotel, dying from a gunshot wound. William Goebel was sworn in at nine o'clock by Chief Justice Hazelrigg as Governor of Kentucky.

> His first act was to issue a proclamation disbanding the State militia and ordering all persons to desist from terrorizing the State Assembly, and his next act was to appoint Brig. Gen. John B. Castleman of Louisville Adjutant General for Kentucky. Then he turned over in his bed and fell into a peaceful sleep.

On February 1, 1900 Governor Taylor and his Republican friends, with the support of the State troops, kept possession of the State House and other official State buildings. The soldiers were standing by Taylor while they waited for proof of the lawful governor of Kentucky, an impossible situation. U.S. President McKinley emphatically stated to Kentucky Senator Deboe and others that there would be no recognition of a dual government in Kentucky. U.S. Secretary Root issued a statement that there was no intention on the part of any Washington authorities to send federal troops to Kentucky until the Kentucky authorities admitted that they were unable to handle the situation and then only upon the request of the governor.

Republicans wanted to submit the question to the U.S. Supreme Court, but the Democrats wanted to have it settled in state courts. Discussions continued. But at least the attorneys were talking, which seemed to indicate that Taylor could be willing to yield, but he was not willing to give up the fight just yet. Democratic attorneys began to find ways to legally oust Taylor.

Goebel's heart weakened in the meantime. It looked like a civil war could erupt in the State. On February 2, Goebel gained strength, giving hope he could survive the shot. The Democrats discussed offering fifty thousand dollars for the arrest and conviction of the Goebel assassin, and Taylor offered five hundred dollars. On February 3, 1900, Governor Goebel died. In the morning, he said to his doctor, "Doctor, I'm afraid now that I'm not going to get over this." Exactly one hour later, he died. J.C.W. Beckham was sworn in as Governor of the State, the oath administered by S.J. Shackelford, Clerk of the Court of Appeals. The news of the death of Goebel was kept secret until Beckham was formally inducted into office.

The assassin who shot William Goebel was never identified, although James Sutton, sheriff of Whitley County, stated that he knew all about the assassination and knew the man who shot Goebel. Sheriff Sutton was arrested and questioned, and he told of a preconceived plot and that the originator was an ex-official of the state, who arranged with three men to do the shooting and showed them the room in the third floor of the Executive building from which the shooting took place. He also told them the hour when Goebel would pass the window to go to the Senate Chamber. William Goebel became the only American governor to die in office from an assassin's bullet.

Several theories were offered. A man named Rodman on a late train from Ironton, Ohio, said he was in Frankfort the day that Senator Goebel was shot and that he knew the name of the man who shot Goebel, and that it was revenge for Goebel killing John Sanford in an 1895 duel.

> I know all about the shooting of Goebel. I can tell you plainly that our people are away off it if they think that Taylor or the Republican Party had anything to do with the shooting. A trap has been set for a long time, and the opportunity anxiously awaited, to kill Goebel for his killing of John Sanford, and the party who fired the shot was a near friend and intimately connected to Sanford.
>
> It was to avenge Sanford's death that the political situation was taken advantage of for the shooting. The idea that the shooting came from the second story of the State House is all rot.

On February 3, Judge Cantrill of the Circuit Court granted a temporary injunction effective for five days, restraining Governor Taylor from interfering with the meeting of the legislature and from removing the seat of legislature to London, Kentucky. The temporary injunction remained in effect until February 8, 1900, when the hearing to make it permanent was scheduled to be heard before Judge Cantrill at Georgetown, Kentucky.

U.S. Senator-elect Blackburn arrived in Frankfort on February 3 to hold a conference with the Democratic leaders and to advise with them regarding the probable attitude of the U.S. Administration toward Governor Taylor. Senator Blackburn was met at the station by Colonel Jack Chinn, Speaker South Trimble of the House, and other prominent Democrats. Senator Blackburn then met with Lt. Governor Beckham and others. Senator Blackburn conveyed the Administration's determination not to interfere in the events at Frankfort unless absolutely necessary. Senator Blackburn strongly urged the necessity of preserving peace at all costs and to allow no acts of violence to take place under any circumstances but to allow matters to proceed to a conclusion in the courts.

The Republicans then generally left Frankfort headed for London. It was a split government. There was a lot of speculation about the effect of Goebel's death on the situation. Then on February 4, 1900, the Democratic seat of government for Kentucky was moved to Louisville. J.C.W. Beckham and the Democratic members of the House and Senate arrived in Louisville in the evening and planned to call the two houses of the legislature to order in the morning of the 5th. A quorum of both houses was present, and the Election Contest Board was also present to decide the contests for offices below that of Lieutenant Governor. The Republican contestants would not be present, and the offices were given to Democrats, including the Secretary of State, Treasurer, Auditor, Commissioner of Agriculture, Commissioner of Public Instruction, and Attorney General. The decision to move the legislature to Louisville was decided at near midnight and kept quiet for fear Governor Taylor would send troops to Louisville to try to prevent the meeting. It was quiet in Frankfort. All the legislators had left the city. The Republicans went to London, and the Democrats went to Louisville.

On February 5, 1900, the train bearing the body of the late William Goebel left Frankfort at four o'clock in the morning, bound for his hometown of Covington. The body was taken to the Odd Fellows' Hall where it lay in state all day. Senator Blackburn rode on the special train along with all the active and honorary pall bearers, a few friends, and Goebel's brothers and sister. Everything was handled simply. It was decided that Goebel would be buried in Frankfort in the cemetery overlooking the Kentucky River, along with the remains of Daniel

Boone, Vice President Richard Johnson, Kentucky Governor Luke Blackburn, and other Kentucky governors, jurists, and soldiers.

The spot is close to the memorial to Kentucky's dead soldiers, near the highest point in the cemetery. Arthur and Justus Goebel, Senator-elect Blackburn, S.J. Shackelford (Clerk of the Court of Appeals), and Warden Lillard visited the cemetery and spent time looking over the ground, selecting the spot for Goebel's final resting place. The Honorary Pall Bearers were J. C. S. Blackburn, General Joseph H. Lewis, Judge W. S. Pryor, J. B. McCreary, Phil B. Thompson, James H. Mulligan, Louis Descognets, Samuel J. Shackelford, Joseph L. Rinnock, Joseph W. Pugh, Zack Phelps, W.B. Haldeman, Charles B. Pointz, and Morton K. Yontz. The active pall bearers were Jack Chinn, Charles C. McChord, Ed Fennell, James M. Richardson, Henry George, Eph Lillard, Willard Mitchell, Charles M. Lewis, John Grayot, John K. Hendrick, John Fulton, Uray Woodson, Joseph Blackburn, Jr., Allie W. Young, R.B. Franklin, and Percy Haley. New York Governor Theodore Roosevelt read of the death of Goebel and said:

> It is to be regretted that such acts of violence can take place in this country, but at the same time, our sympathy must be tempered by the realization that the dead politician himself established a violent and equally fatal precedent. If further bloodshed is to come, it must lie at the doors of those who conspired to accomplish by force what they failed to accomplish by fraud during a State election.

By February 5, 1900 the party Leaders in Kentucky were willing to come together to end the political war. They agreed to the withdrawal of the military from Frankfort, a peaceful meeting of the legislature in Frankfort, and Republicans Taylor and Marshall following the laws and actions of the state legislature.

There was hope for a democratic government being restored in Kentucky once more. Taylor consulted his attorneys, and Senator-elect Blackburn said upon his return from the conference in Louisville that the entire trouble would be settled peacefully.

> It is entirely natural that the other side should wish to take time to consider the agreement and to prepare its statement

> to be issued at the same time the signature is affixed. I have no knowledge of what will be done, but I firmly believe that the agreement will be accepted substantially as adopted by the members of the Louisville conference and that all chance of trouble will be avoided.

On February 7, 1900, Blackburn delivered the eulogy for Governor Goebel at Frankfort.

> Following the death of Goebel, Lieutenant Governor Beckham succeeded him immediately.
>
> Mr. Beckham seemed deeply affected by the position in which circumstances had placed him, and he did not reveal much joy over the congratulations which those in the room showered upon him, although he accepted them gratefully.
>
> 'There is one thing that I would have been greatly pleased to have had done by Mr. Goebel before his death,' he said, 'and that is to have signed the certificate of Senator Blackburn. Of course, I am greatly pleased to have the privilege myself, but I know that it was a matter close to the heart of Mr. Goebel, and I wish that he could have lived long enough to do it. I think I can promise,' he said, with a smile, 'that it will be one of the first things that I will do on Monday.'

Blackburn, who had stood loyally by Goebel and Beckham through the contest, was present at these inauguration ceremonies, which gave the "Goebelites," as they were called, control of the state government. Blackburn received his reward when he was re-elected to the U.S. Senate, beginning on March 4, 1901 for the Fifty-Seventh Congress. The Goebel-Beckham wing of the Democratic Party had a decisive majority. Beckham served out Goebel's term as governor and was elected for another term, ultimately serving from 1900 to 1907, creating a "political machine" and further divisions in the Democratic Party of Kentucky. Blackburn stood and defended against any and all slurs against the party in the state.

On August 18, 1900, ex-Secretary of State Powers was found guilty of being an accessory before the fact to the murder of William Goebel, and the jury's vote was unanimous in favor of a life sentence.

The trial lasted from July 9 to July 31, 1900. When Senator Blackburn heard the Powers verdict as he stopped in Lexington on his way home between trains, he exclaimed: "Thank God for that. I had expected a hung jury. I believed that there were three men on that jury at least would hang it."

Chapter Twenty-Six

National Vision

"That was my ambition; that was my hope; that was my plan—that in the tide of time this great country and Government of ours have accomplished its grand mission and lifted from the ruts and gutters of imperial and autocratic power every government from the north to the south and made a republic where tyranny and autocracy before held sway."

— J. C. S. Blackburn

On May 26, 1900, Senator Blackburn's credentials were presented in the Senate by Arkansas Democratic Senator James K. Jones for the term beginning March 4, 1901 in the Fifty-Seventh Congress, which ran through to March 4, 1903. It was a new beginning in a new century for the country now looking beyond its borders over its realm of influence in the Western Hemisphere. Blackburn was the first Democrat from Kentucky to take office in a new century filled with promise, purpose, and turmoil. He shared the country's vision.

Fifty-Seventh Congress (March 4, 1901–March 4, 1903)

For the first six months of the Fifty-Seventh Congress, William McKinley was U.S. President after he won re-election, but that ended with his shocking assassination on September 14, 1901 at the Pan-American Exposition in Buffalo, New York. The Congress then continued with the first year and a half of the first administration of his successor U.S. President Theodore Roosevelt. The seats in the House were based on the Eleventh Census. The House and Senate each had a Republican majority. Forty-five states were represented in Congress, with five non-voting representatives present for the Arizona Territory, Hawaii Territory, New Mexico Territory, Oklahoma Territory, and Porto Rico.

The Senate approval of a ship canal treaty with Great Britain that allowed the United States to build a canal connecting the Atlantic and Pacific Oceans and then to regulate and manage it once constructed, led the Fifty-Seventh Congress to authorize funds to build a canal in Panama. Discussions on the best way to build a canal through Panama, whether with locks or a sea-level canal, consumed much of the time of the Senate in this Session. In addition, the Senate discussed revising plans for a colonial government in the Philippines.

Republican President Roosevelt launched a vigorous effort to break up monopolies to give every citizen a "fair deal," much in the vein of Democratic and Populist measures, supported by Blackburn and other Democrats. The Senate approved legislation authorizing the federal government to prosecute antitrust violations more effectively, but the Senate was not completely harmonious.

First Session, Fifty-Seventh Congress (December 2, 1901–July 1, 1902)

Tensions erupted on February 22, 1902 on the Senate floor during the First Session when South Carolina's Democratic Senators Tillman and McLaurin had a fist fight on the floor while Congress was in session. They were each censured by the Senate, and new rules of conduct were enacted to ensure some dignity on the Senate floor. Senate Democrats had lacked harmony since the end of the Civil War, which continued on the Senate floor until the following year when Maryland Senator Arthur Gorman agreed to chair the Democratic Caucus in 1903. In order to organize the party and take back the Senate to enable the Democratic party to effectively pass legislation, Senator Gorman adopted a "binding rule" to maintain party unity. In essence, a "binding caucus" rule required all the members to agree to support any issue that received a two-thirds vote of the whole caucus. It worked. Within ten years, the Democrats regained their majority in the Senate.

There were important international events during this session. On May 10, 1902, President Theodore Roosevelt directed Leonard Wood, U.S. military governor of Cuba, to transfer the control of the government of the island of Cuba to Cuban President Thomas Estrada Palma, acting under the authority of their new constitution, which was done on May 20, ending the U.S. occupation of Cuba. The Philippine-American War ended during this session on July 4, 1902. The major legislation that was passed in the first session on June 28, 1902 was the Isthmian Canal Act for the construction of the Panama Canal, supported by Senator Blackburn and many others in Congress. Lengthy discussions were conducted on the Senate floor about the best way to construct a canal during this Session, which provided Senator Blackburn with a thorough understanding of the needs, conditions, and challenges of constructing it, information that would prove very useful to the future Governor of the Panama Canal Zone.

Even though Senator Blackburn was an experienced statesman beginning his third term in the Senate, the Democratic Party was the minority party, and choice assignments to prominent committees were given to Republicans. Senator Blackburn was appointed on the following committees: Census, Corporations Organized in the District of Columbia, Judiciary, Naval Affairs, Pacific Islands and Porto Rico, and Privileges and Elections, as well as one to establish the University of the United States.

Senator Blackburn sponsored many bills in the Fifty-Seventh Congress, including bills for pensions or to increase pensions, bills to grant the relief of persons or companies, a bill for the relief of the Madison Female Institute, a bill for the relief of Cape Fear and People's Steamboat Company, a bill for the relief of the Bardstown and Louisville Turnpike Company (among others), a bill for the relief of the drafted men in the state of Kentucky, a bill to amend the internal-revenue laws, a bill for the reference of claims of certain volunteer soldiers to the Court of Claims, a bill for the extension of roads in the District of Columbia, a bill for the relief of the Russellville and Logan County Agricultural and Mechanical Association of the state of Kentucky, and a bill for the relief of the trustees of the Bloomfield Lodge, Number Fifty-Seven, Free, Ancient, and Accepted Masons, among many others.

The work on the District of Columbia shines throughout Senator Blackburn's third term. There were twenty-five bills referred by the Senate during the First Session. Blackburn's committee made eight reports to the Senate on those bills. During the First Session, Senator Blackburn "schooled" New York's Republican Junior Senator Depew about the Goebel Election Law, asserting that it was reviewed and approved by the U.S. Supreme Court. Soon thereafter, Kentucky's Republican Senator Deboe proposed an amendment to the House joint resolution to amend the Constitution to allow the election of U.S. Senators by popular vote and based his argument on the events that took place in Kentucky under the Goebel Election Law. The debate between Blackburn and Deboe became personal and intimate. It was an extraordinary and lengthy debate in which Deboe used the Kentucky law as a graphic example why it would be better to elect U.S. Senators directly by the popular vote instead of continuing to have state legislatures select them. The debate over the best method to elect Senators continued through this Congress and into the next one. Eventually the Seventeenth Amendment to the United States Constitution was passed by Congress on May 13, 1912, providing for the direct election of U.S. Senators by popular vote. It was ratified by three-quarters of the states on April 8, 1913.

Second Session, Fifty-Seventh Congress (December 1, 1902–March 3, 1903)

This Session passed the Immigration Act of 1903, also called the Anarchist Exclusion Act, which regulated immigration and established four classes of people who were not admissible into the United States: anarchists, people with epilepsy, beggars, and anyone transporting prostitutes into the country. Anarchists were targeted after members of the International Working People's Association (IWPA) exploded a bomb in Chicago's Haymarket Square, inspired by their manifesto, which called for "the destruction of the existing class rule, by all means, i.e., by energetic, relentless, revolutionary and international action." After the assassination of President McKinley by a self-proclaimed anarchist, Congress was more than ready to act to protect the country and passed the Immigration Act in response. President Theodore Roosevelt called for the exclusion of anarchists in his first address to Congress on December 3, 1901:

> I earnestly recommend to the congress that in the exercise of its wise discretion it should take into consideration the coming to this country of anarchists or persons professing principles hostile to all government.... They and those like them should be kept out of this country; and if found here they should be promptly deported to the country whence they came.

In addition, this Session passed the Militia Act of 1903, the Elkins Act, and the Expediting Act. The Militia Act defined when the National

Guard could be federalized and provided funding for its training and equipment, including the annual summer camps. The Elkins Act allowed the Interstate Commerce Commission to penalize railroads if they offered rebates to shippers and made the railroad corporations, their officers, and their employees all liable for the practice. President Roosevelt made this part of his "Square Deal" domestic program, beloved by the populace. Before the Elkins Act was passed, the livestock and petroleum industries paid standard rail shipping rates, but then would demand that the railroad company give them a rebate. The railroad companies felt that they were being forced by the railroad trusts to issue rebates and resented losing the profits. Railroad companies supported President Roosevelt against the Railroad Trusts as did much of the population who did not receive any rebates and felt that they were not treated fairly economically by the railroads and the government. President Roosevelt also introduced the Expediting Act to break up trusts in the railroad industries and the steel, meatpacking, and oil industries promptly. This act allowed the U.S. Justice Department to handle the cases against the railroad, steel, meatpacking, and oil industries first in order to break up the unfair trusts as quickly as possible as part of President Roosevelt's Square Deal program. While President Roosevelt was not a Populist, he supported laws that protected all Americans.

During the Second Session, Senator Blackburn presented petitions against enactment of the eight-hour bill from representatives of several Kentucky businesses in Kentucky, as did many other Senators from companies in their states. Fortunately, their petition failed and an eight-hour workday law was later passed in the Senate.

During the Second Session, Senator Blackburn spoke against the national banking bill that authorized national banks to keep public money deposits while limiting the interest charged or received to four percent per annum. He advocated on the Senate floor, acting as in the Committee of the Whole, that the United States should pay down its debts with the excess money in the Treasury, collected over the years from high taxes and tariffs. He said that:

> The law to-day confers ample power upon the Secretary of the Treasury to invest this plethora of revenue in the purchase and retirement of the United States Government bonds, which are its evidence of debt.

The debate continued in the Senate but was not concluded until a later session when the Senate, as in Committee of the Whole, passed the national banking bill (S. 7301) that authorized national banks to keep public money deposits while limiting the interest charged or received to four percent per annum. Senator Blackburn voted against it. As a member of the minority party, Senator Blackburn knew the chances of changing the Republican and majority party's opinion, but he refused to let bills go to a vote without voicing his concerns, shared by so many people.

Senator Blackburn also made sure that the relative importance of bills was kept in mind when the Senate was asked to vote unanimously in favor of a bill to compile three memorial addresses about three Republican leaders: Lincoln, Garfield, and William McKinley. He thought that the antitrust bill should be considered first because it was more important to the American people. His objection caused the bill to be put on the calendar for debate and discussion on the Senate floor at the regular time. Putting it on the calendar told the public about the work of the Senate on their behalf.

During the Second Session, Senator Blackburn spoke at length about the 1898 act of Congress that limited the prices to be paid for telephones in the District of Columbia, which had never gone into effect because it was contested in the courts. The Senate was considering the repeal of the act, and Senator Blackburn shared his extensive knowledge of the District, gained from his committee work and his work creating The Organic Act of 1878. Ultimately the bill was passed to repeal the 1898 act, limiting and fixing the rates of telephone charges in the District of Columbia.

In addition, the Senate dealt with the issues about governing the Philippines much of the time in the Second Session. Senator Blackburn had more occasions during this Session to instruct junior members of the Senate in proper parliamentary procedure, an area of his expertise due to his service on the Committee on Rules and his long experience in both Houses of Congress.

Fifty-Eighth Congress (March 4, 1903–March 4, 1905)

The Fifty-Eighth Congress met during the third and fourth years of President Theodore Roosevelt's presidency. The number of seats in the House of Representatives was based on the Twelfth Census taken in 1900. The Republican majority continued in the House and Senate. Forty-five states were represented in Congress, with five non-voting representatives present for the Arizona Territory, Hawaii Territory, New Mexico Territory, Oklahoma Territory, and Porto Rico.

The major legislation of this Congress was the Kinkaid Act, passed during the Second Session, and the Transfer Act of 1905, passed during the Third Session. The Kinkaid Act basically amended the Homestead Act of 1862 and allowed a person to acquire one section or 640 acres of public domain land in Nebraska free of charge, except for modest filing fees. It was called the Kinkaid Act because it was introduced by Nebraska's U.S. Representative Moses Kinkaid. The Transfer Act transferred the control of the forest reserves from the Department of the Interior to the Department of Agriculture, Bureau of Forestry. Senator Blackburn maintained his seats on the committees for the Census, Judiciary, Naval Affairs, Pacific Islands and Porto Rico, and the University of the United States, and was added to the committees for Military Affairs, and Organization, Conduct, and Expenditures of the Executive Departments.

Senator Blackburn sponsored many bills, including bills to grant pensions to people and to many churches in Kentucky and the District of Columbia, like the Colored Baptist Church of Lebanon, Kentucky, and the Baptist Church of Crab Orchard, Kentucky, among many others, He also sponsored bills for the payment of certain claims of volunteers of the Civil War, bills for raising the rank of military officers or for claims from volunteer soldiers during the Civil War, bills to authorize busts of former Senators, bills to construct bridges and roads, bills to regulate salaries of assistant postmasters in post-offices of the first class, and others.

Senator Blackburn also introduced a bill for payment to Liliuokalani, formerly Queen of the Kingdom of Hawaii, which was read twice without objection and referred to the Committee on Pacific Islands and Porto Rico. Blackburn sought to compensate the former queen for the loss of her kingdom when it was made a territory and then a state. Unfortunately, it did not pass.

He also presented a memorial of the Independent Tobacco Manufacturer's, protesting the unfair advantage of no internal-revenue tax laws on cigars shipped from the Philippine Islands to the United States. He presented reports of his committees, such as to the Committee on Military Affairs when that committee granted an honorable discharge to a soldier, for example, and many others.

First Session, Fifty-Eighth Congress (November 9, 1903–December 7, 1903)

The Senate noted that the Panama Canal Company began to show its weakness because Mr. De Lesseps was trying to raise money from the French public and had petitioned the French assembly for leave to issue lottery bonds as a way to raise money to save the failing French effort to dig a canal through the Isthmus. Discussions continued throughout the Fifty-Eighth Congress on the Panama Canal, Cuba, the Pacific Islands, and sugar cane production and trade. Much discussion was had defending the actions taken to ensure the independence of the new Republic of Panama and the construction of the inter-oceanic canal across the Isthmus.

Second Session, Fifty-Eighth Congress (December 7, 1903–April 28, 1904)

The Panama Canal discussions dominated the Senate floor during this session and resulted in the passing of an act to provide for the temporary government of the Canal Zone at Panama and for the protection of the canal works. The Senate also continued its ongoing work overseeing the building and development of Washington, D.C., with many bills passed to develop the district under the direction of Senator Blackburn on the District of Columbia Committee, including developing streets, building bridges over the Potomac, and adding buildings.

This Session produced a joint resolution of the Senate and House requiring more testing of education levels of immigrants prior to entry in the country. Another joint resolution authorized the Secretary of the Interior to print an extra edition of the map of the growing United States for 1904, including the latest map of territories. These large color maps may be seen in Senator Blackburn's library today, maintained in the home of the author. In addition, due to public demand, a joint resolution of the Senate and the House was passed that amended the act to regulate the immigration of aliens into the United States, requiring more testing of education levels prior to entry.

In more personal matters to the Senate, Senator Marcus Hanna of Ohio died on February 15, 1904. Senator Hanna was well known as

President McKinley's political campaign manager. Senator Blackburn was appointed to a committee of twenty-five Senators to superintend the funeral. Later in April that year, Senator Blackburn gave a moving eulogy for Senator Hanna on the Senate floor. In many ways, Senator Blackburn's unrehearsed description of Senator Hanna could be used to describe the Kentucky Senator:

> MR. BLACKBURN: It has been truly and eloquently said by Senators who have preceded me that he was an open-hearted, honest, candid man. More than once I have had occasion to go to him to know what his course would be upon a given matter pending before this body. He never refused to answer, and when he answered it was never by evasion. Whether friend or foe, you always knew where he would stand upon any disputed question. His faith once plighted was never violated. His word once given was never broken. Loyal in his friendships, true to his convictions, he commanded in fullest measure the respect and admiration even to his opponents.
>
> I know no higher tribute to pay a departed friend, loyal in every relation in life. He never measured consequences nor considered sacrifices when he deemed himself called upon to stand by his friends.

In March, the Senate passed a bill regulating the erection of buildings on the Mall in the District of Columbia to preserve the vistas from the Dome of the Capitol to the Washington Monument, as originally designed by Pierre L'Enfant under the plan approved by George Washington and Thomas Jefferson.

During this Session, Senator Blackburn had more opportunities to instruct junior Senators regarding the proper time to argue a bill or vote upon a bill or amendment to a bill. He was able to keep track of the procedural status of a discussion on the floor while following the substantive matter of an extensive discussion and argument on the military academy appropriation bill. Wyoming's young Republican Senator Warren attempted to amend the military appropriation bill. Senator Blackburn objected to it because it had the effect of proposing new general legislation that would require the U.S. government to buy lands for permanent military training camp grounds across the country. This type of bill could not be inserted into another bill as an amendment, and Senator Blackburn objected to the breach of the rules and raised a point of order. A Senator raises a "point of order" when it is noticed that a rule has been broken and raises a point of order as a way to insist that the rules be enforced.The President pro tempore agreed with Senator Blackburn, and all three amendments were ruled out of order. The proposed amendment was then voted as not germane by the Senate, and the President pro tempore declared the amendment not germane, ending the discussion.

Third Session, Fifty-Eighth Congress (December 5, 1904–March 3, 1905)

Senator Blackburn was named to the Judiciary Committee, the Committee on Naval Affairs, and the Committee on Organization, Conduct, and Expenditures of the Executive Department, along with his other committee assignments. As a member of the Committee on Naval Affairs, Senator Blackburn spoke passionately about the proposed increase of the battle ships in the navy, arguing that an increase was not needed. He said:

> MR. BLACKBURN: Should any Senator ask me whether I think we have gone too far in the building up of the Navy, I answer and say no. I have been a part and parcel of its construction. I have by voice and vote added to its every appropriation that has been made for its expansion to its present limits, and I apologize for nothing on that score. But I say, to my fellow-Senators we have reached a point where it will require a hundred millions of money every year to maintain the Navy on its present authorized basis if you never vote a dollar for the building of another ship. Is not a hundred millions of money a year enough for the maintenance of your Navy?...
>
> Mr. President, I echo the sentiment I heard from the Senator from North Dakota [Mr. McCUMBER]. I want to see my country grow great and powerful—not by means of aggression; I want the influence of this great Government extended—not by force of arms; I want her territory expanded, not by conquest, but by peaceful methods. I have always believed and do still believe that the greatest and grandest

> mission vouchsafed to any nation was intended for us; that it was not that we should go about browbeating and bullying weaker nations, even when republics. I have always believed that the mission of the United States was to uplift, to liberalize and republicanize every power upon the North and South American continents....
>
> That was my ambition; that was my hope; that was my plan—that in the tide of time this great country and Government of ours have accomplished its grand mission and lifted from the ruts and gutters of imperial and autocratic power every government from the north to the south and made a republic where tyranny and autocracy before held sway....
>
> Mr. President, I have said all I care to say. To sum up in a single sentence, the proposition is whether we will be content to rest for another year without a further increase of battle ships for our Navy. As we have within the last year broken all records of all countries and all governments in the number of battle ships launched, it seems to me we may safely afford to drop this item from the pending bill.

The bill was argued further on the Senate floor, and ultimately, the House disagreed with the Senate amendments, but the Senate insisted, requiring a joint conference on the bill. Since Senator Blackburn had opposed it, he was not named one of the three conferees. Later the bill was passed in modified form, following recommendations from both sides of Congress.

Senator Blackburn also debated the Post Office bill and voted against an amendment that did not pass and against another amendment that was passed by the majority party. He voted to continue the temporary government of the Panama Canal through the beginning of the Fifty-Ninth Congress, which passed.

Sometimes Senator Blackburn even disagreed with the decisions of his committees. For instance, the Military Committee voted to appoint three men as midshipmen who had been charged with hazing in the Military Academy, but Senator Blackburn discussed the hazing charge against the three midshipmen and did not agree that they should be appointed midshipmen and receive an advancement of position. Blackburn wanted the academy to obey the law to prevent and suppress hazing at the Military Academy and thought that the passage of this act negated that law.

Fifty-Ninth Congress (March 4, 1905–March 4, 1907)

The Fifty-Ninth Congress met during the fifth and sixth years of President's Theodore Roosevelt's presidency after he won re-election. President Roosevelt's address to Congress discussed the Monroe Doctrine and its application in Hawaii, Alaska, Porto Rico, and the Panama Canal in the country's realm of influence.

The number of seats in the House was again based on the Twelfth Census taken in 1900. Forty-five States were represented in Congress, with six non-voting representatives present for the Alaska Territory, Arizona Territory, Hawaii Territory, New Mexico Territory, Oklahoma Territory, and Porto Rico.

Congress settled into issuing laws that regulated domestic products for the general welfare of the populace, although there was some discussion about President Theodore Roosevelt becoming too powerful and ignoring the House of Representatives and the Senate. There was much discussion of the chaos at the Panama Canal that needed resolving. The Panama Canal Act passed to provide for the construction of a canal connecting the Atlantic and Pacific Oceans, and Senator Blackburn voted in favor of the bill to make appropriations for the act, authorizing eleven million dollars to build the Panama Canal. Thereafter the Senate debated at length whether the canal should be a sea-level canal like the failed French plan under De Lesseps or a lock-canal favored by American engineers. At first, a bill passed that ordered the construction of a sea-level canal at Panama, but discussion continued throughout this session until it was finally resolved for a lock-canal, favored by Senator Blackburn, President Theodore Roosevelt, and the majority of the Senate.

The Republicans maintained their majority in both Houses of Congress. Major legislation included the Antiquities Act, the Hepburn Act, the Pure Foods and Drug Act of 1906, the Meat Inspection Act, and the Expatriation Act of 1907, to name a few. The Antiquities Act gave the President the power to create national monuments from public lands, put to good use by President Roosevelt, who created national parks and who submitted a report to the Senate on preserving

Niagara Falls. The Senate passed a bill to control and regulate the Niagara to preserve the Niagara Falls in the First Session. The Hepburn Act gave the Interstate Commerce Commission (ICC) the power to set the maximum railroad rates and ended free railroad passes to regular shippers and allowed the ICC to review railroad financial records. President Roosevelt supported this act because it allowed him to achieve one of his major goals, which was to regulate railroads. The Pure Food and Drug Act of 1906 was the first consumer protection law and led to the creation of the Food and Drug Administration that stopped the mislabeling of food products and allowed the government to inspect food products and drug products. Furthermore, drugs had to meet minimum purity standards. Likewise the Federal Meat Inspection Act was a consumer protection act to prevent the spread of adulterated or mislabeled meats. The Expatriation Act allowed the U.S. to renounce a person's citizenship, but it has since been repealed.

During the Fifty-Ninth Congress, Senator Blackburn maintained his seats on the following committees: Census, Judiciary, Military Affairs, Naval Affairs, Pacific Islands and Porto Rico, the University of the United States, and Organization, Conduct, and Expenditures of the Executive Departments. He continued to be active in the Senate, introducing many bills, including many from the Committee on the District of Columbia, speaking on the proper parliamentarian rules of the Senate, voting on the many bills considered and passed by the Senate, dutifully serving Kentucky and the nation as they grew economically and industrially into the twentieth century, and expanding America's role in its hemisphere.

First Session, Fifty-Ninth Congress (Dec 4, 1905–June 30, 1906)

Senator Blackburn voluntarily resigned from the Committee on Naval Affairs on January 20, 1906, and Senator Mallory voluntarily resigned from the Committee on the District of Columbia. Then Senator Blackburn was assigned to the Committee on the District of Columbia and Senator Mallory was assigned to the Committee on Naval Affairs. The work on the District Committee was close to Blackburn's heart.

Senator Blackburn was appointed to be a visitor to West Point and to attend the annual examination of cadets at the United States Military

Academy at West Point, New York, considered an honor among Senators. He debated vigorously against the use of contract surgeons in the United States Army. Senator Blackburn voted in favor of an amendment to a special election bill considering the statehood of New Mexico and Arizona to allow them to vote to determine if they wanted to join as one state, which was passed, though they did not decide to join.

During the First Session, Blackburn introduced a bill to provide for the purchase a site in Versailles, Kentucky, and to build a building surrounded by an open space of at least forty feet on each side upon the land for the U.S. Post Office for Versailles. Two months later, the bill passed, and the price for the site and building was limited to twenty-five thousand dollars. The U.S. Post Office building was constructed at the corner of the intersection of Main Street and Morgan Street and is still standing today. It was used for many years as the U.S. Post Office. Senator Blackburn also introduced a bill to provide for the purchase of a site and the creation of a building in Catlettsburg, Kentucky, which was referred to the Committee on Public Buildings and Grounds. He introduced a bill for the protection of wild birds and animals in the District of Columbia, which was later passed. He stressed the need to pass two important bills in Alaska on the Senate floor, and he was also able to secure the unanimous consent of the Senate acting as Committee of the Whole to pass a bill authorizing the Alaska Pacific Railway and Terminal Company to build a trestle across the tide and shore lands of Controller Bay in southern Alaska and to pass a bill authorizing the same company to build a bridge across the Yukon River.

The tone in the Senate had calmed down considerably among the Democrats since 1902 under Senator Gorman's leadership, assisted by his close friend and supporter, Senator Blackburn. Relations among Democrats and Republicans had improved as well, with the sectional feelings that had ripped the country apart since the Civil War softening between the North and East and the South and West. On April 15, 1906, Senator Blackburn spoke on the Senate floor about the regulation of railroad rates, another major issue confronted by the Senate, and praised the "utter lack of sectionality" in the bill, saying:

> I have never seen in my somewhat extended observance of legislation, a more unselfish, a broader, fairer, more admirable proposition.

Senator Blackburn sponsored many bills in the Fifty-Ninth Congress, including extensive work on the Committee on the District of Columbia. Senator Blackburn was one of the Senators who wrote the rules of the Senate and would become frustrated when Senators would not follow the rules of parliamentary procedure. He was frustrated when three members of a subcommittee of his Committee on the District of Columbia attempted to have a vote on a proposed amendment to legislation to increase the taxation on corporations in the District of Columbia before the vote on a motion to recommit the bill back to the Committee. The Senator's objections were heard, the proposed amendment was withdrawn, and the bill was sent back to the Committee on the District of Columbia for more fact-gathering, as it should have been, but it took Senator Blackburn quite a bit of protesting and educating his colleagues to convey the proper procedure to the Senate.

Blackburn kept the Senate on track procedurally when he could. He protected the rights of both Houses of Congress when one Senator attempted to withdraw a conference report, pointing out that it was the property of both Houses, which required unanimous consent to withdraw or recommit to a committee. The Senate voted in agreement with his motion.

He introduced many bills, including pensions or to grant the relief of people or companies. He introduced a bill to incorporate the East Washington Heights Railroad Company, a bill to authorize the Court of Claims to admit as evidence affidavits in certain cases, and a bill to pay for a claim for cotton from the Civil War days. There were many bills relating to the management, government, construction, business, banking, schools, and the transportation within the District; a bill to provide for the purchase of a site and to build a building upon it at Catlettsburg, Kentucky; a bill for the relief of the trustees of the African Baptist Church of Paris, Kentucky; a bill for the relief of drafted men in the state of Kentucky; a bill for the relief of the owners of certain steamboats; a bill to authorize the Alaska Pacific Railway and Terminal Company to construct a bridge across the Copper River in the Territory of Alaska; a bill to authorize the Alaska Pacific Railway and Terminal to construct a railroad trestle across tide and shore lands in Controller Bay in the Territory of Alaska; and a bill to authorize the purchase of a portrait of Henry Clay, among many others.

Senator Joseph C. S. Blackburn, copied from the March 17, 1896 New York Times, page 1 of 12. (Image courtesy of the author, Blackburn Collection)

Kentucky Governor William O. Bradley, copied from the March 17, 1896 New York Times, page 1 of 12. (Image courtesy of the author, Blackburn Collection)

"BIRTH OF THE TEDDY BEAR (1902), The tubby cub supplanted wooly lambs. TIME, August 21, 1944 – First appearance of the "Teddy Bear" in Clifford Berryman's political cartoon. The cartoonist Berryman was "discovered" by Senator Joseph C. S. Blackburn who then helped him secure work in Washington, D.C. as a political cartoonist. (Image courtesy of the author, Blackburn Collection)

Kentucky Governor William Goebel, first state governor to be assassinated in office in 1900, was a supporter of Senator Blackburn's re-election to a third six-year term in the U.S. Senate.

U.S. Senator Joseph C. S. Blackburn (Image courtesy of the author, Blackburn Collection)

"For President Jo. C. S. Blackburn." Joseph Blackburn's 1896 Democratic Presidential Nomination campaign button. (Image courtesy of the author, Blackburn Collection)

Portrait of Henry Clay given to Senator Joseph Clay Stiles Blackburn by the U.S. Senate in recognition of his eighteen years of service in the U.S. Senate as the longest serving Senator from Kentucky, and six years more than Henry Clay. (Image courtesy of the author, Blackburn Collection)

Portrait of U.S. Senator Joseph C. S. Blackburn, then Minority Leader, given to him by the U.S. Senate in recognition of his eighteen years of service, the longest in Kentucky's history, and his service as Minority Leader. (Image courtesy of the author, Blackburn Collection)

President Theodore Roosevelt on Inauguration Day, September 14, 1901

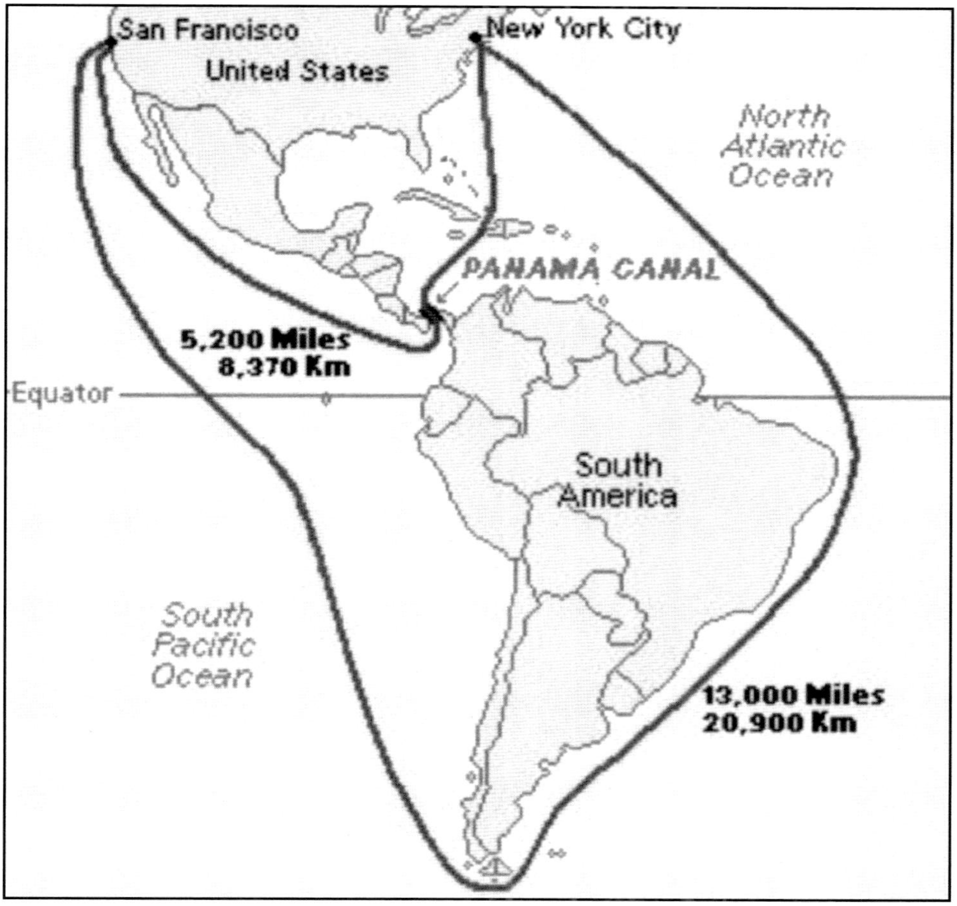

Sailing around Cape Horn vs. sailing through the Panama Canal

The President and Mrs. Roosevelt
request the pleasure of the company of
Miss Lane
at a reception to be held at
The White House
Thursday evening, January the seventeenth
nineteen hundred and seven
from nine to half after ten o'clock.

President Theodore Roosevelt and Mrs. Roosevelt's 1907 invitation to Terese Blackburn Lane, Governor Joseph Blackburn's granddaughter, to a reception at the White House. (Image courtesy of author, Blackburn Collection)

Colonel William C. Gorgas stopped the spread of yellow fever and malaria in the Panama Canal Zone by controlling the mosquitoes that carry the diseases at a time when others were skeptical of his methods, allowing the greatest work of modern time to go forward.

Construction work on the Culebra Cut in 1907.

President Theodore Roosevelt on a steam shovel in the Panama Canal Zone, circa 1906. This was the first international trip by a sitting U.S. President. (Library of Congress, Prints and Photographs Division)

Commemorative Fifty Cent stamp in honor of Governor Joseph Clay Stiles Blackburn, first Civil Governor of the Panama Canal Zone, 1907-1909. (Image courtesy of the author, Blackburn Collection)

Senator Blackburn with his Granddaughter Terese Blackburn Lane whom he raised as his daughter after the death of her parents Thomas and Lucile Blackburn Lane, the Senator's youngest daughter. (Image courtesy of the author, Blackburn Collection)

Members of the Isthmian Canal Commission in 1910. Pictured left to right: Lt. Col. William Siebert, Governor Joseph C. S. Blackburn, Rear Admiral Harry H. Rousseau, Joseph Bucklin Bishop, Colonel George W. Goethals (front), Lt. Col. Harry F. Hodges, Colonel William C. Gorgas, Colonel David Gaillard. (Image courtesy of the author, Blackburn Collection)

Construction work on the Gaillard Cut, 1907, named for Colonel David Gaillard of the Isthmian Canal Commission, who led the work on this section of the Panama Canal.

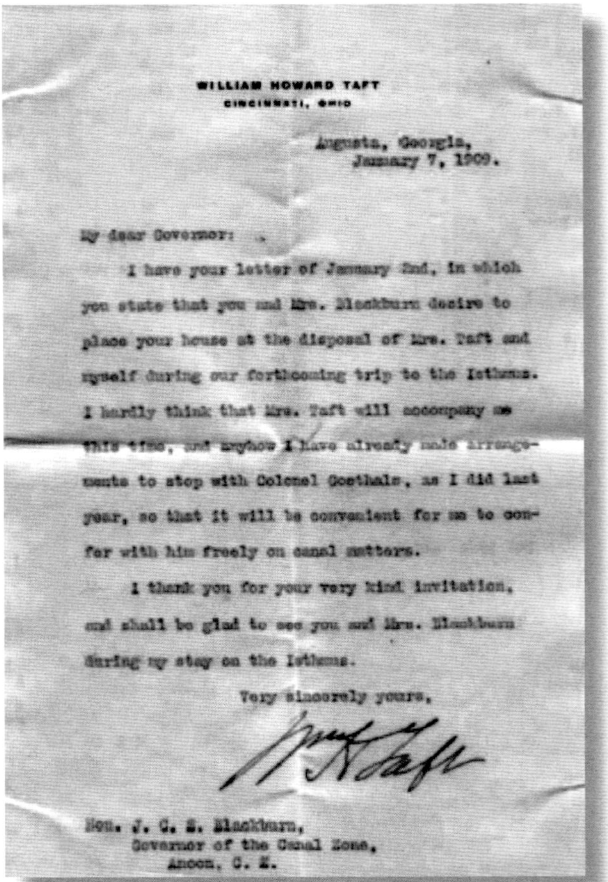

WILLIAM HOWARD TAFT
CINCINNATI, OHIO

Augusta, Georgia,
January 7, 1909.

My dear Governor:

I have your letter of January 2nd, in which you state that you and Mrs. Blackburn desire to place your house at the disposal of Mrs. Taft and myself during our forthcoming trip to the Isthmus. I hardly think that Mrs. Taft will accompany me this time, and anyhow I have already made arrangements to stop with Colonel Goethals, as I did last year, so that it will be convenient for me to confer with him freely on canal matters.

I thank you for your very kind invitation, and shall be glad to see you and Mrs. Blackburn during my stay on the Isthmus.

Very sincerely yours,

Wm H Taft

Hon. J. C. S. Blackburn,
Governor of the Canal Zone,
Ancon, C. Z.

Letter from President-Elect William Howard Taft to Governor Blackburn that reads:
William Howard Taft
Cincinnati, Ohio
Augusta, Georgia
January 7, 1909.
My dear Governor:

I have your letter of January 2nd, in which you state that you and Mrs. Blackburn desire to place your houses at the disposal of Mrs. Taft and myself during our forthcoming trip to the Isthmus. I hardly think that Mrs. Taft will accompany me this time, and anyhow I have already made arrangements to stop with Colonel Goethals, as I did last year, so that it will be convenient for me to confer with him freely on canal matters.

I thank you for your very kind invitation, and shall be glad to see you and Mrs. Blackburn during my stay on the Isthmus.

Very sincerely yours,
Wm H Taft
Hon. J. C. S. Blackburn,
Governor of the Canal Zone,
Ancon, C.E
(Image courtesy of the author, Blackburn Collection)

Mr. Jo. C. S. Blackburn
Governor of the Canal Zone.

REPÚBLICA DE PANAMÁ

PRESIDENCIA

El Presidente de la República
y la señora de Obaldía

Tienen el honor de invitar á usted á un baile que en honor del Honorable Señor - - - - - -

William H. Taft,

Presidente electo de los Estados Unidos de Norte América, y de la señora de Taft, tendrá lugar en el Teatro Nacional el próximo viernes, cinco de los corrientes, á las 9 p. m.

Panamá, Febrero 3 de 1909.

Invitation to Governor Blackburn to the Panamanian President's dinner in honor of President-elect William H. Taft, February 3, 1909. (Image courtesy of the author, Blackburn Collection)

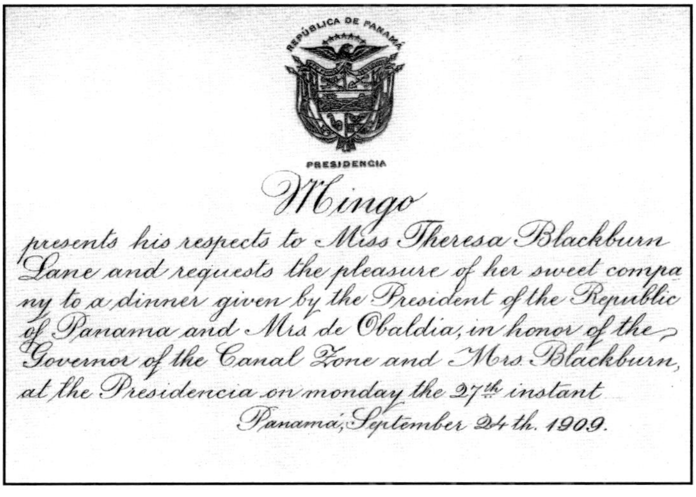

REPÚBLICA DE PANAMÁ

PRESIDENCIA

Mingo

presents his respects to Miss Theresa Blackburn Lane and requests the pleasure of her sweet company to a dinner given by the President of the Republic of Panama and Mrs de Obaldia, in honor of the Governor of the Canal Zone and Mrs Blackburn, at the Presidencia on monday the 27th instant

Panamá, September 24 th. 1909.

Personal invitation to Miss Theresa Blackburn Lane, Governor Blackburn's granddaughter, to the Panamanian President Obaldia's dinner in honor of the Governor of the Canal Zone and Mrs. Blackburn, September 24, 1909. (Image courtesy of the author, Blackburn Collection)

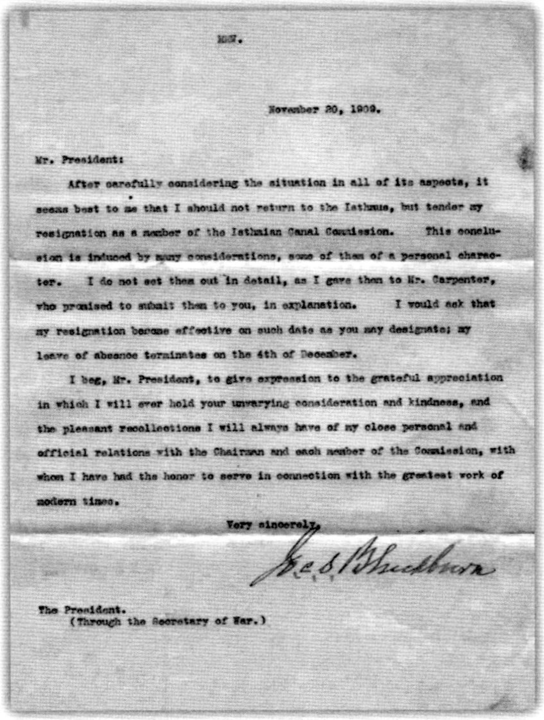

MSW.

November 20, 1909.

Mr. President:

After carefully considering the situation in all of its aspects, it seems best to me that I should not return to the Isthmus, but tender my resignation as a member of the Isthmian Canal Commission. This conclusion is induced by many considerations, some of them of a personal character. I do not set them out in detail, as I gave them to Mr. Carpenter, who promised to submit them to you, in explanation. I would ask that my resignation become effective on such date as you may designate; my leave of absence terminates on the 4th of December.

I beg, Mr. President, to give expression to the grateful appreciation in which I will ever hold your unvarying consideration and kindness, and the pleasant recollections I will always have of my close personal and official relations with the Chairman and each member of the Commission, with whom I have had the honor to serve in connection with the greatest work of modern times.

Very sincerely,

Jo C S Blackburn

The President.
(Through the Secretary of War.)

Letter from Governor Joseph C.S. Blackburn to President Taft offering his resignation. It reads:
November 20, 1909
Mr. President:

After carefully considering the situation in all of its aspects, it seems best to me that I should not return to the Isthmus, but tender my resignation as a member of the Isthmian Canal Commission. This conclusion is induced by many considerations, some of them of a personal character. I do not set them out in detail, as I gave them to Mr. Carpenter, who promised to submit them to you, in explanation. I would ask that my resignation become effective on such date as you may designate; my leave of absence terminates on the 4th of December.

I beg, Mr. President, to give expression to the grateful appreciation in which I will ever hold your unvarying consideration and kindness, and the pleasant recollections I will always have of my close personal and official relations with the Chairman and each member of the Commission, with whom I have had the honor to serve in connection with the greatest work of modern times.

Very Sincerely,
Jo.C.S. Blackburn
The President
(Through the Secretary of War)
(Image courtesy of the author, Blackburn Collection)

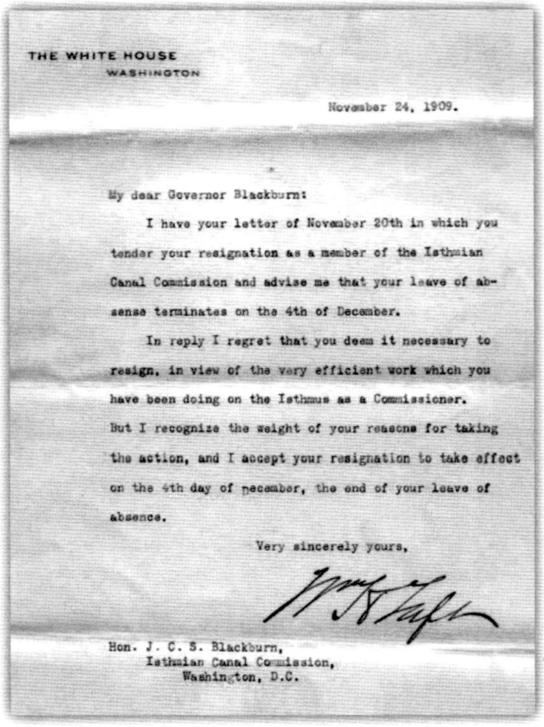

THE WHITE HOUSE
WASHINGTON

November 24, 1909.

My dear Governor Blackburn:

I have your letter of November 20th in which you tender your resignation as a member of the Isthmian Canal Commission and advise me that your leave of absense terminates on the 4th of December.

In reply I regret that you deem it necessary to resign, in view of the very efficient work which you have been doing on the Isthmus as a Commissioner. But I recognize the weight of your reasons for taking the action, and I accept your resignation to take effect on the 4th day of December, the end of your leave of absence.

Very sincerely yours,

Wm H Taft

Hon. J. C. S. Blackburn,
Isthmian Canal Commission,
Washington, D.C.

THE WHITE HOUSE
WASHINGTON
November 24, 1909.
My dear Governor Blackburn:

I have your letter of November 20th in which you tender your resignation as a member of the Isthmian Canal Commission and advise me that your leave of absence terminates on the 4th of December.

In reply I regret that you deem it necessary to resign, in view of the very efficient work which you have been doing on the Isthmus as a Commissioner. But I recognize the weight of your reasons for taking this action, and I accept your resignation to take effect on the 4th day of December, the end of your leave of absence.

Very sincerely yours,
Wm. H Taft
(Image courtesy of the author, Blackburn Collection)

Photograph of the winning Lincoln Memorial Model submitted by the architect Henry Bacon in 1912 to the Lincoln Memorial Commission, signed by Henry Bacon:
"To the Hon. J. C. S. Blackburn with the kind regards of Henry Bacon."
In 1923, President Warren G. Harding presented Henry Bacon with the sixth American Institute of Architect's Gold Medal, the highest award given to one architect a year since 1917. (Image courtesy of the author, Blackburn Collection)

The Lincoln Memorial 2012. (Image by the author's husband, Thomas E. Fielder)

L'Enfant's main east-west axis from the Capitol Dome to the Washington Monument to the Lincoln Memorial. (National Park Service)

Special Resident Commissioner Joseph C. S. Blackburn (center, white mustache, top hat) and others laying the seventeen-ton cornerstone of the Lincoln Memorial, February 15, 1915. (Library of Congress)

he Washington Time

OSS. THURSDAY, FEBRUARY 12, 1914. ONE CE

Senator Gore's Accuser Are

IDN'T NOTIFY ME,' SA

BREAKING GROUND ON MEMORIAL SITE

BREAKING GROUND ON MEMORIAL SITE. In the picture are: HENRY BACON, who designed the Lincoln Memorial; Former Senator J. C. S. Blackburn, resident commissioner of the Lincoln Memorial Commission; M. F. COMER of Toledo, Ohio, the contractor for the foundation of the building; and COL. W. W. HARTS, engineer-officer in charge of public buildings and grounds, who will supervise the construction of the memorial. The Washington Times, February 12, 1914, Lincoln's birthday. (Image courtesy of the author, Blackburn Collection)

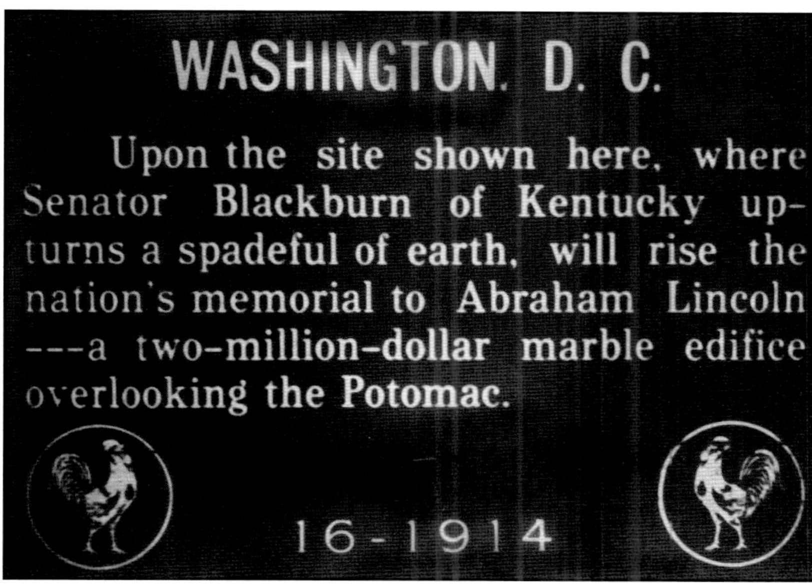

1914 Lincoln Memorial Groundbreaking Plaque, Washington, D.C., commemorating the site overlooking the Potomac where Senator Blackburn of Kentucky broke the ground for the nation's new two-million-dollar marble memorial honoring Abraham Lincoln. (Image courtesy of the author, Blackburn Collection)

The Piccirilli Brothers assembling the marble Lincoln Statue in the Lincoln Memorial in 1920.

Lincoln Statue, Lincoln Memorial 2012. (Image by the author's husband, Thomas E. Fielder)

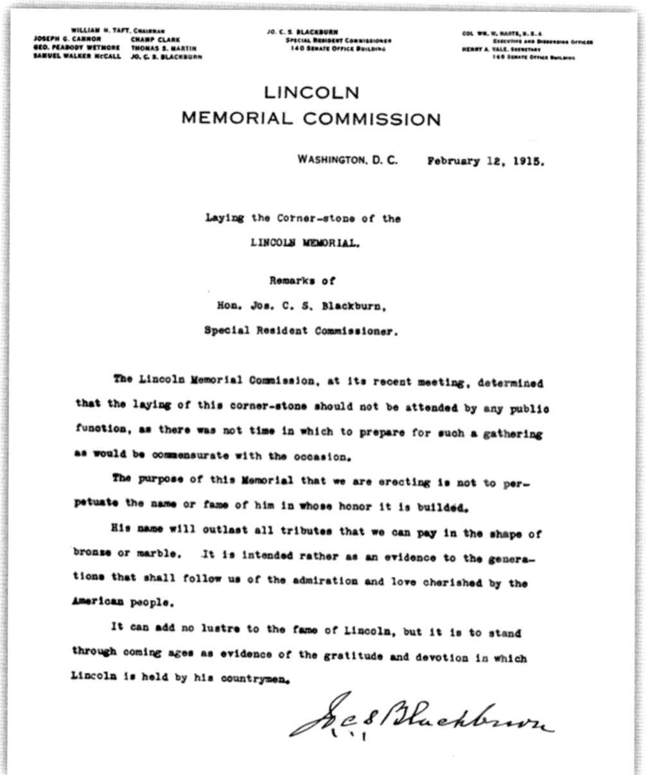

WILLIAM H. TAFT, CHAIRMAN
JOSEPH G. CANNON CHAMP CLARK
GEO. PEABODY WETMORE THOMAS S. MARTIN
SAMUEL WALKER McCALL JO. C. S. BLACKBURN

JO. C. S. BLACKBURN
SPECIAL RESIDENT COMMISSIONER
140 SENATE OFFICE BUILDING

COL. WM. W. HARTS, U. S. A.
EXECUTIVE AND DISBURSING OFFICER
HENRY A. VALE, SECRETARY
140 SENATE OFFICE BUILDING

LINCOLN
MEMORIAL COMMISSION

WASHINGTON, D. C. February 12, 1915.

Laying the Corner-stone of the
LINCOLN MEMORIAL.

Remarks of
Hon. Jos. C. S. Blackburn,
Special Resident Commissioner.

The Lincoln Memorial Commission, at its recent meeting, determined that the laying of this corner-stone should not be attended by any public function, as there was not time in which to prepare for such a gathering as would be commensurate with the occasion.

The purpose of this Memorial that we are erecting is not to perpetuate the name or fame of him in whose honor it is builded.

His name will outlast all tributes that we can pay in the shape of bronze or marble. It is intended rather as an evidence to the generations that shall follow us of the admiration and love cherished by the American people.

It can add no lustre to the fame of Lincoln, but it is to stand through coming ages as evidence of the gratitude and devotion in which Lincoln is held by his countrymen.

Jo. C. S. Blackburn

Laying the Cornerstone of the Lincoln Memorial on Lincoln's birthday, Remarks of Hon. Jo. C. S. Blackburn, Special Resident Commissioner. It reads:
LINCOLN MEMORIAL COMMISSION
WASHINGTON, D.C.
FEBRUARY 12, 1915
Laying the Corner-stone of the LINCOLN MEMORIAL
Remarks of Hon. Jos. C. S. Blackburn, Special Resident Commissioner.

The Lincoln Memorial Committee, at its recent meeting, determined that the laying of this corner-stone should not be attended by any public function, as there was no time in which to prepare for such a gathering as would be commensurate with the occasion.

The purpose of this Memorial that we are erecting is not to perpetuate the name or fame of him in whose honor it is builded.

His name will outlast all tributes that we can pay in the shape of bronze or marble. It is intended rather as an evidence to the generations that shall follow us of the admiration and love cherished by the American people.

It can add no lustre to the fame of Lincoln, but it is to stand through the coming ages as evidence of the gratitude and devotion in which Lincoln is held by his countrymen.

Jo.C.S. Blackburn
(Image courtesy of the author, Blackburn Collection)

Lincoln Memorial under construction (Library of Congress)

Terese Blackburn Lane Rouse, Senator Blackburn's Granddaughter and the author's Grandmother. (Image courtesy of the author, Blackburn Collection)

Clifford Berryman unveiling the portrait of Senator J.C.S. Blackburn that he commissioned in gratitude for the Senator's help securing Berryman's first job in Washington, D.C., launching his career as a political cartoonist. (Image courtesy of author, Blackburn Collection)

"HE PASSED THROUGH LIFE A FRIEND TO ALL." The headstone of Joseph Clay Stiles Blackburn, Blackburn Family Lot, Frankfort Cemetery, Frankfort, Kentucky. (Image courtesy of the author's husband, Thomas E. Fielder)

Senator Blackburn pushed forcefully for the passage of an act to determine the type of construction of canal at Panama during the First Session. He understood how important it was to decide the type of canal before the session adjourned, and he reminded the Senate that the responsibility to decide rested with them, an effort appreciated by President Roosevelt.

> MR. BLACKBURN: Mr. President, there are some facts connected with this situation [deciding whether to build a sea-level canal or a lock-canal] that I think would be well enough for the Senate to realize. I take it that it is an open secret, known to every member of this body, that the preference of the Executive is for a lock and dam canal. It is known by every one that, in reaching that conclusion, he has not followed the advice of the majority of experts, whom he very wisely and very properly summoned to his aid....
>
> That brings me to say what all of us know, or should know, that in the judgment of the American people the responsibility rests not upon the executive, but upon the legislative branch of this Government to determine the type of this canal. Its construction is the most gigantic piece of work ever undertaken by this Government from its foundation down till now. Whether measured by dollars and cents involved in the expenditure, or whether judged in its far-reaching effects upon the commerce of the world, the building of this Isthmian canal is the most gigantic project that this American people has ever undertaken.
>
> Congress, the legislative branch of the Government, is primarily and finally responsible, not alone for the appropriation of the money, not alone for the passage of the act that made its construction possible, but for the method of that construction and for the type that is to be employed. Say what we will, the American people will say, and the American people will be justified in saying, that if we fail, if the legislative branch of this Government fails to determine the type of this canal, it is because that legislative branch of the Government lacked the courage to meet the responsibility that rested on it.

Senator Blackburn actually agreed with President Roosevelt but declined to disclose that opinion during the debate to present a more objective argument about the duties of the Legislative branch, but he was clear that a decision needed to be made during the Session. Thereafter the Senate set the date to vote and decide the type of canal to be built. An amendment to the existing sea-level canal bill was proposed to provide for the construction of a lock-and-dam canal connecting the Atlantic and Pacific, which was intended to be a substitute for the existing sea-level canal bill. That was approved June 28, 1902. The Senate voted on accepting the amendment, and Senator Blackburn voted in favor of it, along with the majority in the Senate, and it was passed. Senator Blackburn agreed with President Roosevelt that a lock-and-dam canal was the best solution for the type of canal to construct across the Isthmus. This was one of Senator Blackburn's most important votes during his third term in the Senate, for the country and the world, and it helped solidify a bond between the President and Blackburn.

Senator Gorman of Maryland died on June 4, 1906. Only Senator Blackburn and one other Senator were his constant companions, discussing the work in the Senate up until his death. Senator Blackburn stepped into the role of Senator Gorman until the session concluded. At the end of this session, the end of Senator Blackburn's third six-year term in the Senate, the Senate gave to Senator Blackburn a portrait of Henry Clay, the famous Senator from the Ashland District, Blackburn's District, because Senator Blackburn had served for eighteen years with distinction, more than the twelve years served by Clay. The portrait of Henry Clay was donated by the heirs of Senator Blackburn to the Kentucky Historical Society and now hangs in the museum in Frankfort, Kentucky, for all Kentuckians.

Second Session, Fifty-Ninth Congress (Dec 3, 1906–March 3, 1907)

Senator Blackburn continued to serve his state and country actively, appearing daily, introducing bills and petitions, voting on the bills and memorials before the Senate, maintaining procedural order where possible in the Senate, and contributing to the debate upon the issues confronting the Senate and the growing country.

Blackburn took a strong stand in support of President Roosevelt's dismissal of three companies of the Twenty-Fifth Infantry after they "shot up" the town of Brownsville, Texas on the night of August 13–14, 1906, killing one citizen and injuring several others. There was extensive debate on the right of the President to dismiss the soldiers from the military without honor. Senator Blackburn believed that the President, as the Commander in Chief, had that right and offered an amendment to a resolution that was submitted to the Senate that stated this, acknowledging the President's right to discharge Army soldiers without honor. The resolution he proposed to amend read as follows:

> *Resolved,* That, without questioning or denying the legal right of the President to discharge without honor enlisted men from the Army of the United States, the Committee on Military Affairs is hereby authorized and directed, by subcommittee or otherwise, to take and have printed testimony for the purpose of ascertaining all the facts with reference to or connected with the affray at Brownsville, Tex., on the night of August 13-14, 1906. Said committee is authorized to send for persons and papers, to administer oaths, to sit during sessions of the Senate, and, if deemed advisable, at Brownsville or elsewhere, the expenses of the investigation to be paid from the contingent fund of the Senate. [Emphasis added to highlight the proposed amendment to the resolution].

It is known as the Blackburn Resolution. President Roosevelt appreciated Blackburn's political skills and "supported it with all his might." This Resolution involved the riot at Brownsville, Texas, where it was determined by the evidence presented to the U.S. Secretary of War Taft that black troops had fired upon civilians from Fort Brown, killing and injuring some of them. President Roosevelt dismissed the soldiers involved in the shooting, based upon the abundance of evidence presented against them. Senator Blackburn's resolution endorsed the President and his actions. The Republican leaders in the Senate tried to get Senator Blackburn and the Democrats to back down, which usually worked, but not this time. Senator Blackburn stuck to his guns in defense of President Roosevelt, and President Roosevelt appreciated it.

> To-day, however, the Democrats stick firmly to their determination. Yesterday [Senators] Spooner, Lodge and Knox, holding a conference, sent for [Senator] Blackburn. They sent for him three times before he would come. When he came it was to refuse point blank to yield.
>
> To-day they were at work on him again, and on other Democrats. It availed nothing. The Democrats had a conference, Tillman being the only one who stayed out, and decided to stand pat. After this was over Aldrich got to work on Blackburn again.
>
> 'It's no use,' said the Democratic leader. 'For the first time in my life I'm a stand-patter.'
>
> Meanwhile the President was building a fire under the Senate oligarchy. As soon as he heard of Blackburn's resolution yesterday he said 'Bully!'

Senator Blackburn's stance was the anchor that firmly supported the President's authority to dismiss men from civil jobs and allowed the President to stand up to those who opposed him, particularly the Republican Senators who were opposed to him. President Roosevelt let them know he was not backing down from his right to dismiss these men from civil employment, with the effect that they were dismissed from military employment. Eventually, the opposition began to come around. Several Republicans joined the Democrats. The Republicans made one last run at changing Blackburn's mind.

> They made one last attempt on Blackburn. The grizzly warrior from the Blue Grass was feeling very fit, so he replied with an alliterative and poetic comeback which he has not surpassed since he uttered, thirty years ago, that wondrous phrase which is still singing down the grooves to time—'He who dallies is a dastard; he who doubts is damned.' Here is the companion piece which Blackburn uttered to-day to his Republican tempters:
>
> 'No power between Paradise and Perdition, Will move the Democrats from their Position.'
>
> When Blackburn dropped into alliteration and poetry in the same sentence Knox, Crane, and Spooner knew the jig was up and tempted him no more.

Some Senators threatened to claim that the men were fired because of race, but this did not scare Blackburn. As Blackburn said:

> The fact is that they realize the race question will be investigated some day, and they welcome it with open arms, for an investigation opened as a result of the Brownsville affair would line them and the President up together as defendants. Never again do they expect to be in such good shape for an investigation.

Senator Blackburn's proposed amendment to the resolution caused an extensive debate on the powers of the United States President, which was continued over several days. He presented his arguments in support of his proposed amendment to the resolution on January 21, 1907 on the Senate floor. His defense of President Roosevelt's authority was greatly appreciated by the President and bonded the two men as allies.

Senator Blackburn said that the only way out of their dilemma that he could see was to have Republican Senator Foraker:

> ...stand up in the Senate and disclaim any intention of questioning the President's authority to discharge enlisted men. It's just a question of whether he is to be compelled to furl his flag here or be empowered to fly it over the White House. If he should make the disclaimer I should say that I was rejoiced to have his adhesion to my proposition, and that the last obstacle had been removed to have a unanimous vote for it.
>
> If they want to go on and pass a resolution for an investigation of the race problem all right. That would open up a situation which in many ways would be unpleasant for the South, but there never could be a better time for it so far as we are concerned. They could only attack us over the shoulders of their President, and if they want to array him squarely on our side we are satisfied to have them. They have been using this argumentum ad terrorem so long that all the terror has been taken out of it. Our stakes are on the table, and our game is open and above board.

The Republican situation was worse after this, and the Senate leaders knew it. The President and the Democrats had them cornered and were closing in. President Roosevelt thought the corporate interests that he had fought were behind the Brownsville business. He thought that they were trying to damage his popularity over the Brownsville incident because they could not attack him directly on the Trusts. "It is not the race question, but the trust question over which the Brownsville battle is being waged." As Blackburn summed it up:

> The President does not favor any resolution which will be satisfactory to the Republican leaders 'who have been against him on corporation questions, and who would now wrest control from him to take the party back to its old affliliatons [sic].'
>
> He is thoroughly disgusted, not only with his Republican enemies, but with those half-hearted Republican friends of his who have not the nerve to take his side. He said Lodge was the only one of the leaders who had backbone enough to stand up for him.

Indeed, the disloyalty that President Roosevelt felt within his Republican Party made his appreciation grow even more for the strong support provided by Democratic Senator Blackburn. The threat of a split in the Republican Party did not deter the President or change his mind. He told the Republican Senators who came to him begging to save them from public humiliation that if the party had to split, he would prefer that as big a fragment as possible should be found on the affirmative side of the Blackburn Resolution. Senator Lodge confirmed after two interviews with the President that the President was firmly committed to the Blackburn Resolution and was prepared to take the lead of the Republican insurgents. Lodge counted the votes supporting the Blackburn Resolution before the roll call and found there were enough to win.

Finally, on January 21, 1907, the Republican opponents of the President's action in the Brownsville affair surrendered to President Roosevelt, a victory for Senator Blackburn, as explained by fellow Senator McCumber, "I think the Senator from Kentucky [Mr. Blackburn] has scored a good home run."

Chapter Twenty-Seven

Personal and Political Challenges

Kentucky Governor Goebel's death in 1900 did not reunite the Democratic Party in Kentucky, as one might have hoped. Former supporters of the assassinated Governor split into two major factions. Each faction had its progressive elements, and each had political bosses and power bases across the Commonwealth. Neither one wanted to support the other, which naturally led to a split vote on the Democratic ticket that provided the opportunity for the Republican Party candidates to win the majority of the votes. The first few years of the twentieth century in the state were confusing. Voters switched parties or simply avoided the voting booth. The party was changing in the state.

Former Lieutenant Governor John Beckham became the governor of the state at the age of thirty. He was tall and handsome and considered a true gentleman, well-bred, attributes that made him attractive on the ticket with Goebel, who was from a working-class family. Beckham was from a prominent family near Bardstown, with a maternal grandfather who had been governor and U.S. Postmaster General, an uncle who had been governor of Louisiana, and another uncle who was a Florida state senator, reminiscent of Blackburn's politically active family. Beckham became a lawyer and followed his father's path into Kentucky's legislature at the age of twenty-four. He was elected Speaker of the State House in 1898 and then became Lieutenant Governor then Governor when the state was in political turmoil and indecisiveness.

Beckham took charge and set about making sure that he would remain in power by building a coalition, led by William Purcell "Percy" Haly of Frankfort who worked behind the scenes, likely because, as a Catholic, he was aware that he could not likely win a statewide election. Haly had worked his way up from newsboy to messenger boy for J.C.S.

Blackburn to sergeant-at-arms in the legislature (when he helped Beckham) to aide to Goebel. Haly had strong Frankfort connections. Beckham was financed by three powerful "bosses": John C. Mayo, who was known as "the *Big Chief*," a man of power; Rufus H. Vansant of Ashland, who had made his fortune in lumber; and millionaire John Newlon Camden, who owned his Spring Hill Farm at Versailles and had interests in banking and various mining companies. All three were important political players in the State. It was said that in some ways Mayo, not Beckham, really dominated and led the state and he was the "boss" who wielded the widest statewide influence and power during the first three decades of the twentieth century. Beckham's next move was to make peace with some powerful enemies like the Louisville & Nashville Rail Road (L&N), who agreed to support the Democrats "if they would not abuse corporations." Since L&N paid forty percent of the railroad taxes in the state, it was an easy deal for Beckham to make, considering the power of this ally that would be useful in the November special election to fill out the remaining three years of Goebel's term.

Then Beckham made additional smart moves to reform the extremely offensive Goebel Election Law that was patently partisan. Beckham called a special session of the state legislature to revise the law, which resulted in an act to regulate elections that placed the power to appoint local officials back in the county where it had been before the Goebel Election Law changed everything. With these allies and reforms in place, Beckham was ready to run for the rest of Goebel's gubernatorial term, which he did and which he won. Blackburn supported Beckham and, in the summer of 1900, issued a call for harmony to all Kentucky Democrats and the will to win again at the polls.

It was an unsettling time. Blackburn suffered personal losses in his family. On October 17, 1900, Senator Blackburn's son-in-law, Thomas F. Lane, who was the husband of the Senator's youngest daughter, Lucile, could no longer bear the pain of Bright's disease, which is acute chronic kidney disease, and committed suicide at the young age of forty, leaving his young wife, Lucile Blackburn Lane, with the sole responsibility and care of their then four-year old daughter, Terese Blackburn Lane. After her husband's death, Lucile made an effort to start a new life for herself and her daughter. At some point in this time period, Lucile met the well-known Italian sculptor, the Chevalier Trentanove. The young widow was seen out occasionally with him during social events when he was working on a commissioned sculptural piece in the country. He traveled frequently between America and Italy to the sites of his commissions, including those in Washington, D.C. While he was in Italy, however, the Chevalier made a surprise public announcement on November 20, 1901 that he was engaged to the widow Lucile Blackburn Lane and that they would wed the following month after he sailed for America on November 30. Unfortunately, he made the announcement without Lucile's knowledge or permission. The engagement was immediately called off when she learned that he was a divorced man who could not re-marry under Catholic restrictions. This had to be publicly humiliating for Lucile and became even more humiliating when she learned that the Chevalier married another woman in Italy soon after their engagement was called off. It had to be a difficult time for Lucile, who was a single mother of a toddler, alone, with no means of supporting herself, and publicly embarrassed.

Sadly, she did not have the time to restart her life anew. Lucile died on July 18, 1902 in Washington, D.C., from complications from a previous accidental pistol wound, leaving her young daughter, Terese, then six years-old, an orphan. Senator Blackburn took in his orphaned granddaughter and raised her as his own. He sent her to a private school in Washington, D.C., and handled all her finances so that when she later married, she was quite a wealthy woman who had inherited Senator Blackburn's farm in the Blue Grass at Spring Station, where she lived for the majority of her later married life. Terese always called the Senator "Daddy."

Senator Blackburn suffered another tragedy on February 12, 1902, when Blackburn's son, Joseph C. S. ("Josey") Blackburn, Jr., died at the home of Colonel Lillard, a family friend. He was only forty-two years of age when he died. The family always stated that he was poisoned for political retaliation for the Goebel affair, although no one ever articulated their unproven suspicions to the younger generation. He is buried in the State Cemetery in Frankfort, Kentucky, next to his mother and father. Senator Blackburn, then, lost two children within five months of one another, just over a year after he lost his wife, all while he was fighting for his political life. The strength it must have required Blackburn to soldier on is incalculable. Only two daughters now survived: Mrs. Terese Blackburn Hall and Corinne Blackburn, but on the positive side, on December 11, 1901, Senator Blackburn remarried Mrs. Mary E. Blackburn, the widow of Judge H. H. Blackburn of West Virginia. Judge H.H. Blackburn was the law partner of the Hon. Ward H. Lamon, U.S. President Lincoln's old friend and law associate. Fortunately for Senator Blackburn, Mary willingly shared the role of caretaker for his young grand-daughter Terese.

Blackburn continued to be active in the Democratic Party in Kentucky, serving as a delegate to three Democratic National Conventions from Kentucky: Chicago in 1896, Kansas City in 1900, and St. Louis in 1904. Despite political battles and personal tragedies, Senator Blackburn still found a way to help his fellow Kentuckians in any way that he could. One example is the help he gave to a young artist from Versailles, Kentucky, Clifford Berryman. Blackburn "discovered" him and then helped him find a job in Washington, D.C. that led to a position at the *Washington Evening Star* as an illustrator. Berryman became famous for creating the famed "Teddy Bear" in 1902 as a joke on President Teddy Roosevelt, who had refused to shoot a young bear cub during a hunting trip in Mississippi. The little bear became a sort of trademark that lives on today in stuffed "Teddy Bears." Years later, U.S. President Harry S. Truman (1945 to 1953) called Mr. Berryman "as much of a Washington institution as the Monument." Berryman won Pulitzer Prizes and many other honors, including the Distinguished Service Medal from the Cosmopolitan Club. Mr. Berryman always credited Mr. Blackburn for his success and even acquired the habit of wearing the black bow ties for which Mr. Blackburn was famous. After his mentor died, Mr. Berryman commissioned a painted portrait of Mr. Blackburn.

In Kentucky, the next major political focus centered on the 1902 Senatorial contest. Senators were still chosen by the vote of the general assembly, on joint ballot, at this time and it would not be until the Seventeenth Amendment was adopted on May 31, 1913 that elections of U.S. Senators were determined by the popular vote of the people of the states. The Seventeenth Amendment had been called for by Blackburn and Bryan in the 1896 campaign and thereafter. The 1902 contest in Kentucky centered on the Republican incumbent Deboe, who had not managed to gain much support since his lackluster election. He faced the elderly ex-governor and ex-congressman Democrat James B. McCreary, the hand-picked choice of Beckham, Haly, and Mayo, who made up the Democratic political "machine." Backed by Beckham's coalition, McCreary easily won the Senate seat in the 1903 election.

This success gave Governor Beckham more support for his run for re-election in a Kentucky gubernatorial race, "that rarest of things," as State Historian James C. Klotter expressed it. There was the slight hurdle of the prohibitions in the state constitution that prohibited consecutive gubernatorial terms at the time, but a "friendly" court decision neatly removed that barrier by ruling that since he had not served a full first term, he could run again. The gubernatorial race was on. The odds were in Governor Beckham's favor because he was backed by his powerful political machine. The only other real contender for governor within the state Democratic Party was the *Courier-Journal* editor Henry Watterson, but it was not enough to defeat the incumbent. Governor Beckham won the State's Democratic nomination and began to campaign in September 1902. The Republicans cheerfully revisited the hated Goebel Election Law in their speeches, but fortunately for Beckham, who was not an inspiring speaker, the Republicans split behind three contenders: Godfrey Hunter, Louisville businessman Morris E. Belknap, and another Louisville resident, Augustus E. Willson. At the Republican convention, Willson withdrew, and Morris Belknap easily won on the first ballot. The Republican candidate Morris Belknap ran as a businessman-governor, and he and his party attacked Democratic Governor Beckham for allowing lawlessness that hindered business, excluded capital, and generally handicapped industry, and for its "odious political machine rule" during his term. But Belknap was not a good speaker, either. Beckham won. For the first time in sixteen years, the Democratic candidate received a majority of all votes cast with fifty-four percent. Young Beckham and his political boss Haly had indeed created a forceful political machine that dominated Kentucky politics for the next three decades.

On the national level in 1903, the *New York Times* reported that most Democratic Senators and Representatives had strong feelings of hopefulness for the success of the Democratic candidates for President and Vice President, but beating a Presidential incumbent, and such a vigorously popular one as Teddy Roosevelt, was a nearly impossible task. Democrats were willing to set aside the lingering hard feelings from the Silver and Gold debate that nearly tore apart the Democratic Party. The Democratic National Convention wanted to choose candidates and write a platform that hopefully would re-unite their Party. They hoped the Republican grumblings about President Roosevelt being bad for business would help their cause.

In 1904, both Democrat William Jennings Bryan and former Democratic President Grover Cleveland declined to run for President. Since the two Democratic nominees of the past twenty years did not seek the presidential nomination, Alton B. Parker, a conservative Bourbon Democrat from New York, was the choice. Parker was respected by both Democrats and Republicans in New York, even though he refused to work actively for the nomination and let his supporters do all that they could. The Democratic Convention met in St. Louis, Missouri, from July 6 to 9 in 1904, and Blackburn participated. This Democratic convention was described as one of the most exciting and sensational in the history of the Democratic Party.

The Democratic platform called for reduction in government expenditures and a congressional investigation of the executive departments "already known to teem with corruption," condemned monopolies, pledged an end to government contracts with companies violating antitrust laws, opposed imperialism, insisted upon independence for the Philippines, and opposed the protective tariff while it favored strict enforcement of the eight-hour work day, construction of a Panama Canal, the direct election of senators, statehood for the Western territories, the illegalization of polygamy, reciprocal trade agreements, cuts in the army, and enforcement of the civil service laws. It condemned the Roosevelt administration in general as "spasmodic, erratic, sensational, spectacular, and arbitrary." Ultimately the Party platform and Parker's unusual ideas were ignored when the election was over.

Parker and Davis lost to the Republican ticket of the incumbent President Theodore Roosevelt and Vice President Charles Fairbanks, allowing Roosevelt to continue to pursue his Progressive Party policies. However, Parker won in Kentucky but only by 2.69% and also won other Southern states like Alabama, Arkansas, Florida, Georgia, Louisiana, Mississippi, North Carolina, South Carolina, Tennessee, Texas, and Virginia. Roosevelt's success in foreign affairs and his firm stance against monopolies helped him carry every region in the nation, except the South. Members of the Democratic Party were still divided on the monetary issue. The divide in the Democratic Party at the national level was reflected in the state level.

In Kentucky, Democratic Governor Beckham had proved to be a weak leader with an unimpressive legislative record in his first term from 1900 to 1904. Democratic Presidential candidate Parker carried Kentucky over Republican Theodore Roosevelt. This victory for the Democrats state-wide was reflected down the line of offices on the ticket. Democrats carried both Lexington and Louisville, after having lost those votes four years before. That success carried over to the congressional races, with Democrats winning nine of the eleven U. S. House of Representatives seats. But the good feelings of unity among the Democrats would not last.

In early 1904, former Senator Blackburn prepared for a fight against the political "machine" in the state run by Governor Beckham and his supporters. Governor Beckham supported Court of Appeals Judge Thomas H. Paynter over the re-election of former Senator Blackburn. Senator Blackburn was not going to give up without a fight. He wrote to his friend, Judge Dedman in Cynthiana on March 8, 1904:

> I have your kind letter of the 7th. I cannot overstate the appreciation in which I hold your kind expressions of endorsement. I never had a doubt as to where you would stand in the fight that I have got to meet in the coming State Convention. You are right in your conclusions. If this machine can control that convention and make permanent its hold upon the party organization in the state; then neither I nor any other Democrat will come to the Senate from Kentucky, but the state will promptly pass into the hands of the Republicans and you and I and all decent honest men will have to admit that by quietly submitting to machine rule the Democratic party has proven itself unfit to govern in the state. No man, nor set of men, have ever yet been able to establish and maintain a system of political bossism in Kentucky and the small calibered politicians that are now engaged in that effort will find the task too big for them. We had just as well make up our minds that after the coming state convention there will either be no Democratic party in Kentucky or if there is it will be a clean and decent one, without the taint or smell of machine

about it. On my recent visit to Kentucky I was assured that so far as these gentlemen were concerned I could come back to the Senate without opposition if I would only keep my hands out of state politics and let them remain in control. I do not need to say to you or any other friend that I have there that I refused to accept any such terms or assurances and notified them that I would add my political fortunes to the stake for which we fight; that I would stand or fall with my friends and the party. I do not want to be in the Senate when Kentucky is governed either by Republicans or by a 2-penny so called Democratic political machine. I cannot tell you how much good it does me to know that you are alive to the situation and have your war paint on. When this state convention meets it's going to be a black flag fight. The machine must go or we will be exterminated, and I know no man in the state who can or will render more valuable service than yourself. You may be sure that I will be there. May God bless and prosper you.

Always your friend,
Jo. C. S. Blackburn

A few family issues intervened in Senator Blackburn's fight against the Democratic machine in the state. On May 15, 1904, the Senator had to stay in Washington, D.C., rather than return to Kentucky to help the Democratic Party during the campaigns in order to probate his youngest daughter Lucile Blackburn Lane's will. He had to delay returning to the fight in Kentucky until the end of May. The political fight in Kentucky prevented the Senator from attending the wedding of his middle daughter Corinne in August of 1905. Corinne married William H. Gale of New York and Leesburg, Virginia at the Ebbett House in Washington, D.C, an event witnessed by a small party of relatives and personal friends. The Gales went to New York for their honeymoon and returned to Leesburg, Virginia, for the summer, before Mr. Gale returned to his duties. Mr. Gale was the Assistant Secretary of State in Puerto Rico (the new spelling) under Governor Hunt. Senator Blackburn was in the heat of the campaign and was unable to attend, but sent his love and congratulations.

By mid-November of 1905, Kentucky's congressmen in Washington, D.C. reported that Senator Blackburn was still fighting the Beckham machine and had a chance of defeating Justice Paynter for the Senate.

But the fight was not over yet and other potential candidates threatened to enter the race. On November 18, 1905, Colonel W.B. Haldeman, the editor of *The Louisville Times*, had "practically decided" to run for United States Senator, opposing Senator Blackburn and Judge Paynter. There was so much ill-feeling between Blackburn and Paynter that many of the party leaders and nominees to the General Assembly had concluded that it would be best to find a compromise candidate and decided upon Haldeman. Blackburn stood for re-election in 1906, but was deserted by the Democratic state administration, which turned to Paynter, a "big business" Democrat, and forced his election by the legislature. The Beckham faction in state government had purged Blackburn, as they intended, when only a few years before, Blackburn's work had played a major role in Beckham gaining the governor's office. Beckham had no loyalty to the Democrats who had helped secure his place in office. Governor Beckham's men had persuaded Senator-elect Charles B. Ecton to represent Bourbon, Clark, and Montgomery Counties and to throw his support from Blackburn to the Beckham choice of Paynter. The editor of the local press soundly denounced the senator-elect Charles B. Ecton for saying he would no longer back Senator Blackburn when he had promised that he would.

Judge Thomas Paynter was nominated on the first ballot by the Democratic Joint Caucus as Democratic candidate to succeed J. C. S. Blackburn as U.S. Senator, beginning in the Sixtieth Congress, which was the equivalent of an election, because the Democrats controlled both houses of the legislature. Senator Blackburn announced his intention of pursuing in the future the same policy as in the past: opposition to the state machine. On June 21, 1906, it was reported that Senator Blackburn had received more than a thousand letters asking him to run for governor of Kentucky. The Senator said: "I am not a candidate for any office, but my sense of obligation to the democracy of Kentucky is such that there is no nomination from governor down that I would not accept if my party thought that by accepting I could save the democracy from defeat." Although Blackburn lost his battle against the big machine in the state Democratic administration, he had ably served Kentucky twenty-eight years, with ten in the U.S. House and eighteen in the U.S. Senate. He had served in the U.S. Senate longer than Henry Clay. "While in the Senate, he met in debate some of the great lights of American political history. . . . It has been said that he said more in fewer words than any other Senator who preceded or followed him." While he served in the Senate, he was a member of the important committees on Finance, Appropriations, Judiciary, Military Affairs, Naval Affairs, and Rules, and served as the Chairman of the latter committee. On the death of Senator Gorman in 1906, he was elected Chairman of the Democratic Caucus, an office that carried with it the leadership of the Democratic Party in the Senate. Senator Blackburn wielded a powerful influence as the leader of his party in the Senate.

Senator Blackburn was honored at home in Kentucky as well. First on August 9, 1906, a large reception was given at *Stonewall*, the home of Mrs. Breckinridge Viley. Everyone of political importance from Woodford County attended to honor Senator Blackburn. He was honored again on McCreary Day, celebrated in late September 1906. A carriage containing Senator Blackburn and others was driven down Main Street to the O'Neal House for a handshaking reception.

Blackburn then traveled to New York for a visit, where his contributions to the Senate and sporting life were recalled by his friends there:

> It will not surprise any one to learn that ex-Senator Joe Blackburn, who is now in New York, drinks whisky. Blackburn, like many other Kentuckians, rather prides himself upon his ability to judge whisky and discriminate between good whisky and better whisky, which is the really difficult task, says the New York World.
>
> Anybody can tell bad whisky, Blackburn says, but that finer delicacy of palate which can differentiate between a really superior brand of whisky and the very best possible brand, is the man of educated taste....
>
> Blackburn's popularity in Kentucky is, in a measure, due to his knowledge of Kentucky's principal sources of pride. The fact that he loves and glories in Kentucky whisky, Kentucky blue grass, Kentucky horses and Kentucky type of female loveliness has made Blackburn a host of admirers, who, like the redoubtable Jack Chinn, are ready to fight for him at any moment he happens to need their assistance.
>
> It was Blackburn who fought the battles of the whisky men and succeeded in keeping the tax upon whisky below a figure

that would have seriously affected the distilling interests and the value of the product stored in bonded warehouses.

Blackburn is the friend of the race horse and the whisky men because he believes both contribute to the enjoyment of life, and that the world is better off when it enjoys itself, even if some go broke and others get drunk.

Blackburn's presence at any race track in the country is welcomed by the officials because he loves horse racing as sport, and is neither a gambler nor horse owner. His long training has made him, however, a hard man to remain with when drinks are coming rapidly, for it is his boast that in spite of his liking for the Kentucky beverage, he never drinks to excess.

He has been known to stay with a party of friends in a restaurant until every other man was ready to go under the table, and then call a carriage and go off to some evening reception.

Upon one occasion, Blackburn and his then colleague, Senator Beck, now dead, spent an evening together. They had with them Connolly F. Trigg, of Richmond, and John Randolph Tucker, of Virginia. Mr. Tucker was then well advanced in years, and it was decided when the hour for going home arrived that the whole party would take the Tucker house.

They reached the Tucker residence all right, and were engaged in an animated if somewhat unintelligible discussion in front of the house. Just then a window opened and a female voice exclaimed: 'This is Mr. Tucker's house.' Always courteous, Blackburn took off his hat with one hand, while he clung to the arm of one of his companions with the other and said: 'We know that very well, Mrs. Tucker, but won't you please come down and pick him out.'

Another oft-told tale about Senator Blackburn was repeated by ex-Assistant Postmaster General Adlai Stevenson, who had been Vice-President for President Grover Cleveland. When Senator Blackburn and others were guests for dinner at the White House, then Vice President Stevenson looked across the table to Senator Blackburn and said:

> 'Senator, do you remember that day we were seconds in a duel?' Senator Blackburn promptly expressed his recollection of the 'pleasant event.' The other guests called for the particulars of a duel that had left in the minds of the seconds such cheerful memories.
>
> 'Well,' began Mr. Stevenson, 'Mr. Blackburn drove me out to the ground. It was before sunrise, but we were the seconds and of course, were first on the ground. But the principals soon arrived. Now, I was very ignorant upon duels. The principals knew very little, too. But Mr. Blackburn was well informed, and in order that everything should be clearly understood and satisfactory he said he would explain the code. So he took the floor, or rather the ground, and began to talk. It was very interesting, for, as you all know, the gentleman from Kentucky is an orator.'
>
> Just then there was an interruption by the bread plate, and Mr. Stevenson paused to help himself to bread. But the pause continued, and Mr. Stevenson was apparently going on with his dinner.
>
> 'Well, but the duel. You haven't told us how it ended,' said several guests, eagerly, and speaking at once.
>
> 'Oh, it didn't end. It didn't begin,' said Mr. Stevenson, solemnly. 'You see, Blackburn began to talk before sunrise, and he never stopped till after sundown, and then it was too dark for the duel.'

Good humor aside, by 1907, the senior Senator Blackburn had matured into an even-handed leader. He had the unusual ability to preserve Democratic harmony, because not only could he preserve his own temper, but he was also remarkably capable of preserving other men's tempers. Trying to find a Democratic leader to replace him became a challenge for the Democratic Party.

Part Four

The Greatest Work of Modern Time: The Panama Canal

Chapter Twenty-Eight

The Greatest Work of Modern Time

The alliance between the fiery Republican President Roosevelt and Blackburn, the Democratic Party Leader, during Blackburn's third term facilitated Roosevelt's choice of Blackburn to serve as the Governor of the Panama Canal Zone, made official on April 1, 1907. It was a good choice. Blackburn had proven his ability to lead over his twenty-eight years in the House and Senate and had organized a government for the District of Columbia when he wrote The Organic Act in 1878 and had helped direct the city's development while in the Senate.

The Panama Canal was completed on August 15, 1914, opening faster, cheaper shipping routes between the Atlantic and Pacific Oceans. Before there was a canal, ships traveling from New York to San Francisco were forced to cover at least thirteen thousand miles traveling around the tip of South America. The opening of the Panama Canal reduced that trip by more than half, connecting the Atlantic and Pacific Oceans. It was a huge accomplishment that symbolized U.S. technological prowess and economic power. President Theodore "Teddy" Roosevelt considered the fifty-one miles of the Panama Canal to be one of the greatest achievements of his Presidency. He also believed that the canal's architectural genius of using three locks on each ocean side to raise and lower boats sixteen meters or about fifty-two and a half feet, up and over the hill between the oceans left an indelible mark on the world. The Panama Canal's contributions to the world more than justified the actions he had to take in order to make it a reality.

Two weeks after taking office, President Roosevelt directed his Cabinet to begin an intensive study of a canal that would be constructed in Central America through the isthmus, that narrow strip of land bounded on either side by the Pacific and Atlantic Oceans, connecting the North American continent to the South American continent. It was daring, but daring defined his character.

Roosevelt believed that the Monroe Doctrine applied to the Pacific and Caribbean regions, a belief that was dramatically demonstrated in the events leading up to the U.S. agreement to build the Panama Canal. It was based on President Monroe's policy that European powers should stay out of the Western Hemisphere because that was the United States' sphere of interest. It had become the best-known U.S. policy toward the Western Hemisphere, and it made it clear that the United States would not tolerate further colonization or puppet monarchs. Roosevelt firmly believed that Spain should be forced out of Cuba, especially given how close Cuba lay to the United States, for the good of Cuba's independence and to show the world the American resolve to enforce the Monroe Doctrine. Just ten days after the battleship *Maine* exploded on February 15, 1898 in the harbor of Havana, Cuba, Secretary Long left the office for four hours, making Roosevelt the Acting Secretary. Not one to waste a moment, Acting Secretary Roosevelt immediately cabled the Navy worldwide to prepare for war, ordered ammunition and supplies, brought in experts, and went to Congress asking for the authority to recruit as many sailors as he thought were needed. In just four hours, Roosevelt helped the U.S. Navy prepare for a war with Spain, which was soon won.

The 1898 Treaty of Paris was signed after the American victory in the Spanish-American War, which granted the U.S. temporary control of Cuba and ownership of Puerto Rico, Guam, and the Philippine Islands, once the U.S. paid Spain twenty million dollars for the Philippines. The acquisition of the Philippines marked the entrance of the United States into the Pacific. Republicans generally supported the Treaty, and Democrats generally favored expansion, particularly Southern Democrats. Massachusetts Senator Henry Cabot Lodge, Roosevelt's friend and confidant, supported expansionism, and Minnesota Senator Knute Nelson said, "Providence has given the United States the duty of extending Christian civilization. We come as ministering angels, not despots."

The Spanish-American War also demonstrated how difficult it was for the United States to maintain a naval fleet in the Atlantic Ocean and another in the Pacific Ocean without a connection closer than Cape Horn. Four full months were required for the U.S. Naval fleet to sail from the waters off Hampton Roads, Virginia, to San Diego, California, and another three weeks before the fleet could reach San Francisco, a total of nearly five months' sailing time. A short-cut was needed for military purposes. Personal and commercial interests begged for a shorter route, as well. By December 1898, American business and military interests in Asia had increased the need for a canal. Within two short years after the Spanish-American War, bi-metallism was dead, the Gold Standard was the law, tariffs were in place, and the need for a canal was pressing for international trade and military access.

The United States and Britain had an agreement that dated back to 1850, known as the Clayton-Bulwer Treaty, to build a canal through the Isthmus, but nothing ever developed under its terms. The U.S. remained interested in developing the canal, however, and continued to explore options and opportunities to do so. Much had been learned since the United States and Britain had first negotiated a treaty to share in the development of a proposed canal through the Central American Republic of Nicaragua. Many hard lessons had been learned from the subsequent French effort to build a trans-isthmian canal.

In 1880, the French had begun to plan and build a canal through Panama in the province of Columbia. Ferdinand de Lesseps, the builder of the Suez Canal in Egypt, had persuaded investors that his chosen path to build a sea-level canal through Panama was feasible. For nine long years, the French worked on digging a canal. It proved to be a disastrous effort, costing over twenty thousand people their lives, mostly to malaria and yellow fever, on top of the millions of dollars expended. The failed effort bankrupted the investors and developers and left behind an unfinished ditch filled with the thousands of bodies of laborers who had perished in the effort. After nine years of suffering in the tropical jungle, the French gave up.

They had failed to understand that removing the dirt and rock excavated was as important as the cut, mistakenly piling up loose dirt in layers that became massive mud slides with the inevitable rains. The mud slides took more time, money, and lives to clear to restart the work. Furthermore, the French failed to make use of the Panama Train that ran through the valley to remove the debris, even though it had cost them a lot to purchase the train. De Lesseps had misjudged the job, thinking the same sea-level canal solution he had used in the desert at the Suez Canal would work for a canal to be cut through the rocky terrain in tropical Panama. It would be his downfall. By 1899, the French had left the isthmus and a trans-oceanic canal was a dream again, haunted with feverish nightmares of the lives lost, money wasted, and French investors ruined, some of whom had invested their life savings.

This meant that the U.S. began with a better understanding of the risks that would be involved in digging a canal when President McKinley began international negotiations. On February 5, 1900, a new treaty was signed, the Hay-Pauncefote Treaty, amending the prior Clayton-Bulwer Treaty, which meant that America was licensed to build the canal on its own without the help or interference of Britain.

President Roosevelt had learned from his experience as Governor of New York that locks and aqueducts could work over long distances like those that were used on the Erie Canal connecting the waters of Lake Erie in the west to the Hudson River in the east. Once completed in 1918, the Erie Canal extended 363 miles from Albany to Buffalo. President Theodore Roosevelt believed that if the Erie Canal could be achieved in 1825 when the country was just thirty-six years old, that a trans-isthmian canal should be possible in 1901 over seventy-five years later. Technology had boomed in the country and world. Engineering advances had been demonstrated around the world in structures like the Eiffel Tower, built for the 1889 World's Fair. If in 1825 the Erie Canal was able to devise eighteen aqueducts to carry the canal over ravines and rivers and eighty-three locks lifting the water level 568 feet, it seemed logical that a similar system of locks could work over the Isthmus and connect the two oceans. Undaunted by four hundred years of unrealized dreams, President Roosevelt made it one of his first objectives to complete a canal through the isthmus once he was in the Oval Office. He was determined to achieve the dream. America had too much to gain from building a canal to give it up.

There was heated debate over the Hay-Pauncefote Treaty in the U.S. Senate. Senator Blackburn joined in the Isthmian Canal debates in the Senate. Initially, Senator Blackburn had opposed the ratification of the treaty, but eventually joined forces with the majority in favoring a later act, the Spooner Act, which established the Isthmian Canal Commission (ICC) and authorized President Roosevelt to purchase the right of way from Nicaragua if the negotiations with Colombia for control over the Panama route ended in a stalemate This vote would prove crucial to Blackburn's career, combined with Blackburn's earlier support of President Roosevelt's agendas in the Senate. Both actions aligned Blackburn with Roosevelt. While Senator Blackburn was concerned about the President's likely intentions to increase U.S. territory at the expense of other republics, he continued to support the Act.

On November 18, 1901, the second Hay-Pauncefote Treaty was signed, which was subsequently approved by both American and Britain and provided, among other things, that the U.S. was authorized to construct and manage a Central American canal; that the U.S. was to guarantee the neutrality of the canal and was authorized to fortify the area if necessary; and that the canal was to be open to all nations and the rates for passage were to be fair and equal. As a humanitarian, Senator Blackburn took a cautious stand on expansionism, but he was far too patriotic to object to the construction of a canal. He recognized the necessity for such a canal in the Twentieth Century, while at the same time, he hoped for fair play in dealing with foreign nations. He wished to avoid a policy of imperialism After much debate, the Senate agreed to build the trans-isthmian canal through Panama, and within six months, a treaty was signed that allowed the U.S. to proceed. This treaty granted the U.S. the leasehold rights to a strip of land six miles wide for what would become the site of the transoceanic canal. The U.S. was to pay Colombia the sum of ten million dollars for the lease, plus an annual payment of $250,000 to begin in nine years, or the estimated time of completion of construction. The lease was to be effective in perpetuity. The U.S. Senate acted quickly to ratify the agreement, even though some Senators argued that the U.S. should receive complete government control over the proposed canal zone.

The Colombian Congress rejected the amended treaty, which triggered a revolution in Panama against Colombia. President Roosevelt responded by sending U.S. Warships to Panama City on the Pacific Ocean and to Colon on the Atlantic Ocean in support of Panamanian independence. Colombian troops were not able to fight simultaneously against the troops and the jungles of Darien Gap, a gap of approximately fifty kilometers (or thirty-one miles) between present-day Colombia and Panama. On November 2, 1903, U.S. warships blocked sea lanes that Colombian troops might have used on the way to put down the rebellion, and the next day on November 3, 1903, Panama declared its independence as a new Republic.

Panama immediately named Phillipe Bunau-Varilla, who was the former engineer for the French canal company, as their new Envoy

Extraordinaire and Minister Plenipotentiary. A new agreement was reached and signed on November 18, 1903 in the Fifty-Eighth Congress and included the following terms: The U.S. received rights to a canal zone that was to extend five miles on either side of the route, plus a one-time ten million dollars payment to Panama and an annual annuity of $250,000. The U.S. also agreed to guarantee the independence of Panama.

President Roosevelt is said to have stated: "I took the isthmus, started the canal and then left Congress not to debate the canal, but to debate me." He justified the American intervention in Columbia and Panama under the Monroe Doctrine, but there was heavy opposition to this act of war on Colombia by members in Congress and in the general public, reflected in the harsh judgments printed in the leading papers of the day. At the time, Roosevelt was concerned that a crisis between Venezuela and its creditors could lead to an invasion by European powers. The Roosevelt Corollary of December 1904 stated that the United States would intervene as a last resort to ensure that other nations in the Western Hemisphere fulfilled their obligations to international creditors. This limited action would not violate the right of the citizens of the United States or invite "foreign aggression to the detriment of the entire body of American nations." President Roosevelt said that the United States might "exercise international police power in 'flagrant cases of such wrongdoing or impotence.' " Since then, it has been called a serious blunder, but one that can be said to have benefitted Panama, North America, South America, the United States, and the world shipping trade.

Roosevelt won in a landslide in the next Presidential election. Remaining in office, he was able to continue his pursuit of the construction of the Panama Canal with gusto. It was apparent that the French effort to dig out a sea-level canal would not work. The Americans came up with the ingenious plan to raise the ships in transit, using three locks on each Ocean side, one on the Pacific side and one on the Atlantic side. The United States took over construction of the Panama Canal by 1904, stepping in and starting the work with the old excavation equipment left on site by the French, which the U.S. had purchased. They had essentially bought a "running operation," but at the time of acquisition it was "limping" along.

When the Americans arrived at Panama in May 1904, they found a jumble of poorly organized buildings and equipment in poor condition. There was a small workforce, several old buildings, and damaged equipment that had suffered from fifteen years of neglect since the French abandoned the project. Ultimately, the U.S. would only use a small portion of what the French had excavated. The U.S. needed a new large workforce to get the project going again, but there were no facilities in place to handle a large workforce.

A newly formed U.S. government Isthmian Canal Commission (ICC) was set up to oversee the construction of the canal and was given control of the Panama Canal Zone that the United States governed. Leaders were needed on the ground. Furthermore, it became apparent that newer and more capable excavation equipment was needed to get the job done. The Americans had to get organized. The early years were the most difficult and most crucial of the project.

President Roosevelt began appointing men to see the project through to its completion, beginning with John Findlay Wallace as the new Chief Engineer of the Panama Canal Project in 1904. Wallace had been the chief engineer and general manager of the Central Illinois Railroad. Wallace resigned from the canal project in June 1905. Then John Frank Stevens took over the task, relying on his former experience building the Great Northern Railroad. First he focused his attention on building and rebuilding the housing, cafeterias, hotels, water systems, repair shops, warehouses, and other infrastructure needed by the city of workers employed on the massive project. In addition, the U.S. bought 102 new, large, railroad-mounted steam shovels from the United States and shipped them to the canal for the work, along with huge steam-powered cranes, hydraulic rock-crushers, cement mixers, dredges, and pneumatic power drills, mostly all products of America's new machine-building technology. New rail lines were constructed or fortified where needed.

Colonel William C. Gorgas was appointed the Chief Sanitation Officer of the canal construction project in 1904. Colonel Gorgas cleaned up the work site to reduce the spread of mosquito-borne diseases, like malaria and yellow fever, using the lessons that U.S. Army tropical disease expert Walter Reed had proven. Reed had shown that malaria and yellow fever were transmitted by the female member of the mosquito species, not poor sanitation. Colonel Gorgas was a Reed protégé who had put the lessons into effective practice in fever-ridden Havana, eradicating mosquitoes and eliminating the disease. Applying the same principles used at Havana, within two years Colonel Gorgas nearly eliminated the mosquito-spread diseases. In Panama, Colonel Gorgas used old newspapers to seal buildings and fumigate them, repeatedly if necessary, and installed ninety thousand dollars worth of wire screens on windows and sent teams of worker's door-to-door searching for mosquitoes and their eggs. They enforced a ban on the old Panamanian custom of keeping water indoors in uncovered containers. They traced the movements of victims and figured out where they had been infected. By December 1905, yellow fever had vanished from the Canal Zone.

Then in 1907, John Stevens resigned as the Chief Engineer. President Roosevelt appointed George Washington Goethals as the Chief Engineer of the Canal Zone Project. Colonel Goethals would apply his strong military training to the task, resulting in surprising efficiencies that enabled him to complete the project ahead of schedule in 1914. From 1907 to 1914, Goethals' work force excavated nearly 215 million cubic yards of earth, nearly three times what the French had accomplished. Goethals also supervised the construction of the locks that former Chief Engineer Stevens had promoted, which were the biggest and most technologically advanced devices of their kind ever built. Roosevelt's trips to visit the Panama Canal Zone represented the first time a U.S. President traveled outside of the country on national business.

Senator Blackburn and President Theodore Roosevelt were alike in many ways: both forthright, direct, energetic, and driven by principle and a belief in the United States' growing role on the international stage. The Senator was known nationally for his vigorous debates and skillful political oratory in the Senate and U.S. House of Representatives. President Roosevelt recognized him as a staunch supporter and ally. Senator Blackburn was fiery, but he could be fair, a fact recognized by Republicans and Democrats alike. Senator Blackburn spoke his mind, but without vitriolic attacks, in a way that compelled others to agree with his authority and logic. He was never afraid to fight for what he believed was right and remained loyal to his friends and family. Like Roosevelt, he stood ready to tackle new challenges, and Roosevelt was about to appoint him to one of the biggest challenges of his life. The bond between President Roosevelt and Senator Blackburn was a bond that would help the two men deal with the challenges that faced them, their political Parties, and the nation at the beginning of the Twentieth

Century as a superpower on the international stage where the country held greater responsibilities.

On January 29, 1907, a plan for the reorganization of the Isthmian Canal Commission (ICC) was considered by the Senate Committee on Inter-Oceanic Canals. It provided for the creation of the post of Director General to be filled by the Chief Engineer in charge of construction. The Canal Commission was made up of the department heads under the Chief Engineer. The proposed plan provided that the Director General's authority was supreme, but that he should act with the advice and assistance of the Commissioners. The ICC met at least six times a year.

Next, President Roosevelt needed someone who could oversee and govern the newly organized Panama Canal Zone. Former Senator Blackburn had not been out of his Senate seat for a month when President Roosevelt had Secretary of War William H. Taft write a letter to Blackburn, telling him of his appointment as the first Civil Governor of the Panama Canal Zone on April 1, 1907. Secretary Taft urged Blackburn to leave for Panama as soon as possible. The appointment meant a major undertaking for Blackburn and his wife Mary and young granddaughter Terese. It was also a strong political statement by the Republican President, who broke all precedent when he reached across the aisle, crossing party lines to select Democratic Blackburn.

When Blackburn assumed the duties as the Governor of the Panama Canal Zone, he faced the tasks of reorganizing and administering the Courts, schools, and public works, and, unofficially, overseeing the adjustment of the intimate and delicate relationship between the Canal Administration and the Republic of Panama. They were like the tasks that he had undertaken when he organized the District of Columbia.

Sixty-eight-year old Governor Blackburn, his wife, and granddaughter, eight-year old Terese Blackburn Lane, sailed to Panama in mid-April, 1907 and arrived on May 6, 1907. The Governor's official residence was a home high on the mountain of Ancon, a suburb of Panama City, where Governor Blackburn began to work vigorously to administer the Canal Zone's schools, courts, civil organizations, and public works. Governor Blackburn supervised the executive work of other divisions, such as customs and revenues, police and prisons, and fire protection and inspection services As Governor, he personally visited every school in the zone and consulted with others on how to improve the education system. "I am giving my very careful personal attention to the matter of schools," he wrote to Taft in January of 1908, reporting that "they are improving, and giving better results every month. He also attended receptions and greeted visitors, tasks that suited the amiable gentleman He represented the ICC and the Canal Zone in their relations with Panama and diplomatic representatives of foreign nations In this capacity, he maintained a close liaison between Roosevelt, Taft, and Panamanian officials. When Congress was in session, he returned to Washington and represented the commission there. He received a salary of fourteen thousand dollars a year, plus use of the Governor's official home that served as the base for directing the work of the commission.

The American Society of Civil Engineers named the Panama Canal one of the seven wonders of the modern world. In effect, the three locks located at each end of the Panama Canal lifted ships up to an artificial lake called Gatun Lake. This lake was created to reduce the amount of excavation work needed to make the canal, sitting twenty-six meters or eighty-five feet above the sea level. At the time the locks were constructed by the Americans, they were thirty-three and a half meters wide or 110 feet wide, which was wide enough for the ships of the day, but since that time, ships and tankers have become much larger and more massive.

One of the greatest barriers to the building of the canal was the continental divide, which rose up 110 meters (360.9 feet) above sea level at its highest point. They had to cut through this wall of rock. When Goethals arrived at the canal, he brought with him Major David du Bose Gaillard of the U.S. Army Corps of Engineers. Gaillard was put in charge of the central district of the canal, stretching from the Pedro Miguel Locks to the Gatun Dam. Gaillard dedicated himself to the Culebra Cut as it was called then, and his successful dedication would be recognized when the name was changed to the Gaillard Cut.

The scale of the work was staggering: six thousand men worked in the Culebra Cut (Gaillard Cut), drilling holes where they placed a total of twenty-seven thousand tons of dynamite to break up the rock. Up to 160 trains per day were used to haul away the rock blasted from the rocky continental divide. The work was treacherous with dynamite blasts and sudden landslides. The underlying iron layer in the rock would oxidize once exposed by the cuts and weaken, which resulted in numerous landslides. Gaillard handled the constant challenges calmly and made steady progress cutting through the rocky divide.

The Blackburns spent most of each year in Panama during the construction of the canal. Governor Blackburn wrote to Daniel M. Bowmar, Editor of *The Woodford Sun* in Versailles on June 20, 1907: "no place has been more slandered than the Isthmus, for it is not hotter there," he says, "than in Kentucky." He told a reporter in 1908 that there were "approximately 30,000 men employed on the gigantic project and that the work was progressing most satisfactorily." His nephew, Captain James Blackburn's son, Judge Samuel E. Blackburn, left his Louisville practice in 1907 to become a district judge in Panama, where he served until 1918. Judge Samuel Blackburn's brother, James, Jr., succeeded him. Other sons of Woodford County families found their positions in Panama due to the Blackburn connection, including Versailles attorney D.L. Thornton's son and others.

The general direction of the canal from the northwest to the southeast results from the shape of the isthmus, where the canal route cuts through it. Two artificial lakes were created and are essential to the working of the canal: Lake Gatun and Miraflores Lake. Four dams were built to create these two lakes: two small dams at Miraflores enclose the Miraflores Lake and a dam at Pedro Miguel encloses the south end of the Culebra Cut, which is an arm of Lake Gatun. The Gatun Dam is the main dam blocking the original course of the Chagres River that creates Lake Gatun.

The size of the locks sets the limit for the size of the ships that can pass through the canal. Many ships are built to the maximum size allowed to maximize the amount of cargo that can be carried. Ships that can fit through the canal are known as Panamax vessels. A Panamax cargo ship weighs between sixty-five thousand to eighty thousand tonnes, with cargo limited to 52.5 thousand tonnes.

On March 12, 1908, Taft sent a secret memorandum to Blackburn in which he discussed Panamanian politics and the approaching Presidential election in Panama. He clearly spelled out his reasons for favoring the Liberal Party for Presidency instead of the Secretary of Foreign Affair, but asked Blackburn for complete discretion regarding the political situation. Blackburn ably served as Taft's special agent and enabled the orderly transfer of executive power, setting a precedent for other Latin American nations, although there was a minor diplomatic crisis when the President of Panama removed from office the governors of three provinces. Roosevelt telegrammed Blackburn to report the "real reasons" for their removal, and Blackburn quickly responded. The Liberal Party candidate was elected without further incident. There were other potential problems, of course, which were duly reported and handled by Blackburn. For example, Blackburn relayed his fears to the President that landowners in the interior might start a rebellion in order to convince Americans to establish a protectorate over the nation, but he managed to handle the crisis to everyone's satisfaction and safety. The professional relationship between Blackburn and Roosevelt became one of personal friendship for both men that lasted until Blackburn's death in 1918. The work of the Panama Canal continued through three Presidential administrations: President Theodore Roosevelt (1901–1909), President William Howard Taft (1909–1913) and President Woodrow Wilson (1913–1921).

Governor Blackburn worked closely with Colonel George W. Goethals, who had been appointed by President Roosevelt as the Chief Engineer of the Panama Canal in February 1907. Colonel Goethals and Governor Blackburn became close friends. Colonel Goethals came to rely on Governor Blackburn's knowledge of men and public affairs. Colonel Goethals said that Governor Blackburn was a "very valuable advisor and counselor," and that "his method of handling matters with the Panama officials in cases affecting the interests of the Canal Zone and the neighboring republic has never been equaled."

It was Blackburn who wrote Roosevelt a long letter recommending he give Colonel Goethals, the Chief Engineer of the Canal, absolute power, a decision that proved to be essential to the completion of the canal. Furthermore, Blackburn recommended to the President that this change should be done immediately. Just two days after receiving Governor Blackburn's recommendations, President Roosevelt issued his famous order telling the seven Canal Commissioners that they would thereafter vote on all questions as Colonel Goethals wanted them to vote, and that any member of the commission that did not feel that he could act in accord with this program would be relieved. It would be the best decision that President Roosevelt would make, all thanks to the advice of Governor Blackburn. Mr. Roosevelt and

Mr. Taft have always received the credit for trusting the Colonel, and it is deserved, but the full measure of credit for recommending this absolute authority, however, belongs to Governor Joseph Blackburn, of Kentucky. Many of the men working on the Isthmus familiar with Canal operations would have agreed.

Governor Blackburn did a service to the Panamanian people, as a people, while he was on the Isthmus. Until 1908, most of the native Panamanians were members of the Liberal party, which had been kept from all practical political power for seventy-five years. The Panamanian Liberal Party had never been able to make their votes count, which prevented them from participating in local political affairs. While Mr. Blackburn was Governor of the Panamanian Canal Zone, the second Presidential election of the Panamanian Republic was held. Panama's Liberal party told Governor Blackburn that if he would put American observers at the polls to secure a fair count of votes, the Liberal party would win.

This was not an easy task. There were charges and counter-charges of political incapacity, double dealing, and corruption. In other words, the local political situation was in a turmoil that threatened to disrupt the work of digging the Great Canal. Governor Blackburn needed to find a way to sort through the confusion and avoid the necessity of U.S. intervention, which would not have been received well in the Canal Zone in 1908. The Conservative Party was the controlling political party in Panama. It was made up of the small conservative mass of white people that had controlled Panama for many years and who wanted to continue to control it. Governor Blackburn had to decide between these two competing political parties. It was a delicate matter.

The U.S. State Department relied on Governor Blackburn to resolve the matter, and after he had dealt with the situation for a few days, a surprising solution arose. Jose Domingo de Obaldia, one of the most distinguished Conservative Party members in the Panamanian Republic, unexpectedly announced his candidacy for the Presidency as the head of a Party composed of all the Liberals and a few of Mr. Obaldia's personal friends. Panamians loved him and his announcement. With Governor Blackburn's representatives at the polls on Election Day, Obaldia was overwhelmingly elected President of Panama. It was a fair election, and there were no complaints then or later. The role of Governor Blackburn's representatives was limited to oversight of voting booths, ensuring that everyone who was entitled to vote could and did vote. The total of those votes put the people of Panama in control of political power for the first time in seventy-five years. Since that day, the new Republic of Panama has succeeded economically and politically.

Governor Blackburn knew politics and he knew men:

> He saw through the party maneuvers; and while talking and with all the suavity of the Kentucky gentleman that is in him, one whom they could understand, he conveyed to them the conviction that he could not be fooled, that Panamanian laws provided for universal suffrage, and that he was going to see the law carried out.

With the skill of an experienced politician, Governor Blackburn was able to move political power from the men who had wielded it for years while simultaneously avoiding the political challenge and danger of putting it into the hands of an inexperienced political party.

> Governor Blackburn, as a past master of political policies and as a profound and accurate student of men, was pre-eminently the man for the hour when, at Panama, both these questions had to be solved. That he did solve it and that under his solution Panama has had political peace and national prosperity ever since is one of the honors that the full and official history of the canal will yet make clear as due to Kentucky.

On October 9, 1909, Governor Blackburn arrived in Washington from Panama for a leave of fifty-six days. Blackburn would not say if he intended to resign when asked, but the rumors were that his resignation was already in the President's hands, and it was a fact that there were two bills before Congress, both of which had good chances of being passed, abolishing the Post of Governor of the Panama Canal Zone and substituting another form of government. Governor Blackburn said:

> The canal will certainly be completed by the latter part of 1913. They have 36,000 men employed on the job, and are taking out 4,000,000 yards of dirt every month. This is an increase of 200 percent over last year's record. The laborers are good, steady men, and their health is exceptionally good. The Engineer Corps says the canal will not be completed before 1915. I believe it will be finished two years earlier, because I have watched the work many months.

Governor Blackburn served from April 1, 1907 under President Roosevelt and continued in that office for a year of the Taft Administration to December 4, 1909, when he was succeeded by another Kentuckian, M. H. Thatcher, a Louisville lawyer. Colonel Goethals often bemoaned Governor Blackburn's resignation as he wrote in a letter to him after his retirement:

> I wish so often for your presence and for one of the cheering talks of yours. One never knows what anyone means to us till they are gone, and I realize more and more as time passes what your resignation means to me.

Colonel Goethals continued to write Blackburn after he resigned. He said the following about Governor Blackburn's conduct in charge of the varied and exacting duties as Governor of the Panama Canal:

> Ex-Senator Blackburn, who has served as the head of the Department of civil administration from April 1, 1907, severed his connection with the work by resignation effective December 4, 1909, and by this I lost one of my supporters. His long public service, his knowledge of men and public affairs, made him a very valuable advisor and counselor, and his method of handling matters with the Panama officials in cases affecting the interests of the Canal Zone and the neighboring republic has never been equaled.

On November 20, 1909, Governor Joseph C. S. Blackburn, at the age of seventy-one, after serving nearly three full years, wrote a letter of resignation to President Roosevelt, which was accepted. It is not clear what the personal reasons were for his resignation, but age and health come to mind, plus the need to properly raise his young granddaughter, Terese, who was thirteen years old in 1909. Former Governor and Senator Blackburn returned to Kentucky and lived on his farm at Spring Station, Kentucky, where he contemplated his next move to continue to take care of his family. On December 10, 1909, it was announced in the press that Governor Blackburn had resigned as a member of the Isthmian Canal Commission After resigning as Governor of the Panama Canal Zone, the Isthmian Canal Commission and the U.S. Postal Service issued a commemorative stamp with Governor Blackburn's image on the fifty-cent denomination of Canal Zone postage stamps.

The United States was an international power now. President Roosevelt had intervened in Latin America to protect the interests of the United States and the world. Colombians were still angry in 1913 with American interference freeing Panama when Roosevelt toured South America and gave a speech in Chile. Colombian students protested, but the President was unapologetic in his defense of U.S. actions:

> Roosevelt considered the Panama Canal to be one of the greatest achievements of his presidency, and he believed that the canal's architectural genius and the indelible mark that it and through it, he would leave on the world more than justified the small South American revolution he had had to foment in order to make it a reality.

The construction of the Panama Canal had profound economic implications for American trade. In just a little over a decade, the United States had redefined its national and international interests to include a large overseas military presence, overseas possessions, and direct engagement in international affairs.

By 1911, there were persistent rumors that Blackburn was restless on the farm. Many people encouraged him to return to seek office and lead the state and country. A cartoon was published in the Washington, D.C. *Evening Star* on Saturday, January 7, 1911, showing Senator Blackburn behind a horse-drawn plow, holding his hand up to his ear, saying, "Did Anybody Call Me Cincinnatus?" The bird, horse, dog, pig, rooster, pig, duck, sheep, and cow shown in the cartoon surrounding Senator Blackburn are each calling out, "Washington." A hand-penciled noted written by one of his friends named "Lampley" can be seen at the top of the newspaper clipping: 'This will please you. I think it is time to listen to the calls. Yours, Lampley." It seems that Blackburn responded to the call. Former Senator Blackburn gave several speeches in support of the Democratic campaigns of 1911-1912. The local newspaper, *The Woodford Sun*, published the note that "Everybody will be in Versailles Monday to hear former Senator JCS Blackburn deliver one of his old time Democratic campaign speeches."

In the United States, Woodrow Wilson and Thomas R. Marshall were elected President and Vice President while Theodore Roosevelt and the Bull Moose Party ended second. President Taft finished a humbling third. Kentucky went for Wilson by nearly one hundred thousand votes. By 1911, ten States had given women the vote. In 1912, Kentucky's Supreme Court upheld the 1912 Act, which allowed women to vote for all offices other than constitutional ones. In Great Britain, George V was crowned King in 1912. 1912 was also the year that the man who took Governor Blackburn's place in Panama, M. H. Thatcher, resigned.

The work on the Panama Canal began on May 4, 1904, and over a ten-year period, approximately fifty thousand people from more than thirty countries came to Panama and took part in the construction of the Canal, which was officially opened on August 15, 1914 with the first official passage of the Panama Railway steamship *SS Ancon*. There were no international dignitaries present, and Goethals followed the progress of *SS Ancon* from shore by railroad. Colonel Goethals became the first permanent Panama Canal Zone Governor after the Isthmian Canal Commission was terminated on April 1, 1914. In August, 1914, a cement boat, the *Cristobal*, made the first actual passage from the Atlantic to the Pacific with Phillipe Bunau-Varilla on board. Two weeks later, on August 15, 1914, the *Ancon* officially sailed through it.

More recently on September 7, 1977, President Jimmy Carter signed the Torrijos-Carter Treaty to ultimately hand over control of the canal to Panama. The treaty became effective on October 1, 1979 and required a twenty-year period during which Panama gained increasing responsibilities for the operation of the Canal. Then, as planned, on December 31, 1999, the United States withdrew from the

Panama Canal Zone completely. Since that time, the Panama Canal Authority (Autoridad de Canal de Panama, "ACP") has operated the Panama Canal. Today the Panama Canal is undergoing widening to accommodate larger ships. In fact the Panama Canal Expansion is the largest project at the Canal since its original construction. A new lane of traffic along the Canal has been created, requiring the construction of a new set of locks that doubled the canal's capacity.

Part Five

Redemption - The Lincoln Memorial

Chapter Twenty-Nine

The Greatest of All Americans

Joseph Blackburn was seventy-five in 1914 and at the end of his long political career when he was appointed by Democratic President Woodrow Wilson to the Lincoln Memorial Commission. The commission was charged with the erection of the national memorial that stands in Washington D.C. On February 7, 1914, Congress passed a joint resolution naming Blackburn as Special Resident Commissioner to represent the commission in overseeing the work. It was a remarkable appointment, because Blackburn was a veteran of the Confederate Army. It was only fitting that Blackburn's career, which began with help from Lincoln, should end with him returning the favor by supervising the construction of the Memorial to honor Lincoln.

Five days after he was appointed, a simple groundbreaking ceremony was held on Lincoln's birthday on February 12, 1914. It was a modest affair because of the tensions over the U.S. being drawn into the great war in Europe. It was a fear that came to pass by August of that year when the U.S. entered World War I. Blackburn turned the first spadeful of sod for the Memorial to Abraham Lincoln in West Potomac Park. Only a small group of persons gathered to witness the significant event, as reported in *The New York Times*:

> With uncovered head, Mr. Blackburn spoke in high praise of the memory of the President against whom he fought half a century ago.
>
> "This memorial will show that Lincoln is now regarded as the greatest of all Americans" said Senator Blackburn, "and that he is so held by the South and the North. To-day we let the country know that this great work has been begun and will be carried on steadily until its completion.'

Several people, including the architect Henry Bacon, took turns with the spade for the honor of helping to break the ground for the memorial. The Senate adjourned out of respect to the memory of Lincoln, after the reading of the Gettysburg Address.

Blackburn had traveled a long road to reach this position of honor. As a young man, Blackburn stood with his family, friends, and community, and when that meant fighting, he did so on the side with his family, friends, and community. When the Civil War ended, he moved up to achieve what Joseph's father had hoped for his family: leadership of this country. His older brothers served their roles too: Dr. Luke became a philanthropist and Governor of Kentucky, and James served as Dr. Luke's Secretary of State. Joseph served thirty-two years in the state and national arenas. In that time, his views had enlarged from the embrace of his family, friends, community, and state to the larger demands pressing the fabric of the enlarging American flag. When Joseph Blackburn started his political career, there were thirty-seven states that did not reach entirely across the continent, and by the time he retired from the U.S. Senate on March 4, 1907 at the end of the Fifty-Ninth Congress, there were forty-five states reaching across the entire continent and additional territories extending beyond the continent. While Blackburn served in the U.S. Congress and the U.S. Senate, he had played important roles shaping the country and ensuring the integrity of its democratic institutions. He had written The Organic Act that established the form of the government for the capitol city of Washington, D.C. He recognized that Washington, D.C. was more than one country's capitol: it was also the international meeting place of world leaders representing the country.

America and its capitol city represented the great shining light of democratic freedom to the world that Blackburn had helped form like his forefathers. His father-in-law Dr. C.C. Graham had inspired and educated Abraham Lincoln. His grandfather had served under General George Washington in the Commander-in-Chief's Guard. Blackburn continued the long line of men in his family who had helped to make this country great. By the beginning of the Twentieth Century, the United States was a world leader, asserting economic and military might, and an international trade partner aided by the creation of the Panama Canal. Blackburn's views were no longer limited to his family, community, and state. Now he embraced the national purpose and importance of the country. His long years of service enabled him to recognize Mr. Lincoln as "the fairest man that ever presided over a nation." He said that Lincoln's assassination was "the most cruel blow the South received from the war."

The architect Henry Bacon of New York City was selected to prepare designs for a memorial on the Potomac Park site. Another architect, Mr. John Russell Pope of New York City, was later employed to prepare additional designs for a suitable memorial for different locations that were ultimately declined.

On February 3, 1912, after careful consideration, the Commission adopted the site in Potomac Park near the river on the axis of the Capitol and the Washington Monument as the most suitable for the Lincoln Memorial. Just two weeks later, the Commission selected Mr. Henry Bacon as the architect to prepare the final design for the Lincoln Memorial, which he did and which the Commission accepted and recommended to Congress. The Commission was particularly pleased with the site because it was comparatively isolated in the middle of a large area of then undeveloped and vacant land with long vistas, providing unobstructed views of the Memorial that would be easy to landscape. Many people objected that a former tidal basin with mud flats was not a suitable site to honor Lincoln, but the Commission defended its choice for its elevation, visibility, and majestic isolation. And they were right. The location of the Lincoln Memorial in Washington, D.C. was upon the main east and west axis from L'Enfant's original layout for the grand city. This line or axis was drawn from the Capitol and the Washington Monument and ended at the Potomac River, allowing it to become as important as the plan of 1791 for the monument to Washington. As the Commission Report noted:

> It is now 10 years since the Potomac Park site was first suggested for a memorial to Lincoln. Among those with whom the location found favor was the Hon. John Hay, one of Lincoln's secretaries and biographers whose rank in statesmanship and whose taste in matters of art combine to give value to his opinion. Mr. Hay expressed in these words the feelings which in one form or another he often stated:

> "As I understand it, the place of honor is on the main axis of the plan. Lincoln, of all Americans next to Washington, deserves this place of honor. He was one of the immortals. You must not approach too close to the immortals. His monument should stand alone, remote from the common habitations of man, apart from the business and turmoil of the city isolated, distinguished, and serene. Of all the sites, this one, near the Potomac, is most suited to the purpose."

Major Pierre Charles L'Enfant developed the first urban plan for the city for George Washington, the first President of the United States. Major L'Enfant was a French engineer who served in the American Revolutionary War and who wrote to President Washington asking to be commissioned as a planner when he heard of the discussions for a new federal city that were underway in 1789. The centerpiece of L'Enfant's plan was a great "public walk" that is today's National Mall, with its straight strip of grass and trees that stretches down the main east-west axis two miles from Capitol Hill to the Potomac River, flanked by the Smithsonian Museum and other national monuments, museums, and memorials and anchored by the Capitol on the east, the Washington Monument in the center, and the Lincoln Memorial on the west along the Potomac River. L'Enfant's design was based on European models translated to American ideals. As L'Enfant's biographer, Scott Berg explained: "The entire city was built around the idea that every citizen was equally important … The Mall was designed as open to all comers, which would have been unheard of in France. It's a very sort of egalitarian idea."

Next came the design of the memorial. Henry Bacon believed that there were four main features to a Memorial of Abraham Lincoln: a statue of the man, a memorial of the Gettysburg speech, a memorial of his second inaugural address, and a symbol of the United States "which he stated it was his paramount object to save and which he did save." The most important object was the isolated statue of Lincoln located in the place of honor in the center of the Memorial, showing his gentleness, power, and intelligence, where visitors can be alone with it. The smaller halls on the side contain a memorial to the second inaugural address on one side and the Gettysburg Address on the other side. Reliefs and decorations represent in allegory Lincoln's qualities, such as charity, patience, intelligence, patriotism, devotion to high ideals, and humaneness. Surrounding the walls enclosing these memorials of the man is a colonnade of thirty-six columns representing each state at the time of Lincoln's death and on the walls above the colonnade and supported at intervals by eagles are forty-eight memorial festoons (a string or chain of flowers, foliage, ribbon, etc.), one for each State existing in 1912 at the time of the Report. The architect Henry Bacon added:

> I believe this symbol representing the Union surrounding the memorials of the man who saved the Union will give to them a great significance that will strengthen in the hearts of beholders the feelings of reverence and honor for the memory of Abraham Lincoln.

The design envisioned Lincoln sitting in the center hall flanked by two side halls that hold large bronze tablets inscribed with Lincoln's second inaugural address on one wall, and his Gettysburg Address on the other wall with its famous last line:

> ~THAT WE HERE HIGHLY RESOLVE THAT THESE DEAD SHALL NOT HAVE DIED IN VAIN~THAT THIS NATION UNDER GOD SHALL HAVE A NEW BIRTH OF FREEDOM~AND THAT GOVERNMENT OF THE PEOPLE BY THE PEOPLE FOR THE PEOPLE SHALL NOT PERISH FROM THE EARTH

The Lincoln Memorial embraced the existing monuments in the city into one harmonious tribute to the founders. At one end of the great parkway stretching from Capitol Hill to the Potomac is the Capitol, a monument to the government; at the other end of the parkway is the Lincoln Memorial, a monument to the savior of that government; and, standing between, is the Washington Monument, a monument to its founder.

The designer of the nineteen-foot high statue of Lincoln was Daniel Chester French, the famous prolific American sculptor who had created a major memorial statue of Lincoln that was unveiled in 1912 for the Nebraska State Capitol in Lincoln, Nebraska. When he was chosen he was famous for his 1884 *Minute Man* statue in Concord, Massachusetts. French and Bacon decided that a statue showing Lincoln seated was best. It is Lincoln's expressive hands that capture the power and conflicting emotions of the President. French paid special attention to Lincoln's hands, using casts of his own fingers to achieve the correct placement. Plaster casts of Lincoln's hands and face were also used to make the statue. The Lincoln statue was carved out of white Georgia marble by the famous Piccirilli Brothers, who were well known marble carvers, made most famous for the colossal and beautiful seated figure of Abraham Lincoln in 1920. The Piccirilli Brothers had worked with Bacon on other projects and were longtime collaborators. It took a full year for French's design to be transferred to the marble in the carvers' studio in New York City. Once completed, the statue had to be shipped to Washington, D.C., and assembled in the Memorial in 1920.

Contractors began work on the memorial's foundation on March 27, 1914 and completed it in April 1915. Before the foundation was completed, the large seventeen-ton cornerstone was laid on February 15, 1915. It was a huge slab, seven feet deep, ten feet wide, and three feet tall. A copper box was placed inside the cornerstone containing forty items, including: architectural documents, photographs, maps, newspapers, magazines, a Bible signed by Abraham Lincoln, the Constitution of the United States, (as amended on May 1, 1913), a leather-bound Rand-McNally world atlas from 1914, the first volume of a biography of President Lincoln by Helen Nicola, (signed by Lincoln's only surviving son, Robert Todd Lincoln), and the signatures of Special Resident Commissioner Joseph C. S. Blackburn and the architect Henry Bacon, along with other members of the Lincoln Memorial Commission and those who worked on the memorial. Inside the box was a document that read:

> We, officers and members of the Grand Army of the Republic, wishing to leave evidence of our love for and appreciation of our great leader during the War of the Rebellion, Abraham Lincoln, who gave his life in furtherance of the Union and whose love for the soldiers was paramount, have signed this paper to be placed in the corner stone of the Lincoln Memorial Building to be preserved for future generations. [Followed by a list of names, not reproduced here].

Special Resident Commissioner Blackburn was given the honor of signing and laying the cornerstone of the Lincoln Memorial because both Lincoln and Blackburn were Kentuckians. Blackburn made the following remarks at the laying of the corner-stone of the Lincoln Memorial:

> The Lincoln Memorial Commission, at its recent meeting, determined that the laying of this corner-stone should not be attended by any public function, as there was not time in which to prepare for such a gathering as would be commensurate with the occasion.
>
> The purpose of this Memorial that we are erecting is not to perpetuate the name or fame of him in whose honor it is builded [sic].
>
> His name will outlast all tributes that we can pay in the shape of bronze or marble. It is intended rather as an evidence to the generations that shall follow us of the admiration and love cherished by the American people.
>
> It can add no luster to the fame of Lincoln, but it is to stand through coming ages as evidence of the gratitude and devotion in which Lincoln is held by his countrymen.

Joseph Blackburn would never see the completion of the Lincoln Memorial that he helped to direct in its fulfillment. He died on September 12, 1918 of heart failure. The Lincoln Memorial was completed and dedicated on Memorial Day, May 30, 1922, almost four years after Blackburn's death. Blackburn had continued his work on the memorial up to the time of his death. When Joseph Blackburn's body was brought back to Kentucky, it lay in state at the feet of a statue of Lincoln in the Capitol (now known as the Old State Capitol). He was the first man to be so honored. The statue of Lincoln had been installed just six years earlier. It was a fitting honor for Joseph Blackburn, given his lifetime of connections with Lincoln.

Chief Justice and former President William H. Taft noted how "peculiarly appropriate" it is that the Memorial was located on "the banks of the Potomac, the boundary between the two sections, whose conflict made the burden, passion and triumph of his life." From this location, the Capitol dome can be seen, that symbol of the Union he saved, and across the river can be seen Arlington National Cemetery, where both Union and Confederate soldiers are buried. Of the Memorial's location, President Taft said:

> [It] marks the restoration of the brotherly love of the two sections in this memorial of one who is as dear to the hearts of the South as to those of the North. The Southerner knows that the greatest misfortune in all the trials of that section was the death of Lincoln. Had he lived, the consequences of the war would not have been as hard for them to bear, the wounds would have been more easily healed, the trying days of reconstruction would have been softened. Rancor and resentment were no part of his nature. In all the bitterness of that conflict, no word fell from his lips, tired as he was, which told of hatred, malice or unforgiving soul. Here is a shrine at which all can worship. Here an altar upon which the [word marked out by Taft] sacrifice was made in the cause of Liberty. Here a sacred religious refuge in which those who love country and love God can find inspiration and repose.
>
> Mr. President, in the name of the Commission, I have the honor to deliver this Lincoln Memorial into your keeping.

Taft presented the memorial to President Warren G. Harding in the presence of Lincoln's only surviving child, the seventy-eight year-old Robert Todd Lincoln.

In 1923, Henry Bacon was awarded the American Institute of Architect's Gold Award for his design. Bacon was the sixth architect to have ever received the honor, the highest given to an architect annually.

Robert Morton, the principal of the Tuskegee Institute, spoke at the dedication ceremony, emphasizing Lincoln the Great Emancipator and not just the Savior of the Union. But liberty was not and has not always been justly or evenly distributed. Indeed, since its dedication, the Lincoln Memorial has served as the focal point for the civil rights marches and speeches seeking the rejuvenation of the promise, long lost in the Reconstruction era of Jim Crow laws denying blacks voting rights and equality to all. Lincoln's influence is still felt today, though. As William Taft said at the dedication ceremony of the Lincoln Memorial:

> Justice, truth, patience, mercy, and love of his kind, simplicity, courage, sacrifice, and confidence in God were his moral qualities. Clarity of thought and intellectual honesty, self-analysis and strong inexorable logic, supreme common sense, a sympathetic but unerring knowledge of human nature, imagination and limpid purity of style, with a poetic rhythm of the Psalms—these were his intellectual and cultural traits. His soul and heart and brain and mind had all these elements, but their union in him had a setting that baffles description. His humility, his self-abnegation, his patience under grievous disappointment, his agony of spirit in the burden he had to carry, his constant sadness, lightened at intervals with a rare humor all his own, the abuse and ridicule of which he was the subject, his endurance in a great cause of small obstructive minds, his domestic sorrows, and finally his tragic end, form the story of a passion and give him a personality that is vivid in the hearts of the people as if it were but yesterday. We feel a closer touch with him than with living men. The influence he still wields, one may say with all reverence, has a Christ-like character. It has spread to the four quarters of the globe. The oppressed and lowly of all peoples, as liberty and free government spread, pronounce his name with awe, and cherish his assured personal sympathy as a source of hope. Their leaders quote [word marked out by Taft] his glowing words of patient courage, of sympathy with the down-trodden, of dependence on God's wisdom and justice, and of his never-ceasing prayer for liberty through the rule of the people. The harmony of his message with every popular aspiration for freedom proves his universality. It was this which Stanton was inspired to predict when, as Lincoln lay dead, he said, "He now belongs to the ages."

Chapter Thirty

The Last Interview

While Blackburn served as the Special Resident Commissioner of the Lincoln Memorial Commission in 1915, James Morrow of the New York *Buffalo Express* interviewed him about his political career. With Blackburn's light hair, blue eyes, and six-foot tall frame, he was still a commanding presence. James Morrow wrote the following in the *Buffalo Express*:

> At six and seventy, he is as trim, jaunty and martial, and certainly as courtly, as he was in the heyday of his life. There is red in his neckwear, as of yore, but his big yellow mustache has turned snow white. Having always spoken his mind with a bluntness that was a delight, he does so yet, but a tranquility which now and then breaks the sharp lines of his words shows that he has grown old cheerfully and tolerantly and that the memories of his adversaries and of his battles, even when he lost, are neither uncharitable nor unpleasant. Like every other gallant gladiatorial spirit, he respects a fair-fighting and hard-fighting man.
>
> 'It seems to me,' he said, and his voice is as strong and deep as ever, 'that it was ages ago when I first came to the House of Representatives. All of my colleagues, then conspicuous before the country, are dead except Cannon—Uncle Joe, he is now called—and Eugene Hale of Maine. Blaine was then a conspicuous figure in the Republican Party and Garfield was gaining the reputation that eventually brought him to the Presidency.
>
> Sam Randall, William R. Morrison, Alexander Stephens, William M. Springer, Fernando Wood, Sunset Cox, Adlai E.

> Stevenson, afterwards vice president, and Roger Q. Mills of Texas, were leaders among the Democrats. Old men habitually look back and praise the years that are past, but the House of Representatives in 1875, as can be shown by the history of their lives, was filled with uncommonly able men.
>
> 'The Speaker was Michael C. Kerr of Indiana. He was ill then with tuberculosis. Had he lived twelve months longer, the Democrats, I am sure, would have nominated him and not Tilden for President. He was opposed to inflating the currency with irredeemable paper money, which pleased the Democrats of the East, and believed in sweeping reductions in the tariffs, which made him strong in the West. He would have defeated Rutherford B. Hayes by a decisive majority.

Blackburn then proceeded to share with Mr. Morrow his memories of individual members of Congress:

> 'I early made the acquaintance of Mr. Blaine—we were both Kentuckians, so he said. He had blown into Lexington on some vagrant wind when he was nineteen years of age. He told me that knew no one in Kentucky at the time and had no plans. A precocious youth, he appeared to be much older and a good deal smarter than was actually the fact.
>
> 'Blaine made the acquaintance of George Duncan, the richest man in the blue grass region, and Duncan got him a teacher's place at a military institute in Georgetown. To the day of his death Blaine would do anything he could to help a Kentuckian get an office in Washington. 'I can never forget the people of your state,' he told me more than once, 'because of the kind treatment I received when I went among them in my youth.'
>
> 'Usually he talked to me with great frankness. On one occasion, however, he put me off with an anecdote. Harrison was President and Blaine was secretary of state. The Republicans had rehabilitated the force bill, controlling national elections in the South, and were trying to drive it through congress.
>
> 'The Democrats in the senate were split up into three shifts of eight hours each to filibuster against the bill. In

that way a senator could be off the floor sixteen hours at a stretch. Gorman of Maryland, and myself, being managers of the filibuster, remained on duty twelve hours at a time. The senate, with only a short recess now and then, was in session continuously for 24 days.

'A piece of strategy, successfully carried out, resulted in the death of the bill. Free silver was just beginning to be a serious issue in the West. We brought a silver bill before the senate and Republicans like Stewart of Nevada and Teller of Colorado, didn't care to sidetrack it by their votes. So the force bill was put aside and we set the silver orators to work on long speeches, addressed mostly to their mining constituents.

'In the thick of the fight, I spent an evening with Mr. Blaine. I knew that he disapproved of the bill which Mr. Harrison, his chief, was trying to have passed. "You have always been a brave and outspoken man," I said to him. "Why don't you come out in the open and assist us to defeat this detestable measure?"'After looking off into space for a moment Mr. Blaine replied: "I knew a man who wrote a play and had it staged in New York. Not wishing to be seen in the audience when the play was produced, he hunted up a friend, who was a dramatic critic of some ability, gave him a free ticket to attend the performance, and asked him to attend and report the results.

'"The dramatic critic, when the night arrived, hied himself to the theatre. At the end of the first act, the audience began to laugh, jeer and hiss. The uproar was terrific. At the height of the disapproving outburst, a man in the next box seat to the critic said: 'Why don't you make a noise like the rest of us?'"

'"'I'll tell you the reason,'" the critic answered. "I am here on a complimentary ticket. I'll stay through the second act and if it is as bad as the first one, I'll go to the box office and buy a ticket and then I'll come back to my seat and hiss as loud as I damn please.'"

'Of course,' Senator Blackburn went on to say, 'I saw the point of Mr. Blaine's story. He was a member of Harrison's administration, on a purely complimentary basis, and didn't feel like hissing the early part of the performance. Blaine was a man of daring courage and loved the battle of debate. The fiercer the attack, the better he liked it. Garfield, on the other hand, the most cultured man in my first, the 44th congress, shrank from rough work on the floor. He would fight ably and politely but if a big, strong Democrat would take him by the neck and jolt him in the ribs, he would gather up his papers and quit the field.

'The strength of Blaine lay in his skill and his weight as an offensive fighter. He was not at his best in the trenches. He knew, for example, that the committee which had investigated his transactions with the builders of the Union Pacific railroad would report to the House of Representatives on April 25, 1876. So he arose on April 24 to a personal explanation and as I sat and listened to him I feared he would have every member of the committee in the penitentiary before night. It was his practice to strike the first blow.

'Yes, I knew Sunset Cox intimately. He was my seatmate for a year. A brilliantly witty man, he was not capable of engaging in long, hard battle. He understood his limitations and, after skirmishing against the enemy and getting them boiling mad, he would retire and let the big guns of the Democracy finish the engagement.

'I remember that he was talking one day and a dozen Republicans were on their feet trying to interrupt him with inquiries and statements. Joseph G. Cannon was shouting for recognition at the top of his voice.

'"Whom shall I let in?"' Cox said to me.

'"Cannon,"' I answered, "but make him promise to keep his hands in his pockets.""Mr. Speaker," Cox called above the clamor, "I will recognize the gentleman from Illinois provided he refrains from shaking his left fist in my face. I am a small man," Cox went on to say, while the house boomed with laughter, "and when the gentleman grows threatening and doubles up and waves his left fist, he makes me nervous."'

'Cannon, looking very solemn, started to speak and instantly his left arm began to fly over his head, in front of his face and in every other direction. The house howled and Cox, saying that the gentleman from Illinois alarmed him by his pugnacious gesticulations, refused to yield longer and went on with his own remarks.

'The ablest leader among the Democrats of the house in those days was Samuel J. Randall of Pennsylvania. I knew his father, Josiah Randall, who was a small man with an immense shock of white hair. Josiah Randall was a lawyer of great ability and wide general culture. But his son wouldn't go to school and grew up to be a bloody Monday fighter at the polling places in Philadelphia. It was said that he had hit scores and scores of men in the face and that in each instance the man went to the ground.

'While Sam Randall had a very limited supply of book education, he had remarkable ability. His speeches were never more than ten minutes long, but they were long enough for an answer to his opponents and for an inspiration to his party friends. He always lived on his salary of $5,000 a year and went to his grave a poor man. He was afraid of no one, big or little, was absolutely honest and as, I said, had great natural ability. That combination of talents and virtues will invariably bring success to any man in public life. Randall governed the wards of Philadelphia largely by his fists. He governed the House of Representatives with his head.

'Most of the potential political leaders whom I have known were men of few words. William R. Morrison of Illinois, was no talker except when he stood up to make a speech against the proposed tariff. A scene in which he figured and in which he spoke only one sentence stands out in my recollections.

'A wildly excited group of members were in front of the speaker's desk. They were ___aming and elbowing one another for recognition. A giant of a fellow named Page, who had been a stage driver out West in his youth and who had whiskers that hung down to the bottom of his vest, was yelling louder than anyone else.

'Walking back and forth, silent but noticeably angry, Morrison was watching what to him was a disgraceful procedure. Page in his pawing about and bellowing came face to face with Morrison, who catching him by the beard, close under the chin, jerked his head in one way and then in another way, saying: "Go to your seat, blankety blank you, and sit down."'I didn't suppose that Page had a pistol, but I expected to see him draw his knife and do some stabbing. On the contrary he shut his mouth instantly and obeyed orders. I never heard whether Morrison smoothed the matter over with Page or not. Anyway, the collapse of the thunderous old stage driver was another illustration of the power of mind over matter.

'Benjamin Hill of Georgia, was also a member of the House of Representatives during my freshman days as a legislator. In my judgment Clay, Webster nor Calhoun was the greatest of our congressional orators and debaters. Silas Wright of New York, I think, was the ablest controversialist ever to sit in the American congress. He never attempted to do more than to state the case under consideration, giving both sides with judicial fairness and doing it so thoroughly that nothing remained to be added. Hill followed the same methods, but his mind didn't always work along straight lines and often his major and minor premises were wrong.

'After Hill went to the senate it was noticed that Roscoe Conkling, vain, talented and aggressive, ready to fly at any Democrat of size who opened his mouth, never dared to impinge himself upon even remote edges of a debate in which the great Georgian was engaged. Hill had Conkling cowed and many a member of the senate was secretly glad.

'The senate in those days, some 30 years ago, was a magnificent body intellectually. Hoar and Spooner, Frye and Ingalls, Gorman and Voorhees, Morrill and Vest, Sherman and Hale, Edmunds and Harrison along with Evarts gave it power and distinction. I respected all of them and was on intimate terms with both Republicans and Democrats.

'I always liked Allison of Iowa, who was most cautious, as is well known, in the expression of his opinions about persons, questions and events. We served together on the finance committee. "Senator," I said one morning while we were waiting the coming of other members, "I am much perplexed about a matter concerning a recent day's legislation and Republican politics."'"Grant," I observed, "was President when I first became a member of the House of Representatives. From that day to this every President, except Hayes, has repeatedly tried to dominate congress. They all failed but Roosevelt. I can't understand why you and your party colleagues have surrendered to him.'"

"'Well,' Allison slowly replied, 'the case does look queer, but it can be easily understood if one, knowing the facts, will think about it for a moment. The threats of all other Presidents were not taken seriously. We know, however, that if we defy Roosevelt and tell him to mind his own business that he will scuttle the ship.'"

"'But,' I interrupted, 'he will go down, in that event, with the rest of you.'"

"'Of course, he will,' Allison answered. 'We know that, but he wouldn't care a damn.'"

'I used to think, all things considered, that Kansas was more symmetrically represented in the senate than any other state,' Senator Blackburn continued. 'Preston B. Plumb was as energetic as the devil and as strong as a mule. He looked after the business of his state and had great influence in the important committees to which he belonged. On the other hand, John J. Ingalls was showy, oratorical, censorious and many thought, superficial, but he was none the less a very able man.

'One of Ingall's eulogies upon a dead senator was found to be the sermon, almost word for word, of a French priest delivered more than 100 years before. Ingalls, answering the charge of plagiarism, said he had been pestered into making the speech, that the dead man was obscure and unknown to him, though a member of the senate, and that to save himself bother and to oblige the dead man's friends, he had dug up an ancient sermon, which reading well and sounding well, seemed to answer the purpose of the generality of eulogies, namely, their circulation through the mails. It was a bloodless answer, I thought, and rather rough on the deceased.

'Ingall's was a cynical fellow. He called me one day while he was presiding over the senate, and handed me a telegram stating that his house in Atchison and all its contents had burned up that morning. "The furniture," he said, "can be replaced but my manuscripts can't." "'Surely,' I remarked, trying to give him a crumb of comfort, 'your neighbors must have saved something.'"

""I suppose," he sneered, "I'll be pulled out of bed at 2 o'clock tomorrow morning by a telegram telling me that, after superhuman labor and great personal danger to themselves, my neighbors succeeded in rescuing the well of cold water that's in my back yard.""

'Oratory is a dead art,' Senator Blackburn said rather mournfully. In his prime, he was famous as a stumper and rough-and-ready debater himself. 'The newspapers,' he went on, 'have killed it. I was fourteen years old when Henry Clay died. Mr. Clay returned to Kentucky once a year and gave us our politics. Barbecue would be held in different parts of the state. Whole beeves, sheep and hogs would be roasted in trenches. As many as 25,000 people would gather to hear Mr. Clay tell what had been done in Washington and to explain the political situation. Those were the golden days of oratory.

'What Mr. Clay told us stuck in our heads and hearts until he returned the next year. It was all that we wanted to know. Now we get the news every morning. And each voter interprets the news for himself. Neither Webster nor Clay, were they alive and following the old methods, could hold an audience in this generation. A big crowd would turn out to see either of them, but when the talking began the crowd would soon evaporate.'"

Part Six

In Memoriam

Chapter Thirty-One

"Our Joe"

Captain Joe Blackburn," as he was called by his friends in Kentucky, died on September 12, 1918 in Washington, D.C. His body was brought to Kentucky where it lay in state in the Old Capitol at the feet of the Lincoln statue, where his funeral was conducted. From there his casket was carried to the Frankfort cemetery and buried in the Blackburn family burial lot. His grave was adorned with memorial flowers from every part of the state and the South, where he was admired as an orator and statesman of unusual ability and powerful influence. Following his demise, the Kentucky congressional delegation, at the call of Representative Swager Sherley, met and paid a fitting tribute to his memory.

Senator Blackburn had been one of the most remarkable men of his time. He was a great parliamentary leader, eloquent, fluent, brave, daring, ready. There was nothing indirect about him. He was a "star of chivalry." He was loved by men of every race, creed, color, and political affiliation. He was one of the few public men that could not be bought with its cash or awed with its power. Blackburn at the age of seventy, was a distinguished-looking man, with broad athletic shoulders, firm step, and spreading gray mustache, which partly obscured his full, massive jaws, expressive of determination of character. "His complexion was florid and keen eyes had that cocksureness and his manner that aggressiveness which were noticeable characteristics of his personality." He always wore a wide-brimmed soft hat, poised at a sporty angle, giving him the appearance of a typical Kentucky colonel, so often seen in those days at the race course in the Bluegrass state.

> He was typical of all that individuality that made the Kentuckian of his generation the most independent man on

> God's footstool and one of the most interesting figures any civilization has ever produced.
>
> This man was born for public life. A handsome, a graceful, an athletic person, his was a glowing mind, an ardent heart, an integrity no seduction could decoy and a geniality no prejudice could withstand....
>
> He had an excellent sense of humor and a memory marvelous for its universality and accuracy.... Joe never forgot what he heard."

Blackburn gave forty-seven years of political service and four years of military service in the Civil War. He served in the U.S. Senate from Kentucky for eighteen years, longer than the notable Henry Clay's sixteen years of service in the Senate. Together Blackburn and Clay make up two of the top five longest serving Kentucky Senators: Mitch McConnell, thirty-four years; Wendell Ford, twenty-seven years; John J. Crittenden, twenty years; Joseph C. S. Blackburn, eighteen years; and Henry Clay, sixteen years. He helped lead Kentucky after the Civil War as one of the central figures in its political rebirth in national politics in the Democratic Party, a remarkable feat for a former Confederate officer. Blackburn's appointment to the Lincoln Memorial Commission is a tribute to his life of reason, patriotism, loyalty, and friendship and symbolizes the healing of the formerly divided country into one nation.

In 1885 after Blackburn served ten years in Congress, Lt. Henry T. Allen of the U.S. Army and later General in World War I, named a mountain in Alaska for Blackburn. Mount Blackburn is the "Jewel of the Wrangells" and the highest peak in the volcanic range in the heart of the Wrangell-St. Elias National Park, the largest national park in the country, and as such, a fitting tribute to:

> A Democrat of the old school who was during his day was considered one of the greatest orators in Congress. He will be looked upon as one of the greatest Democrats since the time of Thomas Jefferson. Everybody knew 'Joe' Blackburn. Everybody loved him.

In 1893, a town in Oklahoma was named for Blackburn. The Post Office for Blackburn, Oklahoma, was established on December 15, 1893.

The town was named for him in gratitude for his work as a member of the Select Committee of Indian Traders for the Fiftieth Congress.

Blackburn lived to be almost eighty years old, and gave fifty of those years to public service, either military or political. He is buried in the Frankfort Cemetery overlooking the Kentucky River and the State Capitol next to his wife, Terese Graham Blackburn; his son, Joseph C. S. Blackburn, Jr.; his daughter, Lucile; his granddaughter Terese Blackburn Lane Rouse; and his great grandsons, Joseph Blackburn Wise and Owen Conner Rouse, Jr.

In honor of Blackburn's exceptional service to the City of Washington, D.C. and his many years of public service to his state and country, the Smithsonian Institute in Washington, D.C., sent a magnolia tree that still shelters the Blackburn family burial lot.

Since his death, the state dedicated the Joseph Blackburn Bridge that crosses the Kentucky River at Lawrenceburg in his honor in 1932. The unique "S" shaped bridge is one of only two in existence. The illness of his granddaughter, Terese Lane Rouse, prevented her from christening the bridge. Instead, Kentucky Governor Chandler's daughter, "Mimi" Chandler, christened the memorial bridge when she broke a bottle of champagne to mark its official opening. A bronze tablet marks the bridge bearing the following inscription:

> JO BLACKBURN BRIDGE
> Dedicated to the memory of Joseph Clay Stiles Blackburn, 1838–1918. Confederate Soldier, Congressman, U.S. Senator, Governor of Canal Zone. Built by State Highway Commission of Kentucky, 1932.

Blackburn was a "hale fellow, well met." In his time he was known as the "Chancellor of Chamberlin," the luxurious hotel in Washington, D.C. that was the favorite 'watering hole' for politicians and the wealthy, long since demolished. He will be remembered for his fiery speeches in favor of his Kentuckian and Southern brethren. He was the chivalrous champion of human equality who fought powerful, corporate foes. He will be remembered for his phrases: "Kentucky is the garden spot of the country and Woodford County is the asparagus bed of the Bluegrass region," a sobriquet that justly and proudly describes the fertility of the soil; and his description of his campaigns "from Mills Creek to the mouth of the Sandy River;" and most famously his saying, "He who dallies is a dastard; he who doubts is damned."

Blackburn was honored by Washington Star cartoonist Berryman who commissioned Nicholas R. Brewer, of Minneapolis, to paint Blackburn's portrait from a prized photograph. Berryman remained grateful to Blackburn for helping launch his political cartoonist career in Washington D.C.

Blackburn was not forgotten even many years later. President Franklin D. Roosevelt's administration named the Liberty Ship *USS Joe C. S. Blackburn* in his honor. It was launched on December 15, 1943, during World War II.

Joseph C. S. Blackburn captured the hearts of his people in his time. He continues to inspire long after his passing.

> His extended experience in the council chambers of the Nation and in the political field has characterized him as a man of rare gifts and great power. He has few equals as a public speaker. Well informed, of instinctively quick perception, he is formidable in debate, whether in the deliberate assembly or before the people. His powers of elocution are exceptionally fine, and his oratory is equaled by few men in public life. Of impulsive and ardent temper, behind a genial and chivalrous spirit, he is a general favorite with his friends, whose admiration rarely stops short of the wildest enthusiasm.

In 2015, one hundred years after the opening of the Panama Canal, his descendant, the author, and her husband Tom Fielder, presented a Kentucky Historical Marker that was erected in front of one of Blackburn's former homes at 215 Rose Hill, Versailles, Kentucky, where he lived for nearly twenty years from 1881 to 1899 while serving as Kentucky's U.S. Representative from 1875 to1885 and Kentucky's U.S. Senator from 1885 to 1897 and 1901 to 1907.

At the end of his life when word came that he was very ill just a few months before his eightieth birthday, one writer said:

> In some respects he is without a fellow in our history, and it is enough even for him to say that those who knew him best loved him most. Old Kentucky will never look on Joe Blackburn as an old man, though he should attain the age of Thomas Parr. He will always be 'our Joe,' the Joe of the seventies and eighties of the last century.

Sources

Brent Altsheler, "C.C. Graham, M.D., 1784-1885," The Filson Club History Quarterly (Louisville, KY, 1933), Vol. 7, No. 2, 67-87, 84-85.

The Lexington Herald Leader, April 25, 1940.

"1,000 Armed Men Invade Frankfort—March into the State House Yard and Stack Arms. Pass Set of Resolutions—Afterward a Majority of Them Were Induced to Leave. All Were Provided with Taylor Badges—Threats Made Against Goebel—Preparations Were Made for Them," The New York Times (January 26, 1900), 1."

"45th United States Congress," http://en.wikipedia.org/wiki/45th_United_States_Congress, (Accessed June 1, 2015). "

"50th United States Congress," Wikipedia, http://en.wikipedia.org/wiki/50th_United_States_Congress, (Accessed June 1, 2015)."

"51st United States Congress," Wikipedia, http://en.wikipedia.org/wiki/51st_United_States_Congress, (Accessed May 31, 2015). "

"53rd United States Congress," Wikipedia, (http://en.wikipedia.org/wiki/53rd_United_States_Congress, Accessed June 1, 2015). "

"A Brief History of Pierre L'Enfant and Washington, D.C., How One Frenchman's Vision Became Our Capital City," Smithsonian.com, http://www.smithsonianmag.com/arts-culture/a-brief-history-of-pierre-lenfant-and-washington-dc-39487784/?no-ist (Accessed August 28, 2015)."

"A Day's Wedding, Lane-Blackburn," The New York Times (October 2, 1895), 8."

"A Great Cartoonist," The Courier-Journal, date not known."

"A Kentucky Combination, Senator Blackburn to be Succeeded by Secretary Carlisle," The New York Times (October 14, 1896), 1."

"A Kentucky Senator Dead. Roswell Weissinger, Leader of the Sound-Money Democrats Victim of Pneumonia," The New York Times (March 10, 1896), 1."

"A Proclamation of Amnesty and Reconstruction, May 29, 1865," Slavery and the Making of America, PBS.org, http://www.pbs.org/wnet/slavery/experience/freedom/docs7.html (Accessed August 16, 2015)."

"A Speech for Blackburn. One of His Kentucky Friends Asks for His Nomination," The New York Times, July 9, 1896."

"A Timeline of Reconstruction: 1865-1877," (https://chnm.gmu.edu/courses/122/recon/chron/html), Accessed February 12, 2014."

"Abraham Lincoln (1920 statue)." Wikipedia, https://en.wikipedia.org/wiki/Abraham_Lincoln_(1920_statue) (Accessed August 28, 2015)."

"Abraham Lincoln and the Border States," Journal of the Abraham Lincoln Association, http://quod.lib.umich.edu/j/jala/2629860.0013.104/--abraham-lincoln-and-the-border-states?rgn=main;view=fulltext, (Accessed July 18, 2015)."

"Address of William Howard Taft, Chairman of the Lincoln Memorial Commission, in Presenting the Memorial to the President of the United States, May 30, 1922," Internet Archive, https://archive.org/details/addressofwilli00taft (Accessed August 30, 2015)."

"Alaska Pacific Railway and Terminal Company," Congressional Record, June 27, 1906 Icr-1906-0627_from_1_to_114.pdf, Accessed June 11, 2016, University of Kentucky W. T. Young Library), 9348."

"Albert Sidney Johnston," Wikipedia, https://en.wikipedia.org/wiki/Albert_Sidney_Johnston, (Accessed July 18, 2015)."

"All For Joseph," Bowling Green newspaper, JCSB Scrapbook, Part (JCSB collection)."

"All Quiet at Frankfort. Another Contest in the Legislature to Take Place To-day," The New York Times (January 29, 1900), 1."

"Alleged Bribery of U.S. Senators," May 21, 1894 (https://books.google.com/books?id=1RMTAAAAYAAJ&pg=PA434&lpg=PA434&dq=which+senate+committees+did+senator+joseph+c.+s.+blackburn+serve+on?&source=bl&ots=z42QDh5yPQ&sig=2XIQQNige-J72PYZ4TavFRgM8sw&hl=en&sa=X&ved=0ahUKEwi1mbK-henMAhVDMj4KHXYnCxoQ6AEINjAE#v=onepage&q=which%20senate%20committees%20did%20senator%20joseph%20c.%20s.%20blackburn%20serve%20on%3F&f=false, Accessed May 23, 2016)."

"Amendment to Interstate Commerce Commission proposed to increase the powers to authorize them to fix rates," Congressional Record, April 15, 1906 (cr-1906-0415_from_1_to_81.pdf, Accessed June 11, 2016, University of Kentucky W. T. Young Library) 6880."

"Another Ballot and No Election—Excitement in the Capitol at Frankfort, Ky., But No Breach of the Peace—The Sheriff on Guard," The New York Times (March 14, 1896), 5."

"Another Duel Averted. The Troubles of Senator Williams and Representative Blackburn." (The New York Times, May 19, 1882), 1, (http://timesmachine.nytimes.com/timesmachine/1882/05/20/102777811.html?pageNumber=1, Accessed June 21, 2015)."

"Antiquities Act," Wikipedia (https://en.wikipedia.org/wiki/Antiquities_Act, Accessed May 22, 2016); "Message from the President," Congressional Record (cr-1906-0327_from_1_to_56.pdf, (Accessed June 11, 2016, University of Kentucky W. T. Young Library), 4328."

"Article Four of the United States Constitution," Wikipedia, https://en.wikipedia.org/wiki/Article_Four_of_the_United_States_Constitution#Clause_3:_Fugitive_Slave_Clause, (Accessed July 21, 2015)."

"Asked to be Candidate, Senator Joseph Blackburn Will Run for Governor," The Citizen, (Berea, Kentucky), June 21, 1906, 7."

"At the National Capital," The New York Times, August 23, 1895."

"Beckham Outwits the Republicans—Decides to Move Democratic Seat of Government to Louisville. Legislators to Meet To-day—Contest Boards

Will Award All Offices to Democrats. Gen. Castleman is Organizing Company of Guards to Aid the Police in Protecting Beckham's Forces," The New York Times (February 5, 1900), 1."
"Beckham Takes Control—Is Sworn In as Governor One Hour After Goebel's Death—He Also Dismisses Collier," The New York Times (February 4, 1900), 2."
"Bills and Joint Resolutions Introduced," Congressional Record, November 20, 1903 (cr-1903-1120_from_1_to_21.pdf, Accessed June 11, 2016, University of Kentucky W. T. Young Library) 398."
"Black Codes," legal-dictionary.thefreedictionary.com/Black+Codes, Access July 13, 2014."
"Blackburn and the Senate, The Kentucky Politician Eager to Get Back into Congress," The New York Times (December 19, 1898), 3."
"Blackburn Chosen By Acclamation," San Francisco Call, Volume 87, Number 34, 3 January 1900."
"Blackburn is Well Again. Denies He Contemplates Fighting a Duel with Logan Carlisle," The New York Times October 19, 1896."
"Blackburn Lauds Lincoln, Ex-Confederate Soldier Turn First Sod for National Memorial," The New York Times, Friday, February 13, 1914, 3."
"Blackburn Looks Ahead, He Talks About Presidential Candidates and Scores Hill," The New York Times (October 26, 1891), 4 ."
"Blackburn Named for Senator, Kentucky Legislature Declares for Him—Bradley May Contest," The New York Times (January 10, 1900), 1."
"Blackburn on the Shooting," The New York Times (January 31, 1900,) 2."
"Blackburn Says Silver Will Win. Confidenet [sic] That Democrats Will Name a 16 to 1 Candidate. Hopes "Money Changers" Will Be at the Convention, as They are His Argument. The Kentuckian a Confederate for First Place, but Second Will Satisfy Him. Backed By His Own State. Does Not Think, However, an Ex-Confederate Can Win—Predicts McKinley's Discomfiture at the Polls," The Journal, Sunday, June 28, 1896, (New York), 3, (Library of Congress, The Journal, June 28, 1896, 3), https://www.loc.gov/resource/sn84031792/1896-06-28/ed-1/?sp=3&q=joseph Blackburn (Accessed August 20, 2016)."
"Blackburn Says,"Thank God for That," The New York Times (August 19, 1900), 1."
"Blackburn Senate Leader. Democrats Propose to Appoint Him Mr. Gorman's Successor," The New York Times, (June 7, 1906), 1."
"Blackburn Will Be Deserted. Sound-Money Democrats in the Kentucky Legislature Will Not Stand by the Senator After Tomorrow," The New York Time (March 3, 1896), 1."
"Blackburn, His Career in Congress-Public Acts of the Kentucky Senator, Extracts from Some of His Notable Speeches-His Course Regarding the Silver Question, An Enviable and Brilliant Record in Both Houses of the National Legislatures (Extracts from the Cincinnati Enquirer, December 30, 1895), 23."

"Blackburn," Encyclopedia of Oklahoma History & Culture, Oklahoma's Historical Society, www.digital.library.okstate.edu/encyclopedia/entries/B/BL006.html, Accessed February 14, 2014."

"Blackburn's Credentials Presented," The New York Times, May 27, 1900."

"Blackburn's Election Duplicated," The New York Times (January 17, 1900), 2."

"Blackburn's Senatorship. Gov. Taylor May Refuse to Sign the Certificate of Election," The New York Times (January 27, 1900), 3."

"Bland-Allison Act," United States History, www.u-s-history.com/pages/h718.html , Accessed February 12, 2014."

"Bluegrass Region," Wikipedia, https://en.wikipedia.org/wiki/Bluegrass_region, (Accessed July 15, 2015) (the Bluegrass Region consists of an eight-county geographic region in Kentucky that encircles about 90 miles around Lexington, Kentucky, making up the Inner Bluegrass. The Outer Bluegrass Region is made up of the northern portion of the State above the Knobs which begins on the western end near Louisville and continues southeastward through Bullitt, Hardin, Nelson, LaRue, Marion, Taylor, Casey and Lincoln counties before turning northeast and running along the Appalachians.)"

"Bourbon Democrats," Wikipedia (https://en.wikipedia.org/wiki/Bourbon_Democrat, Accessed May 8, 2016)."

"Breckenridge for Senator. May be United Upon in Order to Defeat Blackburn," The New York Times (November 8, 1896), 1."

"Canal Commission Plan. Creation of Post of Director General Proposed by Senator Morgan," The New York Times (January 30, 1907), 1."

"Capital Cities of the Confederacy," Civil War Trust, http://www.civilwar.org/education/history/warfare-and-logistics/logistics/capital.html?referrer=https://www.google.com/ (Accessed August 10, 2015)."

"Carlisle and Blackburn. Tariff-Reform Speeches by the Two Kentuckians," The New York Times (September 20, 1888), 3."

"Carlisle For Senator. Impression Gaining Ground That He Will Be Forced to Run," The New York Times (June 28, 1895), 5."

"Carlisle May Oppose Blackburn – The Secretary Will Make a Number of Sound-Money Speeches in Kentucky, and May Be Elected to the Senate," The New York Times, (August 29, 1895), 1."

"Carlisle Not A Candidate, Will Not Enter the Senatorial Contest in Kentucky, Nor Is He Likely to Support Blackburn," The New York Times (January 15, 1895), 1."

"Carlisle's Election Possible," The New York Times (March 10, 1896), 1."

"Chance for Senator Blackburn," The New York Times (November 13, 1905), 9."

"Cheers for the Ticket—Grand Flower Mass Meeting In Chickering Hall—Democrats of the Ninth and Fifteenth Wards Enthusiastic—Speeches by Senator Blackburn, Gen. Sickles, and Others," The New York Times (October 30, 1891), 5."

"Chinese Exclusion Act," Wikipedia, http://en.wikipedia.org/wiki/Chinese_Exclusion_Act, (Accessed May 31, 2015)."
"Cholera on the British Troop Ship Himalaya – Dr. Blackburn," The New York Times, (September 21, 1876), 1."
"Cleveland The One Man, Kentucky Democrats Want Him To Lead Them to Victory," The New York Times May 17, 1888."
"Clifford Berryman, 80, Political Cartoonist, Dies," The Courier-Journal, December 11, 1934."
"Coalition Against Blackburn Proposed," The New York Times (September 17, 1896), 1."
"Coinage Act of 1873," Wikipedia, http://en.wikipedia.org/wiki/Coinage_Act_of_1873, (Accessed June 1, 2015)."
"Committee Service," Congressional Record, January 24, 1906 (cr-1906-0124_from_1_to_59.pdf, (Accessed June 11, 2016, University of Kentucky W. T. Young Library), 1469."
"Comparative Statement of Bills Introduced and Reports Made, First Session Fifty-Seventh Congress (http://library.clerk.house.gov/reference-files/House_Calendar_57th_Congress.pdf, Accessed May 22, 2016)."
"Compromise of 1877," United States History (http://www.u-s-history.com/pages/h396.html, Accessed March 27, 2016)."
"Confederate States of America, History," http://www.history.com/topics/american-civil-war/confederate-states-of-america (Accessed August 10, 2015)."
"Conferee," United States Senate, Glossary, (http://www.senate.gov/reference/glossary_term/conferees.htm, Accessed May 8, 2016)."
"Congress Abolishes the African Slave Trade," History, http://www.history.com/this-day-in-history/congress-abolishes-the-african-slave-trade (Accessed August 8, 2015)."
"Congress Passes the Third Reconstruction Act," History Engine, www.historyengine.richmond.edu/episodes/view/1430 , Accessed February 12, 2014."
"Congress Profiles: 44th Congress (1875-1877)," History, Art & Archives of the United States House of Representatives, (http://history.house.gov/Congressional-Overview/Profiles/44th/ , Accessed April 9, 2016)."
"Congress Profiles: 47th (1881-188)," http://history.house.gov/Congressional-Overview/Profiles/47th/, (Accessed June 1, 2015)."
"Congress Profiles: 48th Congress (1883-1885)," http://history.house.gov/Congressional-Overview/Profiles/48th/, (Accessed June 1, 2015)."
"Congress Profiles: 49th (1885-1887), http://history.house.gov/Congressional-Overview/Profiles/49th/, (Accessed June 1, 2015)."
"Congress Profiles: 50th (1887-1889)," http://history.house.gov/Congressional-Overview/Profiles/50th/, (Accessed June 1, 2015)."
"Congress Profiles: 51st (1889-1891)," http://history.house.gov/Congressional-Overview/Profiles/51st/, (Accessed June 1, 2015)."
"Congress Profiles: 52nd (1891-1893),"Wikipedia, (http://history.house.gov/Congressional-Overview/Profiles/52nd/, Accessed June 1, 2015)."

"Constitutional Convention," Wikipedia, https://en.wikipedia.org/wiki/Constitutional_Convention_(United_States) (Accessed August 6, 2015)."
"Constitutional History of the Kentucky General Assembly," Kentucky Legislative Research Council (http://www.lrc.ky.gov/lrcpubs/IB175a.pdf, Accessed May 9, 2016)."
"Cross of Gold Speech," Encyclopedia Britannica, www.britannica.com/EBchecked/topic/133137/Cross-of-Gold-speech, Accessed February 12 2014."
"Cross of Gold" Speech, William Jennings Bryan, closing debate, Democratic National Convention in Chicago, 1896."
"Custom House Methods, The Senate Sub-Committee at Work in This City, Its First Session Evokes Quite a Variety of Interesting Information," The New York Times, May 25, 1888, 8."
"Daniel Chester French," Wikipedia, https://en.wikipedia.org/wiki/Daniel_Chester_French (Accessed August 28, 2015)."
"Death Comes to William Goebel—Hopeless Struggle for Life Continued All Day Yesterday. Doctors Fought for Times—Tried to Keep Dying Man Alive Until His Brother Came. Patient Lapsed Into Unconsciousness Toward Evening and Died at 6:44 o'Clock—The Brother Arrived Too Late," The New York Times (February 4, 1900), 1."
"Death List of the Day, Joseph C. S. Blackburn, Jr.," The New York Times February 13, 1902."
"Deboe is Chosen Senator—Candidate of the Kentucky Republicans Wins at Frankfort After Two Long Sessions. Goes Right to Washington. Another Vote to Help Pass the Tariff Bill—The New Senator Will Not Materially Change the Present Complexion of the Senate," The New York Times (April 29, 1897), 4."
"December 8, 1863, Lincoln Issues Proclamation of Amnesty and Reconstruction," History.com, http://www.history.com/this-day-in-history/lincoln-issues-proclamation-of-amnesty-and-reconstruction (Accessed August 16, 2015)."
"Did Anybody Call Me Cincinnatus?" Washington Evening Star cartoon, Jaunary 7, 191 (Blackburn Family papers)."
"Did Croker Help Goebel? Republicans Accuse Him of Sending Money to Kentucky. J.R. McLean Also Attacked—Alleged that the New York and Ohio Men Conspired with the Standard Oil to Defeat Taylor," The New York Times (January 21, 1900), 1."
"Direct Election of Senators, Senate History," United States Senate (http://www.senate.gov/artandhistory/history/common/briefing/Direct_Election_Senators.htm, Accessed April 2, 2016)."
"Dismissal of Three Companies of Twenty-Fifth Infantry," Congressional Record (cr-1907-0117_from_1_to_56.pdf), 1252."
"Dismissal of Three Companies of Twenty-Fifth Infantry," Congressional Record (cr-1907-0121_from_1_to_59.pdf), pages 1434–1436."

“Dixie (song),” https://en.wikipedia.org/wiki/Dixie_(song) (Accessed August 9, 2015).”
“Do the people of the South really entertain fears that a Republican administration would, directly, or indirectly, interfere with their slaves, or with them, about their slaves? If they do, I wish to assure you, as once a friend, and still, I hope, not an enemy, that there is no cause for such fears.” The Collected Works of Abraham Lincoln, ed. Roy P. Basler, Volume IV, “Letter to Alexander H. Stephens” (December 22, 1860), 160.”
“Early History of Midway, Col. E. M. Blackburn,” The Woodford Sun, JCSB collection, JBW box Uncle Ned Midway_29.”
“Early Times in Woodford County,” The Woodford Sun, date not known.”
“Eiffel Tower,” History.com, http://www.history.com/topics/eiffel-tower (Accessed August 22, 2015).”
“Election of United States Senators,” Congressional Record, June 28, 1902 (cr-1902-0628_from_1_to_68.pdf, Accessed may 26, 2016, University of Kentucky W.T. Young Library), 7560.”
“Elkins Act,” Wikipedia (https://en.wikipedia.org/wiki/Elkins_Act, Accessed May 22, 2016).”
“Expediting Act,” Wikipedia (https://en.wikipedia.org/wiki/Expediting_Act, Accessed May 22, 2016).”
“Fight Ended, No Choice—Kentucky Legislature Fails to Elect a United States Senator. The Contest Brought to a Close by the Final Adjournment of the Legislative Body—Only Two Votes Cast on the Last Ballot—The Joint Session Dissolved “Everlastingly, Eternally and Forever”—What “Jack” Chinn Thinks About it,” The New York Times (March 18, 1896), 2.”
“For Peace in Kentucky-Chariman’s Ruling as to a Quroum May End the Trouble. Democrats Confident of Success. Police Cleared the House at Yesterday’s Session—Position of the Unseated Members,” The New York Times (March 13, 1896), 1.”
“Free Coinage for the Masses,” Speech of Hon. J.C.S. Blackburn of Kentucky in the Senate of the United States, January 9, 1891, Washington. 1891.”
“Free Silver,” Wikipedia, http://en.wikipedia.org/wiki/Free_silver, (Accessed June 1, 2015).”
“From Hoops to Horse Racing,” (Lexington’s first racetrack opened in the 1830s and was known as “Chittlin’ Switch.” It was located near what is now 5th and Race Streets in Lexington, KY.) www.visitlex.com/idea/sports-articles.php, Accessed February 14, 2014.”
“From the Southwest. The Kentucky Legislature – The Rebel Guerillas Gatewood and Ferguson Committing Depredations in East Tennessee – Jeff. Davis and His Followers,” The New York Times (May 19, 1865), 5.”
“General Notes,” The New York Times (May 12, 1879), 5.”
“Gilded Age,” Wikipedia (https://en.wikipedia.org/wiki/Gilded_Age, Accessed May 8, 2016).”
“Goebel Sworn in as Governor. Justice of Court of Appeals Administers the Oath. Orders of DyingMan—Oust Gen. Collier and Disbands the Militia.

Issues Proclamation. Forbids All Interference with the General Assembly. Gov. Taylor's Action—Declares Kentucky in a State of Insurrection—Orders the Legislature to London," The New York Times (February 1, 1900), 1."
"Goebel to Lie in State—Body Will Be Taken to Covington To-day, But Will be Interred in Frankfort," The New York Times (February 5, 1900), 2."
"Goebel Wins the Kentucky Contest—The Board Finds for Him on a Strict Party Vote. Draws Up Its Report—Legislators Try to Take Immediate Action, but Fail. No Quorum Could be Gathered for Night Session—Republicans Will Resort to Courts," The New York Times (January 31, 1900), 1."
"Gold Standard Act," Encyclopedia Britannica, www.britanica.com/EBchecked/topic/237439/Gold-Standard-Act, Accessed February 12, 2014."
"Gossip," Turf, Field and Farm, April 4, 1903, 322."
"Gov. Brown Would Be a Senator," The New York Times (March 9, 1894)."
"Gov. Roosevelt on Goebel—Says All Decent Citizens Should Support Gov. Taylor," The New York Times (February 5, 1900), 2."
"Gov. Taylor Will Wait. Will Not Sign Blackburn's Commission as Senator Until the Governorship is Settled," The New York Times (January 30, 1900), 1."
"Grand Army Men Thank Blackburn," The New York Times (March 9, 1888), 4."
"Hay-Paunceforth Treaty: The United States and Britain," United States History, http://www.u-s-history.com/pages/h929.html (Accessed August 21, 2015)."
"Hearings Will Begin Monday," The New York Times, (January 13, 1900), page of 30."
"Hearst May Win in Kentucky, Senator Blackburn Urged to Come Home and Fight His Boom," The New York Times (May 16, 1904), 5."
"Hepburn Act," Wikipedia (https://en.wikipedia.org/wiki/Hepburn_Act, Accessed May 22, 2016)."
"History of Immigration to the United States," https://en.wikipedia.org/wiki/History_of_immigration_to_the_United_States (Accessed August 8, 2015)."
"History of Kentucky," Wikipedia, https://en.wikipedia.org/wiki/History_of_Kentucky, (Accessed July 15, 2015)."
"History of Slavery in Kentucky," Wikipedia, https://en.wikipedia.org/wiki/History_of_slavery_in_Kentucky, (Accessed July 15, 2015)."
"Honestly Obtained," Nashville World, JCSB Scrapbook, Part (JCSB collection)."
"I Am Proud of Writing Organic Act,"The Washington Herald, February 2, 1914."
"Immigration Act of 1903," Wikipedia (https://en.wikipedia.org/wiki/Immigration_Act_of_1903, Accessed May 22, 2016)."

"In Which Box Will the Voter of '86 Put His Ballot?" Cartoon of 1896, Missouri State, www.clio.missouristate.edu/wrmiller/Populism/2scartoon/scartoon33.htm, Accessed February 14, 2014)."
"J.C.S. Blackburn Nominated," The New York Times (January 3, 1900), 3."
"J.C.S. Blackburn Resigns. Ex-Senator Gives Up His Place on the Isthmian Commission," The New York Times (December 10, 1909), 6."
"Jim Crow Laws," U.S. History (http://www.u-s-history.com/pages/h1559.html, Accessed March 27, 2016)."
"Joe Blackburn Can't Be Bought," (JCSB collection)."
"Joe Blackburn's Story," E.J. McNatt, The Lamar News, June 2, 1887 (www.newspaperabstracts.com/link.php?id=32200), Accessed February 12, 2014."
"John C. Breckenridge," Wikipedia, (https://en.wikipedia.org/wiki/John_C._Breckinridge, Accessed April 2, 2016)."
"John C. Breckenridge," Wikipedia, https://en.wikipedia.org/wiki/John_C._Breckinridge (Accessed July 15, 2015)."
"John G. Carlisle," Wikipedia, (http://en.wikipedia.org/wiki/John_G._Carlisle, Accessed June 1, 2015). Kentucky's Carlisle served as Secretary of the Treasury during the Panic of 1893 that rocked the country. As a Bourbon Democrat, he was a leader of the conservative, pro-business wing of the party, along with President Cleveland."
"Joseph C. S. Blackburn, Famous Orator and Former U.S. Senator" by Robert T. Barry, Feature, The Courier-Journal, September 30, 1917, Section 4; (JBW box JCSB CJ Kentuckians Who Have Made History 9-30-1917_22.pdf, (JCSB collection)."
"Kentucky Declaration of Neutrality," Wikipedia, https://en.wikipedia.org/wiki/Kentucky_Declaration_of_Neutrality, (Accessed July 18, 2015)."
"Kentucky Factions Patch Up Peace—All Troops are to be Withdrawn from Frankfort. Legislature to Meet There—Taylor and Marshall Are to Abide by Its Action. The Party Leaders Arrive at the Terms of a Truce After a Long Conference in Louisville," The New York Times (February 6, 1900), 1."
"Kentucky Governors," Robert A. Powell, 1976, 52."
"Kentucky Troops Guarding Taylor—Bayonets Bar the Doors of the State House to Legislators. Two Blows at the Governor—Banker and Penitentiary Warden Refuse to Recognize Him. Lawyers Make a Vain Attempt to End the Trouble—Public Men Receive Threats of Assassination," The New York Times (February 2, 1900), 1."
"Kentucky Troops in Arms? Rumored That They are Being Quietly Ordered Out. May Declare Martial Law—Ex-Gov. Bradley, However, Denies that Bloodshed is Feared and Discredits Sensational Reports," The New York Times (January 10, 1900), 1."
"Kentucky," History, http://www.history.com/topics/us-states/kentucky, (Accessed July 15, 2015)."
"Kentucky. Recruiting Slaves Going on Briskly," The New York Times (May 31, 1865), 8 of 8."

"Kentucky's Contest Over," JCSB Scrapbook, Part (JCSB collection)."
"Kentucky's New Senator," Galveston Times, JCSB Scrapbook, Part 1."
"Killed By His Own Crowd? One of the Invaders of Frankfort, Ky., Reported Murdered on the Train Because He Yelled for Goebel," The New York Times (January 29, 1900), 1."
"Kinkaid Act," Wikipedia (https://en.wikipedia.org/wiki/Kinkaid_Act, Accessed May 22, 2016)."
"Knows Goebel's Assassin—James Sutton, a Sheriff, Under Arrest, Says He Knows Who Fired the Shot," The New York Times (February 1, 1900), 1."
"Lenten Events in Washington, Society at a Drill—Easter GayetiesA Spirited Auction for Charity," The New York Time (March 17, 1884),"
"Let the Party Split; Roosevelt to Senate—If It Has to Be, He Wants the Biggest Fragment. Sees the Trusts at Work—Thinks They Are Behind the Senate's Agitation Over Brownsville, and Is Ready for the Issue," The New York Times (January 20, 1907), 1."
"Life and Death in the White House," American History, (http://americanhistory.si.edu/presidency/3d1d.html, Accessed April 2, 2016)."
"Lincoln Memorial Commission Report, Message from the President of the United States Transmitting a Report of the Lincoln Memorial Commission, and Its Recommendations, Upon the Location, Plan, and Design for a Memorial, in the City of Washington, to the Memory of Abraham Lincoln, in Accordance with the Act Approved February 9, 1911," Internet Archive, https://archive.org/stream/lincolnmemorialcunit#page/n0/mode/2up (Accessed August 27, 2015), 9."
"Lincoln Memorial, Washington, D.C.," Full Text, http://archive.org/stream/lincolnmemorialww00alex/lincolnmemorialw00alex_djvu.txt."
"Lindsay's Scalp, Democracy of Barren County Demands Senator's Resignation, MISREPRESENTS HIS PARTY, Promised Both Publicly and Privately That He would Resign His Seat, Representative Instructed to Enforce the Demand in the Legislature, HERE'S THE RESOLUTION," Clipping, (Terese Blackburn Rouse collection)."
"Married Another," The Paducah Sun, (March 26, 1902), 1, (http://kdl.kyvl.org/catalog/xt7tdz030n7z_1, Accessed June 30, 2015)."
"May Offer a $50,000 Reward," The New York Times (February 3, 1900), 2; "Taylor Offers a Reward," The New York Times (February 3, 1900), 2."
"Memorial Addresses of the Late Senator Hanna," Congressional Record, April 7, 1904 (cr-1904-0407_from_1_to_57.pdf, University of Kentucky W.T. Young Library), 4420."
"Milesones: 1899-1913, Building the Panama Canal, 1903-1914," U.S. Department of State Office of the Historian, https://history.state.gov/milestones/1899-1913/panama-canal (Accessed August 19, 2015)."
"Military Academy Appropriation Bill," Congressional Record, April 26, 1904 (cr-1904-0426_from_1_to_72.pdf, (Accessed June 11, 2016, University of Kentucky W. T. Young Library), 5614."

"Militia Act of 1903," Wikipedia (https://en.wikipedia.org/wiki/Militia_Act_of_1903, Accessed May 22, 2016)."
"Miss Blackburn Married. W.H. Gale Weds Senator's Daughter—Campaign Detains Her Father," The New York Times (August 6, 1905), 7."
"Mr. Blackburn Gets a War Club," The New York Times (March 4, 1887), 1."
"Mr. Blackburn on the Commission," The New York Times (February 20, 1877), 5."
"Mr. Blackburn's "Candor,"" The New York Times (October 9, 1893), 4."
"Mr. Blackburn's Platform," New York Times, February 11, 1884, page 3 of 8."
"Mr. Blackburn's Summer Clothes," The New York Times, 5."
"Mr. Goebel's Heart Weak—Unless It Becomes Stronger the Doctors Fear He Cannot Live Many Hours," The New York Times (February 2, 1900), 2."
"My Old Kentucky Home Lyrics," KET, http://www.ket.org/underground/resources/oldkyhome.htm, (Accessed July 21, 2015)."
"My Old Kentucky Home," Wikipedia, https://en.wikipedia.org/wiki/My_Old_Kentucky_Home, (Accessed July 21, 2015)."
"Naval Appropriation Bill," Congressional Record, February 27, 1905 (cr-1905-0227_from_1_to_134.pdf, (Accessed June 11, 2016, University of Kentucky W.T. Young Library), 3482."
"Nelson Act of 1889," Wikipedia, http://en.wikipedia.org/wiki/Nelson_Act_of_1889, (Accessed May 31, 2015)."
"Order of Secession During the American Civil War," American History, http://americanhistory.about.com/od/civilwarmenu/a/secession_order.htm (Accessed August 10, 2015)."
"Original Plan of Washington, D.C.," American Treasures of the Library of Congress, http://www.loc.gov/exhibits/treasures/tri001.html (Accessed August 28, 2015)."
"Orphan Brigade," Wikipedia, http://en.wikipedia.org/wiki/Orphan_Brigade, (Accessed June 1, 2015)."
"Panama Canal by 1913, Gov. Blackburn Cuts Two Years Off the Engineers' Estimate," The New York Times (October 20, 1909), 4."
"Panama Canal Expansion, Canal de Panama, 100 Years Connecting the World," http://micanaldepanama.com/expansion/ (Accessed August 23, 2015)."
"Panama Canal," Congressional Record, June 14, 1906 (cr-1906-0614_from_1_to_80.pdf, Accessed June 11, 2016, University of Kentucky W.T. Young Library), 8476–8477."
"Peace Conference of 1861," Wikipedia, https://en.wikipedia.org/wiki/Peace_Conference_of_186 (Accessed August 10, 1861)."
"Petitions Against Enactment of Eight-Hour Bill," Document No. 189, 68195 Senate, 4430 Senate, 57th Congress, Second Session, February 20, 1903 (Congressional Record, February 27, 1903)."
"Pistols at Frankfort-Riotous Scenes Accompany the Unseating of Legislators. Kaufman, Walton and James Out. The House Decided in Favor of Dunlap After He Had Withdrawn His Contest of Kaufman's Seat," The New York Times (March 12, 1896), 1."

"Political Reflections, Past and Present," The Woodford Sun, 1940; JBW box_25 (JCSB collection)."
"Politics for Everybody, This an Important Year for Candidates and Parties, Thirty Seats to be Filled in the United States Senate—General Elections in Almost Every Commonwealth in Union—An Entirely New House of Representatives to be Voted For—Offices to be Filled, Terms of Service, and Present Incumbents," The New York Times, June 11, 1894, 12."
"Presidential Choice of Democrats in Congress, The Prevailing Opinion is That New York Can Name the Candidates, Gorman Leads in Popularity, With Parker a Strong Second Choice Among Those Willing to Declare a Preference," The New York Times December 26, 1903, 5."
"Prison Cell for Powers—Jury Finds Him Guilty of Participating in Goebel's Murder. Fixes Punishment at Imprisonment for Life—Attorneys Will Make Every Effort to Revese [sic] the Verdict," The New York Times (August 19, 1900), 1."
"Proceedings to Oust Taylor," The New York Times (February 2, 1900),2."
"Pure Food and Drug Act," Wikipedia (https://en.wikipedia.org/wiki/Pure_Food_and_Drug_Act, Accessed May 22, 2016)."
"Random Notes," The Woodford Sun, date not known (1930s)."
"Reconstruction Act of 1867," University of Notre Dame, Open Course Ware, http://www.ocw.nd.edu/history/african-american-history-ii/lecture-notes/reconstruction-act-of-1867, Accessed February 12, 2014"
"Reconstruction Timeline," Harper's Weekly, https://www.mtholyoke.edu/~kmporter/reconstructiontimeline.html (Accessed August 16, 2015)."
"Reminiscences of Prominent Kentuckians with Many Incidents and Anecdotes of the Great and Near Great Never Before Published, Joseph Clay Styles Blackburn," by R. Lee Davis, The Lexington Leader, April 12, 1933, 21–28."
"Remonetization of Silver," Speech of Hon. Joseph C. S. Blackburn of Kentucky, in the Senate of the United States, Wednesday, October 4, 1893, (Washington, 1893), page 4."
"Reports of Committees," Congressional Record, February 27, 1903 (cr-1903-0227_from_1_to_44.pdf, Accessed may 26, 2016, University of Kentucky W. T. Young Library), 2734."
"Reports of the Committees," Congressional Record, May 24, 1906 (cr-1906-0524_from_1_to_64.pdf, Accessed June 11, 2016, University of Kentucky W. T. Young Library), 7337–7338."
"Republicans Vote for Carlisle, Exciting Ballots for the United States Senatorship in the Kentucky Legislature," The New York Times (March 8, 1896), 1."
"Roosevelt Confounds the Senate Oligarchy—Joins Democrats in Smoking Out His Republican Enemies. Aldrich Men are Alarmed—Blackburn Insists on His Resolution on the Negro Troops, and Some Republicans Join His Flag," The New York Times (January 19, 1907), 1."

"Roosevelt Modifies Negro Dismissal Order—Admits Error in Barring Them from Civil Employment. Proves Soldiers Did Riot—Mass of Evidence on the Brownsville Shooting—No Reference to Innocent Men's Right to Court Hearings," The New York Times (January 15, 1907), 5."
"Safe-Keeping of Public Money," Congressional Record, February 28, 1903 (cr-1903-0228_from _1_to_68.pdf, Accessed May 26, 2016, University of Kentucky W. T. Young Library), 2792."
"Safe-Keeping of Public Money," Congressional Record, March 3, 1903 (cr-1903-0302_from _1_to_92.pdf, Accessed May 26, 2016, University of Kentucky W. T. Young Library), 2897."
"Says He Knows Assassin. Man Named Rodman Declares Goebel's Death Was Compassed by a Friend of Sanford," The New York Times (February 3, 1900), 2."
"Says There Was a Plot. Sutton, Arrested Wednesday, Believed by Louisville Police to Know All About the Shooting," The New York Times (February 2, 1900), 2."
"Sculptor Trentanove Engaged, He Will Wed Mrs. Lane, Senator Blackburn's Daughter, Next Month," The New York Times (November 21, 1901), 9."
"Seigniorage," Wikipedia, https://en.wikipedia.org/?title=Seigniorage, (Accessed June 24, 2015)."
"Senate Committees," United States Senate (http://www.senate.gov/artandhistory/history/common/briefing/Committees.htm, Accessed May 8, 2016)."
"Senate Democrats Look for a Leader—With the Passing of Blackburn They are Left at Sea. Bailey Under a Cloud—And His Colleague, Culberson, Would Not Receive His Support for Party Honors," The New York Times (January 30, 1907), 4."
"Senate Fight in Kentucky. Blackburn's Friends Will Carry the Contest to Washington," The New York Times (December 16, 1896), 1."
"Senator Blackburn Beaten," The New York Times (January 3, 1906), 1."
"Senator Blackburn Injured – Thrown From His Carriage While Driving to His Home," New York Times, October 23, 1890."
"Senator Blackburn True to the Soil," The Thoroughbred Record, Lexington, KY., September 15, 1899."
"Senator Blackburn Very Ill," The New York Times (August 30, 1891), 1."
"Senator Blackburn Very Sick," The New York Times (October 12, 1896), 2."
"Senator Blackburn, of Kentucky." JCSB Scrapbook, Part (JCSB collection)."
"Senator Blackburn," JCSB Scrapbook Part (JCSB collection)."
"Senator Blackburn," JCSB Scrapbook, Part (JCSB collection)."
"Senator Blackburn's Recovery," The New York Times, November 5, 1890."
"Senator Hoar in Trouble—An Unseemly Attack on Speaker Carlisle. For Which He is Severely Taken to Task by Mr. Blackburn—Closing Up the Work of Congress," The New York Times (March 4, 1887), 1."
"Senator Joe Blackburn," JCSB Scrapbook, Part (JCSB collection)."
"Serenade to Mr. Blackburn," The New York Times (February 14, 1884), 1."

"Serenade to Mr. Blackburn," The New York Times, (February 14, 1884), page of 8."
"Seventeenth Amendment to the United States Constitution," Wikipedia, https://en.wikipedia.org/wiki/Seventeenth_Amendment_to_the_United_States_Constitution, (Accessed June 22, 2015)."
"Silver Men Again Lose. Their Slate Broke in Kentucky Democratic Convention. Sound-Money Men's Strength Shown. The Second Fight of the Convention is on the Nomination for Treasurer – Completion of the State Ticket," The New York Times (June 28, 1895), 5."
"Simon Bolivar Buckner," Wikipedia, https://en.wikipedia.org/wiki/Simon_Bolivar_Buckner, (Accessed July 18, 2015)."
"Slave and Free States," Wikipedia, https://en.wikipedia.org/wiki/Slave_and_free_states (Accessed August 6, 2015)."
"Social Life in Washington. The Chief Event Yesterday Was a Tea Given to Mrs. Cleveland," The New York Times (January 20, 1894), 3."
"Speakers of the House (1789 to present), www.history.house.gov/People/Office/Speakers/, Accessed February 6, 2014)."
"Tammany's Ovation to William J. Bryan, Regardless of Chill Winds, 50,000 Voters Surround the Wigwam to Greet Him. The Riot of Enthusiasm When He Entered Intensified by His Terrific Arraignment of the Trusts. Sewall and Blackburn Royally Received—Crowds at Meetings—A Gathering Without Political Parallel," The New York Journal, Wednesday, September 30, 1896, 1-2, (Library of Congress, https://www.loc.gov/resource/sn84024350/1896-09-30/ed-1/?q=joseph+blackburn&sp=1), (Accessed August 20, 2016)."
"Taylor States His Position. Declares the Legislature Acted Illegally, and Says He Will Not Give Up the Fight," The New York Times (February 2, 1900), 2."
"The Big Inaugural Ball, Pension Building Transformed by Brilliant Decorations. They Were the Handsomest Ever Attempted in This Country—A Triumph of the Electrician's Skill—How the Wants of the Great Multitude Were Supplied," The New York Times (March 5, 1893), 10."
"The Civil War in Kentucky," Lowell H. Harrison, 1975, The University Press of Kentucky, 3."
"The Civil War in Kentucky," Lowell H. Harrison, 1975, The University Press of Kentucky, 6-7."
"The Civil War in Kentucky," Lowell H. Harrison, 1975, The University Press of Kentucky, 8."
"The Confederate War Department, Confederate Cabinet and Executive Bureau Officers, James Alexander Seddon," http://www.csawardept.com/history/Cabinet/Seddon/index.html (Accessed August 9, 2015)."
"The Enabling Act of 1889," Wikipedia, http://en.wikipedia.org/wiki/Enabling_Act_of_1889, (Accessed May 31, 2015)."
"The Erie Canal," www.eriecanal.org (Accessed August 19, 2015)."

"The Federal Reserve Act," Wikipedia, https://en.wikipedia.org/wiki/Federal_Reserve_Act, (Accessed July 14, 2014)."
"The Fugitive Slave Act of 1793," Wikipedia, https://en.wikipedia.org/wiki/Fugitive_Slave_Act_of_1793, (Accessed July 21, 2015)."
"The Fugitive Slave Clause," Wikipedia, https://en.wikipedia.org/wiki/Fugitive_Slave_Clause (Accessed August 6, 2015)."
"The Goebel Obsequies. Body Will Lie in State at Covington To-day—No Guard Goes With It," The New York Times (February 6, 1900), 2."
"The Gold Rush of 1849," History, http://www.history.com/topics/gold-rush-of-1849 (Accessed August 6, 2015)."
"The Kentucky Senator," Alabama newspaper, JCSB Scrapbook, Part (JCSB collection)."
"The Kentucky Senatorship," The New York Times (March 11, 1896), 5."
"The Kentucky Senatorship," The New York Times (March 6, 1896), 5."
"The Monroe Doctrine (1823)," 100 Milestone Documents, http://www.ourdocuments.gov/doc.php?flash=true&doc=23 (Accessed August 19, 2015)."
"The New Senator from Kentucky," JCSB Scrapbook, Part (JCSB collection)."
"The Noted Race Horse Boston," The Thoroughbred Record, Lexington, Ky, April 16, 1916."
"The Passing of Three Notably Great Men of Kentucky in 1918," Register of Kentucky Historical Society, Vol. 17, No. 49, January, 1919, 45–46."
"The Rebels. Designs of the Conspirators – Interesting Developments," The New York Times, (April 20, 1861), 2."
"The Republic, A Monthly Magazine, Devoted to the Disseminations of Political Information," (The Republic Publishing Company, Washington, D.C., Vol. VI, from January to June, 1876), 254."
"The Republic, A Monthly Magazine, Devoted to the Disseminations of Political Information," (The Republic Publishing Company, Washington, D.C., Vol. VI, from January to June, 1876), 259."
"The Republic, A Monthly Magazine, Devoted to the Disseminations of Political Information," (The Republic Publishing Company, Washington, D.C., Vol. VI, from January to June, 1876), Appendix, 402."
"The Republic, A Monthly Magazine, Devoted to the Disseminations of Political Information," (The Republic Publishing Company, Washington, D.C., Vol. VI, from January to June, 1876), Appendix, 402."
"The Republican Dilemma—Frantic Efforts to Get Out of That Hole. Senator Hale Gets a Scoring from Mr. Blackburn and Mr. Allison Produces Some Doctored Figures," The New York Times (August 29, 1888), 1."
"The Senate Committees – Announcement of the List Yesterday. The Places Assigned to Hill and Vance to be Held for Them by Other Senators Until They Qualify for the Positions," The New York Times (December 18, 1891), 9."
"The Senatorship," JCSB Scrapbook, Part (JCSB collection)."
"The Star Route Thieves, Years of Corruption in the Mail Office Contract Office. Congress Partly to Blame for the Robberies—The History of

Previous Investigations—A Congressional Report on Straw Bids—Money Used to Shield the Ring," The New York Times (April 30, 1881), 1."
"The United States Senate," JCSB Scrapbook, Part (JCSB collection)."
"There Will be No Duel. Senator Blackburn, However, May Try to Chastise Logan Carlisle," The New York Times (November 8, 1896), 5."
"Third Kentucky Candidate, Col. Haldeman to Oppose Senator Blackburn and Judge Paynter," The New York Times (November 19, 1905), 1."
"Thos. F. Lane Kills Himself. Son-in-Law of ex-Senator Blackburn Commits Suicide in Washington," The New York Times (October 17, 1900), 5."
"Toward Racial Equality: Harper's Weekly Reports on Black America, 1857-1874, www.blackhistory.harpweek.com/4Reconstruction/ReconTimeline.htm, Accessed February 12, 2014."
"Transfer Act of 1905." Wikipedia (https://en.wikipedia.org/wiki/Transfer_Act_of_1905, Accessed May 22, 2016)."
"Troops in the Capitol—Kentucky Legislature Guarded by Four Hundred Soldiers. Ballots for United States Senator Practically Without Onlookers—Senator Blackburn, His Brothers, and a Few Women the Only Outsiders Present—No Election—Final Adjournment To-day—Proclamation by the Governor," The New York Times (March 17, 1896) 1."
"Twenty-fifth Congress," Wikipedia, https://en.wikipedia.org/wiki/25th_United_States_Congress, (Accessed July 21, 2015)."
"Ulysses S. Grant, Biography," http://www.biography.com/people/ulysses-s-grant-9318285 (Accessed August 10, 2015)."
"Ulysses S. Grant," Wikipedia, en.wikipedia.org/wiki/Ulysses_S._Grant, Accessed July 14, 2014."
"United States presidential election, 1892," Wikipedia, (https://en.wikipedia.org/wiki/United_States_presidential_election,_1892 (Accessed May 7, 2016)."
"United States presidential election, 1904," Wikipedia, https://en.wikipedia.org/wiki/United_States_presidential_election,_1904, (Accessed June 22, 2015)."
"USS Tallapoosa," Wikipedia, http://en.wikipedia.org/wiki/USS_Tallapoosa_%281863%29, (Accessed May 25, 2015)."
"W.J. Bryan is Shocked," The New York Times (January 31, 1900)."
"Who Was Mrs. Morris," Clipping, JCSB collection, JBW box Mrs. Morris_45."
"1George A. Fuller Company, Reproduction of autographs of the signers of the testimonial, (Press of W.F. Roberts Company, Washington, D.C., 1915), frontispiece; Lincoln Memorial National Memorial, District of Columbia, National Park Service http://www.nps.gov/linc/historyculture/lincoln-memorial-design-individuals.htm, Accessed February 11, 2014."
"1Leonard Schlup, "Joseph Blackburn of Kentucky and the Panama Question," Vol. 51, 357–359."

"A Member of the Order, An Authentic Exposition of the K. G. C. Knights of the Golden Circle; or, A History of Secession from 1834 to 186 (Indianapolis, IN, 1861), 28."
"A Member of the Order, An Authentic Exposition of the K. G. C. Knights of the Golden Circle; or, A History of Secession from 1834 to 1861, (Indianapolis, IN, 1861), 1-80, page 17."
"A Member of the Order, An Authentic Exposition of the K. G. C. Knights of the Golden Circle; or, A History of Secession from 1834 to 1861, (Indianapolis, IN, 1861), 20."
"A Member of the Order, An Authentic Exposition of the K. G. C. Knights of the Golden Circle; or, A History of Secession from 1834 to 1861, (Indianapolis, IN, 1861), 28."
"A Member of the Order, An Authentic Exposition of the K. G. C. Knights of the Golden Circle; or, A History of Secession from 1834 to 1861 (Indianapolis, IN, 1861), 1-80, 5."
"A. J. Halford, Official Congressional Directory, First Edition, Hathi Trust Digital Library , Corrections Made to December 4, 1903, (http://hdl.handle.net/2027/njp.32101072368903?urlappend=%3Bseq=195, Accessed May 23, 2016), 167."
"A. J. Halford, Official Congressional Directory, Second Edition, Hathi Trust Digital Library , Corrections Made to January 10, 1906, (https://babel.hathitrust.org/cgi/pt?id=njp.32101072368853;view=1up;seq=9, Accessed May 23, 2016), 180."
"A. J. Halford, Official Congressional Directory, Third Edition, Hathi Trust Digital Library (https://catalog.hathitrust.org/Record/008885064, Corrected to April 11, 1902, Accessed May 23, 2016), 153."
"Abraham Lincoln, First Inaugural address, March 4, 1861, Washington, D.C."
"Allan M. Trout, "Who Killed Goebel, Research for a new book unveils two new "suspects" but doesn't lift the mystery from the shooting of the Governor in 1900," The Courier-Journal Magazine, May 16, 1954."
"American President: A Reference Resource, The Miller Center, University of Virginia, www.millercenter.org/president/buchanan/essays/vicepresident/1857, (Accessed February 7, 2014)."
"Andrew Eckdahl, "Local Statues Honor Great Men, An Ideal," The Lexington Herald Leader, January 9, 1955."
"Blackburn, His Career in Congress-Public Acts of the Kentucky Senator, Extracts from Some of His Notable Speeches-His Course Regarding the Silver Question, An Enviable and Brilliant Record in Both Houses of the National Legislatures (Extracts from the Cincinnati Enquirer, December 30, 1895), 31."
"Blackburn, His Career in Congress-Public Acts of the Kentucky Senator, Extracts from Some of His Notable Speeches-His Course Regarding the Silver Question, An Enviable and Brilliant Record in Both Houses of the National Legislatures (Extracts from the Cincinnati Enquirer, December 30, 1895), 32."

"Blackburn, His Career in Congress-Public Acts of the Kentucky Senator, Extracts from Some of His Notable Speeches-His Course Regarding the Silver Question, An Enviable and Brilliant Record in Both Houses of the National Legislatures, (Extracts from the Cincinnati Enquirer, December 30, 1895), 34–36."
"Blue Grass Clipper, The Woodford Sun, July 3, 1913, July 5, 2012."
"Bluegrass Clipper, The Woodford Sun, "The Congressman, April 7, 1976 (1876)."
"Bluegrass Clipper, The Woodford Sun, April 25, 1973."
"Bluegrass Clipper, The Woodford Sun, August 25, 1976 (1876)."
"Bluegrass Clipper, The Woodford Sun, August 28, 1974."
"Bluegrass Clipper, The Woodford Sun, August 9, 1906."
"Bluegrass Clipper, The Woodford Sun, December 1, 1976 (1876)."
"Bluegrass Clipper, The Woodford Sun, January 4, 1906."
"Bluegrass Clipper, The Woodford Sun, July 12, 1974."
"Bluegrass Clipper, The Woodford Sun, July 13, 1977 (1877)."
"Bluegrass Clipper, The Woodford Sun, July 19, 1974."
"Bluegrass Clipper, The Woodford Sun, July 20, 1882."
"Bluegrass Clipper, The Woodford Sun, July 28, 1971."
"Bluegrass Clipper, The Woodford Sun, July 28, 1971."
"Bluegrass Clipper, The Woodford Sun, June 16, 1971."
"Bluegrass Clipper, The Woodford Sun, June 2, 1971."
"Bluegrass Clipper, The Woodford Sun, June 20, 1907."
"Bluegrass Clipper, The Woodford Sun, March 15, 1883."
"Bluegrass Clipper, The Woodford Sun, May 14, 1975."
"Bluegrass Clipper, The Woodford Sun, May 17, 1878."
"Bluegrass Clipper, The Woodford Sun, November 23, 1882."
"Bluegrass Clipper, The Woodford Sun, November 6, 1974."
"Bluegrass Clipper, The Woodford Sun, October 19, 1882."
"Bluegrass Clipper, The Woodford Sun, October 26, 1882."
"Bluegrass Clipper, The Woodford Sun, October 4, 1972."
"Bluegrass Clipper, The Woodford Sun, September 27, 1906."
"Bluegrass Confederate: The Headquarters Diary of Edward O. Guerrant, ed. William C. Davis, Meredith L. Swentor, (LSU Press, 2005). 297."
"Boston, The Unofficial Thoroughbred Hall of Fame, www.spiletta.com/THHOF/boston.html, Accessed August 10, 2014."
"Brent Altsheler, "C. C. Graham, M.D., 1784-1885," The Filson Club History Quarterly, (Louisville, KY, 1933), Vol. 7, No. 2, 80. (See, "The Trial of Col. Aaron Burr, on an Indictment for Treason, Before the Circuit Court of the United States, Held in Richmond, (Virginia), May term, 1807: Including the Arguments and Decisions On All Motions made during the Examination and Trial, and on the Motion for an Attachment against Gen. Wilkinson," T. Carpenter, transcribed, (Washington City, 1808), 1-476.)"
"Bryan's "Cross of Gold" Speech: Mesmerizing the Masses, History Matters, The U.S. Survey Course on the Web, (historymatters.gmu.edu/d/5354/) Accessed September 2, 2014."

"Candice Millard, The River of Doubt, Theodore Roosevelt's Darkest Journey, (Broadway Books, New York 2005), 64–66."
"Capital Stories About Famous Americans, a Budget of Tales of Love, Heroism and Adventure On Land and Sea, ed. Rev. Louis Albert Banks, D.D., The Christian Herald Press, New York, 1905, 93."
"Carlos E. Godfrey, The Commander-In-Chief's Guard, Revolutionary War, (Washington, D.C., 1904; Reprinted Janaway Publishing Company, 2014), 34."
"Chicago Herald clipping, JCSB Scrapbook, Part (JCSB collection)."
"Clipping from Terese Blackburn Rouse collection, JCSB cartoons."
"Clipping from THE CRITIC, JCSB defeat 1897, (Terese Blackburn Rouse collection)."
"Clipping, JCSB Scrapbook, Part (JCSB collection)."
"Clipping, JCSB Scrapbook, Part1."
"Clipping, Joe Blackburn tough fight (JCSB collection)."
"Clippings From the Bluegrass-August 15, 1901, The Woodford Sun, August 17, 2000, page A8."
"Colonel Goethals, "Story of the Panama Canal," Blackburn family papers."
"Colonel Goethals, "Story of the Panama Canal," Blackburn family papers."
"Confederate Vets, www.confederatevets.com/mQuery.cgi, (Accessed July 18, 2014)."
"D.M. Bowmar, "Nantura Farm," The Woodford Sun, January 27, 1898; Maryjean Wall, How Kentucky Became Southern: A Tale of Outlaws, Horse Thieves, Gamblers and Breeders, (University Press of Kentucky, September 29, 2010), Chapter 3, 93-112."
"Daniel M. Bowmar, "Versailles Man Put Electric Light in White House, Extreme Heat Sent Senator Jo. Blackburn to Bat for Republican President and Wife," The Woodford Sun, date not known, JCSB collection, JBW box_28."
"David Hirsch, Abraham Lincoln and the Structure of Reason, (Casemate Publishers, June 15, 2010), 158; "Helped Him Out," by James Tandy Ellis, The Tang of the South, The Times-Star, March 10, 1932."
"David McCullough, The Path Between the Seas: The Creation of the Panama Canal, 1870-1914 (Simon and Schuster 1977).
"Elder C. Lewis, History of Big Spring Baptist Church, Woodford County, KY (Now Spring Station), http://baptisthistoryhomepage.com/ky.elkhorn.hist.big.sprgs.html, 1877 (Accessed April 14, 2014)."
"Forty-Fourth Congress, Second Session, Congressional Record: containing The Proceedings of the Electoral Commission appointed under The Act of Congress Approved January 29, 1877, entitled "An Act to Provide For and Regulate the Counting of Votes for President and Vice-President, and the Decisions of Questions Arising Thereon, For the Term Commencing March 4, A.D. 1877, being Part IV, Volume V, 1774 et. Seq."
"Forty-Sixth Congress, Wikipedia, https://en.wikipedia.org/wiki/46th_United_States_Congress, (Accessed April 30, 2016). (According to

Savoyard, "Our Joe," 1918, JCSB collection, JBW box_37, ("During the agitation of the "Nullification" question, Governor Hamilton, of South Carolina, gave expression to the alliteration, "He who dallies is a dastard and he who doubts is damned." While Hayes was President Joe "commandeered" the expression and employed it with electrical effect in the debate on the army appropriation bill in the Forty-Fifty Congress. To a splendid presence and an attractive person, Joe added the finest voice in Congress. On the histrionic stage he might have been a Kean or a Macreary, and when with the matchless voice and superb dramatic pose he threw the Hamilton alliteration into the teeth of the Compromisers on the Democratic side, the effect was tremendous.")."

"Frank H. Heck, Proud Kentuckian: John C. Breckenridge, 1871-1875, (The University Press of Kentucky, 1976) 129."

"Frank H. Heck, Proud Kentuckian: John C. Breckenridge, 1871-1875, (The University Press of Kentucky, 1976), 151."

Frank Harper of Nantura Farm had bought Blackburn's farm that adjoined his farm some years earlier. Frank Harper's will at his death in 1905 instructed that it passed to Blackburn's daughter Lucileand her heirs with a life estate to Joseph Blackburn in gratitude for Blackburn's legal representation in the Harper family murder trial and in recognition of their long friendship.

"Free Silver Movement, Encyclopedia Brittanica, http://www.britannica.com/EBchecked/topic/218360/Free-Silver-Movement (Accessed February 2, 2014)."

"Free Silver Movement, Encyclopedia Brittanica, http://www.britannica.com/EBchecked/topic/218360/Free-Silver-Movement (Accessed February 2, 2014)."

"George A. Fuller Company, Reproduction of autographs of the signers of the testimonial, (Press of W.F. Roberts Company, Washington, D.C., 1915), frontispiece."

"George Blackburn Kinkead was the son of Judge William Bury Kinkead (1809-1894) and Elizabeth F. Shelby Kinkead (1824-1895). Judge Kinkead was the son of Margaret Trotter Blackburn Kinkead (1790-1851) and John Kinkead (1784-1855). Margaret was a sister to Joseph's father Edward, and was, therefore, his aunt, making George second cousin to Joseph."

"Gerald Carson, The Social History of Bourbon, University of Kentucky Press, 1963, 41."

"Greenback Party, http://en.wikipedia.org/wiki/Greenback_Party, (Accessed May 24, 2015) (During the Civil War, the United States issued paper currency that was printed green on one side, thus "greenbacks." They were legal tender but were not backed by gold or silver, only the good credit of the U.S government)."

"Hambleton Tapp and James C. Klotter, Kentucky: Decades of Discord, 1865-1900, (Kentucky Historical Society, November 15, 2008), 331."

"Hambleton Tapp, James C. Klotter, Kentucky: Decades of Discord, 1865-1900 (University Press of Kentucky, November 15, 2008), 348."
"Hambleton Tapp, James C. Klotter, Kentucky: Decades of Discord, 1865-1900 (University Press of Kentucky, November 15, 2008), 370."
"Hambleton Tapp, James C. Klotter, Kentucky: Decades of Discord, 1865-1900, (University Press of Kentucky, November 15, 2008), 348."
"Hambleton Tapp, James C. Klotter, Kentucky: Decades of Discord, 1865-1900, (University Press of Kentucky, November 15, 2008), 348."
"Hambleton Tapp, James C. Klotter, Kentucky: Decades of Discord, 1865-1900, (University Press of Kentucky, November 15, 2008), 348."
"Hambleton Tapp, James C. Klotter, Kentucky: Decades of Discord, 1865-1900, (University Press of Kentucky, November 15, 2008), 365."
"Hambleton Tapp, James C. Klotter, Kentucky: Decades of Discord, 1865-1900, (University Press of Kentucky, November 15, 2008), 370."
"Hamilton Foley, "Joe Blackburn," The Elkton Times, clipping, (Joseph C. S. Blackburn papers)."
"Henry William Brands, TR: The Last Romantic, (New York: Basic Books 1997), 325–326."
"http://en.wikipedia.org/wiki/Joseph_Clay_Stiles_Blackburn, Accessed October 22, 2012; http://pdfhost.focus.nps.gov/docs/NRHP/Text/82001578.pdf, application for National Register of Historic Places for Rose Hill neighborhood in Versailles, KY)."
"http://www.senate.gov/artandhistory/history/minute/War_Secretarys_Impeachment_Trial.htm, Accessed May 18, 2015."
"Interestingly in 1874, widower Thomas Bramlette married Joseph Blackburn's sister-in-law, the widow Mary Graham Adams, sister of Terese Graham, who was Joseph Blackburn's wife."
"J. Winston Coleman, Jr., "The Kentucky Colonization Society," (Register, Kentucky State Historical Society, January 1941), No. 39, No. 126, 1."
"James B. Morrow, "Blackburn Recalls His Friends, Comrade of Famous Democrats and Republicans Alike and a Dashing and Picturesque Figure in Congress for Twenty-eight Years," (The Illustrated Buffalo Express, March 14, 1915.)"
"James C. Klotter, Kentucky: Portrait in Paradox, 1900-1950, (University Press of Kentucky, 1996), 205."
"James C. Klotter, Kentucky: Portrait in Paradox, 1900-1950, (University Press of Kentucky, 1996), 208."
"James Duvall, M.A., "Chronology of the Life and Times of Christopher Columbus Graham, 1784-1885," (http://www.oocities.org/booneencyclopedia/graham/chron.html, Accessed April 24, 2013)."
"Jay Jay, "Four Bits," The Lexington Herald Leader, December 7, 1947."
"Jay Sacher, Lincoln Memorial, The Story and Design of an American Monument, (Chronicle Books, 2014), 45–46."
"JCSB clippings, "Saved the Senator Once, Corinne Blackburn Has Worked Hard in Her Father's Canvass," Corinne Blackburn PDF (JCSB collection)."

"JCSB Collection, "How Blackburn Talked Out a Duel," from the Chicago Herald, Sen B PDF (JCSB collection)."
"JCSB collection, JBW 31- R. Lee Davis, Joseph Clay Stiles Blackburn, 1933, Courier Journal."
"JCSB letter to James Dedman, November 11, 1896, JCSB collection; JBW box JSCB letters_2 (JCSB collection)."
"JCSB letters, JBW box 1898 letters to Judge Jimmie Dedman_21, JCSB collection (JCSB collection)."
"JCSB letters, JBW box 1898 letters to Judge Jimmie Dedman_21, JCSB collection (JCSB collection)."
"JCSB Scrapbook, Part (JCSB collection)."
"JCSB Scrapbook, Part (JCSB collection)."
"Jefferson Davis and His Generals: The Failure of Confederate Command in the West, Steven E. Woodworth, 1990, Lawrence: University Press of Kansas."
"Jefferson Davis, The Rise and Fall of the Confederate Army, Vol 1 (The Project Gutenberg EBook, Release Date November 16, 2006, last updated January 14, 2013), 50."
"Jefferson Davis, The Rise and Fall of the Confederate Army, Vol 1 (The Project Gutenberg EBook, Release Date November 16, 2006, last updated January 14, 2013), 52."
"John E. Kleber, The Kentucky Encyclopedia Eds. Thomas D. Clark, Lowell H. Harrison, James C. Klotter, (The University Press of Kentucky, 1992), 43."
"John J. McAfee, Kentucky Politicians. Sketches of Representative Corn-Crackers and Other Miscellany, The Courier-Journal Job Printing Company, 1886, 19."
"John J. McAfee, Kentucky Politicians. Sketches of Representative Corn-Crackers and Other Miscellany,The Courier-Journal Job Printing Company, Louisville, K 1886: Sketch of Hon. J.C.S. Blackburn, 19; Bluegrass Clipper, The Woodford Sun, October 4, 1906."
"John Stuart Williams, 1818-1898, earned his nickname "Cerro Gordo" for his heroics leading a charge at Cerro Gordo in the Mexican War. He practiced law after the Mexican War and then was elected to the state legislature in 1873 and 1875, and then was defeated for governor in 1875. He was elected for the US Senate in 1878, where, during the secession crisis, he was at first opposed to secession and advocated compromise and Kentucky's neutrality, but he finally supported the Confederacy after he concluded the Union was trying to use force to coerce the South, returned to agricultural pursuits after he failed in his reelection bid in 1885, and later became involved in land development in Florida in the late 1880s where along with his partner, Louisville businessman Walter N. Haldeman, the publisher of the Louisville Courier-Journal, they founded the town of Naples, Florida. He died in 1898 and is buried in Winchester Cemetery in Winchester. (Source: Terry L. Jones, Historical Dictionary of the Civil War (Scarecrow Press,

July 15, 2011), 1609–1610. Wikipedia, en.wikipedia.org/wiki/John_Stuart_Williams, Accessed February 9, 2014)."
"Johnny Green of the Orphan Brigade, The Journal of a Confederate Soldier, Ed. A. D. Kirwan, Foreword by Kent Masterson Brown, (The University Press of Kentucky, 1956, 1984), 134."
"Johnny Green of the Orphan Brigade, The Journal of a Confederate Soldier, ed. A. D. Kirwan, Foreword by Kent Masterson Brown, (The University Press of Kentucky, 1956, 1984), vii."
"Johnny Green of the Orphan Brigade, The Journal of a Confederate Soldier, ed. A. D. Kirwan, Foreword by Kent Masterson Brown, (The University Press of Kentucky, 1956, 1984), viii."
"Jonelle Fisher, Nantura, 1795-1905, St. Crispin Press, 2004; Jonelle Fisher, For All Times: The Story of Lucas Brodhead, St. Crispin Press, 2002."
"Joseph C. S. Blackburn letter from the United States Senate, Washington, D.C., August 24, 1888 to Hon. James Blackburn, Spring Station, Woodford County, Kentucky, (Filson Historical Society, Blackburn Family Papers)."
"Joseph C. S. Blackburn letter to Hon. James Blackburn, Frankfort, Kentucky, from Washington, D.C., February 26, 1880, (Filson Historical Society, Blackburn Family Papers)."
"Joseph C.S. Blackburn, of Kentucky, Reply to Mr. Garfield; House of Representatives, April 3, 1879, Representative American Orators to Illustrate American Political History, ed. Alexander Johnston," G.P. Putnam's Sons The Knickerbocker Press, 1884, 298–310."
Joseph Clay Stiles Blackburn personal papers and letters. (Joseph C. S. Blackburn signed the cornerstone with others).
"Joseph Clay Stiles, "Speech on the Slavery Resolutions, Delivered in the General Assembly Which Met in Detroit in May Last," (Jno. T. Towers, Washington 1850), 21."
"Karl Rove, The Triumph of William McKinley, Why the Election of 1896 Still Matters (Simon & Schuster 2015), 210–211."
"Karl Rove, The Triumph of William McKinley, Why the Election of 1896 Still Matters (Simon & Schuster 2015), 253–254."
"Karl Rove, The Triumph of William McKinley, Why the Election of 1896 Still Matters (Simon & Schuster 2015), 276."
"Karl Rove, The Triumph of William McKinley, Why the Election of 1896 Still Matters (Simon & Schuster 2015), 295."
"Karl Rove, The Triumph of William McKinley, Why the Election of 1896 Still Matters (Simon & Schuster 2015), 351."
"Kelsey Sheridan, "Kentucky Capitol's Lincoln statue turns 100; its tradition nearly as old," The Lexington Herald-Leader, November 10, 2011, http://www.kentucky.com/2011/11/10/1953136/kentucky-capitols-lincoln-statue.html, (Accessed August 29, 2015)."
"Kentuckians Are Bitter—Aroused by the Political Fight in Their State. Secretary Carlisle's Son Inveighs Against Blackburn in Answering a

Challenge to Debate with a Negro—Blackburn Tells What He Will Do with Mr. Carlisle—Gorman Confers with the Managers of the Popocratic Ticket," The New York Times (October 4, 1896), 5."
"Kentucky Bluegrass Country, page 145."
"Leonard Schlup, "Joseph Blackburn of Kentucky and the Panama Question," Vol. 51, 354–355."
"Leonard Schlup, "Joseph Blackburn of Kentucky and the Panama Question," Vol. 51, 355–356."
"Leonard Schlup, "Joseph Blackburn of Kentucky and the Panama Question," Vol. 51, 356–357."
"Leonard Schlup, "Joseph Blackburn of Kentucky and the Panama Question," Vol. 51, The Filson Club History Quarterly, 352, www.filsonhistorical.org/wp-content/uploads/2013/03/51-4-5_Joseph-Blackburn-cf-Kentucky-and-the-Panama-Question_Schlup-Leonard.pdf, (Accessed February 2, 2014)."
"Lincoln Boyhood National Memorial, containing five sculptured panels by E. H. Daniels, was authorized on February 19, 1962 by President John F. Kennedy, http://www.nps.gov/libo/index.htm."
"Lowell H. Harrison, "John C. BreckenridgeL Nationalist, Ccnfederate, Kentuckian," (Filson Club Quarterly April 1973), Vol. 47, 103."
"Mark Grossman, Political Corruption in American, An Encyclopedia of Scandals, Power, and Greed, (ABC CLIO, 2003), 25."
"Mark Twain, Chapter 46, Life on the Mississippi, (James R. Osgood and Company, 1883)."
"Maryjean Wall, How Kentucky Became Southern, A Tale of Outlaws, Horse Thieves, Gamblers and Breeders, (University Press of Kentucky, 2010), 100."
"Maryjean Wall, How Kentucky Became Southern: A Tale of Outlaws, Horse Thieves, Gamblers and Breeders, (University Press of Kentucky, September 29, 2010), 102–103."
"Orlando Oscar Stealey, the Washington Correspondent of the Louisville Courier-Journal, Twenty Years in the Press Gallery, A Concise History of Important Legislation from the 48th to the 58th Congress: The Part Played by the Leading Men of That Period and the Intereting and Impressive Incidents. Impressions of Official and Political Life in Washington, With an Introduction by Henry Watterson, Also Crisp and Vivid Character Sketches of the Men Prominent in Public Life by Well-Known Washington Correspondents, Illustrated by Clifford Berryman, (Publishers Printing Company, 1906), 203."
"Orlando Oscar Stealey, the Washington Correspondent of the Louisville Courier-Journal, Twenty Years in the Press Gallery, A Concise History of Important Legislation from the 48th to the 58th Congress: The Part Played by the Leading Men of That Period and the Intereting and Impressive Incidents. Impressions of Official and Political Life in Washington, With an Introduction by Henry Watterson, Also Crisp and

Vivid Character Sketches of the Men Prominent in Public Life by Well-Known Washington Correspondents, Illustrated by Clifford Berryman, (Publishers Printing Company, 1906), 211–216."

"Orval W. Baylor, "U.S. Senators from Woodford County," The Woodford Sun, December 19, 1946."

"PBS, The American Experience, The Chief Engineers of the Panama Canal, George Washington Goethals,"

"Peter J. Sehlinger, Kentucky's Last Cavalier, General William Preston, 1816-1887, The Kentucky Historical Society (University Press of Kentucky, 2004), 148."

"Populist Cartoons, Missouri State, http://clio.missouristate.edu/wrmiller/Populism/2scartoon/scartoon36.htm, Accessed February 14, 2014."

Preston's sister was married to Confederate General Albert Sidney Johnston.

"R. Lee Davis, "Reminiscences of Prominent Kentuckians, With Many Incidents and Anecdotes of the Great and Near Great Never Before Published, Joseph Clay Styles Blackburn," The Lexington Leader, April 2, 1933."

"Robert E. King, "Alaska's 'Lewis and Clark Expedition,'" National Park Service (www.nps.gov_wrst_historyculture_upload_AllenExpedition.pdf), Accessed February 12, 2014."

"Robert Elkin Hughes, Frederick William Schafer, Eustace Leroy Williams, "That Kentucky Campaign: or, The law, the ballot and the people in the Goebel-Taylor Contest (The R. Clarke Company, 1900), 89."

"Savoyard, "Our Joe," 1918, JCSB collection, JBW box_37 (JCSB collection)."

"See generally www.archives.gov/federal-register/electoral-college/electors,U.S. Electoral College, National Archives, Accessed May 18, 2015."

"Special Resident Commissioner, Jo.C.S. Blackburn Remarks Laying the Corner-Stone of the Lincoln Memorial, February 12, 1915 (Joseph C.S. Blackburn papers)."

"Texas v. White, 74 U.S. 700 (1869)."

"TFF, Keeneland Library, Vol. II, Page 370 (January-June 1866)."

"The American Presidency Project, Political Party Platforms, Democratic Party Platform of 1896, www.presidency.uscb.duc/ws/?pid=29586, Accessed August 10, 2014."

"The American Presidency Project, Political Party Platforms, Democratic Party Platform, Poltical Party Platforms, Parties Receiving Electoral (http://www.presidency.ucsb.edu/ws/?pid=29587) Accessed September 2, 2014."

"The Collected Works of Abraham Lincoln, Volume 2, page 195 (The Abraham Lincoln Association 2006)."

The Congress awarded him a portrait of Henry Clay for his record exceeding the Great Communicator. This portrait was donated by Senator Blackburn's heirs in 2012 to the Kentucky Historical Society and may now be seen hanging in its collection at Frankfort.

"The Courier-Journal, "First One Thing and Then Another," date not known."
"The Flournoy Family, "Blue Grass" (Ky.) Flournoys," The Virginia Magazine of History and Biography (edited by Philip Alexander Bruce, William Glover Stanard, Virginia Historical Society, 1896), Volume 4, pages 97-98."
"The great grandmother of the author, Lucile Blackburn Lane (1871–1902)."
"The Lincoln Memorial, Enchanted Learning, http://www.enchantedlearning.com/history/us/monuments/lincolnmemorial/ (Accessed August 28, 2015)."
"The Memoirs of Thomas Donaldson, Dated 1878-1880, http://www.rbhayes.org/hayes/content/files/donaldsontc/donaldson18781880.htm (Accessed February 19, 2015)."
"The Miscellaneous Documents of the Senate of the United States for the First Session of the Fiftieth Congress, in Three Volumes, Washington Government Printing Office, 1888, 118."
"The New Senator from Kentucky," JCSB Scrapbook, Part 1."
"The split in the Democratic Party in 1860 into the Southern Democratic Party and the Northern Democratic Party may be more understandable to modern readers after experiencing the 2016 U.S. Presidential campaign where the Republican Party appeared to be split between Tea-Party members and conservatives, even though no formal split has been declared to date, as it was declared in the 1860 U.S. Presidential campaign."
"The Woodford Sun, "Political Reflections, Past and Present –" August 29, 1940."
"The Woodford Sun, December 19, 1946."
"The Woodford Sun, Versailles, KY., April 25, 1879."
"The Woodford Sun, Versailles, KY., March 28, 1879."
"Treaty of Paris, 30 Stat. 1754, signed December 10, 1898, ending the Spanish-American War."
"U.S. War Dept, Henry Martyn Lazelle, Leslie J. Perry, The War of the Rebellion, A Compilation of the Official Records of the Union and Confederate Armies, Additions and Corrections to Series II – Volume II, relating to prisoners of war . . . and to state or political prisoners (Published under the Direction of the Hon. Elihu Root, Secretary of War, by Brig. Gen. Fred C. Anisworth, Chief of the Record and Pension Office, and War Department, and Mr. Joseph W. Kirkley, Mr. John S. Moodey, Indexer, Washington Government Printing Office 1902), 817."
"U.S. War Dept, Henry Martyn Lazelle, Leslie J. Perry, The War of the Rebellion, A Compilation of the Official Records of the Union and Confederate Armies, Additions and Corrections to Series II – Volume II, relating to prisoners of war . . . and to state or political prisoners (Published under the Direction of the Hon. Elihu Root, Secretary of War, by Brig. Gen. Fred C. Anisworth, Chief of the Record and Pension Office,

and War Department, and Mr. Joseph W. Kirkley, Mr. John S. Moodey, Indexer, Washington Government Printing Office 1902), cdlx."
"U.S. War Dept, Henry Martyn Lazelle, Leslie J. Perry, The War of the Rebellion, A Compilation of the Official Records of the Union and Confederate Armies, Additions and Corrections to Series II – Volume II, relating to prisoners of war . . . and to state or political prisoners (Published under the Direction of the Hon. Elihu Root, Secretary of War, by Brig. Gen. Fred C. Anisworth, Chief of the Record and Pension Office, and War Department, and Mr. Joseph W. Kirkley, Mr. John S. Moodey, Indexer, Washington Government Printing Office 1902), lxxi."
"U.S. Department of State, Office of the Historian, Milestones, 1899-1913, Building the Panama Canal, www.history.state.gov/milestones/1899-1913/panama-canal (Accessed February 2, 2014). The grand opening of the Panama Canal occurred on August 15, 1914, during the presidency of Woodrow Wilson. There was little fanfare since World War I was erupting in Europe."
"Urey Woodson, "The First New Dealer," 55."
"US Department of State, Office of the Historian, Milestones, 1899-1913, Building the Panama Canal, www.history.state.gov/milestones/1899-1913/panama-canal (Accessed February 2, 2014)."
"William Pope and Duvall Bush, Reports of Selected Civil and Criminal Cases Decided in the Kentucky Court of Appeals, Containing Cases Decided at Winter Term, 1873, and Summer and Winter Terms, 1874 (W.H. Anderson & Co., Publishers 1875), Volume X, 460."
"www.pbs.org/wgbh/Americanexperience/features/general-article/panama-engineers, (Accessed February 2, 2014)."
"Zachary Karabell, Chester Alan Arthur: The American Presidents Series: The 21st President, 1881-1885, (Times Books, 2004), 114–116."

About the Author

Elizabeth Rouse Fielder is the great-great-granddaughter of United States Senator Joseph C.S. Blackburn of Kentucky. Growing up she heard countless first-hand accounts of the Senator's life from her grandmother Terese Blackburn Lane Rouse who was raised by the Senator. Ms. Fielder wrote this book as a way to get to know the Senator and honor his legacy.

Ms. Fielder is an attorney and author who has written a number of articles about Joseph C.S. Blackburn. She is currently working on a nonfiction book about Blackburn's legacy as the first Governor of the Panama Canal Zone and a historical fiction book based on the Blackburn family. She lives in Lexington, Kentucky with her husband, Tom.

INDEX

C

D

M

N

O